Riders of Judgment

Riders of Judgment

by
Frederick Manfred

University of Nebraska Press
Lincoln and London

For William Carlos Williams
who is hacking out a new road up ahead,
all the while singing his come-on song

Copyright © 1957 by Frederick Feikema Manfred
Manufactured in the United States of America

First Bison Book printing: November 1982
Most recent printing indicated by the first digit below:
1   2   3   4   5   6   7   8   9   10

Library of Congress Cataloging in Publication Data

Manfred, Frederick Feikema, 1912–
   Riders of judgment.
   Reprint. Previously published: New York : New American Li-
brary, 1973, c1957.
   "Bison book"—Verso t.p.
   I. Title.
[PS3525.A52233R5   1982]   813'.54   82-8631
ISBN 0-8032-8117-X (pbk.)   AACR2

Published by arrangement with the New American Library, Inc.

Dark and true and tender is the North.
                              —Anonymous

Part ONE

Cain

Cain came riding down through a cloud. He was still very high above the timberline in the Big Stonies. He rode a tall black gelding named Lonesome. Behind him sauntered Animal, his gray pack mule, tied to Lonesome's tail.

Cain let his horse pick the way down the steep slope. Sometimes Lonesome's iron shoes rang on scoured rock. The cloud gave way to clear air very slowly. From the horse's back Cain could occasionally make out varicolored ground: rock blotched over with moss, then bare rock, then carpets of mushy grass.

A single ponderosa pine suddenly appeared out of the mist. It came out of the cloud as if walking toward them. Its orange trunk was just barely visible, while its upper reaches were lost in drifting silver.

For late August the air was cold. Cain drew down his hat, making his stub ears splay out some. He tightened his bandanna snug around his neck. He shivered. He rolled his shoulders. His slicker rustled comfortingly. He walloped his arms around his chest, walloped until finger tips tingled inside his gloves.

Cain was a knobby-muscled fellow. His movements, though quick, were blunt. His face was rough-cut, as if slapped into form with the side of an ax. He had a black walrus mustache, and it gave his face a weathered walnut hue. He wore a black hat, with the wide brim shaped up on both sides against the crown, making points in front and in back. The two dents up front in the crown, into which his thumb and forefinger fit when he handled it, matched the two deep hollows in his cheeks exactly.

Except for a small red heart carved in the leather just below the pull strap, his boots were black too. So too were his .45 Colt and its holster and the cartridge belt, and his pants, shirt, and vest. His Cheyenne-style saddle, bridle, and reins were black. But blackest of all was the kingly horse Lonesome. Lonesome had a coat of somber powder-black and a curling

9

mane and tail that glowed purple in the sun. Setting off all the striking blacks of Cain's rigging was the white sock above Lonesome's left rear hoof and the silver ornaments on the bridle and saddle and the hand-forged inlaid silver spurs.

Cain rode very light, for all his blunt body. He rode with much of his weight in the stirrups, knees taking up the spring, making it easy on the horse. To sit in the saddle like a bag of sand all day long was to kill the mount. He rarely used the reins; drove mostly with his knees. It hurt him to see men rein in their horses with vicious jerks. A horse frothing blood at the bit was enough to set him against the rider.

Behind him, on Animal the pack mule, under a tarp and balanced exactly, rode his bedroll and camp supplies and the remains of a whitetail bighorn sheep. Late the evening before, Cain had finally got his shot and dropped a young buck. He'd butchered in the dusk, shining up his skinning knife with a few quick strokes down his leather chaps, and disemboweling the sheep with easy strokes, the guts welling out like baby snakes, moist and sliding. He'd trimmed out the better meat, all of it smelling deliciously gamy, and wrapped it up in the dust-brown hide. The noble head, with its curling horns resembling hand-carved bench knobs, he'd also saved for mounting later on.

The trail lifted up, to the left, and then crossed over a low neck of rock. The rock was speckled over with various kinds of mosses: brown, green, red, black, orange. The cloud thickened. Old pocked snow lay melting on the left; tiny blue bell-like flowers grew on the right.

Cain smiled to himself. The grimace lifted the ends of his mustache. It creased wrinkles back through a five-day growth of beard. Here comes bachelor Cain Hammett, he thought, a snowball in his left hand and a posy of trueflowers in his right.

They crossed a great open space. The ocher soil was matted over with blooming short grasses, with white and purple and gold flowers. Patches of miniature ferns rode above the grass like diaphanous green veils. Perfumes of the most delicate kind, yet each quite distinct, and weighted with the fresh scent of cloud dew, touched the inside of the nostril no matter which way a man turned his head. It was all a park, almost too good for grazing.

Again the trail sloped down. The cloud thinned out. As Cain came around the shoulder of a huge rock, the cloud suddenly vanished, evanescing up and away, making a solid bank above him and shrouding the blue peaks to the west.

10

Then for the first time he could see, far down to the east, vast throws of eternal rock away, the great Crimson Wall. Forty miles long, it stretched across his path like the Great Wall of China. It ranged from north to south and was as red as geranium-petal rust.

Beyond Crimson Wall the further valley spread out before him like a huge relief map. It was midforenoon, and the full sun struck it with a flood of brilliant light. He could trace the Bitterness River and all its branches as they trickled east through huge breaks in the blood-red Wall, down, down, the Red Fork where Dencil Jager had his horse ranch, the Shaken Grass where he had his own little spread, and then the Bitterness itself where Dale and Rory Hammett had their sheep ranch, all coming together in the violet color of a violent land called the Bad. The Bitterness flowed east, swinging and aggrading through gray alkali wastes, until at last, fifty miles away, it turned sharply north for the Yellowstone. Cain knew it all well, had seen it many times, and yet each time he saw it as a wonder again. This was the country all right. The big open.

Lonesome nickered low. Cain gave the horse its head, and Lonesome immediately headed for a small patch of succulent green growing out of sappy ground. Both Lonesome and Animal were hungry and they snapped at grass to all sides as if they couldn't get enough of it. It was the first good feeding they'd had since leaving the meadow beside the Shaken Grass. The horse moved under Cain, the high shoulders rocking the saddle, making the leather cinches creak. The mule's movements as it grazed stirred up the lifeless head of the bighorn. The horse and mule tromped around in the tender patch. Presently the air was sweet with the smell of crushed greens.

Cain relaxed in his saddle. He let his back hump some and the flesh over his belly fold up. He rolled himself a cigarette. He took a match out of his hatband and lit up. The forenoon sun became warm. After a bit he began to heat pleasantly inside his slicker. The sun also dried Lonesome's damp coat. It left gray streaks in the powder-black hair. Some of the streaks resembled the markings of coastlines on a map.

Once more Cain's eyes could not resist tracing out the great curving escarpment of Crimson Wall far below, scarves of rock sheering down from north to south, from where it curved in a bright red crescent out of the footslopes near Antelope to where it vanished in blue shadow near Hidden Country. Green flanks of land stretched to where Red Fork ran south; deep green hills rolled to where the Shaken Grass

11

ran north. And where the grass ran thin, bare folds of soil lay skinned and fleshy red.

He found himself breathing heavy in the thin air. His nose stung from it. His eyes, seeing so sharply, so widely, and so alive to blood racing within, teared vaguely at the corners. Every now and then his lungs sucked deep of the searing air.

"So dummed high up here, when a fly lights for the night it has to settle on the ground."

Right in the middle of a bite, Lonesome suddenly snorted, once, and lifted his handsome head high, and his raven mane tumbled back, and his ears began to flick. The mule, Animal, jerked up his head too and stood with both of his long gray ears shot forward.

"What's the matter, boys? Somebody around after all?"

Quickly, deftly, with his left hand he opened his slicker and shifted his six-gun around ready to hand on the left, butt up. He also loosened his .38 Winchester in its scabbard under his right leg. With narrowed smoke-blue eyes Cain stared at the falling footslopes below, then up at the soaring cliffs behind. But search as he would he could see nothing. The only things moving were small black spots on a far bench just this side of the red Wall, and these he knew to be Dencil Jager's grazing horse herds.

Once more he examined every ravine, every canyon, every gulch, every cluster of pine caught on a cliff face. Could someone have trailed him this high into the Big Stonies? He'd been careful to double his trail in the waters of the Shaken Grass, and then later in the upper reaches of the Red Fork. He tossed back his hat to hear the better. Both he and the horse, and the mule, listened intently. The falling silence lay around them like a pause between psalms.

If someone had trailed him up that high in the Big Stonies, getting a bighorn for cousin Rory might turn out to be an expensive trip at that. Especially since he'd thought it a foolish whim in the first place. She for asking; he for agreeing to it. And then both saying it was really to be a treat for Gram Hammett.

He was staring down at a brow of black volcanic rock when he saw part of the rock detach itself and assume slow wings. The wings banked and beat up toward him. Eagle. Now what could have choused up that thing? Lonesome and Animal were right. Something or somebody, more than just a stray wild critter, was stirring around below.

Cain studied Lonesome's manner of standing; then Animal's pointing gray tuber ears. Yes. Both sensed another horse below. Both looked as if they were about to break out with a greeting whinny.

Cain checked his guns again; took off his left glove for better handling; had a quick look around. Better get down off the ridge. Against the blue sky they'd be easy pickings for a long-range rifle below. Best to circle home halfway up the sides of ravines and gulches. Though not too low or a man could get hung up in the bottom of some draw.

His wonderful country had lately been not quite so wonderful. Lately it had become full of long riders, full of solitary men who went on long spying expeditions armed with high-powered glasses and rifles. Everywhere a man looked he always saw a hatted head pricking out atop some high hill looking the country over.

"Hup up, Lonesome boy, let's be joggin'. And we'd best take a cross canyon here and streak it down the Red Fork. The same one them Cheyennes took to get out from under the guns of General Plunkett. It looks tough. It is tough. And nobody but a rustling Red Sasher takes it these days."

For all their curiosity about the unseen critter, both Lonesome and Animal were reluctant to leave the little island of green grass on the rock ledge. Cain had to remind Lonesome that he was boss with a very light rake of the rowels just under the quick. The touch made Lonesome crow-hop twice, which Cain rode easy, and then the horse settled into a steady swift single-foot with Animal following patiently along behind. After a bit, Cain slipped on his left glove again.

Once more rock rang under iron horseshoes, like notes struck from stone bells with brass clappers. They brushed around a thrust of light green rock. Again ponderosa pine crowded around them. Lonesome's hooves whispered across thick carpets of pine needles. The scent of rosin was sticky, cloying; it awakened memory of spilled molasses. Lupine bloomed purple in the open parks. A fallen old cottonwood, growing in too high an altitude and dying early, lay off to the left. Brilliant red paintbrush grew near it. Aspen trembled.

They passed through a sloping patch of greenish-gray mahogany brush. Next came a field of deep green juniper. Here and there individual bushes, both mahogany and juniper, had been threshed to bits by bull elk trying to rub velvet fuzz off their new horns. Mahogany brush made great feed for elk, deer, sheep; they favored it the year round. A black butterfly with yellow trim fluttered around Cain for a ways. Petrified logs lay scattered to all sides. The sweet smell of

13

morning rain rose from the ground; it made a man want to hug something.

Silently they rode down, down. The near footslopes of the valley rose toward them. The upthrust cliffs and peaks climbed behind them, rose into distant blue pinnacles frosted over with snow and cloud mist at the very top. There were touches of autumn on the high flanks: yellow and ocher and gold mixed in with the deep green of the pine. Swallows banked steeply over dark abysses. Swift fleeting mirages, like cities seen between eyeblinks, winked over the forests. They rode down into warmth and summer. It became easier to breathe. More and more the flittering leaves of aspen began to show. Buckbrush replaced juniper. And at last, as they rode into the head of Red Fork, sweet spring water welled out of the rocks on all sides and the medicinal smell of sage came up on the wind. The short-grass plains lay below. Both Lonesome and Animal quickened to it.

Cain couldn't help but croon the chorus of his favorite song to himself:

> *"When the Riders of Judgment come down from the sky*
> *And the Big Boss fans wide his great circle drive*
> *And critters come in from low and from high*
> *And critters rise up both dead and alive—*
> *Will you be ready for that Roundup of Ages?"*

The lower end of Red Fork Canyon, where it widened out into a cozy valley, was beautiful. Bluebells and lupines grew thick and tall. Wild primroses and white purple clematis nodded on the low grassy benches. Most fragrant were the larkspur and lobelia. The orange berries of wild rosebushes tossed in the wind. And off in the sidedraws the chokecherries hung a ripened deep red, and the wild plums a turning red, and the wild raspberries a maidenlip red, and the gooseberries an opal blue. And all the while singing meadow larks and scolding magpies threaded through the trees.

Through some cedars Cain spotted the first cattle, most of them whitefaces, a breed of beef with a Texas Longhorn foundation, crossed with Shorthorn and topped off with Hereford bulls. This high on the footslopes of the Big Stonies the cattle were saucy and fat. Grass in the canyons at the base of the mountain was always good and the water was plentiful. During the summer months it was favorite grazing ground. Grass might be as nutritious down on the plains but cattle had to travel too far for water. The color of the cattle before

14

him was deep, rich even, a blood-red with matted white, with sometimes the darker brown of the old Texas base showing through. It was easy to see, though, that the Hereford strain was going to win out. Money spent on the Hereford bulls had not been for nothing.

Cain examined the brands, burnt high on the shoulder so a rider could spot them from horseback, to see if maybe some of his cattle were among them. All he saw, however, were the various brands of Peter Caudle, the Earl of Humberwick: the Derby, ○ ; the English pound, £ ; and the S!R . There were no Mark-of-Cain cattle, as he jokingly called his own brand, ⫐ . He also looked to see if any of brother Harry's stuff was around. But look as he might there were no Rocking Hell, ⊔ , cattle either. Good thing too. With someone looking for him he'd hardly have the time to throw them back toward the hills of Hidden Country to the south, where Harry lived.

The stream of the Red Fork deepened in the slowly opening canyon, at last became a noisy brook galloping from one red boulder to the next, surging up over and around, green over gray fieldstone and pink over slabs of scarlet scoria. The air was sweet with the smell of mountain water. Both Lonesome and Animal fluttered nostrils at it, loud.

"You sure got rollers in your nose today, ain't ye, boys? Well, all right, let's all have a drink then."

Cain threw over a leg and got down. He slipped out of his slicker and folded it up and tied it behind the cantle. He stretched, stretched long, stretched until with a jerk Lonesome, in a hurry to get at the water, pulled him out of it. Cain shifted his gun around and tightened his cartridge belt. He untied Animal's hitch from Lonesome's tail. Then all three went down for a drink, the horse and mule from high shoulders, Cain on his knees. Lonesome and Animal drank on the high side of the stream; Cain on the low. Cain didn't mind. There wasn't a sweeter mouth in all creation than a horse's or a mule's. That was because they ate grass, not meat boiled or rotten.

Cain drank thirstily, mustache touching water, throat tight on each swallow. The water was cool with night. Pebbles rolled downhill under his nose. He could taste the onionlike flavor of the minerals. The cool water restored the throat. It healed bone ache. He drank deep and long, the swallows clicking in his neck.

Finished, water-loggy, he rocked back on his heels. He

15

brushed dirt from the knees of his leather chaps, wiped drops from the tips of his mustache.

Lonesome and Animal went on drinking. Cain liked to watch Lonesome drink. Swallows shot up the underside of Lonesome's long curving neck like rising birds.

After a bit Lonesome had his fill too. Yet he hated to give up the luxury of cool spring water. He continued to lip the rippling water lovingly, an old sage smile wrinkling up his whiskered mug. He played with the water, sucking up a little and letting it run out again.

The three lingered beside the stream, Lonesome switching his tail slowly, Animal still sipping, Cain casually scratching a leg.

Steel chinked on a stone behind them. Cain stood up and whirled around all in the same motion, left hand near the handle of his .45.

Lonesome turned too, nickering, while Animal reared up a long-eared head.

Two men on horseback waited not thirty feet away: Jesse Jacklin and Mitch Slaughter. Jesse was the general manager of Peter Caudle's cattle empire; Mitch was a foreman. And behind them, almost hidden in a fringe of chokecherries, waited a dozen armed cowboys. Lonesome and Animal had been right.

Jesse spoke first. "Hammett, from the rear you and that horse of yours look like a pair of partners in flytime." Jesse had the mocking drawling voice of a Texan, soft yet edged. Jesse was a tall large-boned man, and in blue clothes and wearing a mustache was handsome in a darksome way. He had a red face, of a hue that almost matched the ruby on his left ring finger. He was very high-headed in everything he did and liked running men. When his hide was full of booze he was as touchy as a teased snake. Cain had little use for him, feeling that if a man was a devil and a bastard when drunk he was a devil and a bastard when sober too, no matter how he tried to make up for it with winning talk later on. Booze boiled what was in a man to the top. Jesse added, "Switching each other down like that."

Cain was easy. He allowed a smile to lift a corner of his mustache. "Well, I'm thankful this is a country where a man can switch his tail when he feels a bite."

"Hah!" Jesse spat.

Cain said, "Besides, I always did like horses better than I did a lot of men."

Jesse leaned an arm on his saddlehorn. "How about she-stuff?" Jesse's horse kicked at a fly under its belly and Jesse rose and fell with the motion.

"Now that's close."

Mitch laughed. Mitch was a blond, had a pocked face of slanted ovals suggesting the Mongoloid, and was somewhat round-shouldered. He wore brown leather boots, stiff leather chaps, cowhide vest, cowhide cuffs on his wrists, and tan gloves. A six-shooter showed; a rifle hung ready from the pommel. He was known as a sneering bully to his hands and a braggart to his bosses. He would never admit wrong. When someone brought up a point, Mitch either knew all about it already or didn't consider it worth knowing. Over a drink a man might tell a windy that nobody would much question, but if Mitch were present he'd be quick to come up with a windy that was bigger, better, and windier. Mitch laughed again, and said, "Outside of your cousin Rory, you mean."

Cain moved easy. He decided he'd be better off aboard Lonesome if they were going to throw a gun down on him. He retied Animal's hitch to Lonesome's tail. He put a boot in a stirrup and rose and threw a leg over Lonesome and settled easy in the saddle. He slipped off his left glove, finger by finger, finally the thumb, and stuck the glove in a pocket of his vest. All the while he was very aware that the two, and the cowboys hidden in the brush, were watching him narrowly. Then, when he was set, he looked up. "So it was you my hoss smelled up there. What am I supposed to have done this time, Jesse?"

Jesse's mustache twitched. "Trailed you up there? Nope, not us."

Cain said, "Cut the guff, boys. What's it this time?"

Mitch said, "You in a rush?"

Cain jerked his head at the bighorn behind on Animal. "Meat's heatin'."

Mitch said, lips curling sly, "Lucky for you that thing's got horns like a trumpet. Or some sheepherder over Ten Sleep way might've plugged you."

Cain studied Mitch, and remembered that Mitch, like himself, was left-handed all the way too. Fact was, Mitch was insanely jealous of Cain's prowess as a left-handed shot. Cain said quietly, "Well, it ain't slow elk."

Mitch's round shoulders squared some. "Meanin' what?"

"That nobody can cry thief at me claimin' one of Lord Peter's steers was slow on the getaway."

An eagle broke off of a cliff point, wapping a long trail

17

across the sky, very slowly, its great wings beating like a pair of overbig flags.

Jesse said, "See any Caudle beef on the high meadows?"

"Not on the high. But there's some just back there along the Red Fork."

"How many?"

"Didn't stop to count." Cain settled back in his saddle. "Well, seeing as you don't want me, boys, me and my critters will be moving on."

"Wait up," Jesse said. He touched his horse, a bay with a star, and in a few clopping chinking steps was beside Cain. Mitch and his horse, a chestnut, moved too and circled around on the other side.

Cain could feel dirt under the fingernail of his trigger finger. "Well, throw down. What is it?"

"That proposition I made you last month. How about it?"

"Riding for you and the earl again? Never."

"Why not? The pay is good. Sixty a month and keep. That's already twenty over the usual."

Cain held his horse. "What kind of a tight are you boys in this time?"

Jesse leaned back from his pommel. "This time?"

Cain had once ridden for Jesse Jacklin and he knew his man. He'd even helped Jesse skin Lord Peter. Had been obliged to. When you worked for a boss like Jesse, you followed orders or rolled your tail for home. The skinning of Lord Peter had been quite easy. At the time Jesse owned most of what was now known as the Derby outfit and the earl wanted it the worst way and was willing to pay through the nose for it. That was more than all right with Jesse, since it was also the earl's intention to keep Jesse on as general manager at a good salary. But before shelling out his English money, the earl decided he wanted a rough tally. So Jesse took the earl all across Bighorn County to show him the Jacklin spread. They found Jacklin cattle thick in Lodgepole Canyon and they found Jacklin cattle thick in Red Fork Canyon. What the good earl didn't know was that while Jesse was taking him the long way from Lodgepole to Red Fork, foreman Mitch and his boys, Cain and brother Harry among them, had quick hustled the cattle through a cross canyon, the very cross canyon Cain had just now taken down the mountain, so that the same bunch of cattle was counted twice. Some time after the sale, the very next fall round-up, Jesse hired on as general manager as agreed upon, reported a shortage of some five thousand head. This he promptly blamed on cattle thieves, mostly Harry Hammett and his Red Sash waddies who'd quit the earl's outfit in the meantime. It was true that brother Harry had forcibly parted a few stray calves from mothers that didn't belong to him, and that the Red Sashers had orphaned others, but not to the extent claimed by Jesse. It was more that Jesse, seeing independent cowboys and incoming homesteaders take over the choice land along the streams, knew that his way of life was doomed if he didn't make everybody out a rustler who wasn't working for the earl. And blaming rustlers, Jesse got away with it for a time. The earl believed Jesse readily, since the earl had a low opinion of American cowboys in the first place.

Up on the cap rock, a magpie suddenly began to scold behind them; then broke out, black and white, tail heavy and dipping, and sailed out of sight behind some aspen above them. Ah, Cain thought, so Jesse has more of his boys out that way.

Cain said aloud to Jesse, "Yes, this time."

Jesse swallowed. He forced on a smile, put such effort into the smile that it showed fierce under his mustache. "Plus the ten we'll pay for every loose calf you brand for the earl. Instead of the usual five."

Cain laughed at him. There was another reason why Jesse wanted him back. Cain had caught Jesse in a fast one the past summer. The earl had been thinking of quitting America altogether, and getting wind of it, Jesse had decided to repurchase his old outfit. So he and Mitch choused some of the Caudle beef over the low passes onto the high meadows back in the Big Stonies, so that later, at fall roundup, they could report a low tally. A month before, Cain had found such a bunch high on a ridge, some two hundred unbranded yearlings. Seeing through the scheme, he'd jokingly told brother Harry and his boys about it, and they in turn had promptly put their brand, the Rocking Hell, on them, and had driven them across to their hideout in Hidden Country. In a way Harry had that right, since it was unwritten law on the high plains that unbranded calves without mothers belonged to the first man who could slap his iron on them. Harry and his boys had put Jesse and Mitch in a bind. Jesse and Mitch couldn't very well claim the two hundred as the earl's, since then they'd have to explain how they'd let two hundred mavericks, all in one bunch, get away unbranded.

"Ten bucks? Not enough."

Mitch sneered out of his slanted Mongoloid ovals, "See you left your running-iron home this time." Mitch's horse moved

19

and Mitch jerked it back on its heels, pulling viciously on the reins. The horse huled, once, like a kicked dog.

Anything Mitch said or did just naturally rubbed Cain the wrong way. Especially so when Mitch was mean to his chestnut. Cain warned himself to sit tight, hold tight. That old Hammett ire which he'd inherited from Gramp Hammett was about to get out from under again. What men, and broncs, couldn't throw, it did. Cain said, "I've never made orphans out of calves for myself."

Jesse threw Mitch a look to shut him up. "Cain, your brother Harry bought him twenty cows last winter. That we admit. But now all of a sudden he's got him two hundred and twenty-some calves."

Cain laughed. "Maybe Harry topped his heifers out with a bull jack rabbit last winter."

"The hell you say!"

"Well, now, Jesse, you know how Harry is, a good-hearted kid, and how he hates to see calves wandering around naked without a brand."

"Cain, them two hundred yearlings was our'n."

"The earl's, you mean. Where's his mark on them?"

Mitch said, "Do you know where your brand-changing brother is?"

Jesse threw Mitch another fierce look.

Cain held tight. He looked down at his bare left hand.

It was also true that ornery brother Harry had on occasion altered brands and had done it knowing that to an old cowman a brand was as sacred as a wedding ring. Altering a brand was about the same thing as getting in bed with a cowman's wife. After helping Jesse cheat the earl, and then quitting the earl's outfit, Harry had pulled Jesse's leg a few times by changing the earl's brand to one he had invented for himself, making the Derby, $\bigcirc$, over into the Rocking Hell, $\underline{\mathsf{H}}$. This had infuriated Jesse, and acting for the earl Jesse had ordered his branders to use the English pound sign, $\pounds$. Harry in turn altered it to the American $\$$. When Mitch suggested they use the letters $\underline{\mathsf{SIR}}$, Harry again in turn altered the brand to $\underline{\mathsf{MR}}$. In every case Harry's altering had been perfect. Harry used two tools, a piece of telegraph wire and a short running-iron. The first could be bent to fit any letter or sign, the second was used to touch up the old brand. Jesse had to kill a cow and skin it and look on the underside of the hide before he could tell if the brand had been altered. Harry had been devilish inventive.

"Well?" Jesse finally barked. "Do you join us? Or what?"

When Cain looked up, he found that left-handed Mitch had pulled his gun on him. Looking down the barrel of the .45, Cain could almost see the blunt-nosed bullet getting ready for the jump. The muzzle of the blue six-shooter looked like the entrance to the tunnel of hell itself. Cain said, "Sorry, boys, but I'm afraid you've got the wrong pig by the ear."

Jesse gestured with a high toss of the head, the front of his big hat tipping up. "Mitch, put that hogleg away. Not yet."

Mitch did, slowly. He'd been ready.

"No, boys," Cain said, "I'm throwing in with the little man."

Jesse said, "You're making a mistake, Cain."

"I don't see it that way."

"Cain, we'll run all of you little men out of the country before the snow flies this fall."

Cain glanced over at the dozen armed cowboys half-hidden in the chokecherries. "You haven't got enough guns to bluff us, Jesse, even with them. As you know, we elected us a sheriff last year."

At that Jesse began to curse, loud, profane. "Yeh, that Ned Sine, that mother-forking bastard. If I'd've known he was going to turn traitor on me when he worked for me I'd've drilled him center right then and there. May the Devil fly away with his soul and the dogs water on his grave."

Cain said, "Give up, Jesse. Bighorn County was meant for the small stockman."

Jesse rose in his saddle. His brows climbed his forehead, revealing the high whites of his eyeballs. "It's always been big-spread country and by Grab it's gonna stay big-spread country or my name ain't Billy Hell."

Cain waved a hand at the canyon they were in, then waved down at the Crimson Wall below to the east. "Look at it. Small valleys with the hogback ridges making natural barriers between one spread and another. God meant Bighorn County for the little man. It's not like it is down on the Sweetwater. Or just south of here near Casper, where your friends, Senator Thorne and Governor Barb, has their spreads. Where the country is one big pasture from the North Pole to the Gulf of Mexico and not a stick, no, not even a twig to get in the way. That country I admit was meant for big outfits. But not this. This country here is a little pocket all by itself. Especially this side of the Bitterness."

Jesse's already red face turned a deeper red. He was almost too choked for words. "It was my country before this and it's going to stay my country after this."

Cain said, "You're forgetting something, Jesse. Who really

owns the land you graze your cattle on? We all do. It's public domain. All you own is the three-twenty homestead you built your ranch buildings on. Just like the rest of us who got us a piece of land from the guv'ment too."

Jesse said, "But you forget we big fellers was here first. Why, it was me and fellers like Thorne and Barb that built up this country. And from nothing, too. With beans and whisky. And dirty old dugouts for our wimmen. And with baking-powder bread when they wasn't no wimmen. With Indians hot on our necks night and day. Why, not even the Pilgrim Fathers had it as tough. Why, if it hadn't been for us there never would've been a American territory out here, let alone a state. Cain, I tell you, we're not just going to sit around here like a bunch of big-hearted parsons while a lot of honyocker newcomers and dishonest cowpokes with their hoes and plows and Sunday schools—"

"Hrrp!" Cain cleared his throat loudly, and just barely managed to sit tight. Again he could feel dirt under the nail of his trigger finger. "Listen, if it comes to that, you know we'd all ruther have American big spreads in here if it has to be big spreads. Instead of them high-headed English absentee owners. English absentee owners just naturally ain't good for the country, mostly because they ain't got much heart for the American little man. While the American big man sometimes has. Them English is the worst foreigner we ever let into the States. You know that. And you two especially should know that." Cain did a little dance in his saddle. "But, for a fact now, Jesse, the times have changed. The little man is in this valley to stay. Whether it's the dry farmer like Red Jackson, or horse rancher like Dencil Jager, or sheepman like my brother Dale, or small stockman like myself."

Jesse cursed. "Blast the guv-ment for passing that homestead law. Blast the Immigration Bureau for allowin' all that left-over honyocker riffraff to come in from Europe. And blast the railroads for bringing them all the way here by the carload. A great blasting damnation on them all!"

The brook behind them gurgled over stones. Out of the corner of his eye, Cain spotted a small herd of antelope high on a bench. Cain restrained an impulse to grab the Winchester tucked under his right leg. Then, even as he watched, the head buck in the herd showed his tin-pan tail and with a flick all the pronghorn were gone.

Cain said, "Sorry, Jesse, but them's the times."

"Well, goddam the times then!"

"And maybe you should check it to the will of God."

"And goddam God then too!"

Silence. Saddle leather creaked in the chokecherries. Lonesome and Jesse's horse nosed each other in friendly fashion, lipping each other a little. Mitch's horse, like its master, remained offish.

Cain said, "Jesse, in some ways you and the earl, and Senator Thorne and Governor Barb, got it coming to you. After you fellows was almost cleaned out by the big freeze-out four winters ago, you set a lot of your boys adrift. Nobody worried about them. Well, now that times is better, them cowboys have elected to stay out. And set up on their own like I done. Because they remember."

Jesse said, "Cain, you fellows are crowdin' us and I'm warnin' ye. We're gonna fight back, pronto."

"Better remember we also elected us a judge last fall. With Judge Traves on the bench, there ain't a jury in the county that'll find against a gunfighter or a rustler. So much are the people agin you fellows and your high-headed ways."

"Cain, listen. Trying to squeeze eight married couples into the same bed just don't work. You know that, you old stubhorn you."

"If the bed is big enough, it will. Or if the couples is runt enough."

Mitch broke in with a scoffing snort. "I suppose that's the way you three Hammett brothers cut the bed with kissin' cousin Rory—even if Dale is the only one married to her legal."

Lonesome turned his handsome black head and caught the toe of Cain's boot in his mouth and gave it a tug, as if to say, "All right, we've had enough of this. Let's head for oats and home."

"In a minute, boy," Cain said. Then Cain suddenly turned on Mitch. He rose in his saddle even as his left hand came up with his quirt. He lashed Mitch across the face, once, twice, raising instant welts. "I'll ask you to keep Rosemary's name off your tongue. You have a woman of your own to dribble on."

Mitch threw up an arm; quailed; scrunched down in his saddle. Then, a second later, Mitch's left hand shot down.

"And don't try for it, bud, or I'll burn you down!" Cain's left hand hung poised over his gun too, hovering separate and apart from him, a rattler free to strike on its own.

Jesse abruptly came down. "All right, that's enough! The both of you!" Jesse spurred his horse between Cain and Mitch. Then over his shoulder he said to Cain, with a look of what almost seemed like pleading in his dark bold eyes, "So you ain't acceptin' my invitation?"

"I'm sorry, Jesse, but like I say I'm throwin' in with the little man."

With that Jesse threw up an arm. In an instant the cowboys in the chokecherries wheeled out and thundered off, Jesse and Mitch following, with Mitch, red-necked, turning around, once, to give Cain a glittering look of hate. Higher on the bench another bunch of cowboys clopped out of brush too and joined the first group.

Cain

Lonesome and Animal rolled along swiftly, eight hooves hitting the earth with rocking cadence, with ringing pound on rock, with muted sound on dirt. Leather creaked. Cain's seat clung to the cantle with a soft sucking sound every time Lonesome came down. The dead bighorn flopped behind on Animal's back, head and horns on one side and skinful of choice meat on the other.

The footslopes gradually leveled off into a long troughing valley. Behind and high above were the Big Stonies, the white peaks clear and bluish in the stark midday sun. Ahead stretched the soft red cliffs of Crimson Wall. A cooling wind soughed slowly down the valley, claddering the bottom leaves of the cottonwoods, tinkling the prisming aspen, raising little red whirlwinds off the ground.

The valley earth had the color of dried blood turned to soft red dust. It stived up around them in a gentle rolling following cloud. Cain coughed in it. Lonesome and Animal snorted to clear their nostrils in it. Presently red dust got into the corners of Cain's eyes and they teared red mud, giving him the look of a fleeing Oedipus bleeding from the eyeballs. His black clothes slowly pinked over.

Great herds of cattle began to show. Flows of spotted red hides moved over a thousand hills. The light wind blew all the tails sideways, to the south. The nearest cows wore the Derby brand. They grazed slowly. Their rasp tongues poked in and out between darning-needle grass, gathering in only the more succulent short grasses. Some of the cows, hungry for seasoning, climbed to the foot of the red cliff and nibbled on the pale green leaves of salt sage.

An occasional mule-eared rabbit shot from cover, and sprang long, to the right and then the left, rear legs and high ears showing. Cain remembered that as a boy Gramp Hammett had told him jack rabbits always ran uphill. For a long time he had a vision of mountaintops being overrun with jack rabbits.

Horses began to show next. Dencil Jager's 4̄1̄ lay like a gray crab over their left flank. Bar Forty-one stood for the year when Dencil finally got married. The horses were scattered over the greening redlands in small bands. Some of the colts slept at the feet of their grazing dams, and except for wiggling ears assumed a deathlike pose in the grass. The horses were of all colors: paints, wolfskins, crow-blacks, buckskins, dollar-spots, polecats, blues, sorrels, bays, chestnuts. Most were the new quick quarter-horse bred atop the old mustang base, a specialty of Jager's. Most were tame. Some of the nearer horses looked up with quick heads, manes flowing back, nickering at Lonesome and Animal. But both Lonesome and Animal were all business. They were in a hurry to get home to grain and barn.

Near the turn where Red Fork headed for Shaken Grass, a band of some twenty-odd half-wild ones suddenly threw up their heads with a wild startled look and broke into a shying gallop, the colts with their fawnlike rears chasing far ahead of their dams, hooves clopping, tails popping.

Cain watched them go with a keen eye. It was from just such a band of Jager horses that he'd spotted a little black colt and had fallen in love with it, had fed it from a bottle like he might a bum lamb, had called it Lonesome. He'd had no trouble breaking Lonesome into a good riding horse. Bucky his cow pony had given him plenty of trouble, but Lonesome had just naturally grown up into a wonderful trail horse.

They came up over a rise and below lay the Jager ranch yard: barn, corrals, shed, and house. The circular breaking corral with its high pole fence especially caught the eye. It was built of huge timbers hauled down from the mountains and inside was worn as smooth as a honing stone. The strong smell of horse manure and hoof rind hit the nose. Cain liked the smell most times, but this time it seemed to come a bit too thick for him, like stifling smoke almost.

He saw movement near the house. Dencil. And his wife Clara. In an argument too, if one could trust joggled eyes. Dencil was scuffing the ground with his boot; Clara's head was jerking up and down. Clara was also holding the new

25

baby, with the two other little tykes, girls, underfoot and gawking at it all.

Cain touched Lonesome under the belly, and both horse and mule broke into a lightsome canter down the sage-tufted slope. They slanted through an open pole-gate, stirred up a cloud of manure dust below the barn, clattered around some feedbunks, and then rocked across the barren red yard, coming to a flourishing stop beside the family. "How do, folks," Cain greeted.

Cain hated family fights, and he hoped his showy arrival might break up the ruckus. But Jager, who always had a quiet smile for him, this time gave him only a quick troubled low-eyed look and then stared down at the ground again, while Clara kept up her harangue as if no more than a fly had dropped by for a visit.

"—it was a mistake to come all the way out here to the ends of the earth, Dencil, and you know it," Clara shrilled. "Far better we should've stayed in Antelope, with you running a livery stable, since you liked horses so well, where Sheriff Sine would have been around to protect us, when you know neither one of us ain't much on fighting, let alone—"

"Pah!" Jager spat from under his huge mustache, still glaring down at the ground, scuffing at a horseball with a stained boot. Jager was very bowlegged, and every time he kicked the horseball the side of his boot, not his toe, hit it.

"You go 'pah' yourself, you big boob you." Clara had rashy skin. Her eyes were almost those of a blind one, a hazed-over skim-milk blue. When she became angry the blue in them slowly whitened to the color of frozen milk. "Dencil! If you was to die for it, you wouldn't fight with a butterfly for the sake of your family, let alone an ordinary fly, would you? Dencil, I tell you, I sometimes just don't know what—"

Jager threw back his tan hat, revealing a very high round forehead. He tugged at one of his big flap ears as if he were trying to shake a bug out of it. The tips of his mustache waggled up and down like the broken wings of a blackbird. The big round forehead and the huge mustache made his head seem much too large for his short body and stumpy bowlegs. "Pah!" he exclaimed again.

"Dencil Jager! That's enough out of you! These snotnoses of yours's already got a bad enough start in life without you swearing around them like that!"

"But I didn't swear, Clara." Dencil looked down at his two little girls. "Did I, Sukie? Dody?"

The girls blinked up at him like a pair of baffled puppies.

26

They were exactly what she called them—snotnoses. They were always dripping and the roots of their noses were always inflamed. They had the weak chins of baby squirrels. And like their mother's, their little bodies had the look of being poorly knit.

Watching it all from his lofty saddle, Cain shook his head. If ever a family had the look of doom hovering over it, this one did. That Clara! Man! It was hardly a wonder cousin Rory said of her that she was too dumb to teach a setting hen to cluck. Once again Clara reminded him of an old heifer Gramp Hammett owned back in Siouxland. The heifer had been so poorly, so bony, none of the bulls in the neighborhood would top her. And she was a full ten years old before a half-blind bull, scenting her in one of her romantic moods, finally did cover her. When questioned about it, Gramp said he'd kept the old maid heifer around the place so she might have her chance at sex before she was sent off to the slaughterhouse. Well, the chance almost drove her crazy. Because by great luck she became pregnant. Cracking her ice had snapped her brain. When the little calf came—her dead ringer in markings and also hardly worth a bullet—she went on the prod. No one, not even Gramp, could get in the same pasture with her. Tail switching, she set after anything moving within a mile of her. Gramp finally had to shoot her to repossess his pasture. And so now too poor old Clara. Caught finally by a bull, marrying Dencil Jager in her thirty-eighth year, she'd lost her head. The outrage of having been broken into at last, and of finally having three kids one right on top of the other, had been too much for her. It had made of her a nutzy switch-tail.

Cain swung down from the saddle and dropped Lonesome's reins to the ground. He bowlegged stiffly up beside Dencil. "Well, Dencil, what seems to be the trouble here? Somebody threaten to hang you?"

Clara noticed Cain for the first time. "Oh, so you know about that then too?" With her free hand, the left, she covered her eyes. Two worn rings, a diamond engagement ring and a wedding ring, shone in the sun. Both rings were too big for her, and even as Cain watched, the weight of the setting in the diamond ring made it turn on her finger.

Cain tipped his hat to her. "Hey, that so? What happened?"

Jager ran a hand up and down his pant leg. Stray horsehairs wafted around his boots. Jager wore no gun. Jager had once told Cain that he felt safer admitting he wasn't over-good with a six-shooter.

The vague milk eyes of the little girls staring up at him finally got Cain. He touched the tops of their twine-hair heads. "Don't you think you little tykes ud better . . ."

Before he could finish he heard it. Then saw it. Rattler. It lay in a folded coil of two eights, with the top eight quivering and sliding over the bottom eight, while up through the middle of the whole coil trilled a tufted stalk. The snake's arrow-shaped head wavered back and forth in a slow tense dance.

There was a shot; the head of the snake vanished; dust exploded up around where the head had been; and Cain found himself with gun in hand.

Slowly the rattler uncoiled out of its double eights and in a long lazy undulation stretched out on rocky ground. For a little while its tail rustled softly against a small sagebrush.

Everybody stood enstatued for a moment: Dencil with head shot forward and mustache tips stiff; Clara on toetip with free hand over mouth; the little girls slowly wying their heads around and down; and Cain with smoking six-gun in hand.

"Great granpap!" Cain exclaimed. "That was a close call! The biggest snake I ever seen without likker!"

The baby awoke in its wrappings and began to cry. Only then did Clara come to. She blew sky-high. "Oe! Dencill! Dencilll!" She stooped down, the bawling baby almost tipping out of her stiff arm, and clutched the girls to her flat bosom.

Dencil awoke from his freeze. His voice was a sudden roar on the yard. "Get! In the house! All of you!" He gave Clara such a shove she almost fell down. "Get!" He gave her a second shove and she and the stringy tykes shot through the open door of the log cabin. With a leap he slammed the heavy log door shut after her.

Cain said, "Well, now, Dencil boy, easy there. They couldn't help the snake, you know."

Dencil stood trembling. "She-stuff? Kids? Pah!"

Cain put his gun back. He tried to laugh it off. "Sorry to scare everybody like that." He wiped his lips on his sleeve. "But the darn thing was about to strike." Looking down at the rattler, Cain saw that it was still twisting on the ground, still softly drumming its tail. Except for the bloody raw end, where its head had been, the diamond-check pattern of the snake was hard to make out against the ground. Cain said, "Now there, Dencil, is another reason why you should maybe wear you a gun."

Dencil shook his head.

That instant Lonesome let out a nose-clearing blast. He shied; reared; and then, head held sideways cleverly so his hooves wouldn't tromp on the dragging reins, began to run. Animal, still tied to Lonesome's tail, ran with him.

"Whoa!" Cain called.

But it wasn't enough. Lonesome, then Animal, broke into a gallop across the dusty yard, heading down creek and for home on the Shaken Grass. The dead bighorn flopped live on Animal's back.

Cain ran forward a few steps, heels stumping, spurs chinking on the rough ground. He shot his head out, almost unseating his hat, and sent his voice out powerfully, letting the animal in himself get into it, trying to make the animal in himself stronger than the animal in Lonesome and the pack mule, commanding, thrilling it. "Whoa, Lonesome! Whoa, Animal! Whoa!"

Lonesome ran on, head still held sideways, reins trailing just out of reach of his throwing hooves, Animal following.

Cain ran forward a few more steps. He bent over from the hips, head far forward, veins and tendons ridging white through the dark skin of his neck, strike in the set of his whole body. "Whoa, Lonesome! Whoa, Animal! You wild wall-eyed bustards, whoa!" His shout echoed roaring off the log buildings and the low walls of the little red draw. "Whoa!!!"

The last time did it. Lonesome slowly stopped, Animal with him, with his head still turned to one side, looking back at Cain.

Cain stalked toward the horse and mule, stiffly, slowly, boot heels tumping, spurs chinking, moving full of violent silence, almost bursting in his clothes, eyes furious with white force.

Lonesome stood until caught by the reins. With some difficulty Cain restrained an impulse to punish the two. He led them back to the cabin and tied them to the wheel of a buckboard standing near.

Going back to where Dencil stood, Cain let out some, and he said, apologetically, "That's his one fault. Lonesome still shies at snakes. You probably remember he once got hit while still a colt. Looks like he'll never get over it." Cain looked at a small hairless patch quite visible on Lonesome's left white sock.

Dencil let down too. "I remember," he said. "You'd just bought him from me."

29

Lonesome continued to be snorty. Head lowering, then rising, he pointed his ears at the still-writhing snake.

"Wait," Dencil said. "Guess we better get that dummed dead snake out of sight." With a stick Dencil picked up the long rope of flesh and tossed it into the privy behind the log cabin. "There," he said, "now maybe your hoss won't be so snuffy."

"He'll be all right now," Cain said. He went over and stroked the arch of Lonesome's long black neck. He petted him over the rippling muscles of his shoulders. "Won't you, boy?"

Dencil came over and petted Lonesome too. "Never saw the beat of that. You making him stop running like that. With a running mule tied to him too. I've done some strong things with horses that was a mystery too. But never the beat of that."

Cain held still. He didn't want to go into why it was he could control animals, why he could make his will their will. He knew it was somehow linked with his hot temper, the terrible temper he was supposed to have inherited from Gramp Hammett. He knew the less he thought about such things the better he was able to keep a tight rein on himself.

"Why, Cain, you even scared the devil out of me. If you'd ordered me to, I'd have flown straight up in the air like an augerbird." Dencil stroked his mustache. "What I wouldn't give to have a little of that to shut up that woman of mine."

Cain bit his lip.

Dencil sighed. "It's funny about me. I can raise me horseflesh good enough to win every blue ribbon ever invented. But as for flesh of my own, I get me nothing but egg yolks."

"Maybe you got married too late, Dencil. Both of you."

"Then by golly, Cain, you better hurry. You're going on forty yourself, ain't you?"

Cain laughed. "No, just thirty, thanks be."

Dencil smiled. "Well, anyway, comin' back to that hoss, how did you make him stop like that?" Dencil tipped back his hat and scratched at a pink line made by a tight sweatband.

Cain held still.

"Like I say, by golly, I sure wish I had me some of that. I'd sure take the buck out of somebody I know. That's for sure."

Cain said, "That reminds me. What was all the squabbling about when I rode up?"

"Oh. That."

30

"Yeh, that."

Dencil's round face fell into a sad study. "Jesse and his boys was by."

"Hah."

"Yeh. They told me I better pull stakes, quicklike. They gave me two weeks."

"And the horses?"

"Said they'd take care of them. Shoot 'em down like they once did the buffler."

"Give any reason besides the usual?" Cain's left hand went automatically down to the butt of his gun.

"Said my horses tore up the land too much. Especially along the creeks. Said they were worse on the land than even your brother Dale's sheep. Well, I guess at that it does take more grass to keep a horse than it does a cow."

Cain bit on his mustache. Too bad, but it was true. Horses running in droves were hard on grazing land. Loose herds of horses couldn't help but be playful at times. Their milling around tore up even the toughest of sods. And when they ran at high speed, in stampedes, their sharp hooves cut the green skin of the land so deep it often took a whole summer to heal over. Horses also tore up the grass when they nibbled at it. They tore off the grass, while cows cut it off.

Tears popped into the corners of Dencil's gray eyes. "Sure hate to give this ranch up, Cain. If I was alone, maybe I'd try and stand up to Jesse. Show some sand. Even without a gun I'd try it. But when your own woman undercuts you, and you got kids that can get hurt, why, you've got to give it another think." Dencil blinked his eyes. "And I just yesterday twisted me out a new bunch of horses. So well broke this time I could guarantee 'em even to a Boston schoolmarm."

Cain stood on one leg, silent. His eyes roved over the yard. He observed how neat Dencil kept everything. No litter around the log cabin. None around the barn. The corrals built in neat lines and circles. No litter around the hand-dug well. The privy set well back in the sagebrush. A walking-plow, a wagon, a carriage lined up in a neat row against the fence. Yes, Dencil kept his yard every bit as neat as Clara kept her house.

Dencil scuffed the ground with his boot. "Well, if I go, it won't be to no livery stable, like the little woman wants, that I kin tell you. It's horses out here, in the open red air where they kin run with their manes flying like God wanted 'em to, or it's no horses atall. No stinkin' tangletails in the stalls for me."

31

Cain saw movement in the near window of the log cabin. It was Clara gesturing at him from behind the green panes. He could just make out her face over a red geranium. He caught the meaning of the gestures instantly. She was encouraging him to tell Dencil they should move out. Cain resented the gestures and turned his back on her.

"Cain, blast it, why should Jesse hate hosses so? Why, hosses of all animals is the wisest next to man. Why, hosses teach even men lessons sometimes. I once seen where a hoss took his ears and pointed out trouble ahead, a broken plank in a bridge, where the man was too dumb to see it. In daylight. I once seen where a good cow pony pointed out the right cow when the puncher himself was cuttin' out the wrong one. And many a time I've seen a hoss take a greenhorn kid and in a week make a pretty good puncher of him."

"I know." Cain stroked Lonesome's high black rump. "Lonesome spotted some trouble for me just this morning."

Dencil sniffed up his nose, loud, the sniff so strong it sucked up a few bristles of his mustache. "Course, as usual, Jesse also accused me of rustlin' hosses. Me, rustle hosses? My God, why should I rustle hosses? No one else here'bouts is raisin' hosses. So whose hosses could I be rustling but my own? My God."

"You better get a gun, Dencil."

Dencil stood a moment, bowlegs so wide apart the hole between them seemed wider than the width of his hips. "No, blast it, Cain, that I can't."

Cain said nothing. He was anxious to be on his way. He wanted to be at Rory's early enough so she could prepare part of the young bighorn for supper.

Dencil caught the hesitation. His face clouded over. "Well, all this ain't none of your consarn, Cain." He scuffed the ground. "And say, Cain, I'm sorry I can't very well ask you to step down an' stay for supper. Later maybe, when the old lady's settled her feathers."

"That's all right, Dencil. I know how such things are." Cain smiled. "That's maybe one reason I'm still free." He stepped up and forked himself across Lonesome. "Besides, I had me a big breakfast this morning. Mountain fries. And I want to save room for some more bighorn tonight."

"Should taste good. You must've had a good shot."

"I did. At an angle. Up. With just the corner of his head showing." Cain patted the cherry-wood butt of his Winchester. "Say! Maybe you'd like a piece. Sure you would." Cain stepped down off Lonesome again and went over to Animal and dug out a couple of steaks and a small roast. "Here. And good eating."

"Aw, well, now, Cain."

"Take it. Everybody likes a treat. Bighorn meat is mighty good pickin's."

"Well, thanks, Cain. Much abliged." Dencil looked down at the red flesh in his hands. "The missus will like this."

"Don't mention it." Once more Cain stepped across Lonesome. He looked down at Dencil. "Well, I wouldn't let Jesse scare me too much, Dencil. It looks like we're gonna have to hold us a meeting with the rest of the boys pretty soon now. You see, I ran into Jesse today too. And where I was once pretty much agin playin' along with brother Harry and his Red Sash boys, now I don't know but what I'm for it. If it comes to choosin' between English millions and American hellions, well, you know where I stand."

Dencil nodded.

"Well, so long. Hold hard." Cain touched his knees to Lonesome's shoulders and they were off at a trot, Animal following. Cain let Lonesome pick the trail toward home on the Shaken Grass.

Cain

The sun was hot on his back. He could feel his toes squirming in dampness inside his boots. Even through his glove he could feel heat in the saddle horn. Under him Lonesome began to give off fumes of acrid stink. Wind from their going brushed over his face but sweat still ran down into his mustache.

He examined the horizon ahead, slowly, carefully, using the curled-up point of his hatbrim as something to go by. He studied all the sharp rims and crags in the silhouette of Crimson Wall ahead, looking far to either side. There were no long riders peering out over the hills so far as he could see. Jesse and his boys were maybe done looking for the day.

The sky was completely clear, a very light blue overhead, as if there were no air at all. There was no wind; only heat waves. Red dust puffed up lazily under the horse and mule, and followed after a few feet, and then subsided.

They rode into the red maw of the Shaken Grass canyon, pink dust on hat and shirt, pink light on mustache and mane. Shod hooves rang loud on the rocky trail. Echoes snapped back from the walls. Beside them the brook ran swiftly. The brook ran red as if with spilled Indian blood, sudsing pink over shallow stony fords, streaming bloody in the deeper channels. Red sandstone and molten scarlet scoria glinted in the beaches along the turns. Bluestem grew tall in the low sloughs. Higher up, on the first low bench, grew light green greasewood and wolfberry, and wild rosebush and rough buckbrush and spike cactus. Still higher up the sides, growing in red dirt caught in tiny pockets of rock, clung sagebrush, low, squat, like ruffled nesting hens.

Near the top of the canyon walls, to either side, huge slabs of red sandstone and harder red rock, hollowed out from under by wind and frost, hung threatening over him. His eye naturally followed the possible line of fall. He saw where older slabs of rock had already broken off and now lay shattered in strewn rubble below. His eye followed the flow of the rubble all the way down to the edge of the stream. He recalled the sight of pebbles slowly rolling along in the stream just under his nose back where he'd taken a drink in the Red Fork. First wind and frost broke it off; then water washed it downhill. Night and day, while he was awake and while he was asleep, endlessly, the unraveling of the land never let up. Given enough time, the Big Stonies, the peaks and the cliffs and the footslopes, even the canyon he now rode in, would all someday wash down the Shaken Grass into the Bitterness, and then down the Yellowstone, and then down the Missouri, and finally down into the Gulf, all of it drawing after itself until there would be nothing left but sea washing and washing over the whole round earth. It was enough to make a man shiver and think on God, think even on the Devil, for that matter. What was he? Who was Cain Hammett? What was his horse? Who was Lonesome? Or the dead buck flopping loosely behind on Animal? And much less the sound and the echo of their going down the canyon of the Shaken Grass?

They stopped for a sip of cool red water. This time he was high on the stream; the horse and mule low. They drank together, their swallows clicking in unison. They sighed together. And went on.

He thought he spotted gray movement in the silver sage. Timber wolf. With an easy smooth pull he got the Winchester out of its scabbard. Lonesome felt his knee; slowed to a stop. Man and horse and mule waited. Man looked with his eyes; horse and mule pointed with their ears.

But the gray spot didn't move. And after a while Cain saw that it was but a dying clump of greasewood. It took that

34

long for eyes to make it out. All three of them had been fooled. Too bad. He'd felt like shooting.

He was about to start up again, when he caught, in the corner of his eye, the fleeting image of a man hanging by the neck from a cottonwood limb. He blinked; jerked erect. It took him a good full minute to make out that it was some kind of mangled mirage coming across the barren ground to the southeast. The dancing mirage gave him the shivers; he sweat cold.

Looking backward along the trail, where it wound back through the narrow canyon, he was struck again by all the color of it: the grass beside the creek so green it made a man's mouth water in sympathy for how a horse felt looking at it, and the sides of the red canyon walls specked with silver sage, and the far footslopes beyond on the Big Stonies a light green where mahogany brush thrived and then a deep green where the ponderosa pine grew in groves, and then out of all that, rising more sharply, above the timberline, the purple slopes of the Big Stonies themselves, gradually shading up into pure dazzling white points. He thought it prettier than a picture, and paradise itself.

He rode on, gun over his shoulder, pricking down the canyon. The Shaken Grass kept breaking through successive upthrusts of land, of red sandstone, of gray shale, of volcanic ash, of gray loess. Going down the bed of the brook was like riding into the successive jaws of half-buried saurians.

The canyon widened; became a narrow plain. Along the shallows the bark of willows gleamed red through silver leaves. Rabbit brush flared yellow over the low banks. The coneflower had just begun to shed its purple petals.

Near a turn a dozen small cottonwood saplings were down, all lying one way, cut by beaver. Further on a beaver dam blocked the stream, backing up a considerable pond. Cain had often looked at the dam and had in mind to run an irrigation ditch from it to make a small garden lower down and near his cabin. A thrush, then a flicker, then a flight of song sparrows winged over the pond. Tiny cottonwood with heavy varnished leaves grew along the margin of the pond.

He took a short cut over a low rise, climbing onto a gray slope. Immediately the scene changed. Away from the brook, the land lay cork dry. Rain had fallen on it in early spring, and its surface still lay cracked and open, white fissures cutting through the ocher soil. The rain had encouraged some grass to grow, and it now stood burnt, crumbling to powder at the least touch. The knolls were coarse with stones, vari-

35

colored, some specked with black dead moss. Even the prickle-pear cactus lay limp, its spears brittle red-brown. The huge red-ant hills, with cleared spaces around them, looked deserted. Dozens of clattering crickets, making a racket like rattlers as they whirred straight up out of the sagebrush, glinted in the sun. Yet, despite all the drouth, certain little yellow flowers, very tiny, no larger than pinheads, grew bravely in the drouth cracks.

He came over a low lip of land and below lay his little spread, his bachelor home beside the Shaken Grass: his three-room cabin, built of shiny cottonwood logs, caulked with clay and roofed over with soapmud; his barn built of rough lumber bought in Antelope; his corral made of slim cottonwood saplings. And beyond the ranch buildings, to the south and east, lay his beloved meadow. It all lay cupped within a bowl, where the Shaken Grass made a turn to the north while the low bench made a curve to the south. Cutting across the west tip of it ran the Casper road, coming down off the bench, slipping past the barn, and then crossing the river on the new log bridge on its way to Antelope in the north. Lonely horse-men and men driving buckboards often stopped to water their horses on the golden sand bar under the bridge.

The place had once been a line camp, or "boar's nest," for the Derby outfit, where cowboys wintered to keep the stream chopped open for drifting cattle and otherwise kept an eye out for calves lost in storm. That Cain had got hold of it was a great piece of luck. Before selling out to Lord Peter, Jesse Jacklin had tried to corral all the choice meadows along the Shaken Grass for himself by having his loyal cowboys homestead claims, with the understanding that he would buy them out when the claims had been proved up. But the cow-boy assigned this spot had reneged on the deal, and instead had sold it to Cain. The errant cowboy was known as Timber-line, a huge bald-headed giant of a man, now a member of ornery brother Harry's Red Sash gang.

It was the meadow that had caught Cain's eye in the first place. The meadow was about the size and shape of a park, and every bit as level, and so rich and moist that grass some-times grew an inch in a day, drouth or no drouth. A man could close-pasture his pet horse overnight there and know it'd be fat and saucy no matter how hard it'd been ridden the day before. And when it wasn't grazed, the meadow spilled over with flowers all the summer long: sourdock, windflower, evening star, beardtongue, dandelion. On occasion Cain fenced off half the meadow and let it grow long, and then he got hay so aromatic he could smell it all the way back to Crimson Wall when the wind was right.

Lonesome whickered, and a buckskin at the feedrack near the barn raised its head, its tail shooting straight out, its black mane tossing up, its nostrils flaring. It was Bucky, Cain's favorite cow pony. Bucky still showed he'd once run wild.

Cain was quick to spot his small herd of cattle up on a rise across the Shaken Grass. Good. At least Jesse had not run them off. Cain next spotted his string of horses on the far side of the meadow under the shade of a few tall cottonwoods fringing the stream. But, in spotting them, he noted a strange horse among them, saddle still on.

Cain snapped to in his saddle. Now that was a curious one. Runaway? Somebody hurt back in the hills? The stray had a familiar look.

It was when he came around the side of his log cabin on the bare yard that he found out whose horse it was. A huge cottonwood towered between the cabin and the barn, a good seventy-footer with a four-foot trunk of rough ocher bark, very hale, with leaves so green the time could have been the month of May instead of August. More than twenty feet up, on the south side of the tree, a fat limb grew at right angles to the main bole, and then, further out, it turned straight up to join the main bush of the tree. The limb went up like an arm crooked sharply at the elbow. And from this limb, near the elbow bend, and still in the shade of the tree, hung the body of a cowboy. By the neck. A cottonwood blossom. A huge knot bulked out behind the ear and the face was black with blood. A sash of brilliant red silk fit snug around the waist just above salmon-colored trousers.

"Hell's fire and little fishes! That mirage wasn't mangled after all. It did come true over the hills."

In one motion Cain slid off Lonesome and whirled on high heels, looking to all sides, left hand slipping out of its glove and dropping to the butt of his gun. A trap? He searched the fringe of trees at the end of the meadow, the bushes along the stream, the silver sage on the bench. But all he heard was the creak of the rope as the body turned a little by itself.

Sure no one was around, he rolled up a log and stood on it. Just as he got out his skinning knife, a last convulsive kick shook the body and the dangling legs did a jig. "Great grandad!" Quickly he cut down the body, holding it against his chest to keep it from hitting the ground too hard. He laid it out. Only then did he see that the gorged black face belonged to his ornery brother Harry. Harry actually had a blond face, with silver beard and hair, but choked with blood he'd looked like someone else.

"Man alive, if this ain't Billy Hell!"

Cain slid open the greased slipknot. A blue welt bulged out behind the ear where the knot had dug in. A rope burn lay red across Harry's throat.

Then Cain saw an odd thing. Fingernail scratches showed red all across the throat just above the rope burn. Picking up one of Harry's hands, Cain spotted bits of skin and blood under the nails. Hah. Harry's neck hadn't snapped on the drop afer all, and he'd somehow managed to free his hands. Cain recalled that for all his light body, Harry had a tremendous neck. When Harry got mad it ridged up thick with muscle and tendon like his own. Cain felt of Harry, found the face and neck still warm. So that was why the body could still do a strangulation jig at the end of the rope. "Hell's fire," Cain said softly.

Cain ripped Harry's pink shirt out of the tight red sash, tore it open, and held his ear to Harry's chest. Harry's heart was still beating. Slow, like the slow puff puff of a nearly stopped train.

Cain quick straddled his brother's chest and began to slap his face, both cheeks. He worked his arms. He lifted him up bodily and bounced him on the ground. "Harry! Harry, old boy!" He slapped. "Come around now, boy!" He worked his arms. Bounced him. "Harry, come around now, waddy boy. It ain't your time to go yet."

He heard chinking hooves behind him, and looking up he saw Lonesome coming back from the stream, trailing his reins, Animal following. Cain swore. Blast that snake at Dencil's. Have to break Lonesome all over again to stand ground-hitched.

Lonesome dripped water on his back. The drops reminded Cain of something. He spotted Harry's big felt hat nearby, and quick went over and picked it up, and bowlegged stiffly down to the Shaken Grass and got a hatful of red water. He sloshed it over Harry, over his face, down his neck.

That did it. Harry's chest shuddered; heaved a great sigh. It took a few short dip breaths; at last took hold on its own.

"That's the boy. Come out of it now."

Harry breathed, still unconscious.

Cain kept looking around at the premises, alert to the least sound. A breeze came up out of the north and passed through the upper reaches of the cottonwood. The tip leaves chiddered softly, sounding like the gentle threshing of beaded Indian dresses. Behind him the Shaken Grass purled over the golden sand bar. He saw a vulture winging in. What? How could a turkey buzzard, miles off, get wind of a man just hung and not yet cold? It couldn't be the stink. So how did they know? Cain swore to himself.

Cain sat holding Harry's head in his lap. He watched black blood slowly wash out of Harry's face. He waited until the point of Harry's thumblike nose became red again. Then he shook him. "Harry, old boy."

Blond eyelids fluttered open. Moonstone eyes, still glazed over with death, looked out at the world. "Where am I?"

Cain allowed himself a curving smile. It moved his mustache. "Where else but in hell, lad, for such as you?"

Harry rolled his head to one side; rolled it the other way. He seemed to have trouble understanding that his head and body were still connected. His eye fell on Lonesome dripping water on Cain's back; then on the mule Animal. He tried to focus on the burden Animal carried. "A moose. Where'd you get it?"

"A moose? Man, that's fresh bighorn."

"Guess I'm still bad off." Harry licked his lips. "I'll take some whisky."

"Gosh, boy, for once now I wish I had me some brave-maker too."

Harry continued to lie with eyes like a half-dead rabbit. "My head. Ohh. Feels as big as a salt barrel. And my neck feels like I been in a fight with a wildcat." Again Harry's eye fell on Lonesome, "Ah," he groaned, "I knew it was bad luck to ride you, you black hoodoo you."

"Oh, now, Harry, there's nothing to that now."

"Dencil bred him and Dencil's doomed. I rode him and I just about was doomed."

"What about me? I ride him all the time."

"With you it's different. You and that black horse are two of a kind and cancel each other out."

"Come now."

"You're both black devils."

"How about a drink of water? A good drink of cold mountain water beats all."

"D'rather drink vinegar. That at least has some bite."

Cain got another hatful of cool pink water anyway, and holding up Harry's head helped him drink some of it.

Harry licked his lips. He sighed, deep. "Well. Looks like I'm going to run another season after all."

"Sure you will."

"It's hard to believe I'm still here."

Cain helped him sit against the log. Gradually the sun struck in under the cottonwood. A purplish pallor came and went around Harry's eyes.

"Still got a hunger for a sour, Cain. Pickle or lemon. You sure you ain't got something with bite around?"

"Not a speck."

"How about a brain tablet then?"

"Say, a cigarette would taste good about now." Cain got out makings and deftly rolled two cigarettes, licking them lightly, and struck a match for both.

"Almost as good as a sour, Cain. Almost."

"That's what I say."

Harry rolled his head from side to side. Stare as he might, the haze in his eyes would not clear off: "When I first heard you, Cain, I thought it was the cook in hell trying to get me up for breakfast. Thought I'd made the big jump at last."

"Them damned strangling sons-of-bitches."

Harry winced. "I was just cutting across here when Jesse and two men I never saw before caught up with me."

"What was the reason they gave this time?"

"Said I'd milked one of my cows over one of Lord Peter's calves. So my cow would recognize it and mother it."

"Did you?"

For the first time a smile worked at the corners of Harry's lips. "I did."

Cain glanced down at the red sash circling Harry's waist. "Still a darn fool, I see."

Harry smiled distantly.

"Like waving a red flag at a bull, you jackass."

Harry still smiled.

"Harry, you're my brother and all, but, hell's fire, you've got to cut loose from that bunch a thieves. Or, darn you, you don't need to come around me no more."

Harry continued to smile to himself.

"Why do you do it, Harry?"

One of Harry's dulled-over eyes winked, slowly. "Once a wild one always a wild one."

"I say to hell with that. Even if Gramp said it. Harry, why can't you do like Dale and me? File on a homestead along the Shaken Grass and get yourself a small spread going? Play it honest? God knows we small stockmen got enough against us without adding outright thievery."

"Just a wild one, Cain."

"Harry, I've made my mind up about one thing. Even if

40

you are my brother, I ain't going to let you use me as a fence no more to sell your stolen beef to the stockyards."

"Hey, now." Harry came to life all at once.

"Darn right. And I ain't going to sell your butchered beef to the railroad crews no more either. Them hides I got to show as coming from meat I'm supposed to have butchered is so old now they're stiffer'n tepee skins. From now on, any meat I sell to the railroads is going to be from my own stock. Not Lord Peter's by way of you and Timberline and your boys."

"Cain, ain't you gonna help your dear brother make that one big haul? That one big one?"

"No! I got a strong hankerin' to clean up all around."

"Oh, come now, Cain."

"No."

"Tell you, Cain, if you do help me, you'll be shed of me for good."

"Harry, you're a darn fool twice over."

"If you do, it's off to California for me, to lay on the warm sand with my legs apart in the little waves. Tell you, Cain, I've looked at the back end of a cow all my life and I'm mighty tired of it. I need a change of scenery. Just let me make that one big haul and then you and Dale and Rory will be shed of me." Harry smiled to himself wanly. "And you can be darn sure I'll leave without kissin' the marshal good-bye."

"Harry, that's Saturday mush, and you know it."

Harry tried to sit up on his own; still couldn't quite make it.

Cain said quickly, "Hurt you somewhere?" Again he took Harry's head in his lap. He fanned his ashen face with his hat.

Harry looked up at the top of the cottonwood. A flush came into his cheeks. "Cain, ain't that a black buzzard sittin' up there?"

"Yeh. Does he bother you?"

"He's sitting there waitin' for me to die."

"He does bother you. In that case . . ." Cain drew his gun and fired straight up. He missed the buzzard, but he did clip the twig it sat on. The buzzard fell a ways, then righted itself, and with an angry squawk was off.

Harry tried sitting up again; at last made it.

"Take it easy now. No hurry."

Harry looked around, blear-eyed. "Say! My hoss, Star. It just come to me now. They run off with him?"

"No. He's yonder with my string."

"That bay devil. When here I've trained him to stand hitched to a rattler's tail, if need be."

41

"He probably didn't like the sound of the creaking rope." Harry grunted.

Cain couldn't help but smile to himself when he thought about his younger brother Harry. What a crazy one he was. Always into trouble of some kind. Had been ever since boyhood.

Cain remembered the time Harry had invented the game of pull-the-gooseneck at a family picnic over to brother Dale's. Under just such a cottonwood as the one above them. It was on a spring day right after a roundup and he'd been crocked to the brim with whisky. He'd taken cousin Rory's only gander, against her furious protests, had greased its neck with fatback and hung it by the legs, head down, from an armlike limb. Then he made a bet he'd be the first to snap off its neck riding by it on the dead run on Star. All the boys joined in the fun, even Dale, to Rory's even more furious disgust, and it took no less than fifty runs at it, before Harry, making his sixth try, finally caught the gander's head, popped eyes and gulking orange bill and all, between forefinger and thumb and snapped it off. Riding back, Harry had held it up triumphantly for Rory to take. What Rory had to say to him hadn't been fit for a cat to hear.

Cain got up. "I better help you into the cabin. Till your water runs clear." He helped Harry to his feet. Arm close around his brother's waist, gruff yet affectionate, he half-carried him into the cabin, up over the two-step log stoop and beneath the horseshoe over the doorway, across the puncheon board floor into his own sleeping quarters on the west side. Smells of damp wood and old woolen bedclothes and earth hung heavy in the low-roofed room. Cain helped him onto the bunk. The four log posts groaned as he stretched Harry out on the hide spring. Cain folded up a thick gray blanket and placed it under Harry's blond head.

"Now you take it easy for a spell." Cain pushed back a dusty curtain and light came in through a little square window. The light was barely strong enough to make a gun over the door glint dully. A thin film of dust lay over a trunk and over a stack of magazines and books piled on a pine shelf over the bunk.

Harry said, "What're you going to do with that moose, Dale?"

Cain studied him. Harry's mind still wasn't tracking quite right. Cain shoved Harry down by the shoulders. "Now you lay still for a bit."

Cain went out and got up Harry's bay, Star, and hitched

him to a pole near the door. He untied Animal from Lonesome's tail, removed the burdens and packsaddle from his back, and turned him loose in the meadow. Next he loosened the cinches to Lonesome's saddle and led him beside Star. The two geldings nosed each other in friendly fashion; presently stood tail-to-head switching flies off each other.

That done, Cain shot the loop of the rope out of the cottonwood tree; coiled up what was left of it and hung it on Harry's saddle. Cain thought it a low-down mean trick to hang a man with his own rope.

Cain also thought it a miracle that he'd found Harry alive. If it hadn't been for that Hammett neck of his . . . man! Cain recalled that Gramp had once escaped a hanging too. It was an unjust hanging, because the real culprit was found later on, but it was a hanging just the same. Gramp Mayberry Hammett used to show his grandsons just how he'd kept his neck from snapping when the vigilantes rode the buckboard out from under him. He'd open his shirt and tense up his thick neck muscles and set his chin down hard. With one exception, the thick Hammett neck had been passed on to the grandchildren, Cain, Harry, and Rosemary, by way of Gordon and Raymond Hammett. The one exception was grandson Dale. He'd come up with a gander neck.

The Hammett strain seemed to work down somewhat like the Hereford strain in cattle. Once the Hereford blood got into a man's stock, it gradually pushed out the Shorthorn, even the Longhorn. The stock became baldface, with turn-up horns, and had short legs, and that everlasting stocky neck. In trying to account for Dale's long neck, Gramp had finally decided it had come down through Mother Priscilla. Her father, Gramp Hoak, resembled a long-legged Frisian-Holstein.

Cain remembered that Gramp had been very much against next of kin mating, humans or cattle. Cousins marrying, Gramp said, only made the bad points worse. Gramp said it often made for raving idiots in human stock, six-legged monsters in cattle. Said it was an abomination to nature, one of the unforgivable sins.

"Take us Hammetts," Gramp orated. "We've got us a outlaw streak in our blood. A wild one. And, if I may say so, a beast in us that's wilder than a wild mustang bull. So you young uns be sure to water the Hammett blood down some by marrying strangers. Don't any of you three boys think of marrying cousin Rory, or you'll really whelp you a batch of wild outlaws. Mark my words. I've bred cattle and read Shakespeare, and I know."

Gramp had apparently been in part right about cousins marrying. Anybody could see with but half an eye that Joey, brother Dale's and cousin Rory's boy, had both the thick neck and the wild outlaw streak in him.

Gramp was well known for his old-boar opinions, mostly because he wasn't afraid to talk about them. Another of his ornery notions had to do with firstborn sons. Among other things, Gramp once told Dad Gordon over a glass of rye: "Course, Gordon, if you want to know the truth, and you want yourself a good obedient wife, you should really drown the firstborn son. I know you won't do it, and that's fine, because the boy Cain looks like a tough un, a real Hammett, but there it is anyway. I've bred cattle and read Shakespeare, and that's what I've come to see."

It was this notion about firstborn boys, as much as anything else, that had helped sour Harry some on life. As the middle boy, Harry had mixed feelings about his two brothers—Cain because he had the rights of the firstborn and Dale because he had the petting privileges of the youngest. And Harry was especially touchy about anything that had to do with Cain.

Harry once asked Gram, "Wasn't Gramp teasing Dad Gordon a little when he talked like that about drowning Cain?"

Gram's answer was emphatic. "No indeedy not. Mabry meant every word of it. I know. I can tell you. Euu."

Harry didn't dare mention it at the time, but there actually had been another male in the family, a baby boy who, had he lived, would have been their uncle. Dad Gordon actually was not the oldest boy. Just what had happened to their uncle in babyhood no one knew. Gram would never tell. And while Harry could never quite get himself to believe that Gramp could actually have drowned their baby uncle, or even consider having Cain drowned, Harry did think it mighty strange that the rest of the middle generation, their father Gordon Hammett and Rosemary's father Raymond Hammett, had drowned in a Missouri River flood in Siouxland.

The double drowning affected their entire lives. Their mother, Priscilla, died soon after of a broken heart; Rosemary's mother, Delia, deserted Rosemary. In the end, Gramp and Gram finally had to raise the four grandchildren themselves: the brothers Cain and Harry and Dale, and cousin Rosemary.

There was even a further oddity. Harry had seen with his own eyes that Gram had loved old Mabry to idolatry; that, like a mare parted from her foal at its birth, she hadn't shown much affection for any of her grandchildren.

Much much later, Cain and Harry and Dale found out that Gramp had been a second son. Gramp's older brother and his mother had conspired against him at every turn, so that, even though his family was a well-connected one in the East, he'd had to run away from home to get his freedom. The experience had embittered Gramp for life. Bitterness, the dark secret turnings of fate, and disasters in the form of drownings had left their indelible imprint on the Hammett strain.

It was hardly a wonder that Harry was an outlaw, a Robin Hood rebelling against the mighty. The grandsons could all have been outlaws. Yet, while Harry might steal beef from Lord Peter, and alter the Derby brand to his Rocking Hell, there was one thing he would never do—take as much as a drink of water from a nester without first asking. As an outlaw, Harry had a higher code than the cattle kings themselves did. They consistently stole not only from each other, through hired cowboys, but they often overran, and then took, everything the little stockman and the nester owned.

Thinking about all these things, Cain went into the cabin and shaved and cleaned up and changed clothes.

Finished, he went in to see Harry. He held up three fingers. "How many?"

"It's still a moose, Dale."

"What?"

"Say," Harry said then, grinning, "Cain, what're you going to do with that young bighorn?"

Cain grinned in turn. "Good. I see you're tracking again. That young buck? I promised him to Rory for supper tonight."

A look of disgust wrinkled the groove under Harry's nose. "So that's where you're going in them dude clothes."

Cain looked down at his new outfit: black shirt with white buttons, black pants with silver belt buckle, and fresh black silk bandanna. "Wanna come with?"

"With the shirt even buttoning down the back. Stylish."

"Sure. Makes it easier to get at that unreachable itch."

"New spurs with jinglebobs too."

"Nothing like having a private band along."

"You never did get over Rory, did you, Cain?"

"Ain't we all still cousins of hers?"

Harry sat up, hide spring under him creaking. "Some of the best meat I ever et was a hunk cut from a man's breast." He got out his makings and rolled himself a cigarette.

"What was that?"

45

Cigarette hanging from one corner of his lips, and a match from the other, Harry hopped out of the bunk. "No, after my near trip to hell, a catfight with Rory would be the last straw."

Cain said, "One thing before you run off to your boar's nest in Hidden County. Did Jesse happen to mention my name? Or Dale's?"

Harry's eyes couldn't quite hold up to Cain.

Cain nodded. "I thought so. Well, then I should probably tell you Jesse made the rounds today. He threatened poor Dencil and his wife too."

Again Harry's eyes shifted to one side. "They didn't hang him?"

"Not yet."

"Them strangling sons-a-bitches."

Cain

Lonesome didn't like the idea of going on. Lonesome was home. And Lonesome also shied at the skinful of fresh big-horn meat and the bedroll that Cain got ready to pack behind the saddle. Lonesome showed his disgust by distending his belly, full out, when Cain started tightening up the cinches.

"Dummed hoss always swells hisself up like a poisoned pup when he contraries," Cain muttered to himself. He whacked the flat of his hand under Lonesome's stifle. The whack made Lonesome cough and shoot out his breath in a gush. In that instant Cain jerked up the leather latigo to its usual mark in the cinch ring. "Ah, beat you to it again." Cain next slapped on a new silver-mounted bridle with a chirker in the bit. "All right, now let's ride. Rory will skin us alive if we don't make it by sundown."

Riding along in his shiny leather seat, of a piece with the horse's motion, hat tipped back with buckskin thongs knotted under his chin, jinglebobs on his spurs and the chirker in the horse's bit dingling a steady tune, and Lonesome's tail trailing in kingly style, Cain ahorse was a pretty sight.

They loped down a narrow two-wheel trail on the south or right-hand bank of the Shaken Grass. Grass grew green on both sides of the stream. Occasional high cutbanks showed strata of former floods: black, pink, black. Where the first rise of the bench lifted, the grass gave way to sage and greasewood.

Behind them the sun was almost down, about to be cut to bits by the long-toothed saw of the Big Stonies. From where they rode, some twenty miles east of the footslopes, the full silhouette of the mountains could be seen. The least ridge, the least rise, every prick and peak, became part of the thorny back of vast tyrannosaur risen out of the bed of the earth.

Most prominent were two points on the north end, the Old Man and the Throne. Wind, frost, storm had not been able to emery them off much and wash them down to the sea by way of the Shaken Grass. The Old Man looked like an ancient sage sitting on a stump, deep in thought, back bowed, head down, and crowned over with a great head of white hair, some of it falling far below his shoulders, with a ridgelike arm supporting the head on the near side, the hand or fingers hidden under the snowy crest. The figure sat unmoved, calm, full of stern grandeur. It suggested Old Man Reality Himself resting from his sorrows and labors. The Throne, which towered just north of the Old Man, and some higher by a thousand feet, was something else. It lent itself to ribald as well as reverent regard. From one vantage point it looked like a weathered cowboy privy without a roof; from another it looked like the pure white mount of Ascension. Another version had it that the Old Man was weeping because he'd never been able to climb aboard the Throne. Of the two mountain peaks, the Throne was the most famous, since to the north of it, on one of its rock plateaus and below the summit itself, men had found a curious thing: a gigantic Medicine Wheel made of boulders and slabs, mostly limestone, the whole wheel some eighty feet in diameter. The hub of the wheel was a circular mound of stones, three feet high and thirteen feet across, from which twenty-nine spokes radiated. A stone resembling a buffalo skull, its eyes facing the east, the rising of the sun, rested exactly on the center of the hub. Along the rim of the wheel stood six stone tepees. The stone tepee on the east side was the largest. It stood just outside the rim and its door also faced toward the rising sun. The doors of all the other stone tepees faced inward, toward the hub. Old worn paths, still evident in the forests and the upland meadows above the timberline, led up from the plains. Professors from the East believed it to be a place where ancient Indians had once worshiped the sun, perhaps a people related to the Aztecs. The professors thought the six tepees stood for the six major planets in the solar system, the twenty-nine spokes for the days of the lunar month. Cain himself had once climbed up to see it; and had sat on his horse Lonesome a while, a whole hour in high silence; and finally, shivering involuntarily as his mind slowly went back to that time, had broken off and quick climbed down, a different man for a few days.

Riding along the Shaken Grass, he watched the country flatten out ahead of him, saw it slowly turn to a gray and violent country. Sage and bunch grass grew out of alkali soils. The green along both sides of the Shaken Grass became but a narrow strip, in some places no more than a few feet wide. The color of the trickling splashing water changed too, pink becoming grayish, like dishwater, with the taste of it bitter and sharp on the tongue.

Far to the south a pink butte could be seen just barely riding out of the gray sloping and resloping country. Far to the north a low gray ridge fell away gradually until it mingled with an enormously distant horizon. And ahead to the east, very far, on the other side of where the Bitterness River took its turn to the north, the Cucumber Hills lofted vaguely in the oncoming dusk. The shadows everywhere were long. Except for the gathering regathering throws of Lonesome's hooves, it was very still out, silent, full of wait.

No matter how he tried to push it from his mind, the image of brother Harry's black face hanging down from the cottonwood kept coming back to him, making him shudder to himself now and then. He'd come just in the nick of time. Another minute or so and Harry would have been gone, and no amount of slapping and shaking would have brought him back. He could feel dark anger gather in him, deep down, at the same time that a sick sad feeling worked through him too. For all their wise-cracking talk, he knew, and Harry knew, that bad times were ahead for the three Hammett brothers.

Over a rise of land on the right rose a thin fringe of cottonwoods. It was the Bitterness River coming in from the southwest. The line of trees quartered off ahead to the east where they merged with the cottonwoods coming down with the Shaken Grass.

He followed the dim two-wheel trail over a dusty hummock and below him opened a new view. In the middle of a triangular meadow stood Dale and Rory's flat cluster of ranch buildings—cabin, bunkhouse, barn, sheep shed, fences, corral —all of it weathered brown log. An irrigated garden grew bright green behind the house, so green it was solace to tired eyes. The cottonwoods on both sides of the point of land made a fine windbreak, to the northeast and to the southeast. The evening sun striking underthrough the cottonwoods caught the gleam of slow streaming gray water where the creek and the river met beyond. The further reaches of the sliding

48

Bitterness were in deep shadow. The bitterness was a river spotted with terrors, quicksand in the turns, bottomless silt in the dips.

The two streams coming together made a natural fence to the north, east, and south. Dale claimed all the land inside the triangle back to the first water divide to the west. All Dale and his sheepherder had to do was guard the divide. Looking back, narrowing his eyes to mere slits, Cain could barely make out Dale's sheep on a slope of land a mile to the southwest, just above the Bitterness. The sheep streamed slowly across the evening land, moving over the slope like an army of snubnose maggots on the march, cleaning off the green bunch grass as they went. Every now and then over the sound of Lonesome's hooves, Cain thought he could hear the tinkle of sheep bells. Higher on the slope Cain could see the tiny figure of the sheepherder walking toward his white-canvas sheep wagon. Two collies followed at his heels.

Looking ahead again, Cain saw something else. He reined in his horse. There in the middle of the green irrigated garden stood cousin Rory. She was a good hundred yards away but he could see her plainly. She hadn't heard him come in the soft dust in the trail. What she was doing made him gasp a little. There was glory in it.

Facing the mountains to the northwest, the Old Man and the Throne, Rosemary was combing her long golden hair, first to one side, then to the other, and, lashing her hair forward, also on the underside, whipping it about in the sunset, revealing the nape of the sturdy Hammett neck. With each stroke her hair seemed to gleam brighter. She had on an old dark skirt, a light blue shirtwaist, and a faded gray gingham apron, and she was pregnant, but the glory of the flashing gold hair more than made up for the drab clothes and the laden body. Cain was too far away to see the expression on her face, but he could imagine it. For this one moment, this sunset evening, it would be absorbed, full of distant wonder as well as private thought, the very deep blue eyes in part sad, the lips some turned down at corners. The sight of her there alone, lonely in her garden at sunset and combing her hair while facing the mountains, became a pain, a stone, on his heart. Only a man with a bad conscience could fail to be moved by the sight. He wanted to rush over and crush her in his arms; yes, even bite her.

Rosemary. Rory. Sweetheart. Cousin.

Cain recalled how, because of her, he had killed his one and only man. Cecil Guth. Slim darksome Cecil had been a

49

braggart and a no-good gambling fool. He'd been a bustard to get along with, touchy as a mad weasel, and everybody had agreed he deserved the killin'. Even the sheriff at the time had agreed it was a good killin' and had refused to arrest Cain. "It's the mean thing we don't like," the sheriff told the new reverend, "no matter what it is. If the killin' ain't mean, and the man had it comin', as he did in this case, then we let it go. Out here."

Yet Cain had never felt right about the killing. Darksome Cecil had wanted to marry Rory and that made the killing a bad thing. Cain had not killed with clean hands.

As long as Cecil was courting her, all three brothers, Cain, Harry, and Dale, felt free to see her, even dance with her, and that though all three were in love with her. Had Cecil married Rory, all that trouble about cousins marrying would never have come to a head. But, with Cecil dead, they were back where they started. Many things happened after that killing, with Dale the weakest and the youngest of the three finally getting her.

. . . The killing happened this way. They were all at a country dance: Cain, Harry, Dale, Cecil, and Rory.

The four boys had a few drinks. Cecil needed only a few drinks, and then the devil in him showed. Cecil got to bragging about how good a shot he was, the best in Bighorn County. Cecil picked off the screw on a hanging kerosene lamp. He drilled the drum in the bandstand plumb center. He cut the E string on the fiddler's violin. He shot off the tip of Cain's boot toe.

Cain tolerated it all without comment. Because Cain despised him. Cain's nickname for Cecil was Pretty Shadow. He had often seen Cecil riding along gazing in admiration at his own shadow. A cloudy day was a bad day for Cecil.

It was when Dale was dancing with Rory, with Cecil and Cain and Harry watching, that Cecil finally said something that caught in Cain's craw. Cecil said, fawncing at the bit like an overeager stallion, "I don't know how you waddies feel about it, but that Rosemary, man, now there's the filly for me. I could snort her flanks all days long and not regret a minute of it."

Cain said, "All right, Pretty Shadow, that's it. I've heard enough." Cain backed a step to give the two of them room. "Go for it," Cain said.

"Me?" Cecil said. "You want to shoot it out with me? When

you know I'm the quickest shot in Bighorn County, left or right?"

"Left or right, go for it. You've had your last dirty say of a woman," Cain said, young face dark with rage.

"All right," Cecil laughed, snickering; and went for it.

Cecil's shot came first, because he was the quickest, like he said, but it went wild.

Cain's shot came almost on it, and it hit Cecil in the chest, because Cain was the steadiest, like he knew.

Cain looked down at where Cecil Guth lay on the floor. "Dummed fool should've known better. He saw me shoot down that wild Longhorn steer on the Red Fork last summer." Cain was referring to the time when his cow pony had slid out from under him, pinning down his right leg, cracking it, with the steer suddenly reversing itself and bearing down on him with long wicked horns set. Cain had calmly drawn his gun left-handed and shot the triangular onrushing forehead dead center. Calm. . . .

Even as Cain watched from his horse, Rory was suddenly done combing her golden hair. She turned and walked heavily back along the garden path, past lettuce and onions, past marigolds and petunias, and went around the side of the cabin out of sight.

Cain waited a decent interval. And then, waving his hat, he rode onto the yard with a flourish, whooping, "Ya-hoo! Yi!"

Just as he hoped, his six-year-old nephew Joey came scooting out of the barn to greet him. Joey had hair that was a part of the sunset, with fair tanned face and bold blue eyes. The boy had thin bowed legs, much too light for a heavy head and neck, and running fast he looked like he might at any moment fall on his face. He came riding a stick horse and swinging a looping lasso. It was the circling momentum of the loop which seemed to keep him upright. Around his waist was a belt studded with empty .45 shells and a wooden home-made six-gun. A Hammett if there ever was one. "Hi, Unk! So you made it after all."

"Sure I did, my bucko." Cain stepped down, groundhitching Lonesome.

"I told Mom you would."

"You did, huh? Mom didn't give up on me by any chance, did she?"

Joey examined Cain's black boots critically; then held out one of his own flashy red ones for comparison. "Boy, I wish I was growed already."

"How so, button?"

"Then I would ride a black horse too in black clothes. With silver shining all over like a fair."

"Don't you want to become a sheepman like your paw?"

"No. They stink too much like goats."

"Well, well. Look now, sonny, you go in and tell Mom I just now blew in with the tumbleweeds."

"You go tell her yourself."

Cain slid the skinful of fresh bighorn meat to the ground. "Hey, what kind of talk is that now to your uncle?" He carried the meat to a bench off to one side near the front stoop. The bundle was heavy and his sharp heels cut into the hard gray ground. He grunted as he straightened up.

"Wait'll you see Mom. Then you'll know why I said it."

Cain held. "Oh?" The door to the cabin was open an arm's length away. He sensed someone listening inside. He threw a cautious look at the curtains in the window on the other side of him. "Where's your paw?"

Joey crooked his head in the direction of the sheep corral behind the barn.

"And Gram?" Cain stiff-legged back to Lonesome. He took off his gloves and pocketed them. One eye still on the door, he uncinched the saddle along with his bedroll and slid them off Lonesome too. "Eh?"

"In the bank." Joey crooked his head at the privy in the willows behind the house. "Making a deposit."

"What!" A grin cracked across Cain's walnut face. "You talk like that about your own greatgram?" Cain swung the saddle and bedroll onto the hitching rack, making sure it sat securely balanced.

"Why do you hang up your saddle for, Unk?"

"No cowboy worth his salt throws gear on the ground. You know that. Might get it tromped on. Besides, sand'll stick to the sweaty underside and give the hoss saddle sores."

"Why do you dress up when you come here, Unk?"

"Ain't I company?"

"Why do you wait to water your hoss, Unk?"

"After a run, a horse is too heated to drink water right away."

"Why do you wear a mustache, Unk? Paw don't."

"To strain the color from my language around little buttons like you."

A tall gray Plymouth Rock rooster came cockalorking around the corner of the log cabin. Joey spotted him, and with a quick dextrous turn and throw of his play lasso, roped the rooster around the legs and jerked him to the ground. The rooster let out a surprised squawk. "Calf on the ground!" Joey yelled. "C'mon, you bustard you, slap that dottin' iron on him! We got us another Mark-of-Cain calf."

Cain couldn't help but laugh and join in with the game. He grabbed up an old rusty branding iron leaning against the far end of the cabin and ran for the rooster. "Hot iron comin' up! Hold 'em, cowboy!"

"Ya-hoo! Yi!"

With that, Rory showed at the door. "Joey, you little dickens you, how many times must I tell you not to rope that rooster! He's the only one we got. Oh. Hello, Cain."

Cain turned; stood up; and lifted his hat in mock deference. "Howdy, ma'am. Nice evenin'." Then he added, after a look at her, "Rory, for godsakes, what happened to you? Get caught in a stampede?"

Joey said, "I told you to wait till you see her."

"You shut up you, you little dickens!"

The right side of Rory's face was all brockled over with blue bruises. Her right eye was black and almost shut. From where he'd sat on the ridge overlooking the garden, Cain hadn't been able to make out the details of her face. Cain was shocked. What with being far along in her pregnancy, and her face red, the Rory who stood before him was hardly the slim grass-finished Rosemary he'd once loved. Close up she looked forty, when she actually was but thirty.

"Dale didn't get drunk and beat you up, did he?"

Rory's back arched. She became all horns and rattles. She said, icily, "You know Dale never indulges."

" 'Indulges,' is it? Lady, please. Bite shallow and I'll follow you."

"Joey, take that rope off that rooster right now. Pronto! You hear? And give it here." Stepping heavily, one high-laced black kid shoe at a time, a hand on a knee, she came down off the stoop.

"No," Joey said.

Rory hit him a whack over the ear.

Cain cleared his throat. Hitting the boy he didn't like. "Now, Rory, what's the harm in a little fun? When I was a kid I used to rope roosters too. I once even roped the neighbor's baby."

Rory whirled on him, belly coming around slow. Her mouth squared open. "So you too are out to spoil the little brat, eh? Gram ain't enough, eh?"

Cain swallowed. He looked down at Joey. "Guess we better

53

get that string off that calf, waddy boy, or we'll both be hung as a couple of outlaw hen wranglers."

"Aw, hell, Unk—"

"What!" Again Rory leaned over her burden and whacked Joey, with her right hand and then her left, biff-baff. "Watch your language, you little shitepoke."

Joey jumped, then looked up at Cain from under a throw of gold hair. "Guess it's a case of wrong brand, huh, Unk?"

"That's it, pard."

Lonesome trailed over then, head held carefully to one side to avoid stepping on the reins. He nuzzled Rory's back; her neck.

Rory jumped, heavily, but when she saw who it was, she suddenly smiled, her swollen face opening in a big wide crease. "Why, Lonesome, you old sweetheart you. You still like that perfume, don't you?"

Cain quick blinked his eyes. He remembered a time almost forgotten when Lonesome had first noticed perfume on her, as if he, well-born himself, knew a thoroughbred when he saw one.

"See, Cain, he hasn't forgot my favorite perfume after all this time. I haven't used it in years. Just happened to find the bottle again today as I was cleaning. See, he's nuzzling me where I always put a drop."

Cain held still.

Joey asked, "What is it when Lonesome starts smellin' up them other horses in the corral then?"

To keep Joey out of further trouble, Cain quick said, "Well, Rory, and have you seen what I brought? For supper?"

Rory turned, still smiling. "You did get a bighorn then?"

"Yessiree." Cain pointed to the skinful of meat and the big coiled horns. "And butchered it for you."

"Young?"

"Just turned a year. You kin tell by the growth rings on his horns."

Her face still held bright. Almost she looked again like she had in the old days. It was with pain that Cain remembered the mean words she'd once said to him, that time he took her home a year after killing Cecil Guth. "One night you set and say, yes ma'am, no ma'am, and look like a stuffed owl. The next night you drink up all of Gramp's whisky and make love like a horse. Lord knows what next to expect from you. Cain, if you can't remember I'm a lady, there's the door. Besides, and don't forget it, I'm your full cousin."

54

She went over and stroked the curled horns. "What are you going to do with the head?"

"You want it?"

"We could mount it."

"It's yours."

She looked across at the sun. It was just then sinking behind the Old Man in a great throw of exploding yellow-banded light. It seemed to be burning a hole into the Old Man's white hair. "I won't have time to get a roast ready any more today. But we can fry some up. And we can hang the rest in the cooler for tomorrow night."

"Good. You got you a star boarder."

Rory selected a prime piece from the skin. Still smiling, she climbed the stoop and disappeared into the house.

Cain sighed. He picked up the rest of the meat and the head of horns and went for the well. Over his shoulder, he called, "All right, Lonesome boy, I guess you've cooled enough now to drink. Hup."

"Can I lead him, Unk?"

"Sure. But be careful he don't roll on you."

Cain hadn't more than said it when with a snort Lonesome sank to his knees and rolled over, first on one side, then the other, grinding his neck in the soft gray dust, wriggling in delicious balance exactly on his curved spine, forefeet up like a playful puppy's, rear legs up like an awkward cow's.

Joey held on, allowing Lonesome all the slack he needed.

Presently Lonesome had enough, and got up, knees first, then body, then rear legs, and gave himself a tremendous shuddering shake. A little cloud of dust floated off. It made Joey cough.

After he'd hung the meat and the head low in the cooler beside the well, Cain hauled up a couple of buckets of water for Lonesome. He left the cover off the well thinking Lonesome might need more. One leg up on the drinking trough, he stroked Lonesome's flank lovingly. Dusk turned Lonesome's black mane to a running fire of bronze. Joey stood on the other side of Lonesome, trying to put up a leg too on the wooden trough.

Cain said, "What was Mom so mad about when I first come?"

"I dunno. Paw came home with some news early yestiddy morning that Mom didn't like and they had a fight."

"I can see that."

"You should've heard them. First there was Paw tellin' Mom something. Then came an awful quiet. I could hear 'em

55

in bed laying still as mice, thinkin'. Then slowly Mom started in talkin' low, then she got mad hearin' what she had to say to him, givin' Paw the devil from here to hell an' back. And then finally Paw come to and he got mad and he finally hit her a whack. Then she hit him. He hit her. She hit him. And the noise in the house got to be something awful. I run out like I had to make a deposit in the bank I got so scared. Sounded like they was shoein' a horse inside the house. Pretty soon even Gram couldn't stand it and she came by me in the privy, me on the big hole and she on the little one. Well, when we come back later, after they had enough, both of 'em was so bloody in the lamplight where they wuz patching each other up it was hard to know 'em from fresh hides. Mom was so swole up she looked like she was gonna have two babies. T'while Paw looked like a slunk baked-apple."

Cain didn't know whether to laugh or cry at Joey's lively picture. "Oh, come now, Joe boy, it couldn't have been that bad. You know the Hammett men ain't exactly wife-beaters."

"Well, Paw did hit her though."

"I don't hardly believe it."

Foot still up on the drinking trough, and still stroking Lonesome's black coat lovingly, Cain fell to musing to himself. Yes, the Hammett men were hardly wife-beaters. They were wild and dark sometimes, but they were hardly that.

Cain remembered the days when he and Harry and Dale, besides being just brothers, were also inseparable waddies, calling themselves the Three Mustangs. They were full of the devil then, scorning all women except Gram, "whooping and hollering and raping around," and having themselves a time.

Eventually all three might have married stranger women, and thus have remained jolly kin together at family reunions and family weddings and family funerals, remembering privately and ignoring publicly—if it han't been for Cain killing Cecil Guth.

But he had shot Cecil and that was the end of the brothers as the Three Mustangs. Instead of waddies faithful and true to each other they became rivals wary and watchful of each other. When Gramp wasn't around, he and Harry had played up to Rory for all they were worth, trying to catch her alone, doing her favors, buying her expensive presents, while Dale looked on weakly and sullenly.

Then, before either he or Harry got very far with her, Rosemary all of a sudden eloped with Dale. Just why they could never get her to say. Maybe it was because she knew she could never choose between the two or there would be another

56

shooting. Maybe it was because she was shrewd enough to see that both Cain and Harry would be slow to pick a fight with the weaker brother. And maybe it was because her kind needed the weakest one anyway.

Cain smiled, slow, down at Joey. He asked, quietly, "Your maw and paw fight often like that?"

"No. That's the first I know of."

Cain shook his head sadly.

"Unk, kin I come and live with you?"

"What? Oh, now, my waddy boy, I'd like that of course, but you got your own folks."

"Unk, why don't you get married like Paw?"

The flesh around Cain's smoke-blue eyes crinkled up. "Maybe one of these days I will. Send for a wife out of a mail-order catalogue."

"Paw says what you need is one of them widders what needs her weeds plowed once a week."

"He says that, does he?"

All the while, Joey hadn't been quite able to get his foot up on the drinking trough like Cain. He finally climbed onto a support under the trough and tried again. He got his foot up all right, but the foot he stood on wobbled on the support, and after a moment of tottering he lost his balance. Before Cain could grab him, Joey tipped lengthwise into the open mouth of the well, and in a quick falling streak, a surprised gold face and a blue-clad body and a pair of red boots vanished into the black below. There came a fleeing boy's cry; a muted splash.

Lonesome's noble head popped up from the drinking trough.

"Joe boy!" Cain cried.

Then Cain unfroze. He tore off the remaining planks of the well cover; tried to see down. But all he could make out, some thirty feet down, was a winking surface of liquid ebony. "Balls of fire!"

He saw right away he couldn't trust his weight to the bucket rope. It was too frayed. Quickly he hobbed over to the hitching rack on which he'd set his saddle. A nervous belch broke from him. He grabbed the lasso from the horn and, iron spurs chinkling on the rocky yard, hurried back to the wellhead.

He put his hat to one side and peered down. "Joe? Joe!"

No answer.

He anchored the rope to the trough. He was about to let

himself down hand over hand, when he heard gurgling below. He listened.

Some more gurgling.

Peering down again, he saw whelming rings on the liquid ebony surface.

A weak voice whimpered up at him. "Unk?"

"Joe boy! You all right down there?"

"Oh, Unk!" The boy's voice almost broke. "I'm drownin'!"

Cain finally spotted him—face gleaming up, Joey was clinging to a piece of sprung wooden curbing. Cain hardened; yet spoke very calm. "Hold tight, Joe boy, and I'll be right with you."

"I'm gonna drown, Unk."

The way the boy tried to stay on top of his terror made Cain catch his breath. "Hang on, boy."

"It's awful slidey, Unk."

Cain leaned far into the wellhead, dark hair sliding down in a straight throw over his blunt brow. Swiftly he shook out a little loop. He made his voice land on the water beside the boy; calm. "Joe, I want you to count to twenty. Start in. One, two—"

"I'm gonna drown, Unk."

"Count!"

"One—two—three—"

"That's it." Cain let down the loop, deftly trying to settle it directly over the boy's thin shoulders.

"—seven—eight—nine—"

There was just a foot to go, when the loop slid out through the honda. The knot of it hit the boy on his gold head.

"—thirteen—oh, Unk, I'm gonna fall in!"

"Count!" Cain held back an impulse to roar it. "Hold tight."

There was no time to set the loop again. Cain let the knot settle against Joe's chest. "Joe, listen now. Let go one hand and grab the rope."

"Unk—"

"Try it. Let go one hand and grab the rope."

"I can't, Unk."

"Do it!"

"Unk—"

"Blast it, do it!"

Cain could more feel than hear the boy scrabbling, desperately trying to hang onto the filmy wooden curbing. Cain shot down his voice again, this time powerfully, low, letting the animal in him get into it, letting the animal in him strengthen the animal in the boy, commanding it. "Do it, Joe! Grab it, Joe!"

With a whimper of utmost reluctance, with a creature's whimper, yet having to do it, as if hypnotized, Joey did it. He let go one hand and grabbed the rope just above where the knot lay against his chest.

"Now grab with the other hand!"

Because Cain had set it so strongly in the boy's mind, Joey's other hand also let go and grabbed the rope. With that the lad swung free of the slippery wall and pendulumed awash in the deep water a few times. Curdles of dirt from the wooden wellhead hit the water, setting off little wrinkles across the big ripples.

Again Cain sent down his voice, low, powerful. "Hang tight onto that rope now, Joe! That's it. And up you come. Steady as you go."

Little fists fierce, Joey held tight.

"I'll have you out in a jiff, my boy."

Hand over hand Cain drew him to the top, the boy's soppy gold hair showing more plainly on every haul, until his head rose through the opening, and up into the purple dusk. One look at the boy's pallid face, and Cain's heart bounded in his chest. Cain clutched the boy to his bosom; held him close. Water poured from the boy's clothes. Miraculously his little red boots were still on, spilling water. Cain hugged him. He became sopping wet too. When he thought of what might have happened, almost did happen, his mind burned. This was the kind of lad Gramp Hammett recommended they drown. Because he happened to be a firstborn son. "If you want a good obedient wife, drown the firstborn son." Such monster thoughts. Cain wished Gramp were around right then. He'd beat him up. Drown a dear close bundle of bunny-boy flesh like this? Well, he'd take the boy any day even if it meant living with a Rory on the prod. He hugged Joey close. "My boy, my boy," he whispered, "my little waddy boy Joe." He couldn't see for the tears clotting his lashes.

He didn't hear the sounds coming up behind him. A stringy hard hand grabbed him roughly by the shoulder. Then a man's tight-pitched voice demanded right in his ear, "Great thunder, Cain, you trying to drown my oldest boy?"

Cain whipped around. "Dale! Man, am I glad to see you!"

A long lank of a man, hatless, grabbed Joey out of his arms; hugged him to his own breast. "You better be."

Cain blinked tears out of his eyes. "He's all right, thank God."

"Thank God, bull!" Dale comforted the boy to his skinny chest. "Joey my son boy, you all right?"

Joey drooped. The shock of the fall, the sudden immersion in cold water, the desperate scrabbling up out of the water onto the sprung wooden well curbing, Cain's terrible demands upon him, had emptied him.

"Son?"

"Paw."

Dale gave Cain a fierce incredulous look. His gaunt wind-honed face was blue with it. "How the blazes did you let this happen?"

Cain swallowed. "I guess it was my fault at that." He hated getting caught. "I left the cover off the well thinkin' maybe Lonesome might want some more water. The horse was drinking from the trough and the boy was playing around it. You know. And somehow, before I knew it, he lost his balance and fell in." Cain looked down at the wet rope in his hand. "I guess I'm not used to having kids around."

"I guess you hain't!" A sob racked Dale. "Cain, when you got kids around, blast it, you got to be thinking about where they is every blessed minute of the day!"

"I know, Dale. I was wrong, Dale. Thank God I could still save him."

"Thank God, yes!"

"I'm that sorry, Dale. I am."

"Ohhh . . . forget it."

Outrage slowly drained from Dale's face. With a toss of his head Dale threw back wild dark hair. And presently, as was usual with him, sulk set in and Dale's lower lip came out.

Dale said, "Wait'll Rory hears about this one. The hell I'll catch. She's already got her stickers out for me."

Joey stirred. "Paw?"

Dale looked down at the boy in his arms. "How do you feel, button?"

"I dunno yet."

"Can't you tell me how you feel, Joey my son boy?"

"I dunno." Joey sighed out of the depths of his little belly. "Well, I guess I feel worse all over than anywheres else."

Dale coughed a half-laugh half-sob. "Oh, God, Rory will spot them soppy clothes immediate."

Cain said, "I'll tell her. I'm the one to blame."

But when they went in to tell her, Rory surprised them. One look and she shoved pot and pan to the back of the stove and took the wet half-drowned boy away from Dale and put him to bed for a while in a dry nightgown.

Cain

The coyotes were yowling from the alkali hills by the time the men had washed up. The men hung their guns and hats on the deerhorn rack behind the log door and sat down to Rory's supper.

It was a good supper too. Just as Cain expected, Rory had fried the bighorn meat deep in fat, so that it fell apart at the least touch of the fork while yet retaining in its tender succulent strings all of its mountain-grass savor. She had quick made some flour gravy from some of the meat juice, and the gravy poured over baking-powder biscuits was enough to make a man forget miles of hard riding. She had also boiled some spuds and baked a mess of beans and fried some onion rings. Cain and Dale asked for and got a fresh raw onion each, which they called "skunk eggs" and ate like apples. There was also canned milk for coffee.

The table stood in the center of the big room. Dale sat at the head, near the fireplace. Rory sat across from him, near the hot cast-iron range and the counter on the food cabinet. Cain sat on Rory's right, facing the door, while across from him sat Joey and Gram Hammett, Joey next to Dale and Gram next to Rory.

The room was a large one, serving as kitchen and dining room and parlor all in one. A Seth Thomas clock hung high over the mantelpiece, festooned with old dried pussywillows. Slowly it pendulumed the time away. The woodwork on the clock was dark, with intricate carvings of flying horses and angels and arrows cut into it. Two guns hung under the clock, a .38 Winchester and a .45-120 "Old Reliable" Sharps buffalo rifle. To the left of the clock, in a dark frame, hung the wedding license with its flourish of fancy handwriting: "Know all men by these presents that before me on this day was joined in holy matrimony . . ." On the other side of the clock hung a portrait of Gramp and Gram Hammett, Gram seated on a love seat with a pinched smile on her lips and a baffled look in her eyes, and bullnecked Gramp standing behind her just barely hiding a triumphant smile under his handle-bar mustache. On the mantel itself, just below the clock, stood the favorite family knickknacks: a pot of Wandering Jew, a copper dinner bell, an old-style cut-glass decanter, a cup of lead shot for pen cleaning, a fat gold watch with a key for winding attached to its chain. Fresh logs lay piled on the andirons in the hearth, waiting for the first cold day of fall ahead. A poker shaped like a devil's fork and a small shovel leaned against the bricks. In a far corner stood a high bookcase overflowing with books and magazines: sets of Shakespeare and Dickens, a much worn copy of *Ben Hur,* a set of religious compendiums, a leatherbound set of the World's Best Classics, and a complete file of the stockman's bible, the monthly *Stockbreeder*—most of them former possessions of Gramp Hammett and all of them well read by every male member of the family. Two worn schoolbooks lay on a side table. They were eloquent testimony that while Joey might be a bit pampered by everybody, he still got his daily schooling from mother. Underfoot dark brown bear rugs covered a puncheon board floor.

On the table in their midst a flame licked slowly in a saucer of cow tallow. It cast a low mellow almost red-gold light over their faces and hands. It gave the whitewashed walls of squared logs and moss-and-clay chinking the look of plastering done by a professional. It gave a set of bull-elk horns on the wall an almost live look, as if a real bull elk were eavesdropping on their talk. It set up sparkles in the motto on the far wall, making the lettering easy to read:

Let no stranger leave this house cold or hungry.

Despite the heat of the day, and the hot stove, the log cabin was cool. There was even the pleasant dampish smell of a cave in it.

Joey had been roused to eat. He came to the table in his nightgown. After a couple of bites, he began talking his head off, making bright remarks about everything said, sassing Gram, sassing Mom, even offering Dale some sage advice on how to run the sheep ranch.

"Say, Paw, don't you think we oughter put a better lid on that wellhead? With some regular iron hinges from Antelope? Like Lord Peter's got on his fancy well?"

"We could," Dale said from the head of the table.

"And put a sign on it so everybody kin read it." With only his head and thick neck visible Joey looked a ten-year-old. "And keep it the hell closed."

"We could," Dale said into his meat.

Rory said from her end of the table, "That's enough now with that rough talk, Joey. Little boys should be seen not heard when there's older company present."

Joey chirped on as if he hadn't heard her. "Next time I'm gonna wait till Unk's got it closed afore I—"

"Shut up!" Rory snapped. "Next time. Next time. You're always bright after the fact. Like your father." In the tallow lamplight, under her gold-blond hair, Rory's dark blue eyes, even the swollen one, took on the black glitter of shoe buttons.

Gram looked up from where she was munching on a biscuit with toothless gums. She had hair that was as stringy and as coarse as white horsetail. Her face resembled a hearth with the ashes taken out. She had hands like reversed oak roots. She spoke in a dry leathery voice. "Better listen to your mom, sonny, or as sure as Old Johnny God is in His heavens, I'll get hell for it again." As she talked bits of biscuit crumbled out of her mouth.

Rory said, quiet, eyes dark dots in the low light, "Well, Gram, you sometimes do indulge him too much."

Joey said, "Gram, you mustn't talk with food in your mouth. Yore spittin' in my face and it ain't perlite."

"Hey now," Dale warned. "Respect for your greatgram now please."

Gram laughed, gums showing clay-pink. Her cheeks wrinkled up like old kidskin. "It's all right, sonny." Her old rheumy eyes gleamed. "The days pass by, your blood changes, and gradually you forget."

Rory said, "Gram, it is your fault he talks like that." Rory picked up a white bowl heaped with spuds and passed it around for a second time. "If you'd slap him now and then, he wouldn't dare talk back to you. Fear makes love, you know. Like Gramp used to say."

The laugh vanished from Gram's old face. "Creation alive and mercy me," Gram murmured to herself, as her eyes slowly filled with tears, "I can't slap the boy. Never. Little boys are old so soon."

"What's that got to do with it?" Dale asked, accepting a bowl of gravy from Cain. "If he's bad he's bad and ought to be walloped."

"Oh, what's the use a talking to her," Rory said. "A person is just barking at a knot telling her to quit spoilin' the boy."

Gram hardened up at that. She asked snappish, "A knot, is it? And when have I been spoilin' him?"

"Oh, Lord, Gram, let's not go into that again."

Gram pushed her old face forward. For a moment she looked sixty instead of eighty. "When? When? You tell me. You spoilbutt yourself you!"

63

"Just yesterday, if you must know."

"I did not."

"Why, you did too! You gave him them dried apples I was saving for a Sunday pie. When you thought I wasn't looking."

"I did not."

"You did."

"I did not. Did I, Joey?"

Joey gave them both a pair of big blue eyes; then turned his gold head a little and gave Cain a sly wink.

Rory got mad then. "You see? You see how she lies, Dale? And you see what the boy does then? Even winks, he does. The little dickens."

"Aw, Rory," Dale started to say, "now—"

"But I saw her give them to him with my own eyes. That's how she lies. Right under my nose even. If that boy don't grow up an outlaw, it'll be a miracle to me." Rory shook her head sadly. She was flushed from the stove and the argument both. "Just a spoiled and pompered child, that's what he is."

Gram helped herself to some baked beans. She munched on a few, mouth open. She swallowed noisily. "Never saw such funny beans. Spots on them like that. Look like one-eyed bugs. Never saw such beans with spots on 'em like that. Black."

"They grow that way," Rory said icily.

"Good, though," Gram said, again spraying food over the table in front of her.

"Gram," Joey said, making a show of wiping off his face with a finger, "please don't talk with your mouth full."

"Oh, yes indeedy. I forgot again."

Rory said to Cain, careful to keep her swollen eye out of Cain's line of vision, "See if you can make that little wetnose shut up and behave."

Cain's heavy brows came up; then came down. He'd been eating quietly to himself, determined to keep out of an augering match with his brother Dale and cousin Rory. Two sets of black eyes were enough. Besides, he was one of those who hated talk at the table. Cowboys on the trail rarely talked while they ate. He held his peace.

Rory flashed her one good eye at him. "Well?"

Cain looked across at Joey. Shortening up the lad's stake rope would probably be a good idea at that. But he'd be damned if he said so as long as the boy wasn't his. He loaded up his fork with potatoes and inserted the food beneath his mustache.

Gram said, "Never saw such beans. Must be a new invenshun. Got a spot like a one-eyed bug. Good, though."

Rory hated all bugs—bedbugs, fleas, ticks, box-elders—and Gram's talk gave her a pain. "Oh, shut up about that once, will you, for heaven's sake!"

Joey said, "You can shut up for me too. I'm about as tired of it as anybody."

Dale finally reared up and hit Joey one over the head.

Cain looked on astonished. Not an hour before Dale had given him, Cain, the devil for being careless with the boy around the well.

Dale caught the accusing look in Cain's eyes. "A few doses like that will cure him of sucking eggs, acting smart interrupting folks."

Gram said, "Never saw such beans. Got a spot like a bug. Good, though."

"Please, for godsakes, shut up about those beans, will you please?" Rory said.

Cain quick hid his eyes, staring down at his gravy-streaked plate. It hurt him to look at Gram, to look at departed and fallen grandeur. The wonderful Gram he remembered from back in the old days when they still lived in Siouxland; the Gram who with Gramp raised him and Harry and Dale and Rory; the fierce old lady who goaded Gramp Hammett to start over again by moving into another state; the Gram who in her earthy wisdom took a bucket of Siouxland angleworms with her and planted them in the garden behind the house; the Gram who gloried with Gramp when he came up with a successful breed of cattle by crossing Hereford with Longhorn; the dignified lady who instructed them as to why they should be proud they had Hammett blood in their veins . . . well, here this Gram sat now across from him, mostly an appetite caught in a sack, a few chalk-brittle bones holding it up, decked over with coarse white hair and wrinkled kid-leather skin.

Raising his eyes, he saw that Gram had slipped into one of her cries again. What kind of memory tickled that old unraveling brain now? A vision of Gramp rampant beside his hearth? A fleeting vision of her own lost virginal beauty?

Off to one edge of his vision, Cain felt, almost saw, Rory's dark eyes on him, wondering what he was thinking about. It occurred to Cain that a glimpse of a person caught off to one side of the eye revealed more than a head-on look. For one thing, the other person, not knowing he or she was caught in the vision, let the animal inside look out. For another, one's own animal seemed to see better. At the moment, he could read Rory's thoughts better than she could read his. And what he saw there bothered him.

Gram was saying something. Cain cocked an ear.

"Nobody thinks about me any more. Not even Old Johnny God. Or He would've long ago took me up in heaven with Him. Why don't He take me? I'm ready. I've been ready for twenty years. Ae, terrible it is to get old in old age. One hardly knows oneself any more. With nothing to do but sit on one's one-spot all day, waiting for the ashes to go out. Ae, terrible it is."

Cain cleared his throat heavily. His blunt face was almost black in the candlelight. "Now, Gram, you know we all love you."

"Love me. Hmmph! In a pig's eye you do." Tears wimmered in Gram's milky marble eyes. "You're all just waitin' for me to go. Watchin'."

Cain sucked at a bit of meat caught in a tooth. The grimace gave him a grave reflective look.

The others looked down at their plates.

Joey said, "Unk, you stayin' over for the night?"

Cain fitted on a smile. "I could. Though I ain't had an invite yet."

Joey's eyes opened. He scratched at an itch inside his white nightgown. "Where you gonna sleep? We ain't got but two beds."

"I'll probably sleep in the usual place."

"On the floor?"

"Right. With my back for a mattress and my belly for a blanket."

"You're a liar."

"What!"

"Why don't you sleep with Gram once? And let me sleep on your dream-sack."

Cain almost choked in his coffee.

At that Rory shoved back her chair. "Well, I guess it's time for our treat."

Everybody looked up. Even Gram.

"Betcha it's homemade ice cream," Joey said. "When did you make it, Mom?"

"I bought it the last time we was t'Antelope."

Dale's long head gandered up. "That was over a month ago. Why ain't we had it before?"

"We ain't had us a special occasion before, that's why." Rory couldn't quite look either Dale or Cain in the eye. "I thought with Cain bringin' us a fresh bighorn all the way from under the Old Man . . . well, I thought one good treat deserves another."

Dale's lower lip set out some.

A hand to her knee, Rory got up, heavily. From behind the food cabinet, up in the high window, she took down a tray filled with round dishes. In the center of each dish quivered a mound of translucent red.

Dale's hollow eyes opened very wide. "What is it?"

"Eat it and find out," Rory said. She passed the dishes around.

All looked at the treat with wary eyes: Gram, Dale, Cain, Joey.

"Don't be afraid of it," Rory said. "It ain't poison." Rory sat down and began sampling hers with relish.

They spooned at the quivering red slowly.

When they finished at last, Rory asked, "Well, and how did you like that Jello now, hah?"

"Jello. So that's what it was," Joey said. "Johnny Goodin said he had some last Fourth of July. He said it was a new invention."

"I wasn't askin' you, peckersnap," Rory said. She threw a digging look at Dale. "I was asking that deadhead paw of yours."

Dale raised on that. "Jello be damned," he exploded. "I'd rather stick a funnel in my mouth and run against the wind, for all the good that fancy fluff-duff is gonna do me."

Cain started to laugh—until he saw the look in Rory's eyes.

About that time Gram began to fuss on her side of the table. She tinked her spoon in her dish. She cast eye-rolling looks at Cain.

Cain blinked. What was bubbling in that ancient head now?

Rory, then Dale, noticed Gram's fussing. Quiet settled around the table.

Gram took to eyeing Joey then.

Joey fidgeted. His hide-bottom chair creaked. Finally he said, "I know what Gram wants. She wants for Uncle Cain to read the Bible tonight she told me."

Gram said, "A passage from the Good Book. That would be nice." For all her years, she quick got to her feet, and hobbled to a side table under the north window, where she picked up a thick black volume. Hobbling back, she handed it to Cain, a half-wily smile puckering her wrinkled lips.

Cain recognized the puckering look. In her old age it often

67

appeared on her face. It was a waiting ferine look. Gram knew he didn't care much for churchgoing and such, or reading the Good Book at the table. He read it when he felt like it, when alone, or when remembering some passage he fancied and wanted to savor again. In her sly way she knew she had him trapped in Dale's and Rory's presence, that his sense of courtesy would not let him refuse. She had got her way with Dale and Rory, making them read it as long as she was with them. Now she was reaching out to make him do it.

Or was there another reason? Shame Dale? Show him who she thought most resembled Gramp reading the Word? Show him that if cousins did have to marry, it should have been Cain, the oldest of the Hammett brothers?

Cain fumbled with the Good Book. The gold lettering in the leather cover, Holy Bible, was almost worn off from much handling. He opened it slowly.

Rory abruptly got up and walked heavily to the north window. She stood looking out at the mountains to the northwest.

Cain said, "Don't you want me to read it, Rory?"

"Go ahead. Don't mind me."

Cain looked at her back, at her thickish neck. And looking at her, he noticed the new high windows again. Just a month ago Dale had raised them three feet. As a breeder of sheep in cattle country, he and his family were in danger of being shot at as they sat around the table in lamplight. Silhouettes on the window shades made perfect targets.

Cain asked reluctantly, "What do you want me to read, Old Mother?"

"Psalm Twenty-two."

"Well, let's see if I still know how to find it."

"Glory be. A word from the Lord now."

Cain coughed. He turned his chair halfway around so the reddish light from the low flame in the saucer would fall on the page. The low light accentuated the ax-cut hollows of his walnut face. He riffled through the pages. He noted old finger spots along the margins, some going back to Gramp's time. He paged through the loose pages in the Psalm section. He noted the dark page edge which marked the passage describing the Resurrection according to St. John. The Good Book, like some faithful corncob pipe, had endured the abuse of much loving wear.

Cain found the place at last. He read slowly. He had a fine bass voice. When he rolled off some of the more familiar phrasing, it filled the room and made the chinaware on the mantel murmur.

"My God, my God, why hast thou forsaken me? Why art thou so far from helping me, from the words of my roaring? I cry in the daytime, but thou hearest me not. Even in the night season I am not silent. . . .

"But I am a worm, and no man; a reproach of men, and despised of the people. All they that see me laugh me to scorn. They shoot out the lip. They shake the head, saying, He trusted the Lord. . . .

"But thou art He that took me out of the womb. Thou didst make me hope when I was upon my mother's breast. I was cast upon thee from the womb. Thou art my God from my mother's belly. . . .

"Many bulls have compassed me. Strong bulls of Bashan have beset me round. Like ravening and roaring lions they gaped upon me with their mouths.

"I am poured out like water. All my bones are out of joint. My heart is like wax. It is melted in the midst of my bowels.

"My strength is dried up like a potsherd. My tongue cleaveth to my jaws. Thou has brought me into the dust of death. Dogs compass me about. . . . I tell my bones. The dogs look and stare upon me. Deliver my darling soul from the power of the dogs. Save me from the lion's mouth."

Finished reading, Cain sat a moment looking at the double-column pages of print.

Gram murmured, "I tell my bones. Yes."

Cain looked up then. "Funny old psalm. I don't recall as ever having read it before."

Rory said from the dark near the high window, her back to the table, "Oh, she's out of her mind."

Gram cried it out then, lifting her head. "Yes, Lord, yes, I'm ready. I've been ready, lo, these twenty years now. Yes, Lord, yes. I've lived long enough." Tears ran down her ancient spidery face. "I've lived too long, too long. My God, my God, why hast thou forsaken me? I tell my bones over and over and still thou dost not take me."

Cain and Dale and Joey sat very still. They stared down at their hands.

Rory came bustling back to the table. "All right, Gram, that's enough of that now. Off to bed with you." She shot a red finger at Joey. "And you to bed too. I'll do the dishes alone tonight."

Gram got up and started for bed.

69

Cain went over, then, and put a hand on her old shoulder. He leaned down and kissed her. He didn't mind doing it. She was still his gram and had it coming.

Gram smiled up at him with a wonderful smile and clutched his hand for a moment. Nodding at him, she shuffled off to the lean-to.

Eyes winking brightly, Cain looked the other way.

Joey asked, "Kin I first see Unk unroll his bed, Mom?"

"No."

"Aw, shucks, Mom."

"Oh, let the boy," Cain said, eyes steady again. "I have no secrets to hide."

Joey said, "If I'm gonna be a cowboy like Unk I'd better learn how."

A look passed between Rory and Dale.

Cain got his bedroll from the hitching rack outside. He unfolded it on the plank floor behind the black stove. His bedroll was of the usual kind, a tarpaulin seven by eighteen, made of heavy white ducking and thoroughly waterproofed. It was outfitted with rings and snaps so that the sleeper could pull the top flap over his head in wet or stormy weather. Folded neatly inside the tarp were a couple of suggans or quilts, a woolen blanket, and a warbag. The warbag was a personal sack in which Cain kept his extra clothes and such ditties and dofunnies as a supply of makin's and cigarette papers, pipe, an extra spur, an extra bit and cinch, some whang leather, a carefully wrapped picture of Rory and also one of himself with Harry and Dale as the Three Mustangs, a packet of old tattered letters, a greasy deck of playing cards, a bill of sale for Lonesome, and a bag of silver dollars. Cain often used the warbag for a pillow. Since it was a warm night Cain planned to sleep on top and so did not unfold the bedroll completely.

Many a time on the trail he had awakened in the morning with six inches of snow weighting down the tarp, yet inside he'd been as snug as a baby in a whorl of blankets. Next to a horse, a bedroll was a cowpuncher's best friend. It went with him everywhere. It had been with him up in the mountains while he was getting Rory her bighorn.

Joey watched Cain's every move.

Cain smiled, indulgent. "Think you could make your bed as neat and quick?"

Joey said, "Then you didn't take no surprise along for me this time?"

70

"What!" Cain's smile faded. "No, cuss it, I ain't. I didn't go nowheres near a town, boy."

Dale spoke up from the head of the table where he still sat morose and heavy-eyed. "Never mind now about surprises, you nosy one you. Get to bed. Besides, when Christmas comes in a couple of months you'll have plenty of presents."

In the lean-to behind the kitchen, where Gram had gone to bed, they all heard her suddenly praying in a high leathery rustling voice. "Not my will, O Lord, but thine. I am ready. Let me awaken in the morning with thee in heaven. Let me quit this vale of misery. Let me awaken to the sound of angels playing their silver harps. Let me awaken with my beloved Mayberry greeting me with open arms. O Mabry, Mabry my love, I am coming. Never fear. Not my will, O Lord, but thine. Yet nevertheless hear my plea. I am ready. I have prepared my soul, lo, these many years. Amen."

Cain shivered.

Rory began to rattle the dishware into a pan.

Dale said, softer, "All right, son, bed now, please."

"Aw," Joey began, eyeing each in turn for some sign of weakening.

Cain gave him an uncle's warning look. "Better go."

Joey gave way under the look. "Oh, all right. Night, everybody. See you in the morning." Lip sulky, a little like his father's, he headed for the lean-to, calluses on his bare feet tussing on the plank floor.

Cain stepped outside. The danglers on his spurs tinkled musically on the hard ground.

"Where you goin'?" a voice, Dale's, spoke up behind.

"See if my hoss is set for the night."

"Oh." Silence. "I thought maybe you was looking for a dog to kick."

"Well, that too."

The two brothers stood together under the high starlight. Behind the barn the Shaken Grass and the Bitterness joined in confluence with softly clashing waves. Far to the west heat lightning threw occasional sheets of orange over the white peaks of the Old Man and the Throne. A coyote on the alkali hills yipped lone and mournful.

Cain got out his makin's. "Rory got herself a considerable eye there, Dale."

"She had it comin'."

"What was it all about? Not that it's any of my business."

Dale glanced around in the dark; stepped closer. He stood

71

over Cain a good half-foot. "She went on the prod because I didn't kill Link Keeler the other day."

"What!" Cain's heels almost left the ground. Link Keeler was the young tough who had murdered Gramp Hammett. "Where'd you see him?" Instantly hard, Cain fingered down for his gun in the dark; then remembered he'd left gun and cartridge belt hanging on the deerhorn rack behind the door.

"T'Antelope. Two days ago. He calls himself Hunt Lawton now. But he's Link the killer all right."

"Hunt Lawton, eh? What's he think he's doin' in these parts?" Cain finished rolling his cigarette in the dark. He licked it and stuck it in the corner of his mouth. It bobbed as he talked.

"Took a job with Jesse. Stock inspector. Peace officer. You know what that means."

Cain knew what it meant. As stock inspector and peace officer, Link alias Hunt could shoot down the rest of the Hammetts if he felt like it, and do it knowing he'd have the law on his side. Cain said, "Dale, all these years, you figured out yet why Link killed Gramp? He lived with us a half-year quiet and peaceable, and then all t'once he upped and shot Gramp in the back. There must've been some reason."

"I don't know." Dale let out a deep breath. "I wish I knew myself. It might explain a lot of things."

"So Rory gave you the devil then."

"The devil is right. Said I should have killed him on sight. Not even give him an ask-and-answer chance. Or even say hello. Just pull the trigger."

The coyote on the hill cried long and lone again.

"But did you have to hit her, Dale? We Hammetts ain't exactly been known to beat up on our women."

Despite the dark Cain could see outrage gather on Dale's gaunt face. "Cain, she called me coward."

"Hah."

"You blastin' well right, that's different." Dale began to puff. "I told her if she was so hot for a killin' to go do it herself."

Cain looked down at the ground black under their feet. "Maybe this life here in Bad Country is too tough on the women. Making them overhard." Cain pulled a match out of his hatband and flicked it with a thumbnail. A flame exploded inside his cupped hands.

"Durn her," Dale swore, loud on the yard. "Queen in the house, that I give her. But gunfighter, or foreman tellin' her man how to run his life, no."

72

"Well, there I side with you. As a mother and sister and wife, there a woman is fine. But God save us from bullhead bloomer she-males generally." Cain remembered Gramp's notions on how to handle the women. "Me?" Gramps had said. "Listen, when I've once told a woman what I've got to tell her, she can have as many last words as she wants. She's told."

"Cain, maybe I better tell you all she said." Dale's throat worked. "Cain, you know what that fool woman thinks? She thinks Link killed our dads, Gordon and Raymond, that time they was supposed to have drowned in that great Siouxland flood. Besides Gramp."

"Hah!" Cain took a deep suck on his cigarette. The cigarette lit up fiery pink and almost set fire to his mustache.

"That's what I told her. But she claims she heard it the time Link was around. Said she didn't mention it then because we was riled up enough already."

Cain coughed, and then said slowly, "Well, now that you've mentioned it, I guess I can say that I heard about it too. The boys was talking about it in a poolhall in Sioux Falls. I looked into it but I couldn't find him."

"Hey, then maybe it was true after all like Rory says."

"Could be." Cain drew deep on his cigarette. "But supposin' he did, what has he got agin us Hammetts?"

"Your guess is as good as mine."

Cain's cigarette became so short it began to singe his mustache again. He threw it on the ground and stepped on it. "Well, if he did kill them, I hate to think of what's ahead. Besides all the other trouble we already got."

"Man, so do I."

After a bit Cain said, "Well, now that you've spilled your guts, it's my turn to tell something. Today, coming home, I found our brother Harry hanging from the big cottonwood in my yard there."

"No!" Dale backed a step. "At last then."

"Yes, and in another minute it would have been no breakfast forever for our poor Harry." Cain saw where his cigarette still glowed on the ground. He went over and stumped it out with a sharp heel. "I cut him down and revived him."

"Great thunder!" Dale gasped. Dale's eyes rolled in rapid thought. "Great thunder, that couldn't be Link at work already?"

"No. It was Jesse. And two men Harry says he never saw before. Hired killers, probably."

73

Dale looked down at the ground a while. At last he said, low, "I suppose next they'll be after me. They hate sheepmen even worse than they do Red Sash devils."

"No, I wouldn't quite say that."

Dale cried it out into the night's silence then. "Why does Harry do it? Don't he know enough to play it honest like the rest of us? So them bustards have that much less the hook on us?"

Cain coughed. "Well, now, Dale, see here. We ain't been so holy ourselves. After all, in the past who's been sellin' his stolen beef to the railroads for him?"

Dale fell silent.

"Even if we didn't ourselves kill any of Lord Peter's beef, it's wrong for us to serve as fence for Harry."

Dale pawed at the ground with a sharp toe. "But the butchered beef had no brand. I saw the hides myself."

"Oh, come now, Dale. You got sheep. How could you be sellin' beef?"

Dale swallowed with a loud click. "But the other side ain't been fair either, makin' it so that the little man has got to prove his stock is his to sell." Dale was referring to the fact that the state livestock commission, in the control of the cattle barons, had instructed its inspectors at the various stockyards in the country to hold up all cattle bearing a brand suspected of being a fence for rustlers. This action hit at all the little stockmen, good as well as bad, since every little stockman was looked upon with suspicion by the cattle barons. The little man had to appear before the commission and prove that suspected beef belonged to him and not to rustlers. Dale went on. "It's agin right to make every man prove he is honest. It's always been that a man was honest until he was proved guilty."

Cain said, "Well, Dale, I don't want to argue with you about it. As for me, I told Harry today that even if he is my brother I'm through bein' his fence. Done."

Dale scuffed the ground. "Well, with Link in the country as inspector, maybe I better tell him the same."

Dale

Dale slid in beside Rory in the dark bedroom. The hide spring made a sound as if wincing under the added weight. Dale had on only his summer drawers and his gaunt knees touched the back of her firm legs. She had on a cotton

74

nightgown. Her back was turned to him and he thought he could sense her trying to be distant. Could she be afraid he might ask her to suffer him a moment's pleasure? Holy cow!

He thought about the talk he'd just had with Cain out on the yard. So brother Harry had almost died hanging. It was terrible to think of it. Awful. And that Cain, telling about it so quiet. In a tight Cain always did have more guts than a man could hang on a fence.

Jesse's hard-riding quick-shooting cowpunchers would be after him next then. In his mind Dale could see them coming onto the yard. He could see himself suddenly surrounded by hard grim mouths and dark flashing six-guns. He could almost feel the harsh pricky rope around his neck, with the horse about to leap out from under him.

What was it really like when the brain blackened over?

And Rory, what of her afterwards? Would brother Cain at last have his turn with her? As both Cain and Rory secretly wanted?

Well, in any case he'd had Rory first, when she was pretty and a virgin. Also, he'd had a boy by her. With another coming. Having her first was something Cain could never have.

He groaned softly to himself. The truth was that Rory really belonged to Cain, not him. Cecil Guth had never been in it. Everybody knew Cecil Guth had been just a cover-up.

Cain and Rory. Yes. Otherwise why would Rory urge Cain to go up under the Old Man and get her a bighorn? And Cain agree to get it? There was that treat too, that Jello fluff-duff, she'd saved for Cain.

He groaned softly to himself again. He ran a hand over his long body, down from his lean neck to his hollow belly to his stony kneecap.

His mind turned to the trip he'd made to town two days before. And got stuck there. No matter how he tried to think of something else, something absorbing, something dramatic, his mind would not let go of it.

His mind agonized over it. Searingly. Curse it as he might, his mind burned to make the trip over again, to see it once more and rectify it.

. . . Rory said she needed provisions: salt, sugar, rice, dried fruit, spices, canned milk, canned tomatoes, another rooster if he could get it. He himself needed a pair of boots, some pants, fence nippers, some sheep dip.

Early in the morning, in a light four-wheel spring wagon,

its wheels going irregularly round and round, he left for Antelope some fifty miles to the north. Driving his spanking pair of matched bay trotters, Bill and Doc, hard when it was cool in the morning, pacing them during the heat of the day, and then driving them briskly again in the cool of the evening, he got to town just after dark. After he'd put up his horses at Dad Finfrock's livery barn, he got a room for himself at Ma Deming's. Rory preferred that he stay at the Turnbull Hotel, since Rory believed Ma Deming ran a whorehouse, not a boardinghouse. But he couldn't resist staying at Ma's anyway. He and grass widow Ma got along. She always seemed pleased to see him, always asked with close interest about Rory and Joey and all.

Before he turned in for the night, he had himself a jolly talk with Ma in her roomy kitchen. It was the middle of the week and business was slow, and Ma had all kinds of time on her hands and was anxious for some chin music. Ma had blond hair which she wore brushed up into a bun, with some gray beginning to show.

Dale had a habit of taking a chew when not around Rory.

Ma was sitting across the table from him and she pulled a face. "I didn't know you indulged."

"Well, it's better than smoking. Less chance of startin' a grass fire."

Ma's brown eyes snapped disgust. Her round slightly fuzzed-over face wrinkled up some more. "It's a filthy dirty habit. Who likes to kiss a mouth stained all over with brown like that?"

"Ma! You ain't thinkin' a kissin' me, are ye?"

"Bah! My husband had that terrible habit too."

Dale raised a gaunt brow. He'd never heard her mention her husband before.

"Yes," Ma went on, pecking at the blue tablecloth before her with a fingernail, "yes, I was married once. But the son of a gun wouldn't work." Ma fixed her eyes on Dale. "You know what he did? He run off with one of them poxy whores across the street there. Sister Fannie's."

Dale smiled, a drop of brown juice trickling out of one corner of his mouth. "I take it you didn't get along then either."

"Naw, Bill always played hooky on me when he got the chance. He was always finding some pushover somewhere."

"Oh?" Dale's eyes roved the room. Up on the shelf over the big black kitchen range the alarm clock showed eleven.

A streak of soot went straight up to the ceiling where smoke had escaped from the stove.

"And then too, Bill liked the open-country. He was always traipsing off somewhere. Trappin' wolves for Jesse. Hunting grizzlies in the Big Stonies. Me, I liked the city better." Ma sighed out of her chubby fleshes. "Yes, I sure do like livin' in the city better. Where I can look out of the window at night and see lights. Lights are a mighty comfortin' thing to a lonesome woman." Ma gave him a look.

Dale chewed very slow. "You mind me of Rory. I think she's sorry too she came out to live with me on the Bitterness there. She claims our valley looks like hell with the folks moved out. Except us."

"Well, Dale, all I got to say is—you got you a good woman there. Hang onto her, if you know what's good for you."

"Don't worry. I will. I think a lot of my little Rory."

"And throw that spit-maker away. I'll give you a piece of raisin cake if you will."

"Cut the deck again?"

"I say, throw that wad of tobacco away."

"Oh. That. Well . . ."

"C'mon, throw it away."

"Oh, durn it, I suppose I better give in. All right." Dale caught the chaw in a cupped hand and got up and dropped it in the stove. His lower lip set out some. "You're about as bad as Rory at that."

"Well! If that ain't a nice thing to say! Now you don't get the raisin cake."

For a bit it looked like Ma would get mad and shoo him off to bed. But lonesomeness won out and pretty soon she was chattering away like a magpie that had discovered the season's first ear of sweet corn. She had something to say about everything in town: husbands, wives, lovers, whores, detectives, abortions, miscarriages, and many another item of female trouble.

Ma talked about sex with as much sparkle as a cattleman might talk about bad weather. She hinted, with a cluck of her tongue and a roll of her lively brown eyes, that she'd once been hot-blooded. Yes, and hot-blooded enough to keep Bill steady for the first while. She smiled too when she said that now in her middle years she had sex only as an accommodation for certain of her better friends.

Ma had a juicy story to tell about Sister Fannie's establishment of soiled doves across the street. It had to do with the swindle Sister Fannie had pulled on the lonesome cowboys the previous winter. It seems that on a trip to Sioux Falls, that burg known as the divorce colony of the Dakotas, she'd come across a pretty little kewpie of a girl, hardly more than four feet tall, just divorced yet looking for all the world like an innocent thirteen-year-old. Sister Fannie took her home with her, put her up in a fancy room in back, and casually let it be known around the saloons that Kewpie was her virgin sister. For twenty-five dollars she'd let the right cowboy buy her a friendly beer.

Dale couldn't help but laugh out loud at that. "By Grab, I've heard me many a windy on the trail, but that's the first time I ever heard of a virgin in a whorehouse."

Dale and Ma laughed together a long time over that one.

The next day, Dale awakened to the sound of trains down at the depot doing their usual morning chores, bumping and blowing. He got up; had a good breakfast with Ma of pancakes, ham, syrup, and coffee; and then went around town humping up his supplies.

Antelope was a town of some thousand souls. It had one main street with frame houses and false-front stores lining both sides. It had a courthouse, three churches, a fire department with a hook-and-ladder company, a town marshal, a harness shop, a saddle shop, a hardware store, a post office, and a half-dozen saloons.

Dale liked to go through the back alley and enter a store through the rear door. Dale knew more shortcuts in Antelope than the townsfolks themselves did. And he got to see all kinds of things never seen otherwise: drunks sleeping it off, tomcats prowling for mice and rats, the contents of chamberpots dumped in a pail behind the hotel, cinnamon bears nosing through garbage cans, the latest shipment of Winchesters, a café hand turning an ice-cream freezer, huge piles of empty whisky bottles behind saloons, coils of new rope behind the harness shop, discarded corsets, and best yet the whores at Sister Fannie's sunning themselves on the back porch. One day in town and Dale was up on stuff.

By noon he was done. The spring wagon was so loaded down it looked like a small donkey carrying a haystack. He watered his bays in the town trough and tied them to a hitching post in front of the post office. With luck, he could be home by two in the morning.

Thinking to fortify himself for the long ride home, through the dark night, he decided to drop in for a drink at Butcherknife Bain's saloon.

The moment he pushed through the hand-polished swinging double doors, he knew it was a mistake. A bunch of Jesse Jacklin's boys stood lined up along the bar. All of them wore guns; all were dusty from a long ride in; all had an owly look. The rows of shells studding their flat wide cartridge belts glinted in the dim light. Their leather chaps stood out wide and stiff, shiny from use. Leather work gloves, rolled into tight packs, stuck out of hip pockets. All wore boots of the best make, exquisitely fitted, giving them a chosen look.

The smell of whisky and the stink of decaying cigars in the cuspidors was strong in the saloon, strong enough almost to cut the breath. Green flies buzzed against the dusty green front window. The floor was worn all along the bar, with pine sawdust and bits of horse manure lying in the low hollows a quarter-inch thick. Two rows of tables and iron-rod chairs stood empty in the back of the place. A cat lay asleep above the mirror behind the bar. A framed liquor license hung on the corrugated tin wall beside the mirror. Only the bar looked new; its deep mahogany shone blood-brown from much polishing.

The bartender was Butcherknife Bain, a big bald man dressed in leather apron and striped white shirt without collar. Down in Texas, Butcherknife was supposed to have cut off his wife's nose for cuckolding him. Nobody had proof of it, however, and since Butcherknife was in another state, nobody bothered him about it. Folk were also careful not to use his nickname to his face.

One of the cowpunchers, a wizened wiry runt who wore 'em low and who'd drunk just enough rye to be high lonesome, spoke up from the far curve of the bar. "Here comes that lamb-licker Hammett and his ewe stink."

Dale recognized the voice. Stalker Smith. Dale put a foot on the brass rail and stiffened to his full height.

Butcherknife gave Dale a heavy look. "Well, what'll it be?"

"I'll have some of your wet goods."

"Which?"

"The one with the live snake in it. Something that'll cut the dust in the throat."

"Sure thing." Butcherknife set out a bottle of bourbon and a glass.

Stalker shifted feet on the brass rail. His leathery lips curved back and down into a deep sneer. The bunch standing around him waited. Stalker said, "Bain, better you should give him your special booze. The one what makes a wolf out of a pet rabbit."

79

Dale ignored the taunt as he poured himself a shot.

"Yeh, it's like I always say, boys. Everything in front of a sheep is eaten off; everything behind is killed."

Dale quaffed the snort in one huge swallow and set his glass down with a whack. The whisky cut a glowing passage through the middle of his chest. He smacked his lips. "Good enough to raise a blood blister on a dried-up boot all right."

Butcherknife gave the mahogany bar a swipe with a weathered rag. "We aim to please. Nothing but the best gut-poison served here."

One of the hardrocks next to Dale, an incredibly sun-blackened young fellow, said to Butcherknife, "To go back to where we was before we was interrupted . . . when I first spotted me that crumble of old bones in the gulch, I knew it was time for me to roll my tail for home. I tell you, Bain, I pushed my hoss so fast he was kicking jack rabbits out of the trail."

"Yeh," Butcherknife said, "I guess there's plenty of riders on the skyline these days."

Stalker kept worrying it down at his end of the bar. Tipping back his dented hat, he snarled, "I reckon some folks just never get around to reading the Good Book. Even if they is Sunday School teachers."

Dale took another snort. He was quite aware of how his .45 lay hot against his thigh. He wasn't the best shot in the county, but if it came to shooting he wasn't going to duck it. He wiped his face in his pink handkerchief.

"You'd think," Stalker continued, "you'd think they'd know what they was reading when they was reading. Especially where it says: 'Seems it a small thing when you eat up the good pasture and tread down the rest with your hooves? And drink of the deep water and foul what's left with your arse?' "

Silence.

"That's in Ezekiel," Stalker added. "Or ain't you come that fer yet?"

Silence.

"Hah?" Stalker shot out.

Leather chaps rustled. Green flies bumped against the front window.

The hardrock next to Dale picked up his end of it once more. Remembering something, he started to laugh, and said, "That Grindstone Jen, what a stick she is."

Butcherknife smiled too, revealing big horse teeth with spaces between. "Yeh, Sister Fannie has her times with Jen."

"Nobody takes such a chance as us whores," a bardog laughed.

The sun-blackened fellow whacked his glass on the bar. "You know what that Jen did last week? She showed us a new dance. The can-can."

"What in blazes is that?" still another bardog wanted to know.

"Well, it's a dance where you . . . well, it's a hell of a thing. You have to see it to believe it. Especially the way Grindstone Jen does it." The fellow let fly another laugh. "Jen put so much into it Sister Fannie finally had to snub her down. 'My God, Jen,' she says, 'be careful. You're showing all you got.' "

Butcherknife laughed too. "Yeh, that Jen, there's not much upstairs with her. Just a little whore with a big belly button."

There was a great laugh all up and down the bar. Even Stalker and Dale joined in.

Everybody drank up; set out for another slug.

One of the bardogs was helping himself pretty liberally to the peeled hard-boiled eggs in a bowl on the bar. Butcherknife had set them out for the hard drinkers, and custom decreed that two drinks got you one egg free. Butcherknife gave the bardog a hard look. "I think you killed the nickel you spent for that beer."

The bardog got hot. "What a short-change joint this is."

"Well, you can always get throwed out, you know."

The bardog shut up.

Still Stalker worried it. "By Grab, when we get through with them noble shepherds of the Lord, there won't be as much as a tail feather left of 'em anywhere in Bad Country. Or up in Crimson Wall. Yeh, and all their lousy Plymouth Rock chickens either. Let alone all their stinkin' pink petunias."

Dale knew the time had come for him to make his move. His neck and back sweat frost. But before he could set down his glass, his eye caught something through the dusty green window and across the street.

Getting down off a wet horse and climbing the steps into Great Western Outfitters was Link Keeler, past friend of the family who'd killed Gramp Hammett.

Sudden hate boiled up in Dale. He threw a ringing silver dollar on the bar, and without a word more burst out through the swinging double doors. "Hey, you!" he bellowed into the sun-white dusty street. But the door to Great Western had closed. "Hell's fire!"

81

Dale hobbed on high heels across the rutted street. Hand to the rail, he leaped over the hitching rack, stirring up the waiting horses, and jumped up three wooden steps and pushed inside Great Western.

He went in so fast it took him a moment to make out the dark interior, mounds of sacked saddles and coils of rope and masses of colored blankets. Blinking, he spotted proprietor Homer Fox sitting beside a roll-top desk near the window. Homer was fat and his mouth hung open.

Dale's eyes narrowed back to gimlets deep under gaunt brows. His mouth worked like a fish lipping new water. "Where'd the murderin' son-of-a-gun go, Homer?"

Homer's black eyes rolled to the right.

Dale wheeled, hand over his gun.

Link Keeler smiled at him from between a pile of gleaming blue Winchesters and a stack of new blue Colts. "Something you want?" Link had a high piping voice.

Dale's long head slowly crooked forward. His hand gripped the butt of his .45. Set. For some reason, though, his hand didn't draw. He had the bulge on the other man yet his hand just did not come up.

"Something you want?" Link said again.

Dale looked Link over from head to foot. He hadn't seen him for some ten years, but so far as he could see Link hadn't changed a particle—tall, lean, with as cold a smile under that black killer mustache of his as ever. Link's clear gray eyes with their deep black lashes and strong bold black brows were still hard to hold up to. He was mean handsome and as softly velvet in his manners as a pet viper. From the sweat in the armpits of his gray shirt and in the seat of his brown pants, and the white-gray dust on his brown boots and brown vest, it was obvious he'd just come in from a long hard ride, probably from the alkali desert east of the Bitterness River. His gun and the shells in his belt, though, were shiny and clean.

Dale's lips drew back, showing more teeth to the back and sides of his mouth than in front. "You lookin' for somebody else to murder now, Link?"

The smile widened ever so little under the mustache. The gray eyes opened some, with the black around them sharpening.

"Hah?" Dale shot next.

Fat Homer behind them got up beside his roll-top desk. "Did you say 'Link'?" Homer turned to Link. "I thought you said your name was Hunt?"

82

"What?" Dale snapped. " 'Hunt'? Ah, so the murderin' bustard's got himself a new name, has he? Well, well."

"Hunt?" Homer asked again. "Didn't you?"

Link's smile widened another hair or two.

Still leaning forward from the hips, Dale slowly started for him. "Shootin' is too good for the likes of you."

Link's black-trim eyes took on a hooded look. "Want to make it bare hands then?" For all his cool air, Link's high voice gave him the sound of a man who was always in a scream inside.

" 'Bare hands'? Never!" Dale spat it out. "If the Lord'd intended me to fight like a dog, he'd've give me longer teeth and claws to fight with."

Link smiled.

"Link, or whatever you call yourself now, since you're still probably stinkin' for some kind of crazy-headed revenge on us Hammetts, come on, I'll take you on with guns. You never yet killed you a man but what you shot him in the back. Come on, fight a man what's lookin' right at you."

Link smiled.

"Hell's fire, you are yeller, ain't ye, like we always said. As yeller as mustard without the bite."

"Dale, I got a question to ask you."

"Yeh? Well, fire away. What is it?"

"You sure no one ever did you a favor?"

"What?" Dale's eyes rolled in rapid thought. "Why, you cowardly son-of-a-bitch, you can fill your hand now."

When Link still did not move, just stared back at him with glowing black-edged eyes, Dale started forward again, intending to slap him into action. Dale took two steps—and then fell flat on his face. His elbow hit the floor and his .45 popped from his hand. Cursing, Dale scrambled to his feet; saw that he'd tripped on a loose end of rope spilling off a nearby coil. He spotted his gun and dove for it. When he came up with it, set to blast, Link was gone. The aisle between the Winchesters and Colts was empty.

Dale whirled around. "Where'd he go, Homer?"

Homer's fat eyes flicked toward the back door.

Dale turned just in time to see the door close softly.

"Why, the goddam big coward!" Dale shot out through the door after Link.

But there was no one in sight in the alley. Dale next ran around the side of the building. Still no one. Then, coming around the front side, he was just in time to see dust settling in the street, and where the street curved to cross the bridge over Sweet Creek, he saw a fleeing black horsetail vanish behind a cottonwood. The throwing clop of horse hooves gradually faded away.

"He ran from me. He ran from me," Dale said to himself.

The door to Great Western opened and Homer came out on the steps. "You see him?"

"He ran from me, the low murdering coward. I guess he knew better than to fool with me."

Homer said, "You're lucky your gun didn't go off when you fell on your elbow."

Dale came to. "What?"

"I said you could easy've shot yourself."

"Naw. I never carry more than five beans in the wheel. Hammer is always down on an empty chamber."

"Still was plumb lucky I'd say."

A thought came to Dale. "What'd you say he called himself?"

"Hunt. Hunt Lawton."

"I'll be damned."

"Said he come from Texas, where he was marshal. He took on the job of inspector of cattle for Jesse Jacklin last week. A peace officer."

"No!"

"A deadhard man I hear, Dale. I'm surprised he didn't draw on you. Just yestiddy he brought in Old Man Sims from the mountains. You know, where the old coot's been hiding out after he killed the deputy? Took a lot of sand to bring in Old Man Sims. Alone. But, by golly, he done it."

Dale nodded to himself. "So that's where he went after he murdered Gramp. Marshal in Texas."

Homer said, "What was it you called him? 'Link'?"

Dale said nothing. He looked down at the rutted street. He shivered.

He was still shivering when he got home at dawn the next morning.

The moment he hit the yard, he went for the cabin and burst into the bedroom where Rory was still sleeping. What followed was a case of hair in the butter.

As Rory listened, tense, half-risen from her pillow, her face slowly turned to stone, white, hard. She said absolutely nothing all the while he talked. Nor did she say anything when she got up to get at the work of the day. In fact, she didn't say anything all day. Not a word. Just stone, white and hard.

84

After that first spilling of it, Dale didn't say a word either. It was her turn to begin.

In the evening, after Gram and Joey were asleep and the house was silent, and they were just in bed, she finally opened up. "Don't touch me. As long as that devil Link is still alive don't touch me."

"What!"

"How come you didn't shoot him down on sight?"

"Holy snakes, woman, is it my fault he wouldn't draw?"

"You always wish in one hand and spit in the other."

"But, Rory, he wouldn't draw."

"Link ain't a fool. From what you say, he'd've been a fool to draw after you threw down on him."

"Now wait. First you say I should've shot him on sight. Then you say I didn't give him a chance to draw. When I really didn't throw down on him. I just had my hand on my gun. Waiting for him to make his move."

"He's still alive, ain't he?"

"Yes."

In the moonlight she looked at his long scrawny neck; then turned away from him. "I guess there ain't much Hammett blood in you after all."

"Rory!"

"And that's a pity, seein' that so much Hammett blood's been lost. Gramp first. And later on our fathers, Gordon and Raymond."

Dale reared back. "What? Are you sayin' Link killed them too?"

"I am."

"You are! What makes you think that all of a sudden?"

Rory stirred. "You make me sick. If you didn't figure that out . . ."

"But they was supposed to have drowned."

"Supposed to have, yes. When the truth is Link was around town about that time. He knew they were coming across that flood with a boat. He could easily have laid for them behind some willows, and shot them, and let them drift down the Missouri where only God knows where they disappeared to."

"Holy snakes, woman, if you knew that, why didn't you say something about it afore?"

Rory turned away from him. "Oh, you boys were all riled up at the time, so I didn't want to add more. Besides, I thought you knew."

"Well I'll be goldurned by an angel from hell. You had this all in your head all this time and you never talked up?"

85

"Yes."

"Great thunder!"

"There was plenty of talk about him being around in the pool hall."

"I never heard it."

She lay like a stone next to him.

"My God, Rory, if I'd a shot him on sight today, with Homer Fox looking on right there, why! I'd be gurgling from the end of a rope right now."

Silence. A long silence.

"If you're so hot for a killing bee," he cried, "why don't you go do it yourself? You're a Hammett."

"Coward."

"I don't believe he dry-gulched our dads."

"Coward."

He exploded inside. He bounded up, all knees and balled fists. In the vague moonlight in the bedroom he saw her face half-turned away from him. He struck it. It was flesh to hit and he hit it. "Damn you, Rory," he cried, sobbing, "what do you want? Hah? What do you want?" He bellowed so loud the moss-clay chinking fell out of the wall, pittering bit by bit on the puncheon floor. "What do you want of me, hah?"

Heavy with child, crude from it even, Rory rolled over, and rose up in her white nightgown, and hit him back. The blow struck him as he sat hunched forward on the edge of the bed, teetering, lost in rage and turmoil. It knocked him off the bed. He hit the floor on the side of his face. "There," she said.

He lay hunched over on his knees, moaning more from mortification than from hurt. "Woman, woman, woman, what do you want of me, hah? I married ye like ye wanted it, didn't I?"

Silence.

"You got what ye wanted from me, didn't ye? A willow that'd bend in the least breeze?"

Silence.

"Or are ye sorry now ye didn't marry Cain after all, despite both yer thick necks, the one ye really loved and that we all knew, even if he would've made you walk chalk?" He sobbed on the floor. "Walk chalk, that's right. That's just what he would have made you do had you married him. That stubhorn is a dozen times tougher'n me any day of the week. Than all of us put together. You. Me. Harry. He'd a put you in place. He's got gravel and rock in his gizzard."

Silence.

"Rory, Rory, woman, what do you want of me?" On his knees, beating his head on the floor in terrible mind-blinding mortification, he bellowed in the night. . . .

In the bedroom, and lying lank beside her, with Cain asleep in the other room on his bedroll, and Gram and Joey asleep in the far lean-to, and the single coyote yowling lonesome from the alkali hills, and remembering it all in agonized recall, certain words said by Link suddenly burned across Dale's brain.

—You sure no one ever did you a favor?

If the words meant what he thought Link meant by them, Link had done him a favor killing Gramp Hammett. The old patriarch wasn't around any more to roar about cousins inbreeding.

—You sure no one ever did you a favor?

Fact was fact, hate it as he might. Link had helped him get Rory, had helped him get his son boy Joey, had fixed it so that right now Rory could be lying in bed with him with his own seed planted in her belly once again. No wonder his hand wouldn't come up with that gun at Great Western.

Rory stirred beside him. She groaned a little.

Dale whispered, "What's the matter, Rory?"

"Oh, Dale, the last day or so, this baby in me has got so restless. He's all elbows and knees."

"Poor girl."

"He's tearing me so."

"My love."

"Dale?"

"Yes?"

"Give me a backrub, will you? A long and good one."

"Yes, my love, yes."

She rolled over, partly on her belly, partly on her side. He straddled her, a knee to each side. He reached down and pulled up her nightgown and began working his thumbs into the indentation at the end of her spine.

She groaned in pleasure.

He worked up horny vertebrae by horny vertebrae, pressing through the flesh under her skin, deep into the bone, worked his thumbs in and around each one, rubbing, massaging, setting up a motion on the bed so that the hide spring beneath began to creak rhythmically.

She groaned aloud in delight. "Oh that's good, Dale. Good."

His thumbs climbed, deep up the hollow of her back.

"You don't know how good it is, Dale. You don't know. Oh."

His thumbs worked up between her shoulder blades, pressing in and around each one. He volved the shoulder blades themselves around a few times, fingertips slipping around her chest until they touched where her breasts sloped down.

"Oh, that's so good, Dale."

His thumbs continued up, at last slipped around her full Hammett neck.

"It's such a relief, Dale."

He worked his thumbs all the way up into the roots of her gold hair. The hide spring continued to squeak under their rolling rhythm.

"You're so good to me, Dale."

He wondered if Cain could hear them in the other room. The thought of it made him wonder what stubhorn Cain did for beans. A black horse was hardly enough.

"You're so good to me."

He started over again, beginning at the end of her spine and working up, thumbs screwging around and around, working in, pressing, fingers gathering up her flesh in folds, massaging it.

Well, he thought, each man to his own luck. Me? I'm set.

Cain

Cain could hardly believe his ears.

He listened again. Yes, it was the hide spring creaking in the other room all right. Great grandad!

He couldn't get over it. So far along and yet Dale would bother her. And bother her, with him, his brother Cain, guest in their house. And that too after the black eyes they'd given each other.

Darkness gathered in his mind.

Then he heard a different sound. Ear tight on the warbag on the puncheon floor, he thought he could make out the rhythmic beat of a horse galloping up. He raised off the floor; listened. The coyote was silent. It was galloping hooves all right. Almost without thinking he groped in the dark with his left hand for his .45 where he kept it near his head. The butt of the gun fell easy into his palm.

He remembered Gramp's instruction. "If you must shoot, Cain boy, do it easy. Let your muscles take their own time.

You'll be surprised how quick they can be. And see to it that your grip is firm and your snapdown dead sure."

He listened, head up in the dark, lone predator on the wait. The galloping was still there, though now the sound of it seemed to have faded somewhat. Who could be passing by this late in the night and this far down the Shaken Grass? Link? Or some other of Jesse's men?

This was what a man got for a dark past, for having killed Cecil Guth, for having helped Jesse catch mavericks. The least sound in the night and a guilty man's head raised off his pillow. Yes, and let a waddy like brother Harry mutter in his sleep and the guilty one popped open an ear to hear what he might say. And let a buddy like brother Dale make some joking remark and the guilty one brooded on it for days afterward. Yes, no matter how a man tried to clean up his life after a bad deed had been done, he never came to a time when he could sleep all night long.

The galloping continued to fade off. In its place the hide spring creaking in the other room became louder.

Cain lay back on his warbag pillow. The crazy fools. Had Dale lost all sense? Great grandad.

He covered his head with his forearm, hoping to shut out the sound. But it still came through. He pressed his arm down until his ears roared from pressure. Yet still the sound came through.

He remembered how beautiful Rosemary had been before she got married. At seventeen she'd had a full neck and bosom, a slim firm waist, sturdy legs with the inside line as straight as a string with a weight at the end of it, and oh God in that high wide face of hers such dark blue eyes they were almost black. He'd been crazy-wild about the dark dreamy fury he'd seen waiting in her eyes. Oh, with Gramp's edict against inbreeding hanging over them it had been a tremulous time.

Well, Dale had her now. And what had once been a laughing buddy girl riding the range with him, going along with him on some mad youthful lark, was now just another mother almost thirty years old, fatting up, and as pregnant as a female could get. A regular crab of a wife. Mean even, if what he'd seen at the table was any sign.

That fool Dale had let her get out of hand. Hadn't laid down the law hard enough. Hadn't told her the rules of the trail.

He remembered the way she'd housebroke Joey. Or the way she hadn't. The way to train a boy was to watch for his times, and then, a minute or so before, set him on the pot. Nature worked like a clock, if given half a chance. Like the seasons. Or heat times. Catch what her times was and a man had her tamed. Joey could easy have been housebroke a half-year earlier if she'd taken the time and trouble. She was a good cook, sure. She could ride the range with a puncher, sure. And she was generally kind to the boy, sure. But when it came to training for the rough trail of manhood ahead, there she was a busted cinch. In fact, there she was mean, since like Gramp always said, strict training was true kindness.

He lifted his arm off his ear; listened some more. Hell's fire and little fishes! That blasted hide spring was still creaking.

Of a sudden it came to him what the galloping was. Like a squeaky step in a hotel staircase, the floor under Rory and Dale was giving to the roll of their bed.

Once more he clapped an arm hard over his head; pressed until his ears buzzed. But, like before, the sound of it was still there. And if anything it seemed clearer than when his ear was uncovered.

He rolled back and forth on his hard bedroll. The thought of what they were doing as well as the sound of it was maddening. Burn their horny hearts. Had they lost all good sense and she so far along?

Finally he had enough, and he decided to get out of there. Feeling around in the dark, he first put on his hat, then his vest, and last his pants and gun. From old habit he kept his hindquarters covered in the suggans until the last second.

In one sweep he rolled up his bedroll and threw it over a shoulder. He tiptoed out, timing the touch of his toe to the creak in the other room. He closed the door softly behind him.

It was very quiet out. No coyote call. The leaves in the cottonwoods overhead hung strangely still. Darkness was very deep under the trees. Looking to the west, he saw that the moon was almost down. It rested a full ball of dull gold on a ridge near the Old Man. The Big Stonies loomed up under the old moon like the great hoary hump of a buffalo bull.

He carried the bedroll out to the hitching rack and tied it on behind the cantle of his saddle. From one of his saddlebags he dug out a stick of red-stripe peppermint candy. He stepped softly across the dusty yard, his danglers chinking gently. When he got to the corral gate he whistled low. He listened. No sound. He whistled low again, setting his tongue thin against his upper lip, letting the breath out part hiss and part tune.

Out of the dark black Lonesome hove up over him, head above him like the shadow of a great bird.

"There you are. How about ridin' me home now, huh, boy?"

Lonesome lipped him; searched his clothes.

"You been a good horse, huh?"

Lonesome found the hand with the candy and with soft rubbery lips worked open the fingers and very delicately nibbled up the candy into his mouth. In a second there was a loud crack, and then the sound of crunching as horse teeth ground around and around on the sweet.

One hand under his muzzle and the other over his poll, Cain led Lonesome through the gate and then over to the hitching rack. He threw on the saddle and bedroll in a flowing sweep. This time Lonesome was too busy licking his lips to balloon out his belly against the cinch straps. Cain slipped on the bridle, one hand dividing the wet lips and the teeth and the other pulling down the rubbery ears, each in turn.

Cain stepped across and, reins tight in hand, eased Lonesome off the yard. Lonesome's ears worked back and forth, sometimes singly, sometimes together. When they got beyond the first turn in the trail beside the Shaken Grass, Cain let him out some.

Soon bits of foam from the horse's mouth sprinkled up into his face. For the first time in a long while, Cain rode heavy in the saddle. Not once had Rory given a sign that she'd noticed his new black clothes.

Cain

It was late when he awoke. And he awoke with a cracking headache.

The headache seemed to be all over his brain, not just behind his eyes as he so often had it when looking at the sun-white land too long. He scratched harsh stub nails into black tousled hair as if to dig it up. It burned. It felt thick enough to explode.

For a full minute he had trouble rousing himself to face both the day and the headache. What if he did work up a good-sized spread and became fairly well-to-do? What for? Just to have the money? Who for? Rory? So far as he could see there'd be just more endless unrolling of mornings waking

91

up empty-hearted on a smelly old hide while watching spiders catching flies overhead. It looked very much like his old cabin would remain a boar's nest to the end.

The headache got worse. It spat in his head like a frying pan full of boiling-hot lard. Though he couldn't remember a time when his belly had backed up on game, he decided it must've been the bighorn he ate at Rory's.

There came to him the soft faint sound of water moiling over stones. He licked his dry lips. Fresh mountain water in the Shaken Grass. That would help clear the prickling thickness in the head. It'd be a lot better than a cigarette.

Taking down his old work clothes from a peg—all of them a faded black with weathered gray edges—he once again went through the ritual of dressing in bed: first the skypiece, then the vest over the shirt, then the pants, and finally boots and gun.

To ease his cracking head, he walked as lightly as he could to the front door and then out on the stoop. The sun was halfway up the sky, a good nine o'clock at least. Picking up a pail, boot heels stobbing into the gray dust on the yard, he went straight for the ford by the bridge. He knelt down on a large flat red rock, laid aside his hat, and though the top of his head seemed to burn worse for a second, he stuck his nose and mouth and forehead under the pink water. He drank, gulping, all the while letting the water stream against his face. He could taste, even smell, the exact scent of certain springs high up under the Old Man. The cool water seemed to douse the hot frying in his head somewhat.

He stood up. Water dripped from the end of his nose and the tips of his mustache. He blinked, clearing water out of his eyes. He filled his lungs with a cool breath, drawing it all the way down to where he thought he could feel the cold water in his belly.

He looked around up at the owling brilliant sun again. "I sure slept me a hole in the day all right." He ran a hand over his hollow face. His day-old beard rasped like a rough whisper. As he rubbed his chin, he became conscious of hunger, even ferocious hunger.

He filled the pail with water and went back to the cabin. Quickly he made himself a breakfast of sourdough biscuits, fried steak, fried potatoes, and coffee so black it looked like poured hot tar. He began to feel better.

He managed to keep busy all day, busy enough so that his thoughts wouldn't stray down the Shaken Grass. He shaved. He washed dishes and cleaned up the cabin. He cleaned up on the yard around the cabin. He cleaned out the horse barn.

The work in the barn was hard going. The manure from last winter in Lonesome's stall had dried to brittle shard. He had to break it apart before he could throw it out. Sometimes strands of grass bedding wouldn't let go and then he had to toss out a whole pie of it in one big heave.

By four in the afternoon he was dead-tired. He went over and sat down on a red stone beside the flowing stream. "Not used to the blister end of a fork," he muttered to himself, puffing. "My fingers are straight while the handle of a fork is round. The two just don't go together. Me, I'm a rider, not a dummed homesucker." He skipped a flat stone across the brook. "When I get me my big spread, I'll have some big-footed honyocker work the fork for me."

Presently, as he brooded to himself, black thoughts came swooping back like buzzards smelling decay. Shake his head as he might, shake it until he saw fleeting blue sparks behind the eyelids, he still couldn't keep his mind from going downstream to where Rory and Dale and Gram and the boy Joey lived.

Great granpap! Think of it. A good seven months gone and Dale still bothered her. Seven months. Yes, they were quite a pair all right. Black eyes one day; blind lust the next.

He sat lonesome on the red stone, elbows on knees, face in his hands. He watched the stream flow toward him from under the bridge; watched it flow down to the sea.

He saw where a cross-pole was broken in the corral. "Wish I hadn't seen that. Now I'll have to fix it."

The sun shimmered on the silver sage over the hills. Flies himmed just above the surface of the water. A calf bellowed for its mother behind the barn. An eagle flew high overhead. Its shadow struck him sitting on the red stone; fleeted swiftly over the running pink water.

The shadow roused him. He groaned. And groaning again, he got up and fixed the pole in the corral. Then he went straight for the meadow and got up Lonesome and saddled him. He next led Lonesome to a small separate corral where he sometimes nursed sick beef. The week before he had penned up a lame cow with a fresh heifer calf. The calf had been born out of season and for some reason had hurt its mother aborning. He decided to take the calf away from the mother until she got back on her feed. Steady suckling would only keep the mother poorly, might even kill her.

He roped the frisky red calf; tied up its white feet with

a pigging string; threw it up over Lonesome's back behind the cantle. Lonesome snorted at the extra weight; crow-hopped once to show his annoyance. Cain let fly with a deep-toned "Whoa!" and Lonesome quieted. Cain secured the calf, at the same time making sure it could breathe. Then he swung a leg over and rode off.

They splashed through the ford below the bridge and climbed the far bank. Taking the Antelope road north, they ascended the slowly rising land. Alkali dust puffed up under Lonesome's gray hooves, forming drifting veils of whitish gray in the late afternoon sunlight.

An hour later, they topped a final sage-tufted hill. It was just sunset. The valley ahead was full of thrown purple shadows, miles long.

Below lay a meadow of waving rust-colored bunch grass. Rust Creek ran through it, coming down from the Big Stonies on the left, crossing the Antelope road, and going out to the gray desolate wastes of the Bitterness River on the right.

Just this side of the creek two trails branched off the road, one trail going to a one-story combination store and saloon on the left, the other going to a small one-room log cabin on the right. There were no trees; not a switch.

The brown log cabin on the right was the home of Nella Wells. Depending on who one talked to, Nella Wells was a pard or she was a tramp. Most cowboys thought her a real stick of a woman, hard but good-natured. Most cowmen thought her a loose woman, pretty but good-for-nothing.

Some years before, Nella and a man named Avery Jimson had come riding up from Cheyenne, she on a smart paint mare, he on a jackass. Each led a mule laden with supplies. Nella rode her horse like she'd been born to the saddle. She was a narrow-waisted weasel of a woman, with hair the color and texture of a lion's tail, and with eyes that were always alive with fire, light green, sometimes low, sometimes fierce. She wore diamond earrings. The diamonds were light green and glowed like her eyes, so that she sometimes seemed to be seeing with four glinting eyes. The impression depended partly on her quick movements. She was so quick that brother Harry once said of her she sometimes came awfully close to being in two places at the same time. She fancied green in her clothes, because it went with her diamonds and her eyes. Her chief attraction was a fulsome bosom. Long ago she'd given up trying to hide it. Her breasts were so large, in fact, that some of the more coarse-minded cowboys referred to them as fallen goiters. Also, she carried a tomtit revolver, a pet pistol that had just enough penetrating power to break a man's skin.

Avery Jimson was small too. But where Nella was full of animal quickness and vigor, Avery was slow, even tired, in his movements. Avery was a sick man. He actually did have a goiter. It hung under his chin like a huge purplish gizzard, pulsing with every swallow he took, and getting in the way when he read or ate. Also, he had the popped eyes of a stepped-on squirrel, wet, bulbous, deep brown. Usually he was neatly dressed in blues. He made it a point not to wear cowboy boots. He scorned them. He obviously was not a cowboy and said he'd be darned first before he'd parade around like one. He was a Harvard graduate. He was bookish. And he hated the rich with a sulphurous hatred.

Nella and Avery liked the looks of the meadow beside Rust Creek. After proper inquiry they each took out a homestead of one hundred sixty acres, Avery to the left of the road, Nella to the right, with both homesteads straddling the creek. They built themselves a long one-story log structure, set up store and saloon, and kept a small garden. Later, Avery established a post office. A lean-to served as their living quarters. The place was some twenty miles from Antelope and right on the road to Cheyenne and other points south. While they didn't get rich right away, selling whisky, clothes, stamps, and raising mules from Nella's paint mare and Avery's jackass, they still got along. Both were sure that the site would eventually become a flourishing western city.

Nella worked as barmaid. This was not a new role for her. Some of the cowboys up from Cheyenne remembered her as a waitress in a Union Pacific railroad restaurant. They also remembered her as a choosy woman with a sharp tongue. Rumor had it in Cheyenne that she'd killed her mother back in Sioux City.

No one could quite make out if Avery and Nella were married. They did things together, such as take trips, buy supplies, run the joint. In their attitude toward morality and religion they seemed to be of the same leather too. Yet, somehow, they didn't act married. They were an odd couple. He talked like a professor who'd lost his job; she talked like a lady temporarily down on her luck.

Nella got restless after a couple of years and they had a fight. After a partial reconciliation, Nella built herself a one-room log cabin across the road on her homestead. She

95

proceeded to live in it alone. She got herself a great black dog of an unknown breed, a dog who never barked but who tore things to shreds at her least command. She got some of her cowboy friends to build her a corral behind the cabin. Later she had the entire homestead fenced in with a new invention called barbwire. It wasn't long before a couple of steers were seen butting each other in the pasture. To no one's great surprise, the steers became fertile. In the space of two years the two steers begot themselves some hundred calves. This was ranchland breeding such as breeders Mayberry Hammett and Charles Goodnight had never dreamed of. In fact, not even the cattle kings of old Texas just after the Civil War had had such luck.

How she got the calves and how she chose her brand was always good for a story whenever cowboys got together to spin windies. Everyone knew that Avery was unable. Like a steer all he could do was try. This eventually made Nella quite nervous. One day Avery asked her to do something for him, something she didn't like to do. She told him to go stick it. He got mad and called her a name. At that, right in front of a half-dozen astonished bardogs, she whirled around, flipped up her dress, bent over, and said, snappish, "This to you, dearie, with my compliments." And then, still holding up her dress, she stormed outdoors. Even Avery had to laugh. And with a wink of his big wet bulbous eye, he said to the boys nursing their whiskies, "Down in Old Cheyenne that's what we called the hanging rear hoist." Within a week the phrase, "the hanging rear hoist," was all over the Bitterness valley. But Nella could go along with a joke. She decided to use it as her brand, $\overline{RH}$. . And shortly thereafter she let it be known that she was willing to do certain cowpunchers a favor now and then in exchange for an unbranded calf or maverick. The cowboys were quick to appreciate this gambit and soon quite a few of them contributed to her herd. Most of the mavericks belonged to cattle king Peter Caudle. Presently Nella got herself a title. The boys nicknamed her Cattle Queen, or Queenie.

Cattle Queen, or Queenie, continued to be choosy, just as she'd been in Old Cheyenne. First, she had to like the cowpuncher. She just couldn't find it in herself to be friendly to everybody. She was a lady by instinct. Also, she absolutely refused to let anyone visit her in her brown log cabin. The boys could bring their lost calves to the corral behind the house all right, but the party would be held in the lean-to, or the Hog Ranch as the boys called it, behind the saloon, where

96

she kept a piano and a couch and a pet magpie. Also, she would not let a puncher kiss her until after he'd bought at least two drinks from Avery.

Once, when Harry brought her the present of a calf, she'd met him at the door of the lean-to with the remark, "Well, Harry, honey, I'm afraid I've already got my hands full for the night. I have a party of three in." Then she added in a low whisper, "One of 'em is such a big rough son-of-a-gun I had to give him knock-out drops. I hope the big studhorse never wakes up."

Later Harry played a joke on her. She'd somehow acquired a milk cow, and he and the boys roped the cow one night and led it to the Antelope stockyards. When she gave him heck for it the next time he called on her, he explained, "Well, Queenie, honey, it was this way. After the boys got crooked on Avery's whisky, they began to complain it was wrong for a decent cow to be seen around a whorehouse. So they decided to rescue her from a life of shame."

Still another time, a rich gentleman adventurer from New York staying with Lord Peter called on Queenie. After the usual exchange of civilities, and a coming to grips of sorts, Queenie showed him the door with the remark, "I'm too good a girl to let a lily-picker like you teach me new tricks in this game." The New York gallant said he was surprised that an old whore like her preferred "calf love with cowboys." She snapped back, "Well, maybe at that I prefer a catch-calf from the boys to what you got to offer."

Occasionally Queenie showed that she was bored with her life. Wizened wiry Stalker Smith told of such a time. He said he'd come to in her arms to the sound of someone chewing on an apple in the room. When he turned his head to see who it could be, he discovered Queenie had just taken a big bite out of a red apple. That was as much as it meant to her. Stalker said he let her have a calf in pay anyway. "Because," he said, "it was worth the price of admission just to see them bubbies of hers. How they could get so big on so little a woman is one of the seven marvels of the world. You have to see 'em to believe it."

Yes, Queenie was magnetic, and the punchers mostly did love her. And gradually over the years Cattle Queen built herself up quite a herd. To the growing irritation of Lord Peter and his general manager Jesse Jacklin, her R̄H brand was soon seen high up on the footslopes of the Big Stonies as well as far out on the gray Bitterness plains.

And Avery? His goiter increased; his skin slowly wrinkled

over and yellowed; and his eyes stood out more popped than ever. Also, he took to writing letters to editors in which he attacked the big cattle kings.

When Cain trotted up to the front door of Queenie's brown log cabin at dusk, he saw right away she wasn't home. Her big dog was chained to the door stoop. The dog lay across the path like a black bear, blinking, silent, legs set for the jump. Cain decided Queenie was probably on duty at the Hog Ranch.

He stepped down. He opened the gate to the corral and led his horse through. Some half-dozen calves on the far side of the corral backed into a corner and, tails lifted slightly, stared at him. He untied his own red calf from the cantle and let it slip gently to the ground. Before loosening the pigging string from its feet, he went over and got Queenie's branding iron hanging by the gate, built a small fire out of dry gnarled sage stems, and, heating the iron, scorched her brand onto the left side of the calf. Then he loosened the pigging string.

The calf lay still, all four feet spraddled out. Cain gave the calf a light prod with the toe of his boot. "All right, little dogie, up on your feet." One of the bolder calves on the far side of the corral came up, advancing step by slow step, snuffing, sniffing, finally getting close enough to touch noses with the prostrate calf. The moment their pale noses touched, the calf on the ground bounded to its feet and scampered away. It was still clumsy with stiffness but by sheer crude speed managed to stay on its feet. Its sudden bolt startled the smelling calf, as well as the others, and in an instant all were stampeding across the corral. They hit the far side with a loud whack, like a wave hitting a Missouri River dock, and rose up the side of the corral in tossing splashes of red and white, tails whipping around like bits of flying white spray. They hung up near the top rail of the corral a second, all in a bunch, then gradually receded, falling back, stumbling all over each other like the weltering of little waves settling into each other. They steadied, leveled off, and stood staring at each other on spread-apart legs. Finally, after another moment, they bellowed once, loud, and, pairing off, began butting each other in aimless circles. Gray dust rose in a cloud against the windless purple dusk.

Cain laughed at their antics. Then, brushing calf hair from his pants, he covered the little fire with dust, led Lonesome out, and shut the gate.

He rode across the road and tied Lonesome to the hitching rack in front of the Hog Ranch. There were no other horses around. The dust underfoot was reddish, rusty. A boot scraper was set in a log on one side of the stoop; a withered wisteria bush grew on the other. Clusters of bunch grass grew right up to the brown puncheon door. A bullet hole gaped in the exact center of the near window, cracks radiating evenly to all sides. Someone had tried to fix it with a pair of black coat buttons, one on each side of the pane and sewn together with heavy thread. Behind the one-story brown log building, very far away in the falling blue dark, loomed the white peaks of the Big Stonies. From that point in the valley the Old Man and the Throne looked like a single peak, huge and white.

Cain pushed in. The hinges creaked. The saloon was wide, with a low log ceiling. Kerosene lamps glowed saffron on either side of the bar and along the wall behind the tables. At first Cain could make out only the shine on the bottles on the shelves behind the bar. As his eyes adjusted to the weak light, he saw Avery sitting on a stool beside the bar. Avery was writing a letter. Chin gaggling a little on the great tumor underneath, he mouthed the words as he wrote. As usual he was dressed neatly in blue vest and blue pants and white shirt and black armbands. His gray hair was brushed tight back. In the lamplight his sallow face was the color of aged paper.

Danglers on his spurs tinking musically, Cain stepped forward, step by slow step.

Avery looked up. He blinked. The edges of his eyelids came partway up the sides of his popped eyeballs. "Hammett. Well. Hello."

"The same." Cain put up a foot to the brass rail. He glanced around at the empty tables and chairs. "Business is slow, I see."

"Some." With a sigh Avery pushed pen and paper aside. "It always is this time of the week." An old sadness worked at the corners of his popped eyes, at the edges of his cut lips. "What'll it be this time?"

"Rye." Cain laid down a silver dollar. It rang on the dark shiny bar.

"Chaser?"

"Straight."

Avery set up the drink; made the change; went back to his pen and paper.

Cain took a slow sip. He heard Queenie moving around

99

in back. It bothered him that a man would permit his wife to entertain other men alone in back. A man had to fall pretty low to tolerate that, he thought.

Cain watched Avery scratch his pen across the paper. Avery wrote with intense concentration. Once he swallowed, and the swallow stirred up his blue goiter. The swallowing reminded Cain of a just-born puppy struggling to escape its bag of waters.

After a bit Avery felt Cain looking at him. He glanced up. "Sorry. But I'd like to finish this letter before Johnny Kling comes by on his pony express."

"Don't worry about me." Cain sipped again. The rye glowed in his throat. "I don't mind drinking solitary."

Avery shifted on his high stool. "It's a letter to the *Weekly Bulletin* in Antelope."

"Hmm. Who you rimmin' out this week, Avery?"

Again Avery glanced up, this time with burning eyes. "Who else but that great seizer Jesse Jacklin and his high-headed autocratic boss Lord Peter?"

Cain nodded. "They are a mite troublesome at that."

Avery laid his pen aside. His eyes hazed over. He spoke as if it were a piece he had memorized, something he'd gone over and over again in hate. "Those land grabbers! They run cattle over the public domain like they owned it. Ain't it wonderful to see how much land some of these land sharks think they own? And worse yet, have you noticed how they've organized to prevent this state from being settled up? And oppose everything that'll improve the country? The poor small stockman doesn't have a thing to say about the affairs of his own state any more. It's enough to drive a man to murder to see this whole Bitterness River valley owned or claimed for a distance of seventy-five miles by one man and his hirelings." Avery's voice slowly rose. "I say: change the irrigation laws so that every bona fide settler can have his share of the water. I say: cancel the desert land act. Then you'll see orchards and farms in this state such as the world has never known."

"Now, Avery, now," a cool woman's voice said from a door to one side of them.

Cain turned and saw Queenie. She stood slim in a long green velvet dress and green high-laced pointed shoes. Her wonderful bosom looked like jumbo popovers. Her face was so heavily powdered not a wrinkle showed. Her eyes and her diamond earrings glowed a subdued light green in the dusk of the saloon.

Avery looked around at Queenie a moment. Then, eyes half-closing over, wearily, he lowered his head. "Yes, dear."

"You talk too much, Avery."

"Yes, dear."

Queenie looked at Cain. "Hi, Cain. Haven't seen you around in some time."

"No."

"You been lost?"

"Been busy. Rapin' around."

"Thought you'd forgotten all about us."

Cain smiled. The smile cut a wrinkle across his walnut face. Somewhat to his surprise he saw Avery once again become completely absorbed in his letter writing.

Queenie came tripping over and stood beside him. Perfume bloomed from her clothes. "What you doing up this way, Cain?"

"Thought it was time to cut my wolf loose."

Her eyes narrowed ever so little. Cain could see the animal rise in them, quick, ready. "Well, dearie, you came to the right place then."

"Got a hunger for one of your steaks, too."

"Why, Cain, you poor child."

Cain tried to keep from looking at her bosom. His boot twisted on the brass rail. "Lady, batchin' can get mighty lonesome, I tell you. Besides, I ain't et since I got up this morning."

"Why, Cain, honey, you sound like you really are hungry."

"I am."

"Come. I will feed you all the steak you can hold. Come with me."

Cain threw a look at Avery. But Avery was deep in his battle with Lord Peter. It still made Cain feel queasy inside that Avery could be so casual about his wife's doings. A shiver moved all through Cain's body.

Queenie led Cain into the kitchen in back.

While Cain washed up and combed his hair, she put on an apron and rustled up a hot fire in the range and began frying a huge thick steak. She set out chokecherry jam, bread and butter, salt and pepper.

Cleaned up, Cain took a chair at the table. He leaned back on two legs and rolled himself a cigarette. Though he'd just combed his black hair, it tousled down over his forehead some. The lamplight gave his features a dark and whittled look.

Queenie moved around, slim and busy, with quick light steps. Once she brushed against his shoulder. She did things

101

easy, deftly. There was little waste motion to her. Cain couldn't help but admire the bright mink in her.

—How kin Avery let other men be so free with her, he thought, onless Avery's a pimp at heart?

The fire roared in the range; the steak began to sizzle.

Queenie placed a hand on his shoulder; leaned on him as she placed a steak knife beside his plate.

He permitted the touch.

She went back to the stove and turned the steak. A wonderful smell of seared meat spread through the kitchen.

After a bit she asked, "Cain, dearie, I got a question to ask you."

"Fire away."

"How come you never got married?"

"Oh . . ." Cain puffed on his cigarette, deep. He blew up a rising boiling smoke ring. "Oh . . . I guess it was mostly that I was too nosy about what was on the other side of the hill."

"Come now, Cain."

"That's right. I was mostly too much on the go."

"Somebody else put his brand on your gal first?"

Cain laughed, short. "Wal, that too."

"Maybe it's time you put your running-iron on some other gal."

"Been thinkin' some on that."

She smiled at him, special. "Ah, sounds like good news for somebody."

"Hmm. Don't know as to that. When a man gets it burnt into him like a brand that way once, it lasts him quite a spell. Next time he'll feel his way."

The steak was ready then and with a little show of pride she set it sizzling before him. She'd fried it a deep brown. It had the look of meat that could be cut with the side of a fork.

Cain said, "Now there's one steer that ain't gonna get to his feet again. Mmm. That's just the way I favor it."

She smiled, green eyes and green diamonds glittering. She poured out two cups of black coffee, one for him and one for herself. Then she took a chair across the corner of the table from him.

Left-handed, Cain fell to. He ate heartily. He cut his meat with neat precision. There was style about the way he broke bread and spread the butter and jam.

Queenie watched him eat, pleasure showing in her eyes.

When he sat back to sip his coffee, she reached across the corner of the table and took up his big right hand with both her hands. She studied the lines in his palm. She played with his stub thumb. Very gently, very delicately, she placed a circlet of fingertips around the knob of the thumb and toyed with it.

He suffered it.

"You should come more often, Cain."

He looked up at her with a part-amused part-abashed smile. "By the way, I forgot to tell you, I brought you a leppy."

Again Cain saw the animal in her eyes rise some, far back. This time even her head seemed to move. Idly he wondered if her animal would listen to his animal if it came to a pinch, like Lonesome's had on Dencil Jager's yard, like Joey's had down in Rory's well. Cain guessed Queenie probably had a real wild one in her and that in an emergency even he would have trouble topping it. He didn't envy Avery none living with her. A visit, yes. Marriage, no.

Cain said, "I put him in the corral with the others."

Queenie's bosom swelled. Though she closed her eyes to gimlets, the rampant one showed more than ever.

Cain couldn't look at it. He glanced down at his left hand holding the coffee cup. He felt her finger tips still circling the knob of his right thumb. He thickened. "Yeh, one of my cows came down lame. So I decided both would be better off if I made a orphan of the calf."

Queenie's eyes opened. "You mean, one of your own? A Mark-of-Cain? Not a Derby calf?"

"The same."

"Why, Cain, honey, you didn't have to do that. Not you."

He smiled, more amused now than abashed. "But the boys do, eh?"

Queenie's eyes closed to slits again. She placed a gentle, soft and intimate hand on his thick arm. "Cain, honey."

"Wal, I don't much believe in taking neighbors' beef. Oh, I know it's a custom in these parts, when a fellow is short on meat, to go out and dab him a rope on a neighbor's cow. They all do it. But me, I think that's wrong. It leads to waste. A man is more apt to be saving when he butchers his own beef. But not if he kills his neighbor's."

"You sound like quite a God-fearin' man, Cain."

"Wal, thank you kindly, but as to that, I'd say I was more a neighbor-fearin' man."

"Cain, dearie. You know you don't need to bring me anything. Nothing."

Cain laughed. "Not even any of Lord Peter's, eh?"

103

"Dearie, with you, it's any time any day. And all for love. You know that."

"Wal . . ."

"And another thing. With you, it's over at the cabin. Not here. You're special, Cain, honey, and the latchstring is always out for you there."

A couple of hours later, as he was riding home in the dark, Cain's nose suddenly sprang a leak and he had himself a bear of a nosebleed. It gushed. And it kept bleeding, off and on, all the way home. It took an hour of bathing in the cold pink water of the Shaken Grass before he got it stopped.

Part TWO

Cain

Cain got up early one crisp October morning, made himself a rough bachelor's breakfast of beef and beans, washed dishes, and went out to the meadow to get Bucky, his buckskin cow pony.

But Bucky had picked up a lot of flesh and a bad heart since he was last ridden and Cain had to get out his lasso and try cornering him in the far point near the cottonwoods. He got Bucky into the point too, but at the last moment, long black tail fluttering like a pirate's flag, Bucky slid under the loop and got by him. And once Bucky was out of his reach, he showed his annoyance by popping his tail with four quick loud reports.

Cain smiled, and went back and got another rope. He fastened it to a stout cedar post. He let the rest of the rope lie loose on the ground across the point. Again he chased up Bucky from the far side of the meadow and herded him in, careful not to make him go too fast. He knew Bucky's old trick of going to the far end and then quick turning and roaring back while he was still in the wide part. Cain walked slow, and as luck would have it Bucky chose to walk slow ahead of him too.

It worked. Bucky sniffed the rope, once, and stepped across it. The next second Cain had the rope in hand and had snapped it taut, making a small tricornered corral. He secured it to a yellowing sapling cottonwood. He built a loop in his lasso and feinted a throw. Up went Bucky on two legs, high, rampant, pawing the moon. Just as Bucky's neck was stretched to its furtherest, Cain whirled up an overhead loop and sent it whistling toward Bucky in a wriggling line. It smeared up around Bucky's head and settled neatly around his neck. Cain dug into the grass with both heels and set himself. Bucky hit the end of the rope and almost threw himself. "Whoa!" Cain roared. His shout was like the single bark of a .45. And Bucky gave up. Cain went up the rope, hand over

107

hand, until he could catch Bucky under the chin. Then, with a pinching hand on his ear, Cain led him to the barn.

Next to his riding horse Lonesome, Cain's best friend was Bucky. Bucky stood just under fifteen hands high, had speed to overtake the fastest calf, had weight to hold the heaviest steer—about nine hundred pounds—could run all day, and actually enjoyed cutting out cattle. He was barrel-bellied, had thick shoulders and hindquarters, had a head with a slanting Roman nose, and bright clear eyes that were wide apart and stood out like an alert squirrel's. Bucky was a true buckskin. His coat was the color of deer, an ancient smoke-gray, with a black stripe running down his back, with black ears and mane and tail.

Cain had found Bucky as a colt in a wild bunch on the higher reaches of the Shaken Grass up in the Crimson Wall country. Bucky was tailing a band of mustangs from which the head stallion had just whipped him. The stallion had slashed him with a bite across the back and this slowed him down just enough for Cain to dab a rope on him from Lonesome's back. Cain treated the sore, which eventually healed over and grew a patch of hair even blacker than the mane. After he'd gelded him Cain spent a lot of time getting him used to humans. He breathed in his nose every morning before he handled him. He fed him oats, which Bucky loved. Eventually he broke him to cow work.

Bucky had been a tough one to tame. After lassoing and hog-tying him, Cain fastened a raw swatch of buckskin to each of his legs and an old pair of pants around his belly and then let him up. Bucky swapped ends for most of an afternoon in the round corral. Around and around and around. Without letup. Viciously; furiously; outraged. Then, just at sundown, suddenly, shudderingly, as if he knew he was leaving freedom behind forever, he gave up. Ever since he'd tolerated just about anything, though there were still times, of course, when he'd be a bit waspy, especially early in the morning after a week of running free.

Bucky's natural instincts as a studhorse nipping the backs of straying mares were successfully transferred to nipping the backs of cows. He would take after a snaky cow like a feist or a collie. He could turn so short that Cain's hat would sometimes snap around hindside-fore. He knew the exact moment when the rope would drop over the calf's head or forefeet and was already set back on his four hooves by the time the calf hit the end of the rope. He would keep the rope tight on the downed calf, no matter how it wiggled or

108

struggled to get free, until the wrestlers came up to take it off the rope, or until Cain himself stepped down to tie up the calf. Worked hard, Bucky was very tame, and stuck close to Cain wherever he went night or day.

Near the barn, Cain got a halter and tied Bucky to the snubbing post in the middle of the round corral. He pronounced a low "Whoa!" and put his hand lightly on Bucky's rump. "Steady now, boy." He leaned down and, grabbing the fetlock, picked up Bucky's forefoot. One look and he knew Bucky had to be reshod. The old shoe was worn down to a rind. Even the caulks were down to nubs. Cain growled, "Where the devil you been playin' the past summer, you black-eared son of a wild mare you."

Cain dug up the set of new horseshoes he'd bought the previous week in Antelope. The shoes gleamed a bright iron-black in the sun, with the steel caulks showing up a hard gray. He got out the shoeing tools, some new square nails, hung his cartridge belt and gun on the top rail of the corral, and set to work. He caught Bucky's upper lip in a twitch—a short loop of rope threaded through a hole in the end of a stout stick—and turned up the lip until the horse leaned up off the ground on three legs. Next he fastened the twitch to the snubbing post, holding Bucky to it stock-still. The twitch on his lip kept Bucky from flicking even so much as an eyelid at a fly. Again Cain picked up a hoof by the forelock and caught it between his knees. With a pair of pincers he cracked off the old shoe. When one of the nails broke off at the head, he dug for it, going in deep enough to stir up Bucky in his absorbed contemplation of the lip twist. The nail came away with a squeaky greasy sound. Next he pared down the hoof edges for the new fit. He dug out some of the frog that had worted up in the soft middle of the hoof, careful not to cut down to the quick. Grabbing a rough rasp file, he ground the whole hoof smooth and then tried on the new black shoe. It fit to perfection. Carefully he set the nails to catch through the outer edge of the hard black hoof, and with steady sure strokes of the hammer drove them through and clinched them on the outside. The clinched-over points formed a neat row around the hoof, almost like ornamental work.

He worked steadily, surely. Wet circles grew in the armpits of his old faded black shirt.

When he got to the last hoof, a rear leg, Bucky got tired of it and slyly leaned on Cain, putting most of his weight on the raised leg. It made Cain smile and he cursed Bucky in a low pleasant voice.

He had one more nail to go, when he heard galloping up the valley, coming toward him from Crimson Wall. Bucky heard it too, despite the terrible pinch on his lip, and tried to lift his head. From his bent squat, still holding the horse's rear leg between his knees, Cain craned a look up the creek.

A horsebacker. Dang it. And here he was with his gun over on the top rail of the corral. Then, even as he thought of dropping the leg, he recognized brother Harry's pink shirt and bright red sash. Harry came on in a swift lope.

What now? With a sigh and a grunt, Cain quick drove in the last nail, clinched it, and let go the leg. He walked bent some dozen steps, the distance to his gun, before he could get the stoop out of his back.

Harry came off his bay and dropped the reins to the ground all in one sliding motion. With a quick hoist of elbows, Harry drew up his cartridge belt and then the belt of his hairy chaps. Harry had let his beard grow some and it shone in the morning like a light frost of silver.

"Howdy."

"Hi."

Harry's eyes hooded over. "Cain, where's your beef?" Harry held his head slightly to one side.

"Why, up the valley toward Crimson Wall, where I pushed them yesterday to get ready for our bitty roundup with you boys next week."

"Guess again. Jesse's boys have got the whole bunch."

"Great grandad! Where?"

"With a herd they're holding just inside the Crimson Wall. North of Dencil's place there. Up on that high bench."

"You sure?" A cold shiver ran all over the skin of Cain's body.

"What was your last count?"

"Wal, with the spring crop of calves, about a hundred head."

"Timberline counted over seventy Mark-of-Cains in that herd Jesse's boys are holding. Let alone two hundred of our Rocking Hells."

Cain swore. "The thievin' cowards." A hot throbbing bulb of hate suddenly bobbed up behind his eyes. It almost blinded him for a second. He began to shake; felt thick all the way down to his thumb tips.

"Yeh."

"But I thought Jesse wasn't gonna start his big roundup until late next week?"

110

"He jumped the gun. On purpose. So he'd clean up our cattle as he went along."

"The thievin' sonsa—"

"An old trick we used to help him pull on the nesters."

"Is Jesse himself holding them?" Cain asked.

"No. Mitch Slaughter and his boys."

"Where's Jesse?"

"He's out holding Lord Peter's hand."

"What! Ride over that trail again."

"Yeh, Lord's Peter's come over from England again on a visit. Servants and all." Harry smiled some. "To check into the rumor that Jesse has been shorting him. You know. Jesse's about to buy back the Derby outfit."

"Oho! No wonder they're gathering up all our little herds as they go. To fill out the tally some."

"Yeh." Harry smiled again. "Somebody writ His Bullship a letter."

"You?"

"No. Timberline."

Cain snorted. "That I believe."

"Well, what are you going to do about it?"

Cain tipped back his folded black hat. "Do? Why, get 'em back of course."

"How?"

Cain set his stub legs wide apart. "Where's Timberline?"

"Up at the head of the hole. Just inside the Wall. Watching the Derby roundup through my glasses."

"Where's the rest of your boys?"

Harry tipped back his gray hat and scratched his silver hair. "Guarding what's left of our herd high in Hidden Country. Where I sent them early this morning."

"Hmm. Then we'll have to do it with just the three of us. You, me, and Timberline."

"You crazy? Mitch's got twenty-five armed men holding that herd."

"You got a better plan?"

"Well, I thought we could maybe run a stompede on 'em. Scatter everything all to hell and gone, and then take our time picking out our own."

"No. I'm agin that. I want a showdown with them devils. I got my herd fair. And they can treat me accordin'."

Harry smiled, again looking at Cain with face held to one side. "What about them two hundred unbranded mavericks we took over the past summer? The ones you found hid high in the Big Stonies and told us about?"

111

"Them the ones of yours they're holdin' now?"

"Yeh."

"Wal, each man to his own troubles. They got your brand on and that's good enough for me. If you'd've changed brands on 'em, that'd be a horse of another color."

"But you still think we should take them on with just the three of us?"

"Less'n we get brother Dale to come too." Cain wrung his ear. "Dencil is out of the question of course, since Clara'll have a fit." Cain gestured, blunt. "Listen. Go down and get Dale. In a tight he's a good one to ride the river with. Hurry. It'll take me a bit anyway to get ready and by that time the both of you can be back here. Tell Dale I'll have Lonesome saddled and ready for him."

"Lonesome? That black piece of bad luck? Not Dale too, Cain."

"G'wan, get. Lonesome ain't bad luck. He ain't brought me any yet. And he won't bring anybody else any."

"Cain, as sure as shootin', if Dale rides him, he's sure to land in a mess of trouble like I did."

"G'wan, get. Dale hain't got your kind of conscience. And tell Dale to take both his rifle and .45 along. With plenty of shells."

"Four men is still—"

"You game, Harry?"

"Sure, but—"

"Get then."

Harry galloped off.

Cain let Bucky down out of the twitch and untied him from the snubbing post. When he reached up to slip on the bridle, Bucky gave a funny little whinny, showed old white around the eyeball, and climbed the air, sunfishing, as if to say, "Hey, bozo, ain't you forgot something?"

Cain smiled some. "Sorry, old man, as usual I see you want the saddle on first. The way I first broke y'u, eh?" He slipped on the saddle with its blanket and cinched it up tight. After that Bucky didn't mind the bridle, even parted his mouth to help.

Cain saddled and bridled Lonesome too; dug out an extra rope and bedroll for Dale; filled both saddlebags with greasy shells. He buckled on a set of shiny leather chaps and got out a second pair for Dale.

The boys, Harry and Dale, didn't come, so he took some practice shots with his .45, drawing and firing at a few late fall flies clinging to the sunny side of the barn. The shots cracked loud in the low yard, echoing off the bluffs behind the cabin, and then off the further hills toward Crimson Wall.

"Dummed flies seem to move just as I shoot," Cain muttered to himself. He kept at it until he felt he had the old rhythm down again.

Cain had perfected a technique of his own. He drew and fired in one motion. The moment the muzzle was clear of the holster, he snapped the hammer by jerking down the gun with a hard motion and then stopping the jerk at the exact instant of firing. He held the gun high on the grip and always aimed it some six inches below where he wanted to hit.

He recalled the advice of an old gunman. "When you see you're about to have trouble with someone, make it a point to get up as close as possible. This'll make it easy for you to read the other man's eyes. A man's eyes will always tip off his next move. It also removes the chance of a miss."

The boys still didn't come, so he decided he might as well take the kinks out of Bucky. Bucky saw him coming and his ears went flat on his head. Cain talked low to him, petted him some, and then stepped across. Before the toe of his right boot could find its way home into the stirrup, Cain was aboard a cyclone of muscle and bone. Bucky went off the ground in a great leap, and then, at the very top of it, broke in two and threw the rear half of his body one way and the front half the other, so that when he came down he landed with two separate jolts. Cain knew this maneuver and tried to set himself for it, but with his right foot still not in the stirrup, he wasn't locked in properly. The next thing he knew he was sailing through the air, hind legs kicking around like a migrating bullfrog in full flight. He hit the ground on his belly with a loud wumpfing grunt. And lay there.

He got to his feet slowly. "That dummed wild hyena." He collected his hat and dusted it off. He dusted off his faded black shirt and vest and chaps. He felt over his body for broken bones. With a grim smile he recalled Gramp's advice on how to stick to an outlaw horse. "If you'll just keep the eye of your one-spot glued onto the center of a hoss's spine, you'll never get throwed."

He went for Bucky again. Bucky's ears were still mean down. Cain got hold of the reins, firmly; put his foot in the near stirrup, easy; then bellowed a hoarse and roaring "Whoa!" and stepped across.

Up went Bucky, chinning the moon, swapping ends in

113

midair, swallowing his head as he came down, thumping the ground with four rocking jolts as each hoof hit separately. This time Cain rode him up and rode him down. He'd got his foot in the far stirrup and he and the horse were one.

Cain bellowed another hoarse "Whoa!" and this time he let the heat of his risen bulb of hate get into it. It ripped out of his throat.

Bucky boiled over yet once more—and then had enough. His ears came up and he trotted over to the hitching rack and ranged beside Lonesome. A smile wrinkled back his Roman nose.

Yet still Harry and Dale didn't come.

It got to be twelve noon. Then one. Then two.

Cain cussed. "I knew it. That Rory's went on the peck again. Dummed Dale, lettin' her get her head like that. Interferin' with man's work."

When it got to be almost three, he couldn't stand it any longer. He was hungry. "My stomach's so shrunk now it'll hardly chamber a headache pill." He fried himself some potatoes and steak; opened a can of tomatoes; finished off with some dried apples. It wasn't much of a meal, a simple buck-nun's, but it stuck to the ribs.

It was four when a drumming of hooves sounded behind the barn along the Shaken Grass.

Cain greeted the boys from the low doorway of his log cabin. "What held you up?"

Dale's lean gobbler face split all the way back to his ears. He sat behind Harry, behind the cantle. "Had us a false alarm."

"Oh." That stubbed Cain. The warm bulb in the back of his head lay down some. "Wal! I was awonderin'." He came down the stoop. "How's Rory now?"

"Fine. She forgot the same thing happened this far along with Joey."

"She didn't kick on your comin' along then?"

"Nary a word."

"She knows?"

"She's all for it. Even a killing bee if it's needed."

Cain considered some more. "Harry, when did her false alarm come? After you told her about this deal coming up?"

Dale answered, sharpish. "Before. If you must know."

Cain nodded. "All right. Good. And now let's roll our tails. We're probably too late already for today."

Cain led the way, riding Bucky. Next came Harry on his bay, Star. Dale trailed after on Lonesome. Lonesome snorted now and then at Dale's smell, but Cain settled him with a stern word. They loped briskly up the trail alongside the Shaken Grass. They packed their guns loose, both the six-gun and the rifle. All three watched the skyline above the rim of the canyon.

Fall colors flashed to all sides in the narrow bottom: groves of golden quaking-aspen, patches of scarlet thorn-bushes, clusters of crimson rose briars, webs of whiteball clematis braided through fronds of ponderosa pine. Sage-brush showed the rust of a first frost. Buckbush rattled dry wisp leaves.

The wind of their going bruised in their ears. Far ahead, through the gap of Crimson Wall, reared up the Old Man and the Throne. The snow on them had spread down their sides some. A very thin veil of cirrus clouds worked off the two peaks, spreading out over the wide Bitterness valley like a smoke from a great fire.

The sun fell very slowly toward the range of stickleback peaks to the west. Clusters of tiny dots spread on a far slope like lice across a tawny fur coat. It was where Mitch Slaughter had the last of his boys out on circle.

The three watched the skyline. Horse hooves clopped in rhythmic throws. White dust stived up out of the hard gray trail. The two walls of the Shaken Grass canyon slowly raised, slowly turned pink, then crimson, then blood-crust red. Cottonwoods slowly gave way to red cedars. The three watched the skyline.

Then they were through the gap and inside the Crimson Wall. They wheeled to the right. Red dust rose from the trail under them.

High on a projecting ledge a figure moved. The figure had red hair and beard, a red sash, and dusty red clothes. He blended perfectly into the background of red sandstone. Eyeglasses, catching the late sun, burned down on them briefly. The figure waved at them with a hat, around and around.

Cain drew up. So did the others, coming abreast.

Harry said, "Timberline. On the watch where I put him."

"Wave him on down here."

Harry waved his hat around once, in a big sweep, and down.

Timberline waved again, this time straight up and across, once, emphatic, and started down.

Cain watched Timberline climb down, off one ledge to another, past pink strata, then a layer of yellow clay, then blood-crust red. The blood-crust layers were always the thickest and they gave the great cliff its color. Cain watched Timberline hit the bottom of the cliff; watched him get his horse, a sorrel, from where he had hidden it behind a monster slab of fallen sandstone; watched him clamber aboard and come beating toward them.

Dale couldn't help but make a sliding remark. "Throw a leg of his on each side of a horse and his mind in the middle, and there he'll ride for the rest of the day."

"He ain't so dumb," Harry defended with a flash of eyes.

Timberline's sorrel ran with a paddling gait, front feet winging out on each gallop. Under Timberline the sorrel looked like a runt burro. Timberline's feet almost dragged on the ground and in the dips it sometimes looked like he was holding up the horse between his legs.

Timberline came beating on until he was almost on top of them. Then his red beard parted; a pink-edged hole showed; a large "Whoa!" boomed; and on the instant the sorrel set down on all fours. A cloud of dust stove up all around them.

Close up, Timberline was overwhelming. He was so huge the Red Sash boys swore that, with his red beard, he was a cinch to win first prize at a bull show. No one had ever found out just how tall he was, but he was so much over six feet that everyone claimed at least seven for him. "He's so tall," Harry once said, "he don't even know when his feet is cold."

Timberline dressed rough mostly because store clothes wouldn't fit. He had to make his own pants and shirt from the best parts of discarded clothes of others. His pants might be of as many colors as it took pieces to make them. Luckily he'd once been a shoemaker, so his boots, huge ones, always fit perfect. In fact, his boots were so well made they fit with the elegance and snugness of a lord's, "so fine," as Harry once put it, "a man could almost see the wrinkles in his socks." The grip of his .45 was makeshift—the old butt had been replaced with a plow handle. His hat, to fit, had to be sprung until it was misshapen. Hence he usually hung onto a hat until it was as dark with hand grease as an old family Bible, was as heavy as a pail of lard, and could be smelled all the way across a livery stable. The only store-bought items he could wear ready-made were his belt and vest, though he wore the belt in the last hole and the vest never quite covered the small of his back.

Harry had once tried civilizing Timberline a little. He took him into Antelope to clean him up with a haircut and a bath. "You've been gophering in them hills so long, Tim, you're liable to find yourself without a soul come Judgment Day." They never got to the bathtub. Because the mistake was first made in the barbershop. Long red hairs grew out of Timberline's nose, hairs as long and as stiff as barley beards. The hairs caught the eye of the barber, a finicky Frenchy, and he began work on them first, trimming them away with quick neat snips. It took Timberline, his little red pig eyes rolling, some twenty seconds to catch up with what was happening to him, and then he reacted volcanically, hugely, under the white apron. He rose in terrible rage, and beat the barber to within an inch of his life. He might have killed him with his hairy fists if Harry and the crowd in the shop hadn't pulled him off. "By Grab," Timberline roared, "by Grab, the Good Lord intended them hairs there for a reason! To strain out the wild salt and the flies! Just like He growed a tail off a cow's hindquarters to switch the flies with!" Timberline was so wild after that the boys had to tie him up when it came time to change his underwear each spring.

It was Harry who'd given him his nickname: Timberline. Timberline was hairy from his toes to his ears, and from there on was as bald as the top of Old Man mountain. Harry had seen the resemblance the first time he met him and had branded him on the spot. No one knew Timberline's real name—he'd been known as Big Red until then—not even his summer name. Nor did anyone know where he'd come from. Harry had once heard a rumor in Butcherknife Bain's saloon that back East somewhere Timberline had caught his shoemaker partner in bed with his wife, that he'd tied them together and whipped them unmercifully, then had skipped the country. But Harry had never dared ask him about it.

The top of Timberline's head was the subject of much speculation, though never in his presence. Since he never washed higher than his wrists and only his lips and the point of his nose, a crust of red dust had slowly formed over his bald dome. Harry claimed he'd once seen a wasp sting it with not even an eyeflick from Timberline. Harry was positive that if it could be pried up it would prove to be at least as thick as a U. P. restaurant pancake. Harry claimed that the Good Lord had run out of the same breed of hair when he came to finish Timberline off at the top. Another time Harry argued that the bald dome was probably the scar where the Lord had poured in Timberline's brains. "Except that He poured them in with a syrup spoon and somebody bumped His arm."

117

Still and all, Timberline was probably as clean and as healthy as any wild bull on the prairie. Like them, he was washed by the rains, scoured by the snows, combed and dried by the winds, and toughened by his own accidental vaccinations.

Cain smiled through the dust that Timberline's sorrel kicked up. He tipped back his black hat by the point. "Howdy, Tim. What's new?"

"Nothin's movin' now, Cain. Mitch's hands have about finished ridin' circle for the day."

Cain looked across the width of the red country; then looked it up and down. "Not even a magpie scoldin'."

"That's a gut," Timberline grunted. Timberline leaning forward on the horn of his saddle was still almost a head taller than any of the others.

"Where's Dencil's horses?"

Harry spoke up. "I told Red Jackson and the boys to push them back into Hidden Country until the trouble was over."

Cain lifted a brow. It crinkled the side of his face. "Oh? Did Dencil agree to that?"

Harry said, "No. Nor did Clara. She got as mad as a she-bear with a sore tail when we told her."

"She would."

Harry said, "But we decided to help them anyway. For their own good."

Cain observed that Harry's eyes didn't quite hold up to him when he talked. Something uneasy, something unsaid, lay behind Harry's words. Cain decided to set up a watch in his head. "Poor Dencil. But I guess you probably did right at that. Save him a lot of trouble maybe."

Harry said, "You still plannin' to bull in and cut out what you can?"

"No, not that exactly. I think we'll just ride in easylike and I'll first have my say. After that, the next move will be up to Mitch."

Harry held his face to one side, gray eyes glimmering at Cain in the primrose dusk. "What about your wild one?"

"Try me. The time to let your wild one out is when you know it'll do some good."

"But then it ain't a wild one."

"Mine is."

"All right. I agree. If you got a tight line on it."

"You've got a right to talk, you country jake you." Cain looked at both Harry's and Timberline's red sashes. "I suggest you two take off them eye-catchers. Yeh, them red sashes.

118

Wearin' them in front of men already as touchy as teased snakes will only make them wilder. Like waving a red flag before a bull deliberate."

A dangerous gleam suddenly appeared in Harry's eyes. "Ain't this a free country out here?"

"It's a free country after we get our beef back. So off with 'em, boys, or Dale and me'll go in alone."

"What'll we use for belts to hold up our pants?"

"Use your piggin' strings."

Both Harry and Timberline removed their red sashes with a show of reluctance.

"Stuff 'em in your pokes. Out of sight." When they finished, Cain looked over his little army. "Good. Now. Nobody open his yap or make a move for his gun until I give the word."

A red sun struck the south slope of the Old Man, just at the edge of the snowline. The red sun bounced; burned a deep hole for itself into the rock line; then melted into it. Instantly a vast light-black shadow raced by overhead, climbed up and over the Crimson Wall, then rushed far across all the Bitterness valley beyond. With it came a slowly spreading violet silence.

They rode at a slow trot. A chill night settled down. All four put on a coat over vest and gun.

The moment they climbed onto the bench just north of Red Fork, two campfires popped into view. The fires glittered in the distance like fallen meteors. The four approached rapidly across the parklike level. The near fire glowed under a spreading cottonwood, the farther fire out in the open under the stars. The first fire lit up the under branches of the cottonwood, giving each gaunt elbowing limb a paper-yellow color, with the gold leaves rustling and dancing in an updraft from the jumping orange flames. Off to the left, in the darkness, hovered the horse cavvy, the wrangler riding off to one side. A horse whinnied; was answered shrilly by another in the remuda. The white canvas on the near chuck wagon fluttered in the soft dusk breeze coming down off the blue Big Stonies. Beyond the fires a great herd of cattle lay thrown out on the bed ground. Cowboys rode guard around them slowly. A few calves bellered for lost mothers. The cowboys sang as they rode, raucous but comforting. They crooned with a coarse whooing like the sound of wind blowing across the rough opening of a broken jug.

Cain held up a hand. "At a walk now, boys. And around into the down-wind side along the creek there. So we won't scare the herd. Or the horses. Let alone rile up the cooks with

119

our dust." He waved out a trail for them to ride, along the stream. "Pack your guns loose. Take off your gloves. But keep your hands lookin' innocent." Horseshoes spat sparks on the creek stones. Bridle bits, spurs, gingled gently.

A man rose from the near fire under the cottonwood. His back and sides were aglow, his face in shadow. From the way he rolled on his bowlegs and from his sloped shoulders, Cain made out it was Mitch the foreman. Some dozen faces along the outer edge of the light looked up, teeth and eyes flashing in the gold light. The faces belonged to punchers and all packed guns, loose. They were eating supper from plates set in their laps or placed on their crossed legs.

Left-handed Mitch dropped a hand to his gun. "Hold up out there. Who goes?" Every puncher behind Mitch held his chewing.

Cain reined in Bucky. The firelight played over his hollow walnut face and hollow-dented hat. Harry, Dale, Timberline halted in the darkness behind him. "Cain Hammett. And my boys."

"What do you want here?" Mitch stood with legs apart, set to draw.

"Why, Mitch, you know what I came for. To rep my own beef. Sorry I was late to help you on circle. But I first had to shoe Bucky."

Mitch stood hunched, tense. He growled something to himself. His crimped fingers worked over his gun.

Cain said, "Oh, I know we're a blackballed outfit, Mitch. But we've come anyway. You know my calves are suckin' the right cows."

"Who's your boys?"

"Neighbors. He-wolves on a horse. Come to help me cut out my beef. And help with the branding."

Mitch tried to peer past Cain into the darkness behind him. "Who'd you say?"

Cain settled his left hand over his gun too. "Timberline. And my two brothers. Dale and Harry."

Mitch stiffened. "Harry here?"

Cain said, grim, "That surprise you, Mitch?"

"After what was did to him, Harry still ain't had enough?"

Dale laughed. His fish mouth drew back. "You don't seem to know your Hammetts much, Mitch. You know you can't hang a Hammett."

Mitch glared. "And that peckerneck brother Dale of yours. Don't he know he and his dummed ewe stink ain't much welcome around beef?"

120

The devil in Harry let out some. "Oh, hells bells, Mitch, we've come because we want one hair apiece out of that damned chin of yours."

Mitch jumped. "What's that you say? What's that you say?"

Cain said, calm, "The boys threw in with me because they've got their troubles too. Which they'll tell you about when the time comes."

"Well, if it's stole beef them range bums is lookin' for—"

"Mitch, let's wait until morning with that. When we can see."

"No, the devil with it. Now."

"Hey, slow down a bit, Mitch," Cain said, calm. Bucky moved restless under Cain, fawncing some at the bit. "Now ain't you forgettin' you jumped the gun holdin' your roundup this week? When your boss Jesse announced in the *Weekly Bulletin* it was to be next week?"

A growl from Mitch.

"Now I know that left-handers like you and me like to get the fall work done early. But yet, Mitch, that was hardly fair. You know that. It's hard enough for the little man to prowl through a big roundup and pick his strays, without you first chasin' them out of the country a week early."

More growls from Mitch.

"So let's just say we come for strays that had the misfortune a getting lost in your bunch."

Silence from Mitch.

Then from behind the chuck wagon came an old man wearing a grease-spotted leather apron and an old white blue-striped shirt without a collar. He was totally bald. The top of his head shone in the firelight like a well-licked bone joint. He was cricked forward from the hips and had more the look of one running in one spot than of one shuffling. It was Hambone the cook, or Bon Hamilton, as he signed his letters.

Hambone was the best cook in the valley. No foreman dared buck him. If he fell into a pet and quit, the cowboys attached to his wagon would quit in a bunch with him. Hambone could make fat apple cobblers and bear tracks or doughnuts to such a mouthy fare-thee-well his punchers spoke of them with tears of appreciation. It was said the boys would go to hell itself for one of his pies. Hambone ran a wagon that was home to his boys, bed as well as board. Hambone's wagon was also the puncher's social center. And, in time of trouble, Hambone's wagon was a hospital as well as an underground hideout. When a puncher threw his bedroll into Hambone's wagon, it was as good as saying he'd give his life for the outfit Hambone cooked for.

Hambone approached to where Cain sat easy on his horse. The fire sparked in Hambone's old gimlet eyes, lit up the underside of his whiskery chin. "Cain. Well. And how be ye?"

"Hambone. You old buzzard you. Thought you was going to retire to Old Cheyenne come this fall?"

Hambone shrugged, smiling. "Couldn't resist my own cookin'." Hambone swung his head around from his humped neckbone. "What's the trouble here, Mitch? Why hain't you asked Cain and the boys to step down? We got more than enough chuck here."

Mitch's round pock-blond face worked. He was damned if he didn't and damned if he did. Both Hambone's request and usual camp courtesy demanded that he ask them to stay.

Hambone looked up at Cain again. "Climb down, Cain, and feed your tapeworm. Tell your boys they kin stake their hosses anywhere."

Cain couldn't resist throwing a bad pickle Mitch's way. "Then we can sleep around here?"

Hambone exploded. "Hell yes, you can sleep around here! Anywhere. The world is open."

"Thank you kindly."

"And then come and set down to some grub. I wore out three hats trying to get this fire started and you might's well enjoy it with me." Again Hambone swung on Mitch, who still stood growling to himself. "Cain saved my life last summer, Mitch." Hambone pointed toward the peak of the Old Man looming over them in the dark with purple-white majesty. "Shot a silvertip the size of a load of hay just as she was all set to jump me. While I was out wolfin' for Lord Peter. We owe him that much."

"What's that got to do with me or Lord Peter?"

"By God, the way I read the Scriptures, it was wuth something to me, Mitch."

"Oh, all right." Mitch threw Cain a twisted sneering look out of his slanted Mongoloid ovals. "Step down then and be damned to you, you left-handed saint."

Cain and his boys threw their bedrolls on the ground well back in the shadow behind the chuck wagon and also away from the second campfire further up the creek. They staked out their horses; slid off the saddles and blankets. They gave their mounts a brisk rubdown and then, with a final pat on the rump, left them to graze in what little grass there was around.

Cain drew near the fire, rubbing his hands. The night wind sliding down off the Big Stonies had chilled him. The fire was a good jumping one and it threw waves of warmth over him, over his face and belly and thick thighs. He glanced around at the firelit faces and recognized most of the boys, punchers he'd once ridden with when he worked for the Derby. Hair tufted out over the ears and collar, they were a wonderful hard-looking bunch. He nodded at each in turn. There was Stalker Smith with his crabbed look, and Four-eye Irish with his glinting glasses, and Stuttering Dick with his puckered-up lips. There were also Long Guts Everding, Spade Burnett, Ringbone Sam, Beavertooth Kassen, Dried Apple Bill, Hog Johnson, Peakhead Jim—all of them top cowhands, all of them cut from the same leather.

The upright iron stakes to either side of the fire glowed dull red. The iron crossbar, from which pots and kettles hung on firehooks, was coated with soot. Over it sometimes ran a rim of racing glowing fire. Strongest of all smells was the coffee, but the smell of baking biscuits in the Dutch oven and frying beef in the skillet was the best.

Hambone bowed in mock deference. "He'p yoreself, my lords. The banquet awaits. It's all on the earl."

Dale and Harry and huge Timberline filled their plates and cups and retired to the edge of the lighted area, scratching out a place for themselves in the rusty bunch grass, making sure there were no rattlesnakes or pricklepear cactuses underfoot on the red ground. Furtively they pulled their belts and guns around ready to hand under their coats.

Cain hung back. He was still studying Mitch's glowering face on the other side of the fire.

Hambone bowed in mock deference. "He'p yoreself, my lords." Hambone touched Cain lightly on the elbow. "Grab her, Cain."

Cain got himself a big white plate and a tin cup and a set of eating irons and filled up. He squatted near his boys.

As he ate, half-watching the punchers around the fire as well as the fire itself as it spit exploding wood worms out of burning poplar, his eyes roved the camp. He saw that Hambone ran his usual homelike wagon. The lid to the chuck box was down, set on two props, opening to view various drawers for plates, tin cups, spoons, knives, forks; shelves for coffee, sugar, lard, rice, dried fruit; partitions for salt, pepper, soda, baking powder, calomel, pills, black draught, horse liniment. Under the cupboard lid rested a keg of warm and ancient sourdough. Water barrels hung from the side between the

123

front and rear wheels. Poking out above the wagon box stood various barrels of flour, bacon, canned goods. Freshly slaughtered beef bled from the top rim of both rear wheels. It had been hung out to cool in the night wind. Up front, on top, teetered a weathered spring seat, sagging a bit on the side where Old Hambone always sat while driving across country. A raw cowhide, commonly called the possum belly, had been slung under the wagon, its head and forelegs tied to the front and its rear legs tied to the back. In it the cook stored dry wood and cow chips against a rainy day. A canvas roof or fly stretched taut from the top of the wagon to a lower limb of the cottonwood. Under this, on a barrel, sat Hambone, where he'd retired while the boys ate up. He sat smoking a corncob pipe, musing to himself, eyes milky in the firelight.

A meteor flashed by overhead, almost within hand's reach, leaving a powdery trail of momentary glowing coals, fading out in a trail of pink then ashen smoke. A horse in the cavvy snorted. Some of the mothers in the herd started to their feet. The circling cowboys out on killpecker guard quickly deepened their lowing lullaby songs. All the punchers around the two fires perked up, alert as squirrels and ready to jump for their night horses in case of stampede. Even Mitch momentarily forgot his grudging truculent air. But the night wind continued to slide down off the mountains, pushing softly but persistently against the side of the face, and after a while the cavvy quieted and the mothers in the herd lay down on the bed ground again.

Presently talk picked up around the fire. The boys liked to josh Hambone, mostly because he was the one cook in captivity who'd tolerate much of it. He enjoyed parrying their sallies. This made it all the more sweet.

Ringbone Sam called out from where he sat on the ground, "What's that you got boilin' in the fire there, cookie? Smells bad from here."

Hambone smiled from his throne on the barrel under the fly. He removed pipe from mouth. "Sheep dip. The boss says all you lambs've got a bad case of the scab."

All the eyes around the fire rolled and glimmered with mirth.

Hog Johnson called out from across the winking fire next. "What in God's name did you salt this slumgullion with, cookie? I swear it's worn me teeth down to the gooms."

"Well, son, it got tangled up with one of them dummed sand whirlwinds this afternoon. Eat it. You kin use the grit."

Teeth showed all around the fire.

124

Long Guts Everding called out, "Hey, cookie, how come this warsher"—Long Guts held up a sourdough biscuit—"how come you flavored this warsher with leather?"

"Son, if you'd pay up what you owe Jesse on your new Sunday saddle, you wouldn't have to hide it in my dough barrel no more."

Cain followed the repartee with relief. It meant the boys had relaxed some. Cain guessed that more than one of them might even be secretly on his side, because he'd done what they'd all dreamed of doing someday—quit and set up a spread on his own.

Timberline behind Cain growled to himself. "Burn me, if this ain't the way I like my coffee. Black as night and plumb barefooted. With the real Arbuckle brand comin' through."

Harry nodded, hat bobbing on the back of his head. A throw of silver hair glittered down his forehead, and under it his eyes roved from face to face, alert. "None of that dehorned stuff you get in the town restaurants, hey, Timberline?"

"That's a gut," Timberline grunted. His little red pig eyes roved the camp too. The big plow handle of his gun stuck out plain and its hand-worn shiny surface caught the dancing light. "I once ran out of coffee back in the hills and had to drink milk." Timberline swallowed. Firelight danced orange then scarlet on his red beard. "I'm tellin' y'u, my breath stunk like a young calf's for a week. Even to me."

Dale laughed. His lean cheek muscles bulged and unbulged as he chewed. His eyes were also alert to all around him. "I guess there ain't ary a man on a trail but what he wants his coffee to kick up in the middle and carry double."

Timberline helped himself to a large hunk of fried beef. He ate the beef with his hands, delicately parting the strands of flesh with his finger tips. "Yessiree, one thing you got to say for our old Hambone. He's right free with the chuck. Not like that Neckyoke Jones the coosie over there." Timberline pointed at the other campfire upstream a ways. With his heavy gloves off, Timberline's fingers were white and graceful in gesture, even courtly. "Neckyoke? Why, he's so tight with the boss's chuck he'll skin a flea for its hide and tallow."

Cain chuckled. "You're right about that, Tim. I once worked from Neckyoke's wagon. All we got was mostly beans for breakfast, beans for dinner, and beans for supper. So many beans so often it got ye downright plumb discouraged with life."

"And beans in between times," Harry added. "I remember."

Timberline's eyes rolled. "Wal, now, I'll have to say this

125

for the bean. Except for the bean bein' tiresome, the bean's got a lot of feed in it. Why, out on line camp where I had to eat the bean by the barrel, 'caze there just wasn't nothin' else around, why, I used to wake up in the mornin' with my fists full a strengt'." Timberline rolled his shaggy head. "No, except for the bean that Old Neckyoke serves, the bean is a friend."

Dale bit. "Except for Neckyoke's? Why, what kind of a bean does he serve?"

Timberline's lip twitched. "Why, Neckyoke serves the deceitful bean. It talks behind your back the next day."

Laughter rumbled up amongst the four of them. It spread to the other punchers sitting close by.

Timberline said, "Yep, poor Old Neckyoke, he must've been brung up on sour milk to get that mean." Timberline got to his feet and lumbered over to the coffeepot set in the edge of the fire.

All eyes followed him. He'd barely begun pouring for himself, when a voice, Spade Burnett's, called out, "Man at the pot!"

Timberline slowly turned around and glowered down at Spade. "Durn it, was I the first to go for a refill on the java?" The penalty for getting up first to serve oneself seconds on coffee was to pour coffee for all.

"Man at the pot!" Spade bawled out again.

"All right, all right. Comin' up." Timberline carried the fire-blackened pot from one cup to the next. Even Mitch held out his tin cup.

Beavertooth Kassen was last in line and he couldn't resist making some kind of comment. He asked, coarse front teeth gleaming like a yawning horse's, "Where in hell have I met you before?"

Timberline gave him eye for eye. "I don't know. What part of hell do you hail from?"

Again eyes rolled and glimmered with mirth in the hard-rock faces around the fire.

Timberline put back the coffeepot and went back to his place.

A horse whinnied in the cavvy off in the dark. A nervous steer got up off the herd bed ground. Then Bucky, standing erect, light flowing over his dun coat and black ears shot forward toward the downside of the trickling creek, suddenly shrilled out a high inquiring hinny. Lonesome called then too and shot his ears ahead into the dark.

Cain said, low, "Someone's comin'."

126

Mitch set aside his cup and stood up. "More range bums, I suppose. What the devil do they think this is, a U. P. depot?"

First came the sound of iron hooves ringing on stones; then the bark of a man's voice urging on horses; then the curious scrinching sound of iron rims on sand.

"It's three men in a democrat," Timberline said.

"Crissakes," Mitch sputtered, "it's the boss!" Quickly he turned on Hambone. "Cookie, throw your best foot in the pot, we've got company and lots of it."

The fiddlelike heads of two bay horses came into view of the fire then. The trotters swung sideways, to reveal a light two-seated green wagon behind with blurring sparkling wheel-spokes. Three faces showed up out of the dark: high-headed darksome Jesse Jacklin, mean handsome Link Keeler alias Hunt Lawton, and red-faced Peter Caudle, Earl of Humber-wick, the owner of the Derby. What caught the eye was the contrast between the black curling walrus mustaches on Jesse's and Link's faces and the shaven smoothness of Lord Peter's upper lip.

"Lord Peter in a democrat!" Cain whispered. "Who'd a thought His Lordship would finally come to that? Must've lost his carriage-and-four and his servants in a loaded poker game."

Staring at the three new faces, Dale slowly turned white. "Link! This puts us in a real bind." Dale dropped his hand on his .45.

Cain laid a hand on his brother's arm. "Steady now, Dale. Cattle first and feelings after."

Harry paled some too. "Jesse," he said softly. "I didn't expect to see him here." Harry gave Cain an odd troubled look; then glanced around behind him.

Cain said, "Remember now, you waddies, first things first. You can count cattle but not regrets."

"That's a gut," Timberline grunted. Timberline placed a hand on the shoulder of Dale, who had half-gotten up, and pulled him down. "Pull in your hosses a bit, my laddie."

Dale said, "I think we should slide for home."

Cain said, low, intense, "No, no. Set a spell. We've bluffed them so far and I think we'll come out. We still got Hambone on our side."

"What? With the prime minister of England himself present to make it legal in case they decide to hold a necktie party?"

Cain let some of it go then. He said, low, hoarse, "My hands are clean and I'm stayin'. Alone if need be."

Dale started to get up again, still wild to do something. "But what about Link?"

"Sit!" Timberline said, jerking Dale back to the ground.

Cain said, "The whole trick is to make 'em play the cards our way. It's our deal."

The light green wagon stopped at the very edge of the log fire. The bay trotters were lathered with sweat. Curls of slobber dropped from their mouths. They champed nervously, fawncing on their bits, still running in their heads.

Jesse, sitting on the near side, threw down the reins to Mitch. "Here, hold these ribbons while I help Lord Peter." Jesse stepped across the front wheel and climbed down. Limping badly on his left leg, he went around to the other side and helped the Englishman down. Link followed Jesse out and stood to one side, elbows nervously hoisting up his gun under his long black coat, staring at the faces around the fire. Link's dark-edged gray eyes glittered in the jumping orange fire.

Jesse came limping around to the fire with slim blond Lord Peter in tow. Lord Peter walked with his toes out and quite knock-kneed. His gait was in direct contrast with bow-legged pigeon-toed Jesse's.

Jesse spotted Four-eye Irish and Peakhead Jim. "You two, go around and unload His Lordship's tent and rigging." Jesse spoke in a drawling yet hard voice. "There's a cot in there and a table and cases. Set the tent facing the fire. And make sure there ain't no rattlers underfoot." Jesse rubbed his sore leg. "And you, Ringbone, unhitch the trotters and rub 'em down." Jesse glanced over to where Hambone still sat smoking and musing to himself under the canvas fly, a smile working his old leather-stiff face. "Hambone, how's for chuck?"

Hambone removed pipe from mouth, slowly. "Wal, I reckon I still got a few whistleberries left. Some son-of-a-bitch stew mabbe. A few shot biscuits. Plus a couple of slabs of His Lordship's beef. Later on I was plannin' on servin' a treat."

"Good enough. Dish it out and set it on for His Lordship when the boys've got his tent up."

"Table for three?" Hambone asked, the smile wrinkling up his face even more.

At that Lord Peter came to. "Oh, I say, I'm not accustomed to eating with the help."

Jesse flushed. His dark face almost blackened with it. He said, "Serve His Lordship separate." He bent down to rub

128

his knee again, as if to hide his mortification. Then he said, "Me? I always eat with my boys. Always have and always will. Oh yes, the earl will want his hot tea after."

"Tea!" Hambone exploded, rearing up his humpback. "Tea? Well, I never."

"Yes, tea!" Jesse commanded.

"Wal, we'll see. Clutchbelly stew I'll serve His Bullship. But tea, I'll be durned if I'll set around watching him sip from a cup like he thought it was hot sodder. He can have black java like the rest of us Americans."

"I say . . ." blond and imperial Lord Peter began, blinking.

With a gesture of impatience, as if to suggest that to argue with a cook out in the wilds was the most ridiculous thing he ever heard of, Jesse jerked out a long brown cigar and offered it to the earl. The earl accepted, and casually lit up.

Cain hadn't seen Peter Caudle, the Earl of Humberwick, in some time, not since the day when he and Harry and Timberline had helped Jesse skin the earl. So far as Cain could see the earl hadn't changed much. He still dressed in breeches buttoned at the knee, with high-topped polished boots and hard black derby and oaken cane and pigskin gloves. Cain remembered how in the old days whenever Lord Peter met a lady, he'd stop, catch his cane under an arm, lift his derby, clap himself hard on the head, and move on—all in the way of a formal greeting.

When Lord Peter first came West, he was about as green as a greenhorn could get. Slim, blond, he'd just arrived from Siouxland where he'd visited an English "pup farm" north of Le Mars, a place where the nobility of England sent their socially outcast members, "the troublesome pups." The pups were remittance men, that is, they depended for their existence upon the remittance of money from their families overseas. Lord Peter had been knocking around America looking for fun, when he heard that the pups played very good polo and ran top hounds as well. So out of nostalgia he went to the pup farm. What he found there was not a piece of Old England at all but "a hole with terrible terrible manners" and almost complete debauchery. Lord Peter wandered on, and came to Cheyenne. And there, in the sumptuous Cactus Club, coming across the latest quick-money scheme, cattle, Lord Peter really got bit. For all his hardheaded British caution in matters of finance, he was hardly a match for the shrewd Westerners. The plainsmen outwitted him at every turn. He was cleaned when he bought out Jesse's great ranch;

he was cleaned when he let Jesse run it for him as general manager.

Yet Lord Peter kept at it. He maintained a grand summer ranch house just outside Antelope. He imported furniture, speaking tubes, great clocks, carriage and four, leather-bound books, chefs and valets, hunting and fishing friends, and a pair of mean liver-spotted hounds. He also kept a couple of Boston floozies—he couldn't abide any kind of female coming from west of the Connecticut River. "Lousy. Nits and what-nots, you know."

The Earl of Humberwick always remained very suspicious of American doings. He was especially leery of the cowhands he found working for him. In a letter to his banker he termed them "a real simon-pure, devil-may-care, roistering, immoral, gambling, revolver-heeled, brazen, light-fingered lot."

Curious to know just how he was being duped—it had begun to dawn on him after a time—he began to tromp around a bit on his own. He refused a guide in the belief that the guide would carefully steer him away from question-able ranch practices. The result was he got lost every now and then, and Jesse had to send out a cowboy to bring him back to camp. The Earl of Humberwick's always getting lost got to be a joke and hardly a day went by but what some valley wit would come riding up to the chuck wagon or headquarters and bawl out, loud: "Anybody seen Lord Limber-prick around today?"

Lord Peter had autocratic ways. One time his liveried servant Jeems was asked how come His Lordship took him along on roundup. "Why, to curse me, sir, when he stumps his toe." Another time, on a hot day, Lord Peter ordered Jesse to tell his boys to throw a couple of pails of water over the pup tent every hour or so. Jesse had been very forthright in his reply. "Ask them rannies to get a pail of water from the crick for you? Here in America? Listen, you better not ask that out loud or they'll rope you by the udder and run you off the ranch. Even if it is your own."

Four-eye Irish and Peakhead Jim soon had Lord Peter's pup tent set up and cot and table laid out. They lighted a lantern inside for him, and Lord Peter disappeared within. Presently Hambone brought him his chuck. Jesse and Link alias Hunt, high-headed, alert, sat near the entrance as if on guard. They ate their supper from plates set in their folded legs.

The coming of Lord Peter into the cow camp was like

130

the throwing of an odorous moth ball onto an ant heap. Every face around the jumping orange fire became a sober one, even a stunned one. Every puncher sipped his coffee in silence. Eyes, however, flashed under wide hat brims.

Then Jesse caught sight of Cain and his two brothers and waddy Timberline. He started to his feet as if shot upward. "Well, I'll be go to hell. Look who's here. Mitch, since when did they begin working for us?"

Mitch growled something too low for anyone to hear but Jesse. Every puncher in the circle sat up stiff. Some set down their cups, ready for whatever might come up.

"Cain, yes," Jesse said. "I was hopin' he'd come in. But his brother Harry, never."

Again Mitch growled something meant only for Jesse's ear.

Jesse limped over to Cain, standing over him. "So you ain't quite ready to throw in with us yet?"

With a slow easy motion Cain set down his cup of coffee. A corner of the cup rested on a bent wisp of bunch grass and it almost spilled. He had to quick catch it. "No. I'm still in with the little stockman. Because this is still little-man country." A crack on the knuckle of his trigger finger itched. "Throw a drift fence across a pass and the little man has his little spread."

"Well, what the blazes you doin' here then?"

"Wal, Jesse, maybe you don't know it. But your boys jumped the roundup startin' time a whole week early. And some of my strays had the misfortune of getting lost in your bunch. So I've come to rep for myself and make my cut tomorrow."

Jesse rubbed his sore leg. He grumped, once. Then he looked down at side-kick Timberline. "And you, you big red grizzly, what's your excuse?"

Timberline blinked up little red eyes. "I'm here helpin' my frien' Cain. And to get back some of our beef that had the misfortune of getting lost in your bunch too. About two hundred head, I'd say."

The mention of a specific number, two hundred, checked Jesse. Everybody knew what Timberline meant. Jesse straightened ever so little. "Durn this leg," he said finally.

Harry asked, blandly, "What happened to your leg?"

"Ohh . . . got thrown a month ago and it still ain't healed. Still festering on me."

"Better go see a sawbones."

"What? And have him cut it off?" When Jesse wasn't rubbing his leg, he had the easy gestures of a man who'd

131

used the plains sign language. "Not on your tintype. No, I'll walk it off."

Jesse called over to Link alias Hunt. "Hunt, I want you to take a good look at these pilgrims here. There'll be more doin's with them later and I don't want you to forget the way they button their pants."

Hunt's cold smile deepened. He shifted his gun around under his black coat. His hands moved with a velvet deftness. He said in his high piping voice, "I see 'em." Hunt pointed at his high narrow forehead. "I've already got 'em memorized here."

"Good."

Someone gestured—it was Mitch—and then Jesse turned to look at the tent. There in the door flap stood Lord Peter, blond head leaning out, taking it all in, face as expressionless as the impassive face of an iron lion.

Jesse clammed up, and limped back to his spot beside the fire. Cain and his boys also shut up, and went back to their eating. The affair between them settled into a looking contest.

Fire slowly blackened and grayed the popping logs. Light fluttered gold then purple in the cottonwood leaves overhead. The chill wind flowed down from the mountains. The wind brought with it the smells of newly fallen snow and frost-freshened pines. The stars overhead sparkled like brilliants, just barely out of reach. The horses in the cavvy nickered, and kicked and snapped at each other. The great herd of cows slept on the high bed ground. Behind it all, like a low accompaniment on a mouth organ, water ran murmurous in the stony brook.

Hambone broke up the stiff silence. He did it with a single word. He uncovered a big Dutch oven at the edge of the fire and lifted out five steaming round pans and bawled: "Pie!" Everyone knew pie had been coming. The wondrous aroma of sweet raisins baked with dried apples had been in the air for some time. But the single word did it. In an instant a line formed. Casual joshing started up again. When Hambone gestured for Cain and his boys to come up for their share, no one seemed to think it out of order.

Hog Johnson held up the line arguing for a bigger piece. "Well, now, coosie, it's this way. I was out on the range shootin' a broke-leg bull the last time you had pie. So I really got two slices comin'. By rights."

Hambone denied it.

One of the men at the end of the line, twitching with

impatience, hollered out, "Fire and fall back, Hog. We'd all like a sniff of that spotted pup."

Finished, the punchers dropped their plates and tools in the wreck pan, and went back to the fire for a last smoke before turning in. Hambone meanwhile scraped all the leftovers into the squirrel can and set up the washpan on the cupboard lid and got the hot water.

When Cain saw no one was going to offer to help Hambone, he stomped out his smoke in the red dust and strolled over. "Where's your swamper, Hambone?" Cain was referring to the day wrangler whose duty it was to help the cook in the evening.

"Horses too restless tonight, I guess."

"And the louse, where's he?"

"You know Jesse never allows greenhorns around come roundup time."

"Got a towel handy?"

"Why, now, blamed if I ain't. That's right nice of you, Cain."

After a bit, Lord Peter came out of his pup tent and drew up a canvas chair to the fire and also had himself a last good-night smoke.

By this time the punchers had gotten used to the moth ball in their midst a little. Talk began to flow again. Gradually it built up into firelight taling.

Jolly Hog began it. "Seein' His Lordship here tonight, too bad we ain't got us a fiddle or two around. Or a mouth organ. We could a held us a stomp dance in his honor. Or a bullfrog sing." Hog sucked on his homemade cigarette. "Been a long time since I heard me some music." Hog sucked some more. "Fact is, the last time I heard some, come to recollect, was when I passed Lonesome Tree. Down along the Bitterness there. Where the Sioux bury their dead on scaffolds. Some brave must a fancied him a mouth organ because when I passed by, the wind was just right and I heard one aplayin' in the branches of that tree. Kind of shivery it was. Made me wonder if mabbe there wasn't something to it that a chief's hant hangs around a while after death."

Ringbone Sam pawed his whiskers and had a windy too. "Yep. Seein' His Honor's pup tent here minds me of the time some ranny friends a mine bought themselves one. To live in while on roundup. They'd made up their minds they wasn't gonna get soaked in their blankets under the stars no more come a night of rain. Nosiree. You probably remember them. They used to work with this outfit. Sore-toe

Tex, Gimpy Smith, and that long-legged country jake they called Blowing Florence. Well, they got along first rate the first week. No trouble atall. It rained twice and they woke up in the morning as dry as a cork and as fresh as a daisy while the rest of us had to fight our way out through a rind of mildew. Well sir, the second week, trouble started. One night one of the men began to yell. He claimed somebody had fouled his bed and demanded justice. He made such a commotion he woke up the whole camp, till finally the boss got up and held kangaroo court right then and there. It was Gimpy who'd hollered and he claimed Blowing Florence had done the job. Well sir, with the boss holding Judge Colt in his right hand, it was finally decided that the man who'd first discovered the fouling was the man who'd done it. Gimpy. The next morning the boss told Gimpy to roll his bed and get. 'Poor Blow,' the boss said, 'he's already got enough against him without adding that.' Gimpy rode away with never a word. He didn't even bother to sell his share of the tent."

Dried Apple Bill had something to tell. "Speaking of greenhorns—that was you, Hambone—I remember when I first rode out to camp to begin my career punchin'. I'd bought me a mare, and when I showed at camp, the cook took one look and wanted to know if she was stumpbroke. I didn't catch, of course, but I didn't let on I hadn't either. The cook was a sly devil if there ever was one. He offered to show me where I could picket the mare overnight. Well, in the morning, all the punchers at breakfast claimed I'd lied. They said she wasn't stumpbroke atall and I'd better get her out of camp afore there was a accident. I left camp right after breakfast all right and went straight to town and sold her. What I'd done coming to camp with that mare was a case of mighty poor manners. It took some careful listening in four different saloons to find that out, though. I was just a kid then and wasn't expected to know such stuff. At least not until I'd picked up a few wrinkles of my own on my horn. The mare is hoodoo to a cavvy. Besides being a possible accommodation for some lonesome ranny to lean against, the mare is a bunch quitter. Worse yet, she upsets the geldings. The geldings don't know what to make of her. She just ain't normal to their way of thinkin'."

Surly Mitch tossed a piece of wild sage in the sagging fire. Mitch always had a story handy that was bigger, better, and windier. "Well, you kin talk agin mares all you want. But I had me one onct that I dearly loved. Rabbit was her name.

She was my night horse. I was helpin' a man named Hobie
Parker bring up a bunch of longhorns from Denver. We had
good luck until we hit the North Platte and then all hell
commenced to let loose. One stompede after another. One
night I'd just laid down, it was rainin' hard, and I had my
little mare Rabbit staked near me, when there was a terrible
crack of thunder, and before I could raise from my suggans,
the longhorns was up and going, headed straight for me and
Rabbit. I forked her in the dark in my underwears and let
her run. I let her pick the way through them wild critters.
By jiggity, it was dark that night! Why, it was so black that
night you couldn't find your nose with both hands. I been
out many a night when it was so black the bats stayed to
home, but this night was blacker. Well, pretty soon I could
hear we was in some kind of breaks country, because there'd
be a crash of horns into rock alongside me, and then horrible
groans behind and far down. Was I scared? Well, I'll tell
a man. I was already afraid of badger holes and such, where
Rabbit could break her leg in, and throw me. But here was
rough country t'boot. So I let her have her own sweet head.
She'd stop; start up again; stop; start up again, turning,
slewing around, cutting to this side and that. She did that for
what seemed like ages. Steers was bellering all around me,
every now and then cracking into something, and then dis-
appearing with a horrible groan behind us. Man, I had all I
could do to hold on. I stuck on like a lean tick to a dog's
ear. Pretty soon I forgot to worry about the longhorns. It
was just me and my hoss and my skin. Finally, she stopped
dead, and wouldn't go a step further. So I got off and it being
dry where I lit, and it still being as dark as Jonah's pocket
when he was still inside that whale, and me all petered out,
I decided to sleep right there for the rest of the night. I
slept. Every little while my little mare would come over to
where I was laying and smell me over to make sure it was
me and that everything was all right. Then she'd go back
to grazing. Around three o'clock she lay down at my feet
an hour. I could hear her snore. Well, when light showed,
Rabbit nudged me awake and I found out where I was. On
a point of a cliff. A point only ten feet across. Where it
joined the main mountain it wasn't more'n a horse hoof in
width. Man, I tell you, when we rode along that back trail,
when I saw all them crevasses and gullies and holes we
missed, with dead beef to all sides in the bottoms, I sweat me
big drops of old spoiled vinegar. I tell you, that was one

mare that was a hoss, and the first son-of-a-gun that says she wasn't can begin his spiel right now."

There were no takers.

Timberline started to laugh. "Well, gents—"

Mitch, quick as a flash, had out his gun. "You laughin' at my mare?"

"No. No, I ain't laughin' at your mare, Mitch. No. I was just smilin' about the yarn I was about to spin." Timberline gave Mitch a most abused look.

"The yarn you was about to spin . . . that'll be something, I bet."

Lord Peter, stiff in his canvas chair, blinked and blinked.

Timberline swallowed; then started in. "Speaking of wild ones—which we wasn't—I mind me of the time I tamed me a wolf pup. I got him pretty tame, too, for a wolf. He follered me everywhere. He wouldn't let me pet him, but he'd foller me. Well, one time, I was sitting on a stump by the south line camp there, when a pack of wolves slides by. They spot my pet wolf, and one of the bitches whoos at him. My pet set there a minute, listening, tongue lolly-gagging, and finally he got up and with a sad look at me departs after them. And I thought, yep, there goes my pet. But no, after another minute, he comes lopin' back. When he got near to my feet the same bitch whoos at him again. And again he run after them. Well sir, the short of it was—that pet of mine run back and forth a dozen times afore he made up his mind whether to stay wild or come tame."

"What did he decide?" Harry asked, smiling as if he knew what the answer would be.

"Why! Stay wild a course."

Hambone ambled over from where he had just finished putting away the dishes. There was nothing Hambone liked better than to top Mitch in taletelling. "A stompede I was in once, I had the plumb pleasure of survivin' too. This was down in the Texas Panhandle. It was a black night, as I remember, and the beef was ready to bolt. The air was so thick with electricity, there was a green ball on every horn in the herd. It looked like we was guarding a bogful of them fiery swamp hants. Every time my hoss moved his ears, back and forth, them green balls moved back and forth too. The air was so charged with it our flesh tingled. Why, you couldn't run your hand through your hair but what you'd 'lectrocute yoreself. The cloud above was so low a man went around duckin' his head for fear a getting struck by accidental lightning sparks. It was as close and as hot as an oven full a bakin' mushrooms. The side of a man's face next to the herd almost blistered, as if it had been struck by a blast from a furnace. Well sir, there was a kid with us. A nice kid too. A couple a times I heard him prayin' as we crossed by circling the herd. It was that bad. I finally had to tell him that it was no use to pray. The Good Lord just warn't out on a night like that."

Old Hambone was known for his stretchers and everybody set back on his heels for a real one. Smiles passed around the dulling rose fire.

"Well, we held them crazy critters until just before daybreak. You know, that's when it's always the darkest. All t'onct, a puff a wind comes up and tips a tumblingweed. Now mind you, all this time we ain't even dared spit, let alone swallow or blow. So soft we took it for fear a spookin' 'em. But that little bush tipping over did it. I was on a good hoss, a lightning-striker of a hoss, and it was more him than me that pulled us through. With the first jump he was out in the lead, going lickety-cut for nowhere. Every now and then I see a flash in the night which tells me some poor puncher is pooping off his gun to signal where he is. Shootin' off his Winchester and his Colt all both at the same time. Or tryin' mabbe to turn a few steer so they'd mill and so maybe stop. Boys, the odor given off by the clashing horns and hoofs was so overpowering I thought we'd ridden smack into a glue factory. Man! Well, before I myself could turn any of them spooked critters, I sees ahead in a flash of lightning how we're all heading straight for a damnation of a dropoff, the beef, the hoss, and me. Yessir, there she was. Nowhere. Dead ahead."

As Hambone worked at embroidering his stretcher, the smiles around the fire slowly faded. Everyone, Mitch and his rannies, Jesse and Hunt, Cain and his waddies, all closed their eyes. Only Lord Peter continued to blink at the orating arm-waving Hambone.

Hambone saw what the play was. A smile shot wickedly across his leather face; left it as placid as before. He rubbed his old gourd-bald head once, and went on.

"Well sir, I went over that precipice on my hoss like hell after a preacher. I was dead sure I was headed for my long and happy home at last. I felt like I'd been sent for. Finally. We floated down, down, my hoss and me. After what seemed like a week, at last, we hit bottom. Hard-rock bottom. Well sir, my hoss lit so hard so fierce on that hard rock, on all fours, that she actually bogged down to the knees in it."

All heads around the fire slowly fell forward in what looked to be profound sleep. Only Lord Peter had his eyes open.

Hambone swung his head around from his humped neck bone, looking at all the pretend sleepers. He set his face hard and gently reached over and drew Mitch's .45 from its holster. Then he barked, "All right, you wise rannies! I've had enough insults from you! The first son-of-a-gun that wakes is a dead man! You too, Mitch! This is one hand you ain't droppin' out on." Hambone cocked the gun with a loud click. His eyes flicked back and forth, narrowly watching every face. "And no sweet dreams neither! The first man I see smilin' in his sleep has got to go too."

Here and there a face blanched slightly; became taut.

At that point Lord Peter suddenly spoke up. He turned to Jesse. "Oh, I say, would you have your man bring in a warming pan and warm my sheets? I am about to retire."

"Warming pan!" Hambone exploded.

"Yes. I must have my sheets warm," Lord Peter said emphatically.

Hambone gave Lord Peter a look of outraged astonishment. He tried to stare His Lordship down; couldn't quite make it. "Oh, hells bells," Hambone said at last, and he threw the gun down at Mitch's feet. "All right, you range bums, wake up and stay awake all night for all of me. But after this, Jesse, I want two weeks' notice before you come out with one of them foreign bullships again. That's so I can be in the next county by the time you arrive."

At that, Jesse quick stood up, holding his sore leg. "All right, that's enough! It's time we all turn in."

After a silence, a long silence, Stalker growled, "Well, yeh, I guess at that we've been up long enough. Mitch our boss here is one of them fellers who never needs sleep he gets up so early. It makes him mad to see someone else that does."

"Yeh," Hog said, "guess I've had enough for today too. I'm so sleepy I ain't got enough gumption left to lick my upper lip. When it still has a taste or two of pie left up there. I know, because I can smell it."

Harry

Harry lay coiled in his warm woolen suggans, chin almost into his paired knees. He could smell his own Hammett smell mingled in with the sweat of his horse Star's. There was also the smell of his own breathing, of used air. Faintly, not quite as distinct, was the smell of crushed wild sage. There were also two other smells, stronger than all the others, but those he was used to: fresh horse buns as grassy as old mildewed hay and new cow plotches as rotten rich as soured pudding. Slowly he slid up a hand to make sure the tarp was tight over his head to keep out the chill wind sliding down from the mountains. A man had to make sure it was a cold draft and not a rattler that had crawled in.

A bump in the ground pressed dull but hard through the suggans. It worked into his thigh. He couldn't make out if it was a stone or a clump of bunch grass. He shifted slightly. He felt it through the bedclothes with a cautious slow hand. It was a round stone. He'd overlooked it when he laid out his bedroll.

He lay still, listening absently. Through the ground he could hear the nearby night horses step about as they grazed such grass as was within reach. Further away, duller but still quite plain, was the slow turmoil of horse hooves in the saddle band. He fancied he could even catch the great herd of cattle breathing and chewing cud as it lay on the high bed ground behind camp. Occasionally a coyote sounded off his tarnal lonesome call. He could barely make out on the air a cowhand on guard singing a song, low, hoarse, to keep the mothers and calves and steers soothed for the night. The songs were pitched so low they made him feel drowsy too. Two of them he'd often sung himself: "We go North in the spring but will return in the fall" and "We are bound to follow the Lone Star trail." And underneath it all, like an endless organ tremolo, ran the murmuring of the mountain stream.

He envied the cowhand on guard not a whit. Many a night he too had ridden watch when sleep kept hitting him in the back of the neck like a blow from a boxer. It was only by rubbing the edges of his eyes with tobacco juice, making them smart, that he'd managed to stay awake at all.

Cain coughed near him. The sound of the cough traveled distinct and clear through the ground. Cain awake? Something up? On watch to make sure no Mitch or Hunt would prowl over and, despite cow-camp code, knife them in their sleep?

How did Cain do it? His older brother had a lion inside and yet in a tight was always in complete control over it. When things was easy, yes, then he was apt to explode over some little thing. But let the going get tough, then he was like General Washington himself, cool under fire, thinking galleywest fast. A man of iron nerves. They were in enemy

139

camp and alive right this moment only because every hand in it knew that if it came to a shooting bee Cain would take at least a half-dozen toughs down with him.

A man had to be born that way. Not made. Take this Harry Hammett fellow now, the one talking. To win a point he was more apt to slide around a corner than hit it head-on. To him there was more fun in outslickering a man than in out-fighting him. It took too much out of a man to hold up tough day after day like Cain did.

Cain was born a black walnut; Harry was born a silver willow. Both were trees, yes. But who was to say which was the best in God's great forest?

One thing this fellow Harry had better be careful of. And that was not to talk in his sleep. Because if his older brother Cain ever found out, there'd be all hell to pay.

This fellow Harry had some kind of devil in him to wish Cain dead. Why else would he have considered that deal Jesse offered? Which he didn't go through with? No, Cain must never know how close one of his brothers had come to turning traitor. He must never know that that was why Jesse and his boys near-hung Harry Hammett from that cottonwood in Cain's yard. And why a few minutes later they let Cain go because at the time they thought they already had their man.

Cain believed the little man could win honest if he'd just fight fair. Well, Cain was wrong. The little man would never win fighting fair. Never. The big augers always made the first move and then it was up to the little man to fight back and recover what he'd lost. A man could not match fire with fire if the big nabobs used the big fire first. Nor would backfiring help much either. Because not only would a man clean himself out close around but he would get cleaned out all around. No, when you were the little man you had to use your noodle and outfox 'em. That's what the Red Sash boys believed.

"Cain, man, let me ask you something. In your sleep there, settled down now like low smoke on a swamp, who do you think you are to yourself? Really? A man? A coward? A success? A failure? Good? Bad? What?

"Cain, man, let me ask you something else while I'm at it. With Rory lost, is life worth living?

"Well, it ain't for me.

"Yes, you and Dale thought you two was the only ones in the running for our cousin Rosemary. Let me tell you something. You wasn't. I had a chance there too. And I would have won my chance if I could have kept the fool in me in hand. Not my wild one, but my fool one. You know me. Anything for a good legpull. I'd crack one off even if it meant Gram Hammett's shame. Yes I would.

"I asked Rory, I asked her if she'd like to jump into double harness and trot through life with me. Of course saying it that way made her mad. And I don't blame her. Man, she was so mad she hit me with everything in the kitchen on the old place. Everything that wasn't screwed to the floor. And I left with one eye in a sling. Yes, that's the story here, Cain. That was why, when she saw later what you was like inside—granite along with a boiling heart—she had eyes only for you. Because compared to me you was all heart from the belt up.

"Cain, man, when I saw her kiss you I was sick. I wanted to kill someone. I wanted someone to kill me. That's why I went into rustling—to get either one done quick.

"Cain, man, for a little while I hated you something awful. Awful, I burned at nights with it. So I couldn't sleep. I've got over it now. But for a little while there I could've as easy killed you as not.

"Dale I laughed at. I always have. He's a mutt face. Rory's got him whipbroke. She's out for sheriff. That's why I have no regrets that Rory really don't know for sure if Joey is his boy or my boy.

"What? That surprise you? Why should it? Don't you know a married woman will always step out once? Once? Don't ask me why. Rory ain't the only one I know about. Personal. You know that most of the women hereabouts was once either schoolmarms or out-and-out whores off the U. P. Most men picked the hard-boiled hookers for their sociability. You know that. They're easy.

"Wait, wait. I'm not sayin' Rory is a whore. Far from it. Like them schoolmarms from Boston, she's high-class. But let me tell you something. Even them high-class ones will step out once on their men. Once. Just to be doin' it maybe. I don't know. Or just out of curiosity like a cat. Or to be one up on the husband. Or to make sure she's even with him in case he should happen to step out on her when she don't know about it. Or to be shoppin' around to make sure she got a bargain in the first place. I don't know. But anyway, once.

"And that once for Rory was once with me. That time Dale went to Cheyenne for a sheepmen's convention.

"Yes, Rory finally got two out of the three of us brothers.

141

And if what I hear is right, she'll soon have all three of us. You, Cain.

"No, so far as Dale is concerned, I have no regrets. But you now. That's a horse of another color. Because I really took her from you; not Dale. Dale and me has stole your life from you. We're thieves.

"Cain, man, you don't know. Oh, you don't know how I sometimes hate you something awful. Just last month this ranny turned down Jesse's offer to get rid of you."

. . . Harry went to visit Queenie. He was in a mood to be a king for a night.

When he walked into the Hog Ranch, instead of Queenie in green velvet at the end of the bar, there was Jesse packing a gun. Beside Jesse ranged Mitch, Stalker, Hog, and Ringbone. While behind the bar, bulb-eyed Avery nodded solemnly over his purple goiter.

Harry swallowed and bellied up to the bar anyway. For once he was of a mind to be daring. A wee drop of the critter sometimes gave him that. Or a sudden change of weather off the mountains. Or memory of that week with Rosemary.

In the low kerosene light, from his end of the bar, deliberately and tauntingly retying the knot in his red sash, Harry said, "Why, Jesse, I didn't know you went in for calf love too."

At that, Jesse got as hot as a wolf. His dark face blackened. He hoisted up his high belly and chest and leaned on the bar. "Yeh, and what brings you here, you range bum? Last time I saw you, you was hanging to a tree."

Harry laughed a silver laugh. He lifted his Stetson and brushed back fair silver hair. "Yeh, and I bet you're still wondering if I'm hant or real." He reached for the bottle Avery had set out for him and helped himself to a big snort.

Jesse blazed white eyes at him. So did Mitch and Stalker. Hog and Ringbone looked down.

"What you probably forgot, Jesse, was that we all got that Hammett neck. You can't hang a Hammett."

Jesse snarled. "Lord save me if the next time I don't butcher you. In fact, just to make sure, by the Lord the next time I will eat you. Without salt and pepper too. Just to make sure that when I see you after's you got to be hant."

"Do it and you'll have you as fine a case of the skitters as ary a man ever had in Bad Country."

Jesse whacked his glass down on the bar, bottom first,

hard. "Set 'em up again, Avery. Five. Some more of your kill-me-quick rye. Mitch, Stalker, Hog, Ringbone, and me here."

Nodding solemnly over his neck bloat, Avery slid off his stool and poured.

Jesse drank up. He smacked his lips. He twirled the sweeping ends of his walrus mustache. "Harry, I tell you plain. You're a goldurn rustler. And not only that, you're a goldurn coward. And not only that, all of you goldurn Hammetts is cousin lovers. Your tough brother Cain included."

Harry looked at Avery. "This Jesse here, when he gets snockered, he really gets low-down mean drunk, don't he?"

Avery shrugged. His neck bloat rolled.

Harry said, "Avery, pour me some snake poison. Two. For me and myself here."

Jesse lowered his head. His darksome face became savage. "A thief. A coward. And a cousin lover."

"Too bad my brother Cain ain't here to speak for himself."

"Thief. Coward." Jesse picked up the bottle and poured himself yet another shot. "Thief. Coward. Burn me, there it is, Harry Hammett, if you want it. And if you don't want it, burn me, there it is anyway."

"Durn if it ain't."

Jesse hung his hand near the butt of his .45. "You ain't gonner fight?"

"Draw on you here? Five agin one?"

"Why not? You're Hammett, ain't you?"

"If I did, I'd have about as much sense as last year's birdnest."

Jesse studied a while.

Mitch whispered to him under a pudge hand.

Jesse brightened, eyes opening high in his darksome face. "Harry, I hear ye're a heller with your fists."

"I ain't never bragged about it."

Jesse placed his right hand on the bar. The ruby on his ring finger glowed like a geranium petal. "If I took off my gun, would you fight me then?"

"No."

"If all of us here took off our guns and stored 'em behind the bar with Avery there, would you fight me then?" Jesse spoke low, drawling.

"No."

"Harry, I'm going to stay here all night for my meat if I have to."

Harry swore. "You galvanized Yankee you. Go hunt yourself a hole and pull it in after y'u."

Jesse's face screwed up fiercely savage again. Calling a former Confederate soldier a "galvanized Yankee" meant the death gobble. Such a critter was a captured Confederate turned loose by the Union on the promise that he'd go West and stay West for the duration of the Civil War. Jesse roared, "That did it! Goldurn you, will you fight with yore fists or must I just shoot you down like a gramma-whore?"

Harry's wild one lunged around inside; finally broke halter. "Sure I'll fight you with my fists if it comes to that. No man on this old earth can insult me, as you've just did, not even if you had you a hundred stars on your vest."

"Done! Boys, unpack your hardware and hand it all over to Avery. We're gonna have us a fun."

Heels stumped hard on the wooden floor; guns clunked down on the bar; tables were pushed back for more room.

Jesse and Harry squared off. Jesse held up his arms in the old-fashioned style, fists balled up in front of his face. Harry stood with his fists at his sides.

"You ready, cowpuncher?"

"Ready."

Jesse made a bull's rush for Harry and tried to catch him with a lifter. Harry sidestepped to the right and as Jesse went by tipped up a boot toe and tripped him. Jesse fell hugely, piling up against the log door, hat falling off and rolling away in a curve under a table. Jesse got up, bellowing. He rushed Harry again, this time with head down and with his arms spread out like the pincers of a great crab. Again Harry sidestepped, to the left and further away, except that this time he leaned forward some, and just as Jesse was upon him he jammed up a knee. The knee hit Jesse in the middle of his black hair. Taut kneecap cracked against bony pate. Jesse went down, face landing in a brass cuspidor. Jesse lay still.

Avery leaned forward, looking down over goiter and bar both. Avery smiled.

Mitch began to curse softly. He clawed for a gun that wasn't there.

Slowly Jesse got to his feet. Tobacco-juice slop ran off the tips of his mustache. Slowly a cunning smile creased across his face. Jesse started another bull's rush; stopped it just short of reaching Harry; waited for Harry to make his move; then swung from his crab position. The blow caught Harry click on the chin and he sank like a sack of mud.

144

Harry lay.

Jesse came up and stood over Harry. Jesse puffed, swelling high. "Get up and fight, you cowardly pup."

Harry lay curled up. Harry thought: "I've just got to get up off this floor and hit him at least one good one with my fists. I've just got to."

Harry got up, bone by bone. He wavered. Jesse seemed to be doing a kind of dance in front of him. Harry tried to cock a fist; fell down again. He could see, and hear, but the rest of him was numb.

Jesse stood over him. Jesse made as if to stomp him.

From over the bar Avery threw something, whistling. It cracked Jesse across the shin. It was Avery's stool. Jesse fell down, clutching his shin, groaning.

Avery said quietly, "That'll learn you to keep your opinions under your hair."

"Goldurn you, Avery," Jesse groaned, "I'll get you for this too."

Avery nodded over his goiter. "You forget I got all the guns. Also, you forget this is my homestead. There'll be no shooting."

Then the back door opened and Queenie stepped in. She was slim in green velvet and high green shoes. Her light green eyes and light green diamond earrings sparkled in the low kerosene light. Queenie said, "Aren't you boys a bit old to be playing leapfrog?"

The next Saturday, in Antelope, Harry had the luck to run into Jesse and his bunch again, this time at Butcherknife Bain's saloon. It looked like an exact repeat.

Jesse sneered from his end of the bar. "Well, well. Look what the cat just drug in."

Harry laughed, silver. "You again, Jesse. Deuce take it, but this luck of mine is spreading faster than a secret among women."

Jesse said, looking him up and down, "All duded up too, I see. Mitch, go over and smell him and see if he took whore perfume up there where the end of his neck is haired over."

Harry said, "There's men who'll tip you their hole card. Or help you out in a bind. Such men are long rides apart. And you ain't one of them."

Jesse whacked down his glass, ugly. "By the Lord, I still say somebody I know is a thief and a coward. And a cousin lover t'boot. I ain't mentionin' any names but his front name is Harry."

"I see you're still a bully when you drink, Jesse."

Jesse glared. "I'll say more. I'll say you can't even ride a hoss. Why, you couldn't even ride a sawhorse snubbed down to a stump."

Harry raised at his end of the bar. This was a new deal. "I'll ride anything you've got to put up. Just so long as it has four legs. And a head to put the bridle on."

"Want to bet on it?"

"Sure I want to bet on it."

"A hundred silver dollars says I got a critter you can't ride ten seconds."

"Has it got four legs?"

"It has got four legs."

"Has it got a head?"

"It has got a head. With an arse to balance."

"All right, a hundred silver dollars it is."

Jesse hove up on his sore leg. "Stalker, go get Old Blue. It's moonlight out tonight, so I guess Harry can see to ride."

Old Blue was got. When Harry and Jesse bowlegged through the swinging saloon doors out onto the main street of Antelope, half a hundred bardogs crowded after them. Harry found Old Blue to be a wild longhorn steer from Texas. It was one of the last of the old longhorns, and also one of the toughest meanest-looking critters he'd ever cast eyes upon. It had a horn spread of at least seven feet. It stood almost as high as a horse. It breathed slow like a mad bull-alligator. And but for the tensile strength of half a dozen hemp ropes stretched taut from half a dozen pommels, it would have cleaned the town. It stood pawing slowly, bellowing in a low guttural primeval moan. The low bellowing hurt a man all the way up into his belly.

Harry smiled some. "Old Blue."

"You'll ride him?"

"You won't get a bridle on that head."

"You'll ride him?"

"Hell, yes, I'll ride him. If somebody will side me I'll ride Old Blue to a finish."

Jesse waved a kingly hand. The ruby on his ringfinger burned like a red coal in the blue moonlight. "Drop him, you cowpokes."

Two expert ropers, each with legs as bowed as warped rain-barrel staves, stepped out of the crowd. One made a gesture, and Old Blue reared. The other whirled his loop and caught Old Blue around the front feet. The two ropers grabbed the rope together and down went Old Blue on his side. The half-dozen ropes from the various pommels held

146

Old Blue's head steady. Every rope hummed as Old Blue jerked convulsively. Four more punchers leaped in and helped hog-tie him on the ground. Dust rose a blue smoke in the moonlight.

Jesse let the dust settle some and then turned to Harry. "Well, cowboy, she's yours. Ride 'im."

Harry stepped over to where his horse Star stood hitched to the railing in front of the saloon. He uncinched the saddle and slid it off and carried it over to where Old Blue lay. He set it on Old Blue's back. He placed his boot on Old Blue's ribs and drew the cinches up tight. The tighter he drew the cinches the more the backbone of the old steer began to crack and undulate. The spine of the old steer moved like a stiff bull whip.

Harry set his Stetson on firm. He looked up at the bright and shining silver moon. He bowed elaborately to it, hand across his pink shirt. "This is for you, my dear," he said softly. He turned to Jesse. "Boss, if you'll just tell some of your boys to haze that critter a ways, I'll sure as blazes make them one-hoss Antelopers sit up and take notice for once. They'll know they're livin' in a town with hair on at last."

"The boys are at your service," Jesse said.

Harry handed Jesse his gun and holster. He tightened up his bright red sash. He made sure of the buckles on his silver spurs. Then he stepped across.

The boys on foot slipped off all the twines and ran for cover, crowding in through the swinging double doors along the street. "Now," they all breathed, holding back wonder and wild laughter.

Old Blue lay, throbbing and undulating.

Harry raked him with his rowels, once, lightly.

Old Blue lay, vibrating violently.

Harry said to the punchers on horseback, "Haze him some. Snap a knot at 'im."

One of the cowboys whirled an arm, and a long rope whizzed through the moonlit air and whacked Old Blue across his whirling tail.

Old Blue surged. He came up off the ground like a blue whale surfacing and trying to stand on its tail. There was a great shout, a quick one; then, equally quick, a great shut-off silence.

Harry rode out the mighty leap and except for his hat came down all of a piece with Old Blue.

Old Blue bellowed. He jumped around in a circle. He swapped ends. With every jump he got madder and madder,

147

bellowing and bawling. The louder he bawled the louder the cowpunchers began to whoop it up. Some shot off their forty-fives. The boys on horseback hazed Old Blue from behind with stinging ropes. Harry reefed him from stem to stern with his spurs.

Suddenly Old Blue had enough at the spot and he headed down main street. Old Blue roared. Old Blue bucked. Old Blue ringtailed. Old Blue jumped for the moon. Sudden dust boiled up. Dust came down the street like a fierce prairie fire. Townsfolk in nightshirts and nightgowns who had popped out of doorways to see what all the commotion was about popped right back in when they saw Old Blue and his great spear horns headed their way. Antelope had been taken over again by them crazy shooting whooping cowboys.

When Old Blue hit the end of main street, out where the trail from the south came in over the bridge across Sweet Creek, he startled everybody by doubling back. The townsfolk in nightshirts and nightgowns who'd ventured forth after he'd passed by, suddenly had to reverse themselves and pop back inside again. The bardogs following on foot, whooping and shooting, scattered for cover too, behind rain barrels, under front porches, behind wagons, into strange doors, even underthrough strange nightshirts and nightgowns. The boys aboard the ponies skittered out of the way the best they could. All the while laughing, silver hair throwing this way and that at every jump, Harry reefed Old Blue from stern to stem and back again, waving one wild hand free while the other clutched leather.

Then, just down the street from Butcherknife Bain's saloon, at the end of one of his ringtailed jumps, Old Blue happened to land face-first in front of the new plate-glass window in Alberding's Mercantile. The plate-glass window was the new thing in town. Old Blue stopped dead. Dust settled slowly. Gradually Old Blue began to make out another steer, just about his size and exactly his color, glaring back at him in the moonlight. Old Blue stared long and steady. Old Blue seemed to be sizing up the length of the other blue steer's great seven-foot horns.

Silence fell along the street. Everybody wondered what next, bardogs, nightgowned townsfolk, dogs. Harry's arms hung at rest; his silver hair hung down his forehead.

Old Blue bellowed, once. The echo bellowed back at him, once.

That was enough. Lowering his head, bawling, waving his tail, Old Blue rammed into it. His long horns hit the huge

148

plate-glass window with a ringing crack. The glass shivered; exploded inward. Old Blue's momentum carried him inward too. Glass rattled and fell all over him. Ducking his head, still hatless, Harry rode him in. The two disappeared through the black prickle-edged hole. There was a milling and a moiling inside. And a terrible bellowing, sometimes smothered.

On the boardwalk outside, a man in a nightshirt began to jump up and down, bawling, "Get 'em out of there, you crazy galoots, get 'em out of there!"

Two cowboys spurred their ponies, urging them toward the prickle-edged hole. But the ponies shied off, refused to jump through it.

The man in the nightshirt covered his face and began to sob. "My God, my God, there goes all our life's savings!"

The next moment Old Blue suddenly reappeared, coming out through the black hole, bawling and ringtailing, his great long horns decorated with clothes, mostly black bloomers and a stack of new wide-brim Stetson hats. Harry was still aboard, laughing and reefing. Old Blue turned a sharp right and went heels-over-head out for the country again.

The man in the white nightshirt took his hands from his face. "My God, stop 'em! There goes all our life's savings!"

A great whoop rose. Some pistols went off. The boys on horseback set out after Harry and Old Blue. Two blocks down the street, ropes whizzed through the moonlit air. Out of six thrown, five connected. Five ponies set back on their heels and dug in. Old Blue managed one more leap and then hit the end of the five ropes. He came down hard, with a tremendous belly-whack. Just as he was about to hit ground, the sixth rope caught Harry around his thick neck and shoulders and jerked him off, up in the air, so that when he landed he lit on Old Blue's rump. It saved him. Harry quick jumped for safety. The boys on foot with ropes got in their licks next and tied Old Blue down.

When dust and horns and boot heels stilled, bareheaded, silver in the moonlight, Harry stepped up to Old Blue. Carefully he pulled the wide-brim Stetsons off one long horn and the black bloomers off the other. The hats had all been punched through the crown. The bloomers were intact, though dusty. Harry dusted them all off and stepped across to where Jesse stood leaning on his sore leg.

"Maybe bloomers don't go well with Stetsons, Jesse," Harry said, looking down with a modest smile, "but I didn't get much of a chance to shop around." Harry smiled again.

"Though I think there's plenty to go around. One apiece for each of you." He dumped the merchandise in Jesse's arms and took back his gun and holster.

The man in the white nightshirt came running up, bawling. "You'll pay for this, you golderned wild-eyed—"

Harry held up a hand. "What's the damages, Alberding?"

Alberding's wild eyes rolled in the moonlight. "You crazy peerootin' golderned—"

"Tally it up, Alberding!"

Alberding's mouth closed to. His mustache worked, first one end up then the other end down. "One hundred dollars and I'll forget it," he said suddenly, low.

Harry turned to Jesse, silver, still laughing. "I won the bet fair and square?"

Jesse nodded slowly, thoughtfully. "You won fair and square."

"Then pay it all over to Alberding. I had a fun and that's enough for me."

Later, back in Butcherknife Bain's saloon again, Jesse limped over and had a drink with Harry. "Harry," he said, putting an arm over his shoulder, "you can ride. I'll never question that again." Jesse lowered his voice confidential. "Harry, boy, how about letting bygones be bygones, and riding for the Derby again?"

Harry smiled under the heavy arm.

"Tell you what, Harry, tell you what. I know how much you prize them cows of your'n. And I admire you for it. Harry, listen, ride for me and I'll let you run your cows with mine at one dollar the head per year. Then we both win."

"What about Cain and his little spread? Will you let him come in too?"

"I'm talking to you, Harry. What do you say?"

"The offer don't hold good for my brother Cain?"

"No, it don't hold good for your cousin-lover Cain."

"But why not?"

"He ain't our kind, that's all. You know that."

Harry shrugged off Jesse's arm. He laughed him in the face. "Jesse, I'll see you in hell first, further than a wedge can fall in twenty years, before I hold hands with you. After this."

Jesse reared back and began to cuss the country blue. . . .

Lying on the ground in his bedroll, with brother Cain sleeping next to him, Harry laughed about it all again, reliving the wonderful ride on Old Blue in the moonlight.

Harry laughed—until he remembered the look that had passed between Jesse and himself that evening while Cain was looking on. Had Cain caught it? Both Jesse and Harry knew that despite Harry's terrible oath at Butcherknife Bain's, Harry had considered Jesse's offer—and in a way, off to one side, was still considering it some.

Cain

At dawn a voice murmured, "Cain, lad, she's breaking day." A hand next touched him through the tarp and rocked his shoulder. "Cain, boy, chuck's on."

Cain's mind awoke like a sprouted bean and rose out of black soil and blossomed into pink petals. Slowly he folded back the flap of his tarp. He saw the bald gnome head of Hambone against the stars. He murmured, "Comin', Ham." He sat up in his bedroll.

"Good. God helped me make the coffee this mornin' and you might like it." Hambone vanished.

Cain began dressing automatically: first his folded dented hat, then the cigarette he'd carefully rolled the night before which now needed only another wet lick of the tongue and a match, then his vest and coat, then his socks and pants, then his boots, and last his gun belt and chaps. The brass buckles of the last two were slippery with frost and worked stiff. Inhaling deeply, enjoying the crisp curling scent of the first smoke of the day as well as the fresh breeze off the snowcapped mountains, he leaned over and called low against the ground, "Arise and shine there, Harry boy, and give God the glory." He touched Harry through the tarp, It was an old, and safe, range custom to call first and then touch a sleeping hand. A cowhand trained on the trail was always ready for instant action in the night. The least touch without warning and he'd come up shooting.

Harry stirred. "Comin'," Harry murmured. Harry's movements under the tarp reminded Cain of a huge muscle stirring under a sleeve.

"Make sure now. Cookie's given us a good hole card wakin' us first."

Harry's tarp flipped back. He sat up.

Cain put a finger to his mouth. "Wake Tim soft there. And I'll root Dale out of his velvet couch."

By the time Cain finished his smoke, the boys were dressed. Together all four stepped softly to the splashing mountain stream and, stooping, washed hands and face and up around the neck in the ice-cold water. They splashed until faces were flushed and glowing. Minds clear, they next hit for the fire, where Hambone had coffee ready. The coffee was great; God had helped in the making of it; it woke a man all the way back to his animal. The boys wolfed down masty beans savored with bacon and fresh warm biscuits.

The air was crisp with frost; the nose cracked with it. Every now and then the nose dripped a string of fluid as clear as the white of an egg. The men snuffled as they ate. Fingers worked numb. The men took turns warming their hands over the fire, eating with one while warming the other.

Dawn opened vaguely beyond the Crimson Wall. The downside of the wall still lay in shadow. The morning star glittered bright. To the west, above the white crowns of the Old Man and the Throne, night's late stars still twinkled lively. A coyote let go a last call from a nearby butte, a series of sharp staccato barks slowly merging off into a long dying call, to which another coyote from another hill sent back an echoing call. The second call came so close behind the first the two sounded like a pack of coyotes might have surrounded the camp. Behind the camp, the horses in the cavvy began their morning cavortings. Mothers in the herd on the bed ground called for lost calves. Some of the steers were up and grazing. The sliding wind coming down off the mountains brought the sounds straight into camp.

The horse wrangler and one of the morning cattle guards came in for breakfast. The sound of their tomping heels on the hard ground wakened Jesse and Mitch in their blankets.

Hambone spotted Jesse and Mitch stirring, and immediately threw back his head as far as his humpneck would allow and bawled, "Hurrah, boys! She's breakin' day. Roll out, you snakes, and bite a biscuit!"

Jesse and Mitch rose on their elbows, hair tousled, faces in the firelight as slack and as pale as brine bacon. It took the pair a couple of seconds to clear sleep-blurred eyes. All of a sudden both realized that Cain and his boys were ready to roll. They sat bolt upright. Their faces hardened. Quickly they slipped into their clothes. Some of the other Derby punchers, Stalker, Hog, Spade, were right behind them. Jesse got to his feet and with a groan limped over and poured himself a cup of coffee from the fire-blackened pot. Mitch and the others followed suit.

One swallow and Jesse had his horns back. "Hambone,

what in tarnation is the idee wakin' Cain and his bunch first?"

Hambone smiled from the chuck-box lid where he was already pounding bread dough for dinner. "Why, Jesse, such swearin'. If you ain't careful, you're liable to melt the frost off the morning afore it's here."

"Answer my question." Jesse lifted his sore leg and stroked it slowly.

"Why, boss, I stepped accidental on Cain when I went for fresh water for your coffee."

Jesse's face colored in the firelight. "Accidental, bull."

"Well, ask Cain."

"A little thin, Hambone, a little thin."

A boss didn't easily squash Hambone. "Jesse, I've never seen it to fail. The minute you get that first swallow into you in the morning, you get a bad rush to the head."

Jesse turned on Cain. "Anyway, there'll be no workin' the herd today."

"No?" Cain faced Jesse. Red light from the fire danced over his hollow face. "My cattle is comin' out."

Timberline turned too, standing over them, beard waggling. "So is our'n."

Jesse glared at them over his cup of coffee. "There'll be no workin' the cattle until the reps from Senator Thorne's and Governor Barb's outfits get here. I'm not going to first cut out your beef, then Thorne's, then Barb's, then work over what's left for ourselves. We do it all at once, or nothing. Working them that often keeps 'em too ginned up."

Punchers on the ground all around them began to sit up in their bedrolls. They rose up like prairie dogs, each alert from his private nest. A few began to dress cautiously in the half-dark; some put on a hat and lit up smokes first; others carefully laid their forty-fives ready to hand. Stalker, Hog, Spade, already by the fire, warily made a point of facing Cain and his boys.

At that moment full dawn broke over the high rim of the Crimson Wall. It limned all moving things with vague blue-pink haloes. For a few moments the eye saw all objects as double images. Cattle, horses, and men moved as if wading slowly through veils of violet fog.

Jesse looked down at where Dale still sat on his heels before the fire. "And you, you better go home to your woollies and that cousin-wife of yours. We don't like the smell of ewes around here."

Dale rose to his feet like a long-legged grasshopper coming up rampant. The corners of his mouth drew back into his

153

lean cheeks. He tossed his cup into the bunch grass at his feet. "By thunder, Jesse, you say cows won't feed where sheep have fed first. Well, by thunder, Jesse, I wish you'd let your durn cows in on that. It'd save me from having to chouse your damned lousy stuff off my range every day. Solve my grass problem."

Jesse backed a step. He hadn't expected the weaker Hammett to come up at him in a sudden rage.

"Jesse, will you tell me why it is your damned pesty cattle is always grazin' on old sheep bed grounds? Hah?"

Jesse stooped down to help himself to another cup of coffee. "All I say is, I don't want your ewe stink around here."

"Jesse, burn me down if that's your mind, but my sheep is my business."

Jesse sipped his black coffee.

Slowly the violet fog of dawn subsided. Double vision came back to single.

Jesse looked around for another dog to kick. He saw Hunt was still asleep. He limped over and lightly kicked Hunt's bedroll with the toe of his boot. "Wake up, inspector, time's a drawin'."

Hunt rose out of his cocoon with eyes ablaze, hair wild, and .45 caught in working claw. The gun gleamed blue in the rose dawn. Hunt snarled, "Blast you, Jesse, don't you ever do that again!"

"Hells bells, Hunt, trouble is bustin' out all over this cow camp and you're still snoozin'."

Hunt glanced over to where Cain and his boys and Mitch and his men ringed the fire, stiff, waiting. Hunt's black eyes half-closed. He lowered his gun. "I see," he said. "That's different." He began to slip on his clothes.

Hambone came wandering over, bald head aswing from his hump. "I jes' wonder," he said in a low voice. "I jes' hope people ain't forgot cow camp is holy ground." An ancient smile worked his old leather face. "Holy ground to the cook." Hambone waved his arm around, sudden. "For fifty feet around, by God. Let alone I don't intend for it to be a horspital. Or a funeral parlor neither. So I say, if you want to fight, goddam it, go down wind a ways and shoot it out there. All both a yous."

There wasn't a word from anyone.

"All right," Hambone said, "jes' so that's understood." He turned and wandered back to his chuck-box lid and began pounding bread dough again.

154

The men ate in silence.

After a bit, Cain and his boys withdrew to one side.

Harry shivered in the chill wind. He drew his red bandanna tight around his thick neck. Dale trembled more from the excitement than from the cold. Timberline stood with his shirt open. His coat of red hair kept him warm.

Day-lily yellow burst high over on the mountains to the west of them; then cascaded down onto the footslopes of evergreen below; then streamed all across the high bench of red bunch grass.

"It's going to be a sunny blue-eyed day," Cain mused.

Timberline looked up, sniffing. "Yeh, the sun's burning off the fog in the valley. The weather is gonna fair off nice."

Dale said low to Harry, "You look like you're gettin' cold feet."

"Me?" Harry exclaimed. "Not at all. Put a rimfire cigar in my mouth and I'll admire to meet the President himself."

Cain glanced at his two brothers. "What's this? Ain't I got men with me? Or is it just boys grown tall?"

Dale said, "Just wanted to make sure Harry was going to side us all the way, is all."

"He will. You kin lay to that. Let's saddle our ponies."

Jesse bulled up with horns again. "Oh, no, you don't." Jesse dropped his right hand to the butt of his six-gun. Mitch and Hunt followed suit.

Cain faced them, stub legs set apart. He kept his wild one in hand. His face assumed a rocklike cast. He said, calm, "Jesse, don't forget you've got a visitor." He nodded at somebody behind them.

Jesse and Hunt and Mitch whirled. There in the flap to the pup tent stood Lord Peter. His Lordship was up and fully dressed: riding boots, pants, coat, cane, and derby.

Jesse held. He looked at Lord Peter. He looked at Cain. He was as one being torn by two horses pulling in opposite directions. After a long second of time, Jesse said, "Mornin', yer Lordship."

Bland Lord Peter looked at Jesse, at Cain. He studied Cain. His smooth blond face and blue eyes were expressionless. Then he nodded to himself, once, quick.

Cain turned and went straight for his horse Bucky where he'd staked him the night before, beside the tumbling mountain stream.

Dale and Harry and Timberline followed him.

Dale kept one eye alert for any move Hunt might make. Dale said, low, "Cain, I still smell a mice."

"It'll be all right." Cain growled. "That darn Jesse. He knows blame well he can't push me too far. Because I know all about them times he shorted His Bullship on the yearly tally. I know for a fact that he sold yearlings and heifers as two-year fat beef, that he sold off both ends of the Derby herd. He got away with it so long's His Bullship warn't around. But now that Lord Peter wants to sell, Jesse's got to quick fat up the tally. Which he's trying to do with our little herds."

Harry began to sing a tune, tauntingly, loud enough for Texas-born Jesse to hear:

> *"Abe Lincoln was our president,*
> *Jeff Davis was a fool;*
> *Abe Lincoln rode a big gray horse,*
> *While Davis rode a mule."*

Cain couldn't help but smile some. "That ain't the way I heared it."

Harry laughed. "Well, it ain't the way I heared it either. But when I see a Texan that tune just naturally comes to mind. With the names reversed."

"Abe ridin' a mule is funnier. Forgettin' that he's Lincoln the President, that is."

"High-vested Jeff on a mule is mighty funny too."

Timberline began to curse his sorrel behind them. "So overnight ye've changed yore mind about the cow business, has ye?" Timberline had got the bridle on but the horse refused the saddle, explicit. Timberline jerked down the jawbreaker bit so hard the sorrel almost kneeled and its bright bulb eyes half-closed. But only for a second. The next second the sorrel was up again and sunning his heels. Timberline lunged for his head and managed to get one of the horse's ears in his hand. He gave it a vicious twist. The horse tried to circle away from him. At that, Timberline caught the tip of the ear in his teeth and bit in, fiercely. That instant the sorrel stood still, trembling.

With his free hand Timberline gestured for Cain to throw on blanket and saddle. Cain didn't like Timberline's brutal earing tactics much, but he went over anyway and picked up Timberline's rigging. He was about to slide it on with a throw, when he suddenly saw something. He dropped the rigging on the ground. "No wonder your mount is ringy, Tim. Why, he's got a saddle sore on his back as big as a freighter's pancake. Full of maggots."

156

Timberline still had the horse's ear in his mouth. He grimaced fiercely for Cain to throw on the rigging anyway.

"And your blanket. Man, it's crawling with maggots. You can't treat a horse that way and expect him to let you ride him all day without a kick." Cain drew up his nose in great disgust. "Wash it."

Timberline's red pig eyes rolled in his red whiskery face. He turned slightly, teeth still sunk into the horse's ear, and gestured for Harry to throw the rigging on.

Shrugging at Cain, Harry did so.

The horse shivered with pain; would have bucked it off except that Timberline had taken a deeper bite into its ear.

After Harry finished cinching the girths tight, Timberline let go the ear, spitting sorrel hair from lips and tongue. "What a bunch a Monday wimmen I woke up with! I suppose the next thing, Cain, ye'll be recommendin' we scrub the hosses down with Cologne soap. Sspt!"

"You and your hoss could stand it," Cain said flatly.

Timberline let out a great snort. He stepped across and socked his spurs in.

The sorrel jumped straight up and broke wind with a loud report. Then, despite Timberline's great weight, the horse exploded in all directions like a Fourth of July celebration. In the flick of an eye Timberline was flying through the air. Both Cain and Harry had to run for it or Timberline would have fallen on them. Timberline hit the ground hard on his back. A burst of red dust rose up around him.

Harry laughed and whacked his knee. "I've heard of it rainin' cats and dogs, by golly. But I'll be go-to-grass if I ever saw it rain old red bulls."

Timberline grunted. He got to his feet. "This time, you devil, I'll haul back on the lines till the bit splits your mouth clear back to your brains." Once more he grabbed the sorrel by the reins and climbed across. But the sorrel had given up after that one outburst. He stood quietly, four legs astraddle to sustain heavy Timberline.

"Yahh," Timberline said, eyes glinting with satisfaction, "so I've got you finally where you're plumb tender about a bite in the ear, eh?"

By the time Cain, Harry, and Dale finished saddling up and tying on their bedrolls, Jesse had his boys routed out for their mounts too.

Some of the hands formed a rope corral around the cavvy, and the expert ropers, with quick low almost casual throws, caught the mounts one by one for the others. No matter how cleverly a cow pony might duck its head behind another, the roper always guessed the exact moment when it would show ears again, and with a long slurplike motion the loop was around its head. Dust boiled up in rolling columns of pink from the hooves. The cowhands became vague figures in it. Only their bright gay bandannas and the shining silver on their belt buckles and spurs showed through.

The crisp cold morning put springs in most of the ponies and presently, mounting, the lads were falling off like wormy apples in a high wind. It made Cain laugh to see it. And laughing, a vague regret shot through him. Those good old carefree days when, except for hoss and rigging, a man hadn't a worry in the world were done for him. It was the boss who worried about a herd them days.

Off to one side of the camp, the branders were busy too, sharpening knives and cleaning irons. The low morning sun caught the side of their bronzen faces, giving their cheeks a rich healthy color not unlike the cherry red of polished riding boots. Above the moiling of the bucking ponies, Cain could hear the wet snick of knife edge on emery stone. Liskh. Liskh. The sound always gave him the shivers. He had never quite got himself used to the idea of castration. The sound of a knife being honed was always the same to him as the actual slice of a knife across a testicle. It was a sound no woman could ever come to appreciate, let alone understand.

Harry called across to the branders, gaily. "Put it on good, boys. She'll wear it all her life."

One of the men threw Harry a mean look from under his hatbrim. "We'll put it on so you won't be able to mistake it in moonlight, ye blinkin' night rider."

Cain and his boys rode to the edge of the great herd, with Jesse and a dozen of his men following close behind. The cows and calves, the steers and the other market stuff all were up on the bed ground. Red dust twisted high. Only whites showed through: white faces, white legs, white patches over the spine, slick horns. Red hair was impossible to make out. A few of the mothers nosed for grass. In some areas the grass was completely cropped off or pulverized underfoot. Cow plotches dotted the ground everywhere, thin dark green pies sprinkled over with cinnamonlike dust. The sky over the bench seemed but shoulder high all around.

Cain held up a hand. They stopped. Jesse and his men held up behind them too. Gun butts shone dully in the red morning sun.

Cain slipped on his leather work gloves, a finger at a time

158

and then the palms and wrists. "Harry, you and I will go into the herd and prowl. Dale, you and Timberline make this your holding ground. It's low here, where you can watch all around from any position."

Dale sat stiff on black Lonesome. He kept looking over his shoulder. "I still smell a mice, Cain, them following us like that."

"They won't bother us. They may even have trailed along to help. Jesse has probably decided to let the tail go with the hide since we got him into such tight papers with the earl."

"But that Hunt is on a hoss too. And he couldn't chouse a lice down the back of his finger even if his life depended on it."

Out of the corner of his eye, Cain saw Jesse come riding up beside him. He decided to be the first to talk. He turned in his saddle; sat with half a leg over. "Jesse, I'll have to say this for your Mitch. The son-of-a-gun can shape up a herd to a fare-thee-well. They're all up but they're all steady. And the calves have mothered up. Which'll help."

Jesse cocked his head to one side, bold eyes hooded, watchful. "Just how many do you claim, Hammett?"

"I'm missing about fifty mothers, some forty calves, five bulls. All Mark-of-Cains. With split ears."

Jesse nodded toward Harry and Timberline. "And them?"

"Harry!" Cain called. "How many for you?"

"Some two hundred steers, plain. Rocking Hill. With cropped ears."

"No mothers?"

"Not one. Not even an uncle."

Again it was understood just what two hundred was meant. Cain said, "Them reps from Thorne's and Barb's outfits here yet?"

"No," Jesse said, grim.

"Well, that's too bad. But we can't wait."

To keep out the dust, Cain fastened his black bandanna high over his nose. He touched Bucky lightly in the quick with a spur. Bucky moved forward into the herd. Harry followed.

After a moment Jesse suddenly waved an arm in a circular motion. It was not the motion for the men to surround Cain and his boys, but to join the guard in holding the herd while Cain and Harry made their cut. Cain saw it and sighed in vast relief. Cain saw also that Jesse had placed two of his best men on quick horses between the great herd and the place where the cut was to be held.

Cain and Harry prowled. In the turmoil of red dust and fly-

ing tails and mean glinting horns, it was sometimes easier to
spot a split ear than a brand on the hip. Within moments
Cain spotted a split-ear cow with its calf. He leaned over and
next made out his brand: ⌐⫐. "Ha," he said. He nudged
Bucky with a knee. At almost the same instant Bucky veered
slightly; stepped along as if half-asleep; then suddenly darted
and with a rush took the cow and calf out at breakneck
speed. The two dodged this way, that way. But Bucky was
quicker and stayed right on the heels of the snaky pair,
once even laying his nose on the mother's rump, as if to
steer her in the right direction. Cain finally got the two
halfway across and then Jesse's two throw-back men took
over and ran them to where Dale and Timberline were to
hold the cut, some two hundred yards away.

Twice Cain found three of Harry's crop-eared Rocking
Hill, ⟨H⟩ , and with luck shot them across to the cut. Another
time he found two of his bulls fighting. He broke up the
fight and before they knew what hit them they too were in
the cut.

Bucky never worked better. The buckskin had caught the
urgent nature of the work from Cain's voice and manner.
Again and again, like an aroused collie, Bucky bit a steer or a
cow on the back, or in the tail. Once Bucky nipped a calf
in the leg, growling like a dog.

Cain followed Bucky's every move as if born part of the
horse. Cain rode light, flowed with every turn of the neck
and spine. Sometimes Bucky stopped so quick Cain had the
feeling that if he had not foreseen it he would have turned
through himself. It was a delight, a great joy, to work with a
cow pony as expert as Bucky. Bucky was the best. Working
with a horse as good as Bucky took all a man had. There
was little room for thought about other things, such as lilies
or ladies, petunias or cousins, or whatever. Working with a
cow pony was full living. It was life brimming over. It was
life lived down to the hilt, sometimes even with the hilt sunk
in.

The main herd began to surge some inside the circling ring
of cowboys. Calves bawled for mothers; mothers lowed for
calves. Bulls bellowed in outrage when chased from some
favored heifer in heat. Steers roared. Dust puffed up like
sudden rages in a smoking prairie fire. The ground quaked.
Ponies became white with sweat; after a while turned slowly
pink from the stiving red dust. From within the eyeball a
man fancied he could see dragging pink clouds hanging from
his eyelashes. The ponies puffed like ganted lizards. Buzzards

floated high overhead, just outside the edge of the rising red cloud. It was driving dirty work for man and beast, for chaser as well as chased.

Dust worked in under Cain's bandanna. He coughed; coughed hoarsely; coughed until he seemed about to blow out his ears.

Twice Cain saw a calf become separated from a Mark-of-Cain mother. Each time Cain shook down his rope and snaked a wriggling turning loop through the red air and caught the calf in a figure eight, catching the head in one end of the loop and then, as the loop turned over upon hitting, the forefeet in the other. He dragged both calves out of the herd and over to the cut. He saw Jesse rise in his stirrups as if to protest, but then also had the satisfaction of seeing the calves, upon being released, run for their mothers in the cut.

Working like Turks, Cain and Harry finished by noon.

Jesse came riding over, Mitch and Hunt to either side of him.

Cain waved for his boys to stay put around the cut. He would handle the parley alone.

Jesse scrutinized the cut carefully, examining the critters one by one. Finally Jesse said, "You satisfied now, Hammett?"

"I am." Bucky puffed under Cain. Bucky was plumb winded and had thrown up his tail.

"I suppose you expect me to feed you chuck this noon too?"

Cain took off a glove. His hand came out pale, as if from under an old bandage. The palm had deep rope bruises across it. The fingers tingled with a curious kind of buzzing sensation. Cain said, short, "We'll get by."

"You know of course you won't get away with this. Forcing my hand under Lord Peter's nose."

"Jesse, all I can say is—dammit, leave my beef alone!"

"I've already sent wires to all the regular stock markets with orders to impound all beef showing up with your brand on it. As well as Harry's. Cheyenne, Chicago, Omaha, Denver, St. Paul. Everywhere. Also with orders to sell such beef at the best price and to bank the money for the Association."

"Backing us in a corner, are you?"

"I am." Jesse forced himself to smile. "Cain, why don't you vent your brand and ride for me and the Derby again? I'll never hold it agin you that you helped your brother Harry here today cut out cattle that really belonged to us."

161

Cain's dark chin set down.

"I'm giving you your last chance."

Cain looked up at the owling sun. "That money they're banking for the Association . . . I suppose you'll use part of it to pay his salary?" Cain pointed his quirt at Hunt.

"Might."

Cain moved his prat around in its seat. He was soaked through to the crotch and his pants stuck to leather. "You know who Alias here really is, don't you?"

"I think so."

Cain whacked dust off his pants, then his shirt, then the bedroll behind him. He said slowly, "Little more than a tin-horn outlaw operating under the protection of a tin badge until he was run out of your state of Texas."

Hunt's lips thinned back.

Jesse looked from one to the other.

Cain turned his back on both of them. He touched a spur puffing Bucky and trotted off.

When Cain got to where his brothers and Timberline were holding the bawling bellowing cut, he yelled, "All right, boys, let's get high behind."

Harry cried gaily, "It's for the hills, ain't it, Cain?"

"You bet. For Hidden Country. Where they'll never find them. At least not until this all blows over."

Cain

It was late October. Cain and Harry were asleep in a one-room log cabin high in the hills, in Hidden Country where white clay overlay red earth, where white modes overlay Indian ways.

Cain slept in the bunk behind the door; Harry in the bunk across the room. The fire in the red-stone hearth had long ago fallen to a gray-edged mound of amber coals. The cabin smelled of warmed-over pine pitch. A slow wind moaned low over the chimney opening above.

Something awoke Cain. In the dark he could hear it rustling across the board floor. Cain raised off his blanket pillow to hear better. He was still on the alert for Jesse or one of his boys. They just might have got past Timberline the lookout and trailed them into Hidden Country.

Finally he made out the princing of small feet and the brush of a tail across a floor board. He heard nibbling. That was enough for him. He reached across to his hat on the chair beside the bed and pulled a match from the hatband. With a strike along the board side of the bunk, he lit it, a spitting glow breaking into a blue flame surrounded by an orange halo. He looked around. There lay brother Harry sound asleep in his bunk, blond face in innocent repose like a baby's, arms crossed over his chest as if laid out for a funeral. Cain raised in his blankets a bit more. And saw it. On the floor at the foot of his bunk burned two eyes set close together. Sachet kitten. Nibbling on his saddle-cinch strap. It took Cain a moment to understand the skunk had paid them a visit for the salt in the sweated portions of the leather. It'd probably come in through the breathing hole to the root cellar.

He stared at the skunk. "Wal," he thought, "ain't much point in kickin' a loaded polecat in the arse and out the door. It'll probably leave in a minute if left alone." Yet a half-chewed cinch strap wasn't much good to a man either. Cain glanced back and up at the corner post of his bunk where he'd hung his .45 and cartridge belt.

As if sensing Cain's thoughts, and just as the match was about to go out, the skunk turned leisurely, even lazily, and on soft light pads princed for the door to the root cellar. The long white stripe down its back and along its tail showed like a streak of snow on ebony. Its bright black bead eyes winked at him. Then the lucifer was out.

Cain settled back on his pillow. With a sigh of relief he nuzzled under gray horse blankets. It was good to know there were still a few hours' sleep coming.

He heard Harry stir; heard him mumble in his sleep. He heard the low wind outside moan in the chimney opening. The towering Stonies outside seemed to be moaning too, with a sound like a very low hum, as if barely moving wind were playing a vast comb.

He recalled a story Harry had told at supper. A cowboy keeping lonely line camp came home one day to find a stranger eating at his table. The stranger, as was custom, had helped himself and had fixed up a good meal. The cowboy noticed a fresh batch of biscuits on the table. "See you had good luck with the sourdough," the cowboy said. "I did," the stranger said. The cowboy pointed to two identical jars on the shelf over the stove. Both had white powder in them. "Which a them two did you use?" "The one on the left," the stranger said. "Good," the cowboy said, "you're all right then. That other'n's got strychnine in it."

He slept.

Dawn was breaking, when the heavy log door at the foot of his bunk suddenly shoved in with a loud screak and quick boot heels tapped on the floor.

"Who's there?" Cain called out.

"Tramps," a high voice said.

Cain opened his eyes and looked directly into the black eyes of two guns. It was still somewhat dark inside the cabin and he couldn't quite make out the two faces behind the guns.

Across the cabin there was a rustle in Harry's bed and then the thump of a body hitting the floor.

Cain really woke then. Almost without thinking, he faked an elaborate yawn and asked as sleepily as he could manage, "What do you want, boys?"

The same voice said, "Better give up, Hammett, we've got you this time."

The voice behind the other gun said, "So you thought it safe to play king-on-the-mountain up here, eh?"

Again almost without thinking, all in one motion, Cain suddenly rolled to his right and left-handed snatched his .45 from the bunk post and fired. One of the bundled-up forms grunted and the gun nearest Cain let go, roaring and flaming, the flame singeing his mustache and the bullet tearing into the pillow under his head. The other gun let go then too, bellowing and blazing, the slug ripping through the center of the bunk where a moment before his body had lain, whacking into the floor beneath. The smell of burning powder and smoke filled the low cabin, sharp, acrid, like burnt sulphur.

Before Cain could thumb the hammer of his gun again, the two forms, one of them still grunting, hit the log doorway together, crashing. They struggled, both trying to get out at the same time; at last managed it. Cain swung out of bed, and in shirt and socks was after them, firing as he went. By the time he got through the door, in the gray dawn, he saw only the tails of two coats vanishing around the corner of the cabin. He was about to take after them, when two men jumped from around the other corner of the cabin and let go at him, both guns bellowing and flaming. Somehow they missed him completely. He whirled and threw down on them, but they too ducked and ran. He jumped after them in his socks, hobbling as best he could across the iron-cold ground. Again he was disappointed to see only the tails of coats vanishing, this time into gray-green mahogany brush beside tumbled red boulders. He fired a parting shot after them. The echo of the shot bounced back and forth several times between the high red walls looming overhead.

After a few seconds he thought he could make out the sound of galloping hooves in the distance. He remembered a trick of Gramp Hammett's and quickly whipped out a silk handkerchief from his shirt pocket and spread it on the frozen ground. A kerchief put to the ground became a long ear and magnified all distant sounds. He knelt and put an ear to it. He listened closely. Yes. Horse hooves were beating the earth somewhere. The sound was diminishing; finally faded out altogether.

Coming back, he was surprised to find a gleaming well-oiled Winchester rifle leaning against the side of the house near the steps. "I'll be dogged." He went over and picked it up. He snicked it open. Loaded. He turned it over in the gray light. There on the stock someone had carefully, even quite neatly, burned an initial: L.

"L for Link. Or Lawton, his summer name. Either way, I'll bet that's who one of 'em was," Cain said softly to himself. "I thought I sort a recognized that voice. The tall one. The sonofa." He looked the gun over some more. "Wal, looks like I'm one gun ahead. The owner will never dare come around and claim this one. Not onless he wants to be arrested for attempted murder." Cain shook it for heft. "Light and handy. Just my kind of gun. A jimdandy .38-56, 1886 carbine."

He was about to step inside when he spotted some blood on the doorsill. "Yessiree! I did nick one of 'em then. The one that grunted. The short one that sort a sounded like Mitch. That'll make even better evidence in a tight."

Then, inside the cabin, after he had lighted a lantern, he saw something else that surprised him. There under the other bunk, eyes bleering out big and scared and moonstone gray, lay brother Harry. "Wal, I'll be go-to-grass. Harry! I been wonderin' what'd happened to ye all this time." Cain remembered he'd heard someone fall to the floor when the strangers first popped into the cabin. "All right. You can get out from under. I've chased them off."

Harry crept out. He too was in shirt and socks. He was bacon pale.

Cain laughed. "Harry! You look so white with fright a man could easy cut off your head at the neck and not shed a drop of blood."

Harry trembled. "Put out that lantern, you fool!"

165

"Oh, for godsakes, Harry, they're all of ten miles from here by now. I heard them go ahorseback."

Harry ran three quick steps and grabbed up the lantern and shoved up the chimney level with a thumb and blew it out.

"Wal, Harry, by golly now!"

Cain

A few days later, at cousin Rory's, Cain sat tipped back on two legs of his chair. Rory sat across the table from him. They were having a midmorning cup of coffee together. Dale and the boy Joey and the herder were out tending sheep. Gram with her old leathers lay breathing in the lean-to, taking a nap. The fire in the hearth threw soothing warmth over the side of Cain's face and body.

Cain was telling Rory about the attack in the hills. "The way I figure it, they must've wanted to catch me alive. So they could hang me. Otherwise they'd've drilled me plumb center afore I woke up. They had the drop on me."

Face swollen red from pregnancy, Rory looked down at her black coffee. She stirred it. She said, dispirited, "Like they tried with your brother Harry."

"Yeh."

"Make an example of you."

Cain nodded.

"Like they'll probably try with Dale next, now that this Hunt-Link devil has come north."

Cain picked at the tablecloth with a blunt thumbnail.

Rory tolled her head. "And here I always thought you Hammetts was men." She sighed. The burden in her lap moved.

Cain fired up. "You tell us what to do then, since you're so sure."

With a slow pendulant motion Rory leaned across the table. Her lips curled back, chalkish teeth showing. "You boys should have got rid of him years ago. And I know this much, by Grab, if you boys don't fix him soon now, he's going to kill you off one by one. All three of you."

"Rory, you ain't suggestin' we up and shoot him down in cold blood, are ye?"

"Yes."

"The law won't let us. In fact, the law probably won't even arrest him with just that initial to go on."

166

"Yet you know it was him there in the hills," Rory said.

"Wal, yes, I guess we do. Just the same, you got to catch a man making his move out in the open where everybody can see him make it."

"Ugh! You men."

"We Hammetts ain't exactly in the habit of shootin' a man in the back."

Rory continued bitter. "Yet you'll let him shoot you in the back."

"Oh, Rory."

"Just you watch. That Hunt'll shoot all of you in the back yet. One by one."

Cain grunted. "I'll watch, all right. You can bet your sweet life on that."

Rory looked down. Her swollen lips and swollen eye pouches sagged. "Yes, I guess I might as well get used to it. Yes, all my menfolks dead."

"Now, Rory, we'll hold the thought."

"Yes. Like he killed Gramp. Like he killed our dads."

"We'll hold the thought."

"All in the back."

Cain drank the last of his coffee. "Oh, shut up about that now. Got any more Arbuckle?"

Rory got up and poured him some. "Dale. Harry. Joey. Let alone this one when he comes."

Cain dropped a spurt of canned milk into his coffee. He stirred it. He watched the yellow-brown fluid swirling. "One thing bothers me. Been puzzling on it a whole week. Why those strangling sons-of-bitches didn't go for Harry. Why, they never even looked his way this time. As if he warn't around." Cain shook his head. "Guess I'll have to turn that over to my brownie back here." Cain tapped the back of his head. "He usually tells me what's what when I give him some problem to work on."

Rory looked up from her coffee. "It's about time you wondered about that."

"Oh, come now." Cain blinked. "Another funny thing was how they got past Timberline. The best sighter in the country."

"Yes, and it's about time you wondered about him, too."

"Come now. Harry and Tim are all right when it comes to that."

"Can you tell me where Harry is right now?"

"Wal, no."

"Antelope. Whooping and yelling and having a high old time."

"Wal? Ain't that his right? He's got to have some fun some time."

"He told Dale yesterday afternoon he was going into town to sleep on a regular goose-hair piller for a couple of nights." Rory had to smile in spite of herself.

"Wal, why not? Blanket pillows get oncommon hard after a time."

"You don't think nothing of it then that he's contrary one day and friendly the next? And in between times full of the devil?"

"No." A smile cracked across his hard face. "Whooping and yelling. I mind me of the time he led his horse Star into Butcherknife Bain's saloon and give him a bottle of wine. Sheriff Sine finally had to tell him that pullin' up the town to look at its roots hardly helped the town's growth much."

"Don't it scare you the way he can get so terrible drunk sometimes?"

"Not atall."

Rory tolled her blond head. "So terrible terrible drunk. Like that time at Red Jackson's shindig. Me and Dale'd just been married a year then, remember? You boys finally had to put him to bed."

Cain nodded. He remembered. "You know what Harry said when he come to that time?"

"No."

"Wal, he come to looking Mrs. Jackson's commode mirror in the eye. He said it was the first he knowed he had a twin brother."

"Cain, I tell you, he scares me with them awful drunks of his."

"Wal, it probably only means his brownie ain't happy."

"I could tell you some things, Cain."

"Wal, maybe we all could."

"Cain, I'd be careful of him even if he is your brother." She placed a work-reddened hand over his stub hand, warmly. "Cain."

Cain let the hand rest on his a moment; then, quietly, eyes closing against a thought, withdrew his hand.

They sat a while in silence. They sipped coffee. Time tocked away. The fire in the hearth spat; sagged; rustled. Gram's breathing came to them with the sound of someone pumping stiff old bellows. The soil roof overhead moved under the November cold.

168

All at once Rory began to talk a blue streak about a dream she'd had. "It was so strange. I was trying to cross the Bitterness. The river was rising. On my side all around the land was low and I saw that if I didn't hurry and get across I'd drown." Her sad face slowly brightened, became almost a young girl's again. "On the other side was a high red bank with green grass and green trees. Like it was a park kind of. Birds singing. Pretty birds, not magpies. Fiddle music calling from somewhere. A kind of a paradise almost." Her dark blue eyes lightened and sparkled. Right before Cain's eyes dullness seemed to wash out of her blond hair. "Well, I saw I couldn't walk across like a Jesus. Like Peter my faith was weak. I knew I'd sink and drown. So I knew I had to get a boat from somewhere."

Mention of the boat made Cain slowly stiffen in his chair.

"I looked all up and down the river. Then I spotted one. A hollowed-out log like you and your brother Harry once made when we was kids. I saw it tied to a tree up the river a ways. I went up to it and looked it over. To my surprise I found it lined with fur. Beaver fur. Even the seat was covered with it. Soft, like velvet."

Cain's smoke-blue eyes widened until the whites showed like onion rings.

"Well, I got in and started paddling across to where all the shindig music was. Then the next thing I knew there was a man. He looked like someone I knew real well. He took the paddle out of my hands. He smiled gentlelike and started paddling me over. Then there was a flash like lightning in my head and I jerked awake."

" 'Tain't possible!" Cain exploded.

Rory frowned. "What do you mean 'tain't possible?"

"Why! I had the very same dream myself the other night. To the leaf almost."

Rory sat up. "What!" She ran a hand around and over her swollen belly.

"Hell's fire and little fishes, Rory! If that ain't the darnedest thing I ever heard of."

"You—dreamt—that—too?"

"Last Thursday night."

"Why! that's when I had mine!"

"The night after the attack."

"Well, I never."

They stared at each other. Her eyes became milky with inner thought. His eyes closed over secretively.

"Funny," he said.

"Funny," she said.

After a moment he let his lips crinkle at the corners. "There was one thing different though in my dream."

"Oh?"

"In my dream I warn't the woman."

"Oh." She laughed, short.

"But I did see the woman standing beside the river, awondering if she dared to go across it or not. I felt sorry for her, so I—"

She broke in. "Oh, now I understand! It was you, you who called my attention to the hollowed-out boat. It was you who took the paddle from me and smiled gentlelike and then paddled me over to the green park. You."

"Why, yes, it was."

They stared at each other.

Then they began to study to themselves some, he with his eyes down, she with her eyes to one side.

Part THREE

Rosemary

Rory was picking up one of Dale's cigarette butts in her frost-killed garden, and was stooped over, when the first pain seized her. It came from behind the child-weight and seemed to hold the weight a moment and then slowly tickled away.

"That darn Dale," she said. "Still throws them butts of his in the petunias when he knows they'll kill Gram's angleworms. He's hardly better than our sheepherder with his tobacco cuds."

She straightened up and dropped the burnt butt into the pocket of her gingham apron. "I've told him a thousand times if I've told him once, that when it rains, or when the snow melts in the spring, the juice from the tobacco soaks into the ground and discourages the angleworms." Her dulled-over eyes focused on a row of limp frost-killed petunias. "And if there's one thing this river-bottom dirt needs it's angleworms. Loosen it up. Give it air holes so it can breathe."

She passed both hands around and over the low huge bulge in her belly. "But he never thinks of my flowers, let alone my vegetables. It's all sheep with him. All sheep."

She felt life stir. It was like a kick from a bed partner in sleep. "Guess I better call him up from the sheep shed."

She moved slowly toward the house. Her dark blue skirt hung low in back, almost dragging the ground. The ground felt rock-hard to the foot.

It was still early in morning. A slow cold wind swept through the barren cottonwoods lining the Shaken Grass and the Bitterness. It chased tumbleweeds across the narrow point. The sky was overcast with gray hurrying clouds, bulging low like ruptured bowels. The mountains to the west were hidden in them.

Her glum eyes ran. Her red nose dripped. "We'll never have a garden here if we don't keep them angleworms going. Gram's carrying them in a pail of dirt all the way from Siouxland will be wasted."

Hand to knee, she climbed the log stoop and entered the

brown cabin. The place was doggy with the old-hair smell of buffalo robes and bear rugs. She picked up the poker from the hearth and went back to the front door and reached out to hit a string of horseshoes dangling on a wire. The home-made gong bangled loud on the yard. When Dale didn't show right away, she hit the gong again, harder. Once more the jumping iron horseshoes bangled loud, this time setting up discordant echoes between the cabin and the sheds.

Dale's long head and neck, hatted, popped out of the door of the sheep shed. His face gaunted toward her in question.

Another inner quickening and then a knotting up of muscle behind the burden worked her belly. She gripped the door jamb, tight, until it passed. The pain seemed to have sharpened some.

Dale held his head down to one side to hear the better. He seemed to think she'd already called; that he hadn't caught it.

"Come up," she called. "Hurry."

"Hah?"

"Come up!"

"Be right with you." His head withdrew; the shed door closed.

She put the poker back by the hearth. She threw a couple of cottonwood logs on the fire. She wound the clock on the mantel. She noted Dale had been careless with the Winchester shells again—left a couple out where the boy could find them. She filled the black range with chopped wood and set on a kettle of water.

She longed for a bone to chew. She loved chewing a bone close, sucking off all the delicate tastes, tonguing out the soft marrow. When alone she often sat working and gnawing over a soupbone. It was her one secretive delight, something she kept even from Dale and the boy Joey.

Next she dug out an old sack full of leftover clothes. She chose an old white shirt of Dale's and ripped it into neat strips and folded them neatly and carried them into the half-dark bedroom.

Another inner quickening closed like a fist just behind the child-burden. It held her, deep, almost fierce. It had the feel of someone squeezing chyme, a half-digested ball of green-black grass, out of a cow's intestines, fist by pressing fist.

"Ahh!" she cried, clutching her tuberant belly with one hand while grabbing the corner of their hide-spring bed with the other. "Ahhh! It's coming fast this time."

174

The front door opened. Boot heels clicked on the puncheon floor in the other room. "Rory?"

"Ahhh," she whispered.

"Rory? Where be ye, woman?"

"In here."

The boot heels entered the bedroom. "What's my long-haired partner up to now?"

She half-turned to him. "Dale, I'm afraid it's . . ."

"Rory, my love." Dale took off his big hat and set it on a chair. "What ails ye, woman?" His wild dark hair slid across his high narrow forehead.

"Help me on bed."

"Sure, my love." He wrapped his long hard arms around her, his hands catching her tenderly, even delicately, under her distended paps. She suffered the smell of sheep on him. She let herself be hoisted onto the bed. She suffered the sound of creaking hide spring.

She said, "It's like my whole bottom's fell out." She felt a smile tickle at a lip corner; felt it pass away. She spread her legs. "I'm so wide." She drew her skirt to her knees.

In the half-dark bedroom Dale's eyes became big hollows. He suddenly seemed to have trouble looking at her.

She sighed. "Good thing I sent Joey to Cain yesterday. With Gram."

Dale shivered. "It's on the way then?"

"Yes. And this time it feels like it's going to come quick. Not like last time with Joey, when I fought three whole days and nights."

Dale's face slowly whitened over. He stood stiff. With a rough hand he combed back his wild hair.

"Dale? What's the matter? Having a baby ain't as bad as all that."

He started for the door.

She roused. She said sharply, "Here! Where you going?"

"Get Gram of course."

"Oh, no, you don't. Not her. I don't want her again."

"Lord, Rory, ye want help, don't ee?"

"Sure I want help. But not hers. She almost lost the baby and me both last time. She's too old to be of much help."

"But you got to have someone. There ain't no doctor. Less'n you want me to quick ride to Antelope for one."

"It's too late for that." The big fist behind the child closed and squeezed again. "Ahhh," she hoarsed, low. "Ahhh."

Dale jumped. Again he started for the door.

Hardly able to see him for the pain, yet out of her need,

175

she cried, "Dale! Don't you dare leave me! It'll be here in a . . . Dale!"

Dale's gaunted throat worked. "But I just got to get you someone, Rory. I can't let you suffer alone."

The fist let go of its grip and she came back, clear. "Listen. There ain't time." She gasped for breath. "Listen. Light the lamp. It's so dark and cloudy out."

"Oh." Dale jumped to do it. Trembling, he had to scratch three matches before one took hold on the wick under the raised glass chimney. Slowly orange light diffused through the bedroom. It gave some color to Dale's cheeks. It lighted up the browns in the black bear rug on the floor. It helped the light coming in through the single window high over the bed.

She lay panting. She suffered it. She said, "It's almost here, Dale, dear. There'll be no time to get help. Will you get the hot water and some soap? This second one . . . And over there is some clean strips I made."

He lashed around at her. "But ye can't have it alone, woman? I won't let ye."

She tried to smile. "My good husband. Of course I won't have it alone."

"You don't mean for me to help ye, do you, for godsakes?"

"Yes."

He almost broke up. When vision came back to his eyes, he made for the door a third time.

And once more she had to rouse herself out of birthing slumber. "Here! Where you going?"

"Get help."

"Come back here!"

He covered his face with his arms. "If you mean for me to help you, I can't."

She sat up, first on one elbow, then on the other. "What? And you brag how you've helped ten thousand ewes at lambing time? How you've got a vet's thin arm?"

"I'll try and face up to most anything, Rory. You know that. I've done real good with most things. But oh, God, not this . . . my own wife."

Her eyes hardened. Her mouth squared. Her face became haggard with rage. Summoning up all she was, she swung her legs over the edge of the bed and got to her feet. Straddling more than walking, she staggered toward the door, pushed past him, and went to the mantel. She took down the Winchester. She picked up the couple of shells she'd earlier noticed

176

Dale had carelessly left on the mantel. She snapped the shells into the carbine; levered one into the chamber.

Dale heard the snicks and peered around at her from the bedroom door, mouth agawk. "Hey! Woman! What the hell's fire you up to?"

She aimed it from the hip. "You long-legged cowardly Hammett, get over to the stove there and pour that hot water in a basin. And then take it into the bedroom with you. You ran out on me the last time, leaving me in Gram's hands, who hardly knew what she was doing any more. But not this time. You're going to help me whether you want to or not."

"But Rosemary, my girl, a man can't help his own woman!"

"You've always lumped me in with your ewes. Well now, darn you, you're going to help me like I really was a ewe."

"But Rory—"

"You ain't my man any more. Between us that's done. You're a stranger to me now. Like a doctor might be. And if you don't help me like a doc might, by the Lord, Dale Hammett, I'll shoot you down like a dog."

"Rosemary woman—"

"Shut up. And don't you Rosemary me any more. After you've helped me with this child, you'll never touch me again. Never. I'll be damned first before I'll be the loving wife to a coward. Never." She harsed up a great breath. "You damn men think this country is too tough on the women. Not at all. It's you men that can't stand up to it." She almost snarled it. "I let you take up with me again after Joey was born. Because maybe Joey wasn't your'n and you didn't owe me the help. But this one I know is your'n and by the Lord you're going to help me have it."

"What! 'Because maybe Joey wasn't . . .' My God!"

"Get!"

"Now, Rory, now." He jumped up and down. "Don't shoot now. Rory."

"Get that hot water!"

"All right, all right. But at least let me first have a couple stiff jolts of hooch. Oh, my God."

"And let you get so snockered drunk you won't know what you're doin'? Oh, no." She cocked the hammer. "Get!"

He got.

Within an hour the baby was born. It was another boy. She named him after his uncle: Cain Hammett.

Jesse

With Mitch beside him on the democrat, Jesse led the way. Behind them trailed a dozen tough punchers on horseback.

It was just noon. Though the sun was out, bright, it was biting cold. It was November and all shadows leaned long to the north. Each shadow glinted with night's lingering hoarfrost. The gray ground rang like a great stone bell under the iron horseshoes and iron rims of the wheels. Every man was bundled up in winter clothes: overcoats with fur collars, heavy gloves, and hats tied down over the ears with varicolored silk bandannas.

They breasted the final hill. Jesse held up a gloved hand. "Whoa!" Mitch hauled back on the lines and the spanking pair of bays stopped. The horsebackers behind stopped too. Horses puffed. Men breathed deep. Bridle bits and spurs gingled gently.

Below and to the left of the trail lay Avery Jimson's Hog Ranch; to the right lay Cattle Queen's spread. Rust Creek under the little wooden bridge sparkled in the noon sun. There were no birds. Wolves and coyotes lay hidden. West of them loomed the Big Stonies, high and pure and white, with new snowfall reaching far down the slopes, into the near canyons and low passes. The white peaks glinted against the sky like icicles against a vast silk bedspread, blue, fine-spun.

Jesse stroked his game leg. He was careful to stay well away from a big bandage covering a pussing pulpy wound. "Well, there she lays." Jesse's face was beetling red in the cold. "Now, boys, I want you to get this straight. No killing bee today. We can't afford it. Lord Peter is ready to back out and bolt as it is now. A killin' would queer him sure. Hangin' or shootin', one."

Mitch glowered beside him. Mitch was for the killing bee. His wife had been eating him out for tolerating a whore in the valley.

Jesse turned in his seat and looked up at wizened soureyed Stalker on horseback. "All we're going to do is go in and scare the daylights out of 'em. So they'll pack up and leave. Got it?"

Stalker spat. "Got it."

Jesse looked at the rest of the boys one by one: Hog, Ringbone, Spade, Beavertooth, Peakhead, Dried Apple Bill, Stuttering Dick, Four-eye Irish. "You boys got it too?"

178

"Got it, boss."

Again Jesse examined the valley below. Gray smoke rose in slow and wafting spirals from the chimneys of both buildings. Whiteface cattle browsed on rusty bunch grass in Queenie's pasture. A solitary cowboy's pony waited at the hitching rail outside Avery's place. Jesse snorted, high-headed. "Take her pay in my calves, will she? Write letters to the paper about me being a crook, will he? The blinkin' buzzards."

The boys sat quiet. Their horses chafed under them.

Jesse smiled some under his dark mustache. There wasn't a waddy in his bunch who hadn't contributed at least one calf to Queenie's herd. Even Mitch who was now all for killing her. Silently Jesse thanked his lucky star that he hadn't got around to asking her for a private viewing of her famous breasts. He was the only one free to do what had to be done.

"Sorry, boys," Jesse said at last. "But I'm afraid our Queenie's got in the way of progress."

Stalker spat. "Will her little herd be enough to fill out the tally for the earl?"

Jesse's smile held. "It'll help."

"How many you figure she's got in there?"

"Mitch, how many? You had them counted last week."

"About a thousand."

Jesse whistled. "She and Solomon would have made quite a pair."

At that all the boys smiled, even Stalker.

"Remember now. No killin'," Jesse warned again. "Just a durn good scaring bee is all we want."

"Hell, boss," Spade said, "if it was to be the other bee, you wouldn't a got us with. You know that."

Jesse nodded. "I know, boys. And I appreciate it. I almost took titty there myself. But you know she's been putting on a style we just can't tolerate in this valley. It's got to be done."

Yes, it had to be done. From somewhere he had to pick up a thousand head or the deal was off. Lord Peter would go elsewhere for a buyer. Jesse felt he was right in taking Queenie's calves away from her. Hadn't they all originally been the earl's? Besides, wasn't it high time somebody did something to put a chill into all them homesteaders coming into the valley? Let alone them goldurn overbold rustlers Harry Hammett and Timberline? And especially that king rebel of them all, Cain Hammett? Yes, getting rid of Queenie and Avery would be just the thing to start the ball arolling.

Jesse rubbed his bad leg slowly. "All right, you saddlestiffs.

179

Mitch and I'll drive up to Queenie's cabin. While Mitch holds the horses, I'll shoot down that goldurn big black monster she's got for a dog. Then you boys cut the pasture wire and drive off her beef. Head them for the hills under the Horn where we'll vent her Hanging RH and put on the Derby brand. Got it?"

"Got it."

Jesse waved his arm again. Mitch slapped the reins over the rumps of the bays. Off they went. Wheels cracked on stones. Green spokes shone whizzing in the sun. Throwing hooves kicked up sparks. The two men rolled with each lurch of the green democrat as it careened down the irregular roadbed. The cowboys racked after them. Hoarfrost held down the dust.

Slope-shouldered in his heavy black winter coat, Mitch held the bays firm in hand. A smile worked his wily Mongoloid face. He laughed short, once.

Jesse saw the smile, and he yelled over the noise, "What you chokin' on?"

Mitch shrugged. He yelled back, "Heard tell that if you can't find no weapon on Queenie, look for a derringer hid on her somewheres."

"What!"

"They make them tomtit guns mighty small these days. No bigger than a thumb."

"What?"

"I wouldn't put it past her to hide it there. A woman will do anything when she gets in a tight."

Jesse grunted. "We'll make her keep her hands high."

Mitch pulled slightly on the right rein and they whirled into her lane on two wheels. Small red rocks shot out from under the twisting spinning wheels. Behind them trotted the pack of tough punchers.

Jesse saw the big black dog rise to its feet in front of Queenie's door. Even from where he sat on the tossing democrat, Jesse could see the big black devil blink its cold evil eyes. Jesse picked up the Winchester from the floor of the democrat; levered a shell into the firing chamber.

When they got to within fifty feet, Jesse commanded, "Hold up."

Mitch drew back on the lines, hard. The bays reared up, forefeet pawing the air; then stopped so sudden both Jesse and Mitch slid forward off their seat some.

Jesse took off his right glove. He stood up and brought the carbine to his shoulder. He caught the center of the dog's head, just above the blue nose, in the sights of his gun. He pulled the trigger. There was a roar; the bays reared again; the dog dropped to the ground.

Almost the same instant the cabin door opened and out stepped Queenie. As usual Queenie wore a light green dress, narrow at the waist and bosom enormous. Her hair, the color of a lion's tail, was done up in a bun on the top of her head. She'd apparently been napping and had quick slipped on a pair of beaded moccasins. She burned hell's own light green eyes at Jesse. "What goes on here?"

Jesse waved an arm. From behind him swept the cowboys. One of them stepped down off his horse and got out a pair of blue nippers and cut the barbwire pasture fence. The next thing the horsemen were all in the pasture, spreading out on circle drive.

Queenie looked down at her dead dog. A final wink closed its eyes. A trickle of scarlet blood ran down its blue muzzle. It stiffened slowly in the cold. Queenie looked over to where the pasture fence was cut. The ends of the barbwire had been ripped off the fence posts and dragged back a good hundred feet. Queenie's face convulsed a moment, showing wrinkles and age; then smoothed over. She made as if to dart back into the cabin.

"No, you don't!" Jesse yelled, throwing down on her from the green democrat, aiming the Winchester straight for her big breasts. "Reach for the sky! Reach!"

Queenie glared at him. Slowly she raised her small white hands as high as her face, palms out.

Jesse said, "I've heard tell you been expectin' me on a private visit for some time."

"Go to grass."

"Well, I finally have come for a private look-see at them wonders of yours." Jesse looked at her bosom while at the same time he nodded toward her cattle. "Steers that use the multiplication tables like them do should go under the name of mule-eared rabbits."

She turned slightly and stared out to where the punchers had just finished rounding up the herd. They had them bunched for the opening. Little triggering movements jerked at the corners of her eyes. "Them sonsa! So this is what I get for being goodhearted to poor lonesome cowboys."

All of a sudden the bays on the democrat smelled blood. They snorted; shied away from the dead black dog.

"Whoa, boys," Mitch growled, "easy now." Mitch held them steady.

Jesse stepped down off the democrat, careful to keep his carbine trained on her bosom. "All right, Queenie, step right up."

She shivered, dress rippling all the way down to her moccasined feet. "Won't you at least let me get a coat and shawl?" She looked down at her feet. "And something warm for them?"

"Get aboard!"

"But, my God, Jesse, I can't ride this way, wherever it is you're taking me. I'll freeze to death."

"It'll be plenty warm where you're going."

Calves and young steers bellered behind them and in a moment all of Queenie's wealth began to chouse past, around both sides of the democrat and the brown cabin. Jesse looked at them admiringly. Choice whitefaces. Chunky. Almost all of even weight. Lord Peter couldn't kick on them.

Queenie watched them go, one by ten by hundred, and she cried. Tears in her lashes gave her light green eyes the look of just fallen hailstones. "Them sonsa!"

Despite heavy hoarfrost, hooves slowly began to kick up red dust. The boys in the drag soon had to cover their noses with silk kerchiefs.

Jesse waved for Stalker and Ringbone and Spade to come over. They came at a gallop and pulled up almost on top of him and Queenie.

"Yeh, boss?" Stalker said, leaning on the pommel of his saddle, face sour, hard. He ignored Queenie.

"Get over to the Hog Ranch and corral Avery before he gets wise. And whoever else that waddy is with that lone horse at the hitching rail there."

Spade held a hand over a frost-pinched ear. "What if the lone waddy is one of our boys, Jesse?"

Ringbone broke in. "It's Harry Hammett."

Jesse's eyebrows raised. "No!"

"It's his hoss. Star."

"Well, well. Now we will really have us a necktie party. We'll string him up too."

"Why, you strangling sons-a-bitches," Queenie said, low. "So that's your game."

Stalker and Ringbone and Spade gave her a sliding look; then galloped toward the Hog Ranch. They were afoot and had gun in hand before their horses had stopped. They popped into the front door, one right after the other. But they had hardly vanished inside when out of the back door darted Harry in his flashy rigging. With a run and a flying leap, Harry forked his bay and was off, heading for the hills. As he disappeared over the rise, he stood up in his stirrups and thumbed his nose at them. Then he fired his gun at them, once. The bullet skipped across the ground in front of the bay team. Once again Mitch had to steady the horses with a sharp haul on the lines.

"Hah! Good!" Queenie said, "Now he'll bring his Red Sash boys on the run."

"Won't do you much good, Queenie. The party'll be over by then." Jesse gestured with his Winchester. "Get aboard!"

"You won't let me get a coat and shawl? Or some shoes for my feet?"

"Get aboard!"

"Jesse, my God, where are you taking me? You're not really going to hang me?"

Jesse smiled, mean. "Well, if you really want to know, we're running you out of the country on a rail, hive you back to where you came from. To Old Cheyenne and your old biscuit-shooting job in that U. P. restaurant."

"If that's where I'm going, please let me change clothes first, Jesse. As a woman I have a right to show up in my best."

"No."

"Haven't you any respect for a woman atall? I look a fright in all this dust."

Jesse considered a moment. "All right, where's your coat hanging?"

"Just behind the door."

"Mitch, hold down on her."

Mitch put the reins in one hand and with the other held down on her. His blue gun glinted in the sharp sunlight. "Up," Mitch said, "and no reaching under the dress on the way up either. I know your puncture tricks."

Queenie swore. "Mitch, you Judas you. I knew I should've had at least one good talk with that poor wife of yours."

Mitch's round face reddened. He held steady on her.

Jesse went in and got her coat, a long black affair, velvet, voluminous. He also got her a shawl, a light blue woolen one.

"And my overshoes, Jesse. And a muff, if you please. And oh, yes, my diamond earrings."

Jesse said, "Goldurn, no. I've already been enough of a gentleman as 'tis." Jesse glanced across the road. "Ah! I see they got Avery ready for us at the Hog Ranch. C'mon, get aboard."

Queenie still balked. "I won't feel dressed unless I have my diamonds."

"Durn you, Queenie, get in or by the Lord I'll rope you and drag you out of the country. Instead of just ride you out. All the way to Cheyenne."

Queenie got in.

"Sit down on the floor just back of the seat. Facing me. Hands up."

Queenie got down on the floor.

Jesse climbed in. He sat facing her, back to the horses, Winchester still aimed for her bosom. "Let 'er rip, Mitch, across the road and we'll pick up Avery next."

Humped Avery stood waiting for them. Avery showed fight. His bulbous brown eyes were burning mad. He looked up at Jesse. He had on his overcoat and hat, but still looked cold. The wattlelike goiter under his chin was purple with it. "Stalker says you got a warrant for my arrest, Jacklin."

"I have," Jesse said. "Climb aboard, you blinkin' wedger-in."

"Let's see it," Avery said. "I want to see with my own eyes just who signed a complaint against me." Avery gave Queenie the merest flick of a glance.

Mitch drew his gun again. "That's warrant enough, I reckon. Straight from Judge Colt hisself."

Avery looked into Mitch's gun barrel. "You going to dry-gulch us in the hills, Jacklin?"

"Might. Climb aboard."

"You don't have the warrant then, Jacklin."

"Get in. I didn't come here to have a chin with you, Avery."

"You don't have the warrant then, Jacklin."

A new rope of pain tightened around Jesse's bad leg. It was almost a doubling of the usual searing twinge. It gripped his whole leg, down into each toe, up into his groin. Jesse already resented the way in which Avery used his last name and the sudden increase of pain in his leg didn't help any. It was Avery who had given him the bad leg in the first place, whacking him in the shin with his stool the night he fought Harry Hammett. He took dead aim with his Winchester on Avery's brow. "By the Lord, Avery, we can end it right here, if that's your mind. I'll put this carbine to your head and scatter your college-warped brains all over the ground."

Queenie spoke up from the floor of the democrat. "Better get in, Avery, dearie. They're giving us a free ride to Cheyenne, is all."

"Free ride to hell, you mean," Jesse roared, high-headed.

Queenie added, "We can look up the law later, Avery. Climb in."

Avery thought it over a moment; finally climbed in beside her.

Jesse pointed with the barrel of his gun. "Mitch, follow Rust Creek up the gully a ways."

Mitch drove. Stalker, Ringbone, Spade followed on horseback. The trail became rough with red stones. Iron hooves and iron rims rang loud in the bitter cold.

Jesse watched the two narrowly for signs of weakening. Except for that one moment back at the cabin, Queenie was taking it calm. She seemed to have guessed it was only going to be a scaring bee. Avery meanwhile sat nodding over his purple wattle. His thin humped body rolled with each pitch of the democrat. Avery was burning but he had dampered it down some.

Jesse hated them and their guts. It always made him as mad as the devil when people dared stand up to him, and especially so when they did it after he'd got the drop on them. He cursed them silently to himself. They'd upset the smooth and orderly flow of what had been the first real paradise on earth—big-time ranching in Bitterness valley. Life had gone along as merry as a marriage bell for him and his family and his friends until these two satans had crept into his Garden of Eden. It enraged him that a smart painted cat like Queenie and a smart ornery cuss like Avery could get his very own boys to play the game of grab against him. A settler or two he could have tolerated. But not an out-and-out calf-stealing whore and a college-warped letter-writing saloon-keeper both of whom went out of their way to encourage his boys to traitor him.

They rode in silence. The stone-pocked gully deepened into a rocky red canyon. They followed a crude dugway along the cliff edge. Junipers, then stunted pine, appeared along the upper edges of the crimson canyon cliffs. With every twist and jolt the wheels of the green democrat cracked like they might dish and collapse. Sometimes the twisting jolts were so violent Jesse had to hang on with one hand while with the other he held the carbine. Queenie and Avery rolled away from each other; rolled against each other. Once they cracked heads. Mitch had the advantage of hanging onto the lines. The three horsebackers followed along slowly behind.

Queenie finally had enough. "Jesse, if this is your idea of a shortcut to Cheyenne, you can stop."

"Blast it, if that ain't just what we will do. Hold up, Mitch, this is far enough."

They stopped on a narrow ledge. There was just enough

185

room for the bays and the democrat to pass along the dug-way. Above them on the left climbed the south wall of the canyon, straight up, overhanging them, red, tipping, with gray-green mahogany brush sticking out of an occasional crevice. Below them, on the right, some twenty feet down, ran Rust Creek. The mountain stream gurgled like the sound of someone faintly choking. A single tree, a sturdy mountain ash, grew at the edge of the ledge, rising some twenty feet above them. The sun had begun to fall and in the shadow of the south wall the wind seemed a bit more cold and bitter. Teeth chattered. Jesse was jumpy from both the cold and the tension. High and far to the west rode the pure white blunt icicle peaks of the Big Stonies. The Old Man and the Throne were just barely in view.

Jesse looked up and around and down. He gestured with his gun. "Get out."

"Jesse—" Queenie began.

"Get down." Jesse prodded them both with the barrel of his gun.

Slowly they rolled to their knees; then rose to their feet. They were stiff from the jolting ride. They shivered. They looked around at the sky and then down below at the canyon. A wonder turned in their eyes. Their eyes seemed to say: "Is this it? Is this the place?"

They climbed down slowly. Queenie winced once when her moccasined foot touched on sharp rock.

Jesse climbed down with them. "All right, you mullygrubs. Here's what we'll do. If you'll promise to leave the country, and stay out, we'll let you loose. But if you don't, so help me God, I'll have you drowned in that stream there like you was rats in a sack."

Queenie glanced down at the thin but noisy stream. She shivered. Then she laughed, short. "Why, Jesse, there ain't enough water in there to give me a decent bath even if you was to dam it up for a week."

Jesse boiled over. He realized he'd been a jackass to men-tion the water at all. He should have set himself to kill them in the first place. Then they would have caught from the tone of his voice that he wasn't bluffing. Jesse said, "Climb down there and we'll see if there's enough water or not. We might just want to hold your heads under until you've drowned. Like a calf in a bucket of milk."

Avery looked up. "You got a warrant for our arrest, Jacklin?"

"Oh, I got warrants for you two all right, which I'll serve

186

on you, hot, from this muzzle, if you don't get down on your knees by that stream."

Queenie said, "Jesse, be careful how you joke us."

Avery shivered from the cold. "You can't start your lead pump any too soon to suit me, Jackin."

Jesse shook his head like a baffled bull. Tarnation, they sure were the cool ones, wasn't they?

Mitch couldn't stand the palaver any more. Again taking out his .45 he said, "Shall I cut the dirty buzzards in two, Jesse?"

For the first time Avery showed a trace of fear. The thin lids to his bulb eyes flickered some; his head sank a little. Queenie still wore a pinched smile, though she too showed that Mitch's move had given her check. She looked back at the boys on horseback.

"Stalker," she said, appealingly, "Stalker, you ain't going to be a party to my murder, are you? I know I was sometimes cold to you, but I sometimes wasn't feeling overgood."

Stalker couldn't hold up to her. Neither could Spade or Ringbone.

"Boys, I'm surprised at ye. After all the favors I've done for you too."

Stalker said, "Aw, now, boss, hain't this gone far enough? They ain't really hurting anyone in the valley."

Ringbone said, "Yeh, boss. What's a few measly calves for fun? And as for the homesteads . . . I see Queenie and Avery ain't got any kids or kin to pass it on to."

Jesse reared back. His red face blackened. "This brigazee has gone far enough. Stalker, Spade, toss down your ropes."

Stalker and Spade said nothing. Neither moved.

Queenie's warm smile came back. "Jesse, you really wouldn't joke us now, would you?"

"Boys, get them ropes down here. Pronto!"

Two coils of rope whirled down into the democrat.

"Mitch, keep holding down on them while I set the knots."

Mitch held down on them. Jesse built a noose for each of them and then with thirteen wrap-arounds built the knots. He kicked around under the seat and dug up a pail of grease. He grabbed a handful of it for each noose and slicked the rope up and down. "This should slip like a heel in fresh prairie mustard." Jesse dropped one of the nooses around Avery's neck. Avery stood very still. He quit shivering from the cold. Avery's fat goiter kept the noose from fitting snug. Jesse got it up as tight as he could under Avery's chin. He threw the other noose over Queenie's neck. Her smile

187

once more went back to being pinched. Yet she helped him by holding out her head some. Then Jesse threw the ends of the two ropes high up over a limb in the mountain ash and tied them to the base of the tree. The ropes hung with some slack in them, with the crude knots lying on the shoulder blades of the two. Both Avery and Queenie could breathe with ease, could even take a step or two.

A gun boomed on the canyon wall opposite. Everybody jumped. Jesse swore. "I'll bet it's that thievin' Harry Hammett!" Jesse saw a bright spot move on the opposite wall, behind a red boulder. Jesse raised his carbine to his shoulder and sighted carefully and fired. Mitch fired then too. Stalker, Spade, and Ringbone held. They looked on. Bullets whistled back across the canyon, the canyon quickly filling with loud echoes. The echoes jangled together; then boomed up and out. After a moment the bright spot behind the boulder moved; rose; became a man; and then became Harry leaping around a corner out of sight.

Queenie smiled. "I knew my Red Sash boys would come to the rescue."

Jesse got desperate. "Durn you, Queenie, Avery, play the game. If you'll just promise to leave the country, and stay out, I'll let you loose."

Even with the rope snug around her neck, Queenie laughed him bold in the face. "I know you now, Jesse. You really don't dare."

Avery asked quiet, "Have you got a warrant for our arrest, Jacklin?"

Jesse stomped around, black, almost beside himself. This wasn't going right atall. "Queenie, if you don't promise to leave the country, balls of fire, I'll just have to kill you. I hate to do it but I must."

Again Queenie laughed bold. "I know you, Jesse." She toddled her bosom at him. There wasn't the least trace of fear in her eyes or in her face.

It was finally too much for Mitch. He let go of the lines and jumped down to the ground. In a single leaning motion, with his sloping shoulders hunched high, he gave first Queenie a shove, then Avery.

Both lost their balance; twisted half-around. Then, with faces suddenly drawn taut in surprise, eyes shuttering wide, mouths sucking air, they fell backwards off the ledge; and down. The ropes snapped tight; two cries were suddenly choked off; two separate neck-popping sounds followed as of a giant cracking his knuckles.

"Holy suffering Jehoshaphat!" Jesse exclaimed.

The two bodies momentumed back and forth, slowly, above the gurgling stream. Both heads hung crooked, as if both Queenie and Avery were craning around to get a good look at something that could only be seen with the head bent to one side. Queenie's light green eyes and Avery's dark bulbous eyes slowly closed, dulled over sleepily.

"Holy snakes, Mitch, now you've gone and done it!" Jesse cried out. "You goddam fool you—that wasn't in the plan atall!"

Stalker and Spade and Ringbone cried out too. "Goddam!" All three dropped hands to their guns. But they didn't quite draw.

Mitch laughed, shrill. "Last time I saw Queenie she complained about how she'd got off on the wrong foot in life." Mitch laughed some more. "Haw. Look at her now. She ain't got no footing atall."

That very moment both of Queenie's moccasins slipped off her small feet and fell into the flowing water below. The moccasins floated down the tossing stream like toy canoes, unmanned, whirling around and around.

Cain

The last week in November and the first week in December were strangely hot. Warm winds soughed up from the south; mellow Chinooks poured over the low passes to the west. One afternoon it actually became eighty-one in the shade. For ten straight nights the temperature stayed above fifty. Ice in the stock tank melted. Frost came out of the ground. Snow on the lower slopes of the Big Stonies vanished. In a few places, on sandy knolls above the Shaken Grass, Cain even saw a few purple pasques show hairy dwarf flowers.

"Dummed funny weather," Cain muttered as he chopped wood for the winter ahead, "things've been upside down all year."

Around eleven one morning, while trying in vain to split the braided strands of a particularly tough cottonwood log, he heard a wagon come rattling down from Crimson Wall. He smacked the ax partway into the log and ran for his belt and gun on a nearby stump. Hurriedly he buckled it on. Then, looking around, he was startled to see that it was switchtail Clara Jager driving a pair of blacks. The blacks were lathered with sweat.

Something was up. Instead of the usual look of outrage pulling her face all out of shape, she now looked calm. Too calm. With his sleeve Cain wiped sweat from his hewn walnut face and walked toward her.

Clara hauled back on the lines with thin pale hands. "Hooa!" She pulled so hard she raised herself off the spring seat. "Hooa!" The blacks were going so fast they had trouble stopping.

Cain reached out a hand, slow, gradual, and caught the nearest black by the bit. "Whoa!" he commanded. They set down on all eight legs. With a clatter of chains the doubletree rose partway up over their rears. They stopped.

Cain stepped around the nearest black and tipped his hat. "Why, Clara, what can the matter be?"

Clara sat indrawn like a stunned mouse. Her skim-milk eyes whirled white, once; then hid behind red lids. Her rashy face was pale.

Cain gave her a steady calming look. "What's wrong up your way?"

Clara took a brown envelope out of the front of her dress and handed it to him. "Look in it," she said. Again her milk-blue eyes whirled once, furtively.

Cain took the brown package wonderingly. He saw her name and address written on the outside. He felt a lump inside. He glanced up at her again, in greatest delicacy, as if to say he didn't like reading other people's mail. But she nodded, once, for him to look anyway. So he did. At first he thought it but a dried half-pear. But then he saw the hole in the middle and felt the gristle and knew it for what it was. A human ear.

"Dencil's," he said, low, deadly quiet.

A convulsion almost exploded out of her face. She fought it back. She managed to nod, once.

Cain put the ear back in the brown package and returned it to her. "When did you get that?"

Clara tried to talk; couldn't; grimly held onto the lines.

Cain rolled down the sleeves of his black shirt. "Better try tellin' me about it, Clara."

Her teeth chattered. "And he ain't back yit."

Cain pitied her. That she still should expect him back. "Where'd he go, Clara?"

With a single hunching motion, Clara scootched herself forward on the spring seat. "Some men come for him a week ago."

"What!" Cain's smoke-blue eyes widened some. His legs set apart automatically. "Some men? Who?"

"I don't know. They come at dark. Just as we set down to supper."

Cain's head slowly thrust forward. Blood began to pulse with a clicking sound in his ears. "You didn't see them?"

"No." She swallowed. The swallow loosened her tongue. "There was a knock. Dencil went to answer it. I heard him talk in the dark with someone outside. There was three men but I heard only one talk. Then Dencil come back and said he had to go with them men. I said, 'What fer?' He said, 'They got a warrant for my arrest.' I said, 'What fer?' He said, 'It's all right, Clara. It's just a mistake of some kind. I think I better go along and get it straightened out before it gets worse.' I said, 'What fer, Dencil?' He said, 'Well, they claim I rustled some hosses from the Derby outfit.' I said, 'What? When just last week the earl himself drove up and bought a pair of trotters?' He said, 'That's just it, Clara. That's why I think it's just a mistake. I'll be back soon. Just you finish supper and put the kids to bed.' "

Cain's stub body slowly knotted up all over. "Then what?"

"He ain't back yit."

"That was a week ago, you say?"

"A week."

New sweat gathered on his heavy brow. He wiped it off on his other sleeve.

Clara said, "I warned him. The first time they come I told him he should quit horses. I warned him. I told him he should take that job at the livery stable."

"Clara—"

"But oh no. Not Dencil. He knew better. He always knew better. He had to be a big-time—"

"Clara—"

"—rancher. A big auger. Well, now he's murdered. Like I warned him."

"Now, Clara—"

"Murdered." She sat small, indrawn, quivering as if she had the knotted ague. "Murdered."

"Where'd you leave the little tykes?"

"Home. I locked them all up in the bedroom. With the new dog we got."

"Good." Cain hitched up his pants. His left hand settled around the blue butt of his .45, lightly, experimentally, "Clara, I want you to listen close now. I want you to turn right around and go back to your tykes."

191

"But Dencil—"

Cain held up a hand. "Wait. Wait. Meantime I got a hoss up in the corral. I'll go rustle up some help and we'll go hunt him up. And, Clara, look. If there is any righting to be done, we'll do it. It ain't much comfort to ye mabbe to say that, but at least it's somethin' to take with you." Cain looked down at the ground; slowly shook his head. "I can't see Jesse orderin' this one though. Jesse knew Dencil was honest. As honest as the day was long."

"Dencil is dead," Clara said.

Once again Cain and Dale rode up the canyon of the Shaken Grass, this time just the two of them, Cain on Bucky the dun horse and Dale on Lonesome the black horse. They rode through where the Shaken Grass parted the Crimson Wall; trotted across a low swell of red land; racked past Dencil Jager's ranch buildings. Clara had beat them home. Cain saw her in the single window and waved to her. Her wagon stood in the middle of the dry yard, empty and horseless, tongue down and doubletree hanging, all of it waiting, once again slowly weathering into gray.

Behind the stable they found a few tracks, three horses coming, four going. The tracks were old, almost erased in places, erased not so much by wind or rain, or even distending and contracting frost, as by slow relentless myriad diffusion, particle by particle. They found the tracks more by guess than by sight.

Cain climbed down and knelt beside one of the clearer tracks. "Odd shoe work."

Dale hadn't much to say. "What's the matter with it?"

"Wal, 'tain't a Derby shoe. Jesse's blacksmith makes his caulks three-cornered. And 'tain't Governor Barb's outfit neither. Nor Senator Thorne's."

Dale grunted. He leaned his arms on the pommel of his saddle.

"Looks more like the caulks Timberline makes."

"Naw."

"That's a fact. Except it's a little too pointed. Too much like a spear point. Instead've a blunt round point with a kind of a mouse tit on the end of it to keep it sharp."

"How can you tell so close after two weeks?"

"That's just it. If these caulk holes showed less point after two weeks I'd agree. But they don't."

Dale grunted.

Cain searched around for more sign. Finally, when he

192

couldn't find any, he climbed into his saddle again. He glanced across at his brother. "Say, what are you mumpish about?"

Dale made a face. His fish mouth drew back at the corners, showing teeth tips.

"Personal, I'd be riding on clouds if I had me two colt boys." Dale ganted a breath.

"You got a hard for me again, Dale?"

"No."

"Wal, what are you mumpish about then? Forgettin' Dencil for the minute, that is."

"Oh, I guess maybe it's just that I got me a headache built for a hoss this morning."

"Drinking?"

"No."

"What then?"

Dale hauled back head and shoulder. He swallowed loudly. "Oh, I guess it's just that I'm tired of this country at last."

"Oh? How so?"

"Cain, a man never answers a knock on his door any more without he has to have a gun in hand. If that's God's country, I'll eat it."

Cain cocked his head at his brother. "You still afraid that Alias Hunt fellow will get you?"

"Cain, I say it's come to a terrible time when men we've known all our lives can ride up to our door and grab us and hang us from the nearest tree without fear of the law. We can elect as sheriff all the Ned Sines we want to, but it don't seem to do us much good."

"Hah. You've had another fight with Rosemary."

Dale's eyes wouldn't hold up to his. "Oh, it ain't that." As if to rid himself of a mask he'd been wearing too long, Dale bruised a hard hand down over his face, starting at his brow and ending at his chin. "Cain, I say hell has come to earth when men known to us all can hang a woman and never stand trial for it. Yeh, and her husband with her."

"Now, Dale. Steady there."

"When men known to us ever since we was kids can change their name and get in behind the law and take potshots at us. Rory is right, we shouldn't wait. We should kill such on sight and not wait until we have to shoot in self-defense."

"Hah! You did have a fight with Rory then."

Dale stared out across the red valley. Slowly his face grayed over. "Dencil is dead," Dale said.

They searched for miles around. Up dry coulees. Down wet draws. Along cross-canyons. All across the Crimson Wall

193

country. Every tall tree became suspect. Still they couldn't find Dencil.

The third day out, around one o'clock, getting hungry, Cain suggested they ride up a draw where it cut high into the side of a hogback. A few chokecherry trees, now leafless, grew at the head of the draw and under them waved thick masses of rusty grass. The head of the draw would make a good place to stake out the horses, while they themselves could sit on the hogback above, eating and looking.

While Dale scratched for dry wood in the draw, Cain took over the horses. He tied Lonesome and Bucky each to the end of a catch rope, slipped off their bridles and saddles, and let them roll in the dry grass and red dust. In examining their soaked saddle blankets, he found a wet hair-fringed spot on the underside of Lonesome's padding. He smelled it. Pus. He went over and examined Lonesome and found a small sore in the black hair just over the spine. He felt around it carefully. There was no bump under the skin so it couldn't be a grub in the hide. Nor did it look like a bite by Bucky. Cain spread Lonesome's blanket over the top of a small wolfberry bush to let it air out in the sun. After thinking about the sore spot some more, Cain decided Dale had ridden with a loosely cinched saddle. Dale had been fooled by the way Lonesome always swelled up his belly the moment a saddle touched his back.

Dale got a small fire started and soon had the coffee boiling and the bacon searing. Dale still had a few of Rory's biscuits left over in his saddlebag, two each, and he set them out on a tin plate. Both Cain and Dale fell to wordlessly. There was only the occasional pop of a working jaw. The sun shone warm on them. There were no midges to swipe at. The mountains waited above them, serene, holding high and white.

After wiping the pans and tin plates with a rag, and shaking the tin cups dry, Cain broke the silence. "It's so danged peaceable around here, I got half a mind to help myself to some shut-eye."

Dale sat on his heels, glum, staring down at the red country below.

"Lonesome's sore back could stand the rest too. And his blanket could stand a dry."

Dale's lips moved. But there was no sound. He turned on his heels, still squatting, and looked across toward the blood-raw cliffs of Crimson Wall.

"We can ride late tonight before camping. Be cooler for both hosses and us."

Dale let go then. He worked his mouth at Cain as if to cut him with his teeth. "It's crazy, I tell ee. It's wrong. All wrong."

"What is?"

"Everything." Dale waved a long hook-ended arm. "The weather, hot like this. The law, with Hunt part of it. Women, asking for revenge. Everything." A high haunted look passed over Dale's face. "Why, you dassent even laugh to yourself miles away from anybody any more." Dale's lips thinned back; his teeth worked.

"Go on."

"And then there's our sheriff we elected. Ned Sine. Why hain't Ned arrested somebody for the murder of Queenie and Avery? Hah?"

"Maybe Ned couldn't find any witnesses or evidence so he could prosecute."

"Aw, hell, Cain, I'm afraid our Ned is in with Jesse and his boys by now. Bought over."

"Well, you know he did question everybody in the valley about it. And he pushed himself too, doin' it."

"Cain, you know very well he ain't man enough to do the job. Now don't you?"

"The trouble was, nobody would talk."

"That's just it," Dale cried. "Everybody's too scared to talk. Cain, it's gettin' so people don't even go to the law any more when they get in trouble. Like Clara. She came to you, not the sheriff."

"Soon as we find out what happened to Dencil, we'll make it a point to notify the sheriff," Cain said, grim.

"But we should a done it in the first place, Cain, don't you see? We should be helpin' him find Dencil as part of a posse. Instead a doin' it on our own."

"Wal, I guess you're right at that."

"Cain, even if we do find Dencil, and then tell the sheriff about it, what can the sheriff do? Who can he arrest? Because they won't be any witnesses this time either."

Cain fell silent.

Dale nodded sadly. "Yeh, I can just see Ned Sine writing in his little book. 'Dencil Jager came to his death by parties unknown to the jury.'"

"Now, now, Dale."

"Cain, I'm getting out of this country. Whether Rory wants to go along or not."

"Where will you go to?"

"Back to Siouxland. At least there they hang you legal."

"Dale, you got dyin' on the brain."

Dale picked up a red stone and threw it into the bushes below. The fall of the stone startled both horses. Their heads came up with a jerk, ears pricking back and forth. When nothing further happened, they went back to cropping rusty grass.

Dale said, "And always ridin' that dummed black hoss ain't helpin' my luck either."

"By golly now, Dale, black or buckskin or bay, what's the color of a hoss's hair to do with luck? A good hoss is a good hoss."

"That ain't what Harry says about a black hoss."

Cain looked at his brother's suffering eyes. "Dale, why don't you go off and end it all somewhere? If that's your mind."

"Cain, I've often thought of doin' just that. It would save Hunt Lawton from having to shoot me in the back. And Rory could then bother you about getting revenge for us Hammetts."

At that, Cain shut up.

The gloomy talk with Dale chased sleep away. Looking around, Cain spotted behind them, some three hundred yards back, a small red butte sticking up out of the hump of the hogback. Without a word to Dale, he got up and slowly sauntered over to the foot of the red teat. It was some fifty feet high. He looked it up and down. He saw he could climb it without much trouble and get an even better view of the country.

Puffing, sweating some, he made it up. He sat down, and rolled and lighted himself a cigarette. He took off his boots. He wiggled his toes and straightened out his tan cotton socks. He lazed back against a small red boulder. He let his eyes rove, taking in the grand sights. He narrowed his eyes up at the glinting white peaks to the west; let in the light again when looking down at the raw red wall to the east.

An hour later, as he was finishing his third cigarette, his eyes caught movement far away and below, some three miles to the north and along the mountain stream where he and the boys had cut their cattle right out from under the noses of Jesse and his armed band of toughs. Cain tipped his hat down over his piercing eyes and made peepholes of his hands. Then he saw what it was: a couple of buzzards circling a cottonwood tree, the very tree under which they'd eaten of Hambone's grub. Studying it some more, Cain thought he could make out still other buzzards flapping near the ground.

"Old Hambone sure must have thrown out a mess of leftovers if they're still scavenging that place," he muttered to himself. "He probably had a mad on after that night and went out of his way to be extra careless with Lord Peter's property. Cooks is an awful touchy kind of critter. An Almighty in human flesh if there ever was one. Not to forget Christ of course."

Cain looked up at the sun. "Hey, time is runnin' out the bottom end. We better roll again." Setting his heels deep in the soft dirt, with pink stones rolling down ahead of him, he stomped down the little red butte.

He found his brother Dale still moping to himself, writing doodles in the ground, working at it almost harshly, as if in a fret just how to shape a last will and testament upon the very earth itself.

"We best go, Dale," Cain said. "We're burning daylight."

"Yeh, guess we better."

Cain found Lonesome's blanket dry. He broke off a handful of leafless little twigs and gave the black horse a brushdown to get rid of the light powdery red dirt it had picked up while rolling with a wet hide. He also brushed off Bucky. When they saddled up, he made sure that this time Lonesome got his saddle on tight despite his ornery trick of puffing out his belly.

They headed toward Hidden Country where brother Harry and Timberline lived. They rode along in silence.

A half mile, and Cain abruptly reined in. "Hell's fire and little fishes! How blind can a man get! Looking it right in the eye and still not see it."

"What?" Dale sat sagged forward in his saddle.

"That was two months ago when we ate Hambone's grub under that cottonwood. Them leftovers wouldn't't've lasted them buzzards that long. Dale, I think we've found him."

"Dencil?"

"Dencil."

"Oh."

"Come on." Cain turned Bucky around and touched him lightly with his spurs. Bucky gathered legs under him and took off as if shot from a chute. Dale followed at a slower pace.

As Cain approached the cottonwood, the buzzards circling in the air above it climbed a rung higher, squawking, while those flopping on the ground scattered into the bushes upstream. Something was hanging under the tree, all right, and from the highest and fattest limb too. Bucky snorted at the terrible smell, so did Lonesome, and both refused to go in

197

close. Both Cain and Dale finally had to climb down and tie the horses to a bush near the stream a good hundred yards away and down wind.

Coming close, they saw the body clearly. It was Dencil Jager. Hung by the neck until dead. Head craned around sharply sideways. Ears missing. Eyes pecked out and nose sheared off by the buzzards. Shirt ripped off by the vultures. Body already badly decomposed. Green bottleflies buzzing around in clouds. Wide black mustache just beginning to slide off the face. Right leg separated from the body and fallen out of pant leg and on the ground, lower end still booted and upper end eaten away. Black dripping out of open hip socket from which it had fallen.

Dale looked at it all for a couple of seconds, then ran for the stream, gushing gray as he went.

Cain quick got up Clara Jager's wagon and brought a big store box. He found it impossible to handle what was left of Dencil, so he placed the box directly under the body and cut the rope and let it fall in. He picked up the leg with a scoop and put that in the box too.

Just before he closed the box, Cain noted a curious thing. The whole chest of the man, about eighteen inches square and including the vestigial teats, had been skinned away. He saw knife cuts, not the slashes of buzzards' beaks, along the outer edges of the raw area. Also, the corners were square. Cain stared at the marks. He had trouble believing someone hated Dencil enough to want to make leather out of his hide.

Then, sure that the vultures couldn't further molest the body, Cain rode hard for the sheriff. As he rode, a few words from the Good Book came to mind: "My God, my God, why hast thou forsaken me? Why art thou so far from helping me, from the words of my roaring? But I am a worm, and no man. I am poured out like water. All my bones are out of joint. My heart is like wax. It is melted in the midst of my bowels. My strength is dried up like a potsherd. Thou hast brought me into the dust of death."

Dale

Late in December, a cold snap came down from Canada and pushed the unusual warm weather out of the country. Dale, reading the signs, decided that before heavy winter set in he'd better make a last trip into Antelope for supplies. Early one morning, long before dawn, he hitched the matched bays onto the box wagon, put on his heavy winter coat with its beaver collar and cuffs, and headed north. He drove steady and got into town late that same night. The next morning, also very early, he bought two dozen sacks of grain for the horses, a dozen big boxes of groceries, and, because Christmas was only a few days away, several packages of toys for Joey and rattles for baby Cain. Dale also bought Rory a present, a potted pink begonia, something she could fuss with during the long white months ahead. He hoped the begonia would help her get over her mad. He was willing to forget that someone else might have fathered Joey if she would forget that he still hadn't shot down Hunt. The wagon was mounding full.

He finished making his last call in town right after the noon meal. It was still snappish out, despite the clear sun, and he decided a shot of rye would be just the thing before beginning the long ride home.

A sight of mustached men were boiling around inside Butcherknife Bain's saloon: new settlers just come in from the States trying to get acquainted the quick way, chuck-line riders from Montana looking for a winter nest, range bums from the Dakotas trying to sponge drinks. Looking them all over Dale couldn't find a face he knew. Everyone was a stranger. The wool-hat people with their plows and kids were really moving into the valley at last.

He drank alone, at the far end of the bar, near a door going off to a back room where men sometimes played poker. He listened to the roaring talk. It was easy to see that most had been drinking hard.

"I tell ee," one old bearded cowhand next to him orated, "middlin' folk can't survive in this country. You've got to be good at whatever you are. Good good or good bad. And you either get better at it, or you get worse—fast."

"The God religion is played out in this part of the world," another bearded puncher roared. "All that's left around here is a man's word and a steady hand."

"So there I sat, helljuice running out of my mouth with all the while a preacher sitting across the table from me takin' it in."

"Well, a preacher can kiss my foot and go you-know-where. Anytime."

A big pot-bellied stove, red with heat, roared in the middle of the whisky mill. The air inside the saloon was full of strong odors: fumes of raw whisky, melting horse manure caught under boot heels, soft new sawdust, steaming acrid

199

sweat in the armpits of old coats, tobacco quids squishing underfoot, body smells all the way from tar soap to nicotine. Tolerating it all on the sober side of the bar, a scowling smile holding up his mustache, was big bald Butcherknife Bain. As always he was wearing the usual striped white shirt and leather apron, and also as always he was pocketing money hand-over-fist into the voluminous folds of his baggy gray pants.

Dale had a foot up on the brass rail. His elbow rested on the bar. He mulled over his troubles to himself. There was that dummed Hunt fellow still in the country. There was that Rory who still had not let him touch her. There was that confession of hers that Joey wasn't his boy. There was Dencil's terrible end. And there was that business as to who Joey's father really was. Cain? Harry? Probably Cain, since Rory had never really got over him. That was probably why she'd named the second peckersnap after him. Dog-nab it, what a sad life it was. It made a man feel as lonesome as a lone stud on a butte. "Right now," he muttered to himself, "right now, not having had a drink or a kiss for a couple of months, I kin say I never yet tasted bad rye or saw an ugly woman."

He had another drink. And drinking, began to wonder if beating Rory wasn't the answer. Better yet, a licking over the knee, even if she was as strong as a bobcat. What in Goshen had got into the woman? Dale whacked the bottom of his glass on the bar. Blast that Cain anyway for having addled her heart in the first place. Yes, it was probably Cain who done it.

Still another drink and Dale knew he could lick her even if she was two bobcats. He was a man. Y'u durn right. Her secret strength lay in that short-choked Hammett neck of hers. If a man could somehow get around that, say maybe get a scissorbill hold on her belly and get one of her arms crooked up around behind her back, high, maybe a man could get her to say uncle. Yeh, and maybe in the wrestling around she'd get worked up some and come around to seeing it his way. Yeh. It had happened before. A wrestle worked about the same way on a woman as a backrub.

Butcherknife stopped for a word. "You dyin' off here, Dale?"

"Just mopin' to myself a little."

"How's she down your way?"

"Boiling,"

"Well, it's boiling all over the valley, let me tell you."

200

Dale looked at the crowd jammed tight against the bar and around the tables behind them. "I can see that."

"Well, Dale, you fellows figured out yet who red out Dencil?"

"Got a pretty good idee."

"Who?"

"Same ones as tried to kill Cain and Harry in their beds back in the hills," Dale said. "Hunt and Mitch. And two others."

"Has Cain and Harry reported it to Sheriff Sine yet?"

"Sure. But he's too scared to move, even if we did elect him in. Says there ain't enough evidence to make out a warrant for their arrest."

"Not even with that gun Cain found with the initial L on it?"

"Oh, so you know about that there too?"

Butcherknife was about to reply, when he caught sight of someone behind Dale. He winked, quick, at Dale.

But Dale, studying the amber fluid in the bottom of his glass, missed the warning. Dale said, "Shooting people in the back, trying to kill people in their beds, ganging up on lone men and hanging them, scaring the wits out of women and children—I call that low coward's work."

Again Butcherknife tried to warn him with a wink.

And once more Dale missed the signal. He was in a sod-pawing mood for fair. "Why, not even the worst of the Red Sashers has ever stooped to that kind of stuff. When they want a man out of the way, they give him fair chance. They come at him from the front side and give him a chance at his chips. In self-defense. While this Link Keeler that now calls hisself Hunt Lawton, that snake-in-the-grass coward, he brags about shootin' people in the back."

"Dale—"

"Don't tell me. He shot Gramp Hammett in the back. He drygulched our dads, Gordon and Raymond Hammett. Oh, that Hunt is a sly one all right, making hisself a peace officer and then as the law getting his revenge legal, the cowardly murdering wall-eyed bustard. I tell ye, Butcherknife, he's as yellow as mustard without the bite." Dale's gaunt head shot forward off his long neck so sudden that some of his black hair escaped from under his hat and fell across his eyes. "I begged him to draw on me once. Last fall right there across the street in Fat Homer's store."

"Dale—"

"And I don't care if anybody's listening to me neither. No,

201

I say, shooting people in the back, drygulchin' 'em, that's the lowest of all cowardly work."

"Dale—"

"The blood of a snake runs in his veins. Why, he's so mean he has to sneak up on the dipper to get hisself a drink of water."

Butcherknife finally gave up. His gray eyes fell, he made a swipe or two more at the bar with his rag, and then without another word slunk away.

"The cowardly bustard. Rory was right. I should a killed him on sight that fust time. There at Fat Homer's. That was a mistake all right."

Dale was working on yet another drink, and getting madder by the minute, at the whole rotten world, when, through the roaring in his head as well as the roaring in the saloon, he heard behind him, in the poker room, a light high voice. The voice bothered him; pulled at him. He cocked his ear. The next thing, he heard his name mentioned. Then he really became all ears. Slowly he set down his glass. Slowly his haunted eyes opened as he turned around. Standing just inside the door to the poker room was Hunt. He was talking to Jesse.

Hunt stood with his back to Dale. "Jesse, if you think that lamb-licker needs killin', killin' he will get. I'll hand that snoozer a deadhead ticket to hell. Direct."

Jesse stood sideways to Dale, favoring his game leg. "He needs it all right. Along with his brothers and all the rest of them thieves." Jesse flexed his bad leg. "Hunt, I want you to make sure about one thing, though. Make him draw on you. Before witnesses in the right place. Our side wants to keep it legal."

Hunt said, "So he complains about some people getting shot in the back, does he? Why! That's all he and his bunch deserves. You shoot a rattler in the back when it lays on the ground, don't you? Well, he don't deserve any better."

"Hunt, I'm sure glad you ain't got it in for me."

"Well, Jesse, it is a long story and it goes back a long ways. Someday I'll tell you about it."

Dale thought: "This time he ain't going to get away. And then I kin go home to Rory and get her back from Cain, Joey or no Joey."

Dale dropped his hand on his gun inside his overcoat; softly cocked it; whipped around and drew.

But Link alias Hunt was gone. So was high-headed Jesse.

It was Butcherknife who recalled Dale to himself. Butcherknife had been watching. "Why, Dale, what made you skin your gun? Don't you like my saloon?" Butcher gave him a grave wink with his offside eye, the one away from the crowd of bowlegs at the bar.

Dale saw all eyes along the bar on him. Slowly he put his gun away. He swallowed. It seemed to him the click in his throat popped loud enough to be a pistol shot. He mumbled, "Guess I was just seein' if my gun was still there."

A bit later, after a final drink, Dale asked, "Butcherknife, tell me, where did them two disappear to? Or did I dream them in the fust place?"

"Oh, they were there all right. No, I tell you, Jesse heard you cock the gun and he grabbed Hunt by the arm and they beat it out the back way."

Dale shook his head. "And here I thought I done it soft-like."

Butcherknife whispered under his handlebar mustache. "Maybe somebody has good guilty ears."

When Dale stepped outside, he found the sky all scudded over with rolling wool. He slipped on his heavy gloves and pulled up his fur collar. He untied the bays from the hitching rail, climbed onto the spring seat, backed the horses, then clucked them down the main drag. He shivered.

He had just driven past the livery stable at the edge of town, rolling some with the load of provisions and Christmas gifts, when a woman darted out of a tar-paper shack and came running toward him, skirts lifted for easier going and shawl ends flying.

"Oh, Dale Hammett! Yoohoo! Yoohoo!"

He hauled up on the lines. "Whoa, boys, whoa."

"Dale?" The woman waved her hand at him. The rings on her left ring finger jiggled round and round. "Yoohoo!"

He looked down at the woman. "Why, Clara Jager, it's you, is it?"

"Dale?" Clara's eyes were so screwed up into tight little gimlets the pale-milk color in them became near-blue. "Dale?"

He saw right away that poor Clara was worse addled than ever. Them devils killing Dencil had really knocked her off her rocker. "Yes, Clara, what it is?"

"Will you be seeing your brother Harry on the way home?"

"I might."

"Will you tell him for me that my children thank him kindly?"

"Why, Clara, I sure will. But what for?"

"Tell him we're all beholden to him for the meat and the clothes and all that his boys brung me."

Dale stared down at her. So that crazy Harry had been around showering gifts on the poor again. You just never knew what he'd be up to next. That crazy bustard.

Yes, and that was exactly why the poor folk and the little stockmen in the valley were beholden to him, why they found it hard to take sides against him and his Red Sash gang when doing jury duty. Harry was the Robin Hood of the West, robbing the rich and giving to the poor. It was hardly a wonder that the dummy candidate for sheriff the big augers put up in the last election lost to little stockman Ned Sine, helpless as Ned might be.

Dale slowly wagged his head. He said, more to himself than to her, "What a sly devil he is. First he keeps Jesse's boys from rimrocking your sheep. Then, just as you feel properly thoughtful about it, he turns around and asks you to sell his beef for him to the railroad crews. He's got all us honest duffers in a bind. Even Cain. So what happens? Jesse and all them big augers lump us all together and call us thieves. Including our sheriff."

"We're beholden to him," Clara repeated.

He blinked. "Yes, Clara. Sure." He looked down at her. She looked so pathetic, so beaten down, so broken-winged if not broken-willed, that tears began to sprinkle down his weathered hollow cheeks. He tried winking them away; couldn't; finally had to wipe them off in his fur collar. "I'll tell Harry," he said. "I'll be sure to."

"We can make the winter now," Clara said. "I'm going to sew hard for some extra money and maybe by next spring we can go back to the States."

"I hope you can, Clara, I hope you can."

"Beholden."

" 'Bye."

" 'Bye."

Dale drove along. He nodded to himself under his broad-brim hat, mulling things over, burping fumes and so enjoying the rye once more, shaking his head at all the strange doublings in the trail of life.

The afternoon faded. The north wind got colder. The sky became darker. Luckily he was driving south and had the wind at his back. By keeping the fur collar well up around his neck and his hat down, and taking turns driving with either hand, warming one inside his overcoat while the other held the lines, he managed to stay fairly warm. Occasionally a

204

flake of snow wisped past, hitting the ground and sticking, until in some of the frozen draws the gray sage took on a strange hoary aspect, from one side a silvered white and from the other a whitened silver. Flakes fell on the rumps of the bays too. Sometimes the wind whipped them off; sometimes they slowly melted and vanished into dusty hair roots. Gradually the backs and rumps of the bays darkened over with damp.

"All them settlers there at Butcherknife's . . . dreaming of the great days to come . . . what they don't know, if they want to stay alive in this valley, is that they better cut their windows high in the ranch house or someone is liable to shoot them down in the night. In bed or sitting on the pot."

The bays trotted along smartly. The trace chains jingled musically.

"Poor devils. The government is betting them one hundred sixty acres they won't live on it eight months." He nodded inside his fur collar, his hat flopping in the wind. "Well, it looks like the valley will be full of deserted ranches in time to come. Dried coffee grounds on the stove and the bed empty."

The trail fell away ahead. The bays picked up speed as they went through the dip. Just as they hit the bridge, a short wooden affair built of cedar logs and bolts, the bay on the right pricked up his ears and whinnied, once, as if to a friend horse somewhere up the draw out of sight around a corner. Dale hardly noticed it. The bay whinnied once more and then both horses plunged up the other side of the dip, the dragging weight of the heavy wagon once again taking up the slack in the rattling chain tugs. Both bays breasted into the sudden weight with spirit.

Dale had just changed hands on the lines, had just got the cold hand well inside the warm overcoat, when a rifle whoofed behind him, and something, a thing like a small twig, caught at his overcoat on the left in back. It was more like a tick than a blow. He looked down at the new round rent in his black coat even as his chilled hand reached for his gun. Letting the lines go, he instinctively tried to roll forward and down into the front part of the wagon box. The horses, already going at a good clip, doubled into it. But his cold hand in its stiff glove was too slow, and he knew it. He knew too Link alias Hunt had cached himself under the small bridge, had raised and shot at him after he passed by, that it was Hunt's horse his bay had whinnied at.

"I knew it," Dale said aloud.

The second bullet caught him in the middle of the back, well up. It shoved him forward a second, and then, as the suddenly loose horses began to gallop wildly, the wagon caught up with him and he toppled over backward.

"I knew it," he gurgled aloud again. "But little good it does me now."

One of the lines caught under the broad iron rim of the right front wheel. There was a vicious jerk and the bays veered sharply to the right. They turned a half-circle and plunged into the draw with the wagon cracking after. The horses and the wagon came to a stop in a narrow part of the draw where the turn was choked with red willows.

Two more shots whoofed under the low sky. Then the kicking hooves of the bays stilled too.

Dale lay back, blood spilling slowly, trickling, over the Christmas packages, over the toys for Joey and the rattles for baby Cain and the potted pink begonia for Rosemary. Dale's haunt eyes, wide open, stared up at the gray snow-sprinkling skies; gradually dulled over.

Cain

Cain said to himself: "I will not think of it."

Cain rode up to Rory's door and got off Lonesome and went to the door and knocked.

"Who's there?" a quivering leathery voice called out.

"Open up, Gram. It's Cain."

"We don't know any Openhammetts."

"It's me. Cain. Open up."

"They killed my husband Mabry and my sons Gordon and Raymond and my grandson Dale," Gram's ancient voice keened, "and now I suppose it's to be my baby greatsons next."

Cain tried the door; found it barricaded on the inside. "Rory? Joey? You there? Open up. You don't need to be afraid. It's just Cain. I'm alone."

Gram wailed on. "I suppose we might's well get killed one time as another. You'll get us anyway." Gram began removing the cordwood barricade, heavy piece by heavy piece. After a bit the door opened and bowed white Gram, tears twinkling on wrinkled kidskin face, stood shivering in the blasting January wind. "Shot at. Killed off one at a time. And still no sheriff at the door to arrest the killers. Nothing is done to protect us."

Cain placed a gloved hand on her shoulder and turned her about and gently pushed her inside. He closed the door after them. Warmth from the blazing fire in the hearth breathed over him. It was good to get in out of the terrible cold. He kept his hand on Gram's shoulder and shook her, gently, respectfully. "Now, Gram, now, Gram, it's only me. Cain."

"No one left to avenge our shame. No one. All my grown men killed."

"Gram."

"I've asked my Lord to take me, receive me, but now I suppose He'll hardly let me live long enough to see my great-sons avenge our shame." Gram stood shaking under his hand. Coarse wisps of horsetail hair brushed the back of his wrist. "They mean to wipe out the Hammett name."

Cain heard a noise in the lean-to. "Rory?" he called.

There was more noise, a scrambling and a heavy thump as of someone removing yet another barricade. Then the door opened. The black barrel hole of Dale's old Sharps rifle showed first. A pair of very grave blue eyes looking steadily from under a throw of gold hair followed.

"Joey!"

"We thought you was a Derby rider, Unk, come to wipe us out to the last man." Joey came forward, still carrying the old heavy rifle at ready.

Cain quick glanced at the mantel over the hearth; saw where the lad had dragged up a chair and got down the gun. Cain's eye went back to the old gun. Lucky for the boy he hadn't fired it. The Sharps would have kicked him out of the county. Cain said, calm as he could, "Where's your mom?"

"She went to get you. Gram heard yestiddy they was coming for us next. We hain't slept all night."

"I see." Cain pushed back his black hat. Shadows moved in the fore dents of his hat as well as in the hollows of his cheeks. "I just now come back from town, so Rory'll have missed me. How long has she been gone?"

"About an hour."

"She walk over?"

"What else? They killed Paw's horses too, you know. Them drygulchin' devils." Joey set the gun on the puncheon floor, stock down. His face was blue from anxious watching. "Boy, Unk, it's a good thing you hollered out. I was all set to let the lead fly. Nobody was going to get me and Baby and drown us. We got work to do when we grow up."

Cain held the boy's eye steady in his. He saw there was already more manhood in the lad than there'd ever been in Dale.

It was Hammett blood by way of Rory plus some by Dale making the man in him.

"Gram kept sayin' that we was their next move. Like they done in Bible times."

Cain's belly knotted up under his cartridge belt. He had trouble breathing. He loosened his leather jacket and took off his gloves and stuffed them in a pocket. Then he settled on his heels and put an arm around the thick-necked towhead and hugged him. "What a wild-eyed tough waddy you're gonna be someday."

Joey drew back, gently, with fine childish delicacy. "I dunno about that now, Unk. I'm afraid I ain't much tougher than baby Cain. I filled my pants too a little when I first heard you come riding up."

A laugh burst from Cain, ripped through the middle of his tears, shaking drops from his mustache like a dog wringing its hide after a dip. "Oh, come now, Joey. I don't smell nothing."

"You're just being perlite, Unk." Joey gave him an adult shake of the head. "Oh, Ma's told me all about you. Too good for your own good. Wouldn't say son-of-a-bitch if you was to see one come out from under the Devil's tail itself."

"What!"

Gram hitched old knobs across a bear rug and touched him on the shoulder. "Are you Cain my grandson then?"

Cain stood up. "Why, Gram, don't you know me?" Cain saw something pass across her old gray eyes, a thing like a shade. Cain thought: "Ah, she's gone blind. That last killin' must have snapped something in her."

"Ijam? We don't know any Ijams."

Cain thought: "And she's gone deaf some too."

Cain leaned down, gently, respectfully, and yet with a ringing voice tried to reach her mind, far back as it might have retreated behind ruggled brow. "I'm Cain all right," he said, pointing to himself. "Cain Hammett."

A laugh rasped up from her old lungs. "Why now, 'y Johnny-god how times does fly. Ye've grown."

Joey still held the gun stock down on the rough board floor. "Don't mind her, Unk. Lately she's had rats in the attic."

Gram tugged gently at Cain's leather sleeve, catching it between gnarled thumb and forefinger. "Cain, you will take this shame away from us? My husband Mabry will never forgive us if we don't remove this blot from our name. It's four of our men now."

Cain caught her crooked hand in his. "Sure we will, Gram. Don't you worry about it now."

"They've killed off all my menfolks and I have no one to help me protect my baby greatsons."

Cain looked around at the door of the lean-to. "By the way, Joey, how is my namesake getting along? The little weaner."

"Shhh." Joey quick held up his hand. "He's sleeping. The pore innercent thing."

"Ah. Good. He's best off asleep." Cain tiptoed over and softly closed the door.

"I left him warm and covered up. Though he's wet again," Joey said.

"Yes," Cain said, "I know. I just now got a whiff of him."

Joey lowered his blue eyes. "Maybe it was just me."

"No, Joey, it was the baby."

"I'm glad you're perlite to think so, Unk."

Cain's walnut face blackened over. "This is a terrible thing they've done here," he muttered to himself. "Terrible."

Steps sounded outside on the frozen ground; crunched on the log stoop.

Quick as thought both Cain and Joey had their guns ready.

"Who's there?" Cain called, sharp, cocking his .45 and setting himself so that he'd be the first to get shot if there was to be a shooting bee.

The door pushed open.

"Rory!"

"Mom!"

Rory's face threw open like a hand hit from behind. "Creation alive!" she gasped. She closed the log door and leaned against it. "You almost scared the wits out of me! All them guns." Her dark eyes flared wide with deep flooding blue.

Joey said, "Doggone it, Maw, next time answer when you're spoke to, will you? Cain and me like to shot you down. These days a man never knows what kind of mean saddlestiff is at the door."

She looked at Cain. "You're here," she whispered. "Cain."

She had been grieving, was pale from it, and it became her. All spraddled out in her best duds—blue shawl cowled close around blond head and long black velvet coat pulled close around her sloping waist and black kid shoes snug on trim feet and fluffy muff carried in one hand—she looked like the grandest woman in the world.

Cain thought: "She's changed. With the baby born she's slim again. Almost as pretty as the grass-finished Rosemary I once tried to kiss. A beautiful widow."

Gravely, courteously, he took off his black hat.

Again with pain he remembered the mean words she'd once said to him, that time he took her home a year after killing her boy friend Cecil Guth: "One night you set and say, yes mam, no mam, and look like a stuffed owl. The next night you drink up all of Gramp's whisky and make love like a horse. Lord knows what next to expect from you. Cain, if you can't remember I'm a lady, there's the door. Besides, and don't forget it, I'm your full cousin."

He suppressed a groan and turned away from her. He thought: "I will not think of it."

She swept forward to where the orange-tipped fire burned warm in the fieldstone hearth. She slipped out of her velvet coat and blue shawl. "My, it's cold!" she said. "I near froze to death. I was already bad off when I got to your cabin. And then I had to come all the way back." She stood before him in long purple velvet with white frills at the neckline and wrists. She was pale, drawn, shivering. Yet there was also the air about her of one who at last had been relieved of a burden, and was glad of it.

Joey leaned the old Sharps against the stone hearth. "Maw—"

"Hey, there, Joe boy," Cain broke in, "I don't think I'd set that old cannon so close to the fire. It just might let go. I'd set it behind the door there."

Joey threw him a look. "You bossin' me around, Unk?"

"No. Just trying to uncle you a little, son."

"That's all right then." Joey set the gun down easy behind the door. Again Joey turned to Rory. "Maw, is it all right if I go to my room now?"

"Is Baby still asleep?"

"I won't wake him."

"Well, all right."

"Well, if you don't want me to go in there, don't blame me if your nose raises a fuss."

"Why, what's wrong with you?"

Cain said, managing to keep a straight face, "I still don't believe it."

"Thanks, Unk. But I better change pants anyway. I'm closer to it than you." Joey sidled into the lean-to and closed the door behind him.

Gram sat down in her black rocker in her corner by the fire. "I don't know what's wrong with me these days. I just seem to be rotting off at the ends. Last summer, when I was ready to go to Mabry and my Lord, He wouldn't take me.

Now, when I'm not ready, He all of a sudden seems to want me."

Cain said, "Gram, you know you'll be around a long while yet."

Gram pulled a woolen sock off her left foot. A thick bandage came with it. "Rotting off at the ends. Yes. Leakage of the toe." Her big toe was swollen and as gray as a lump of suet, with the old ribbed nail lifted askew. With each beat of her old heart watery yellow pus slowly pulsed from under it. There was a sudden stench in the room, and it was strong, as bad as very old fly-specked swill. "Leakage of the toe," she murmured. "Tried everything for it. Mabry my husband told me in a dream th'other night I should soak it in a sack of fresh cow mustard to dry it out. But all we got around here is ewe stink."

Joey came back out of the lean-to. His face was round with surprise. That's sure funny, Unk. My pants was as fresh as a June daisy. Must've just passed some dewy wind instid." Then Joey suddenly grabbed his nose and his eyes half-closed. "There it is again," he said with a hairlip's nasal sound.

"Joey," Rory began, running a hand down her purple velvet dress, somewhat tense, "please, Joey—"

"Oh, so that's it." Joey caught sight of Cain looking down at Gram's foot.

"Leakage of the toe," Gram muttered. "Must ask Cain for a sack of it. My grandson Cain is a fairish boy and he'll help me." Gram looked around suddenly, furtive, crimped forward in her black rocker. "Openhammett? Can't say as I do." Gram gave her big toe a squeeze and more pus ran out.

Cain bit on his teeth. "Gram, maybe you better put on some mutton tallow. A mutton poultice."

"Justice? Never heard of him."

Rory threw Cain a look. She touched Gram on the shoulder. "Now, dear, just set still there while I go get a pan of warm water with some salt in it." Rory scolded her gently. "How come you didn't soak it in salt water like I told you to in the first place? While I was gone."

Joey said, "Her and me was too busy fightin' off them Derby riders."

Rory gave Cain another look. The look said: "You see? This is the kind of life we lead now."

With a sigh, Cain took a chair and sat down before the crackling fire. He thrust the toes of his black boots almost into the flames.

211

Rory set out a pan of warm salt water. Gently she took up Gram's knob foot and placed it in the pan.

"Euu! Glory be! How good that feels," Gram said. "It's like bein' washed in the blood of the lamb."

Rory next filled the coffeepot and set it at the head of the range. She set the table with her finest: blue cups and saucers, the best silver, and an Indian-made sugar and creamer set.

Cain thought: "What's she spreadin' on the mustard for? Them fancy eatin' tools. Fresh spit curls. Chalk on her nose."

The smell of boiling coffee was sweet in the log cabin.

Cain thought: "Ain't this instead a time for puttin' on sack-cloth and ashes? Like the Old Book says?"

She brushed past him, once.

Cain thought: "I cannot think of it."

Rory poured coffee for Joey too. Joey took his new role as head of the house in stride. Cain had to smile to himself. What a strong little skimmy he had turned out to be. Out of Rory.

The coffee was rich, dark; and sipping and blowing and swallowing, everybody enjoyed it, Cain, Rory, Gram, and Joey.

Rory poured Cain a second cup; then hit him with it. "When are you going after him?"

Cain's ax-graven face darkened over with thought. He ran a stub hand through his tangled hair. He said nothing. For a second he didn't know what to say. Trust Rory to bring up the hard thing.

Joey said, "We elected Ned Sine to office. Ain't it about time he did something?"

Rory said, "There's no use'n goin' to the law in this country."

Cain drank up. He stirred the grounds in the bottom of his cup. "To swear out a warrant you got to have evidence, Joey. And this time nobody saw it happen. At least not that we know of. So the sheriff can't do anything just now."

Rory said, "But we know this Hunt Lawton is around."

Cain went on, explaining. "And even if someone had seen it, Joey, the one seeing it might be afraid to talk."

Rory's mouth drew down at the corners, mean. "Then there ain't no Hammett men left after all."

"Wait. Listen. The killer knows. He can't get away from himself. You know that. And one of these days he'll make a slip. Then we'll go after him legal."

"Just us Hammett women and children left."

"Listen. Most of us here along the Shaken Grass is just

shirttail outfits. We can't afford to make any mistakes. One slip and all the big papers in the state will blow it up to make us look like crooks. Except for one paper down in Cheyenne, the *Tribune,* they're all on the side of the big augers. The big augers can make all the mistakes in the world and yet never have to blush for it. Because it never gets printed. The whole world, the big wheels in Washington and London and New York, they believe only what the papers print. They have to. They've got money sunk in the big ranches. The first thing, if we do something wrong, they'll be in here with the Army to protect the peace. And you know what that'll mean for us."

"Then this ain't a country for the little man?"

"We ain't made it that yit, no." Cain's heavy jaw set out. "But we will. Given time. And we'll do it the right way. The big way."

"Time. Time." Rory's wrath was suddenly in the room like a she-grizzly let loose out of a cage. "And what good is 'time' to your brother Dale now? And Dencil? And Cattle Queen and Avery Jimson? And our dads? And Gramp? And all the other murdered ones? Or even you after tomorrow?"

"I'm sorry, Rory, but I don't aim to be stompeded into joining Harry's wild bunch. Which I will be if I take the law into my own hands."

"Even if it means you may be shaking hands with St. Peter tomorrow morning?" Rory choked with it. "And my little boys next?"

"I can't."

"Dale must be avenged."

It slipped out of him before he could catch himself. "He meant that much to you then?"

Rory rose in her chair. Terrible were her dark beautiful eyes. Her gold hair flashed like a mane. "What! What!"

Cain felt himself cowing. He resented it. He held up a hand as if to ward her off. "Wait. I didn't mean it that way."

"Cain, let me ask you this: Are you afraid to kill when this time you really will be in the right?"

"Wait. Wait. Yes, I did kill a man once. Yes. And I'm sorry for it. Terrible sorry for it."

"Even when the sheriff and everybody said you done right?"

"Yes. I killed wrong then. He was a no-good, yes. But my reason was wrong. And I swore then, as I swear now, that I will not kill without good reason again. Neither for pleasure nor profit. But will prefer peace."

"Even if it is all our revenge? And not just yours?"

"No. I cannot. I remember how Cecil Guth looked afterwards."

"And you won't do it for my sake then either?"

Then Cain's wrath was suddenly in the room too. His neck swelled. The weathered part of it darkened over. "What a question!"

"So all along you too have been a coward. Acting like you was a tough one with that big noisy mouth of yours."

" 'Big noisy mouth'? When I was careful—"

"Like Dale was. Like Dale did."

"Rory, the way you want it, it ain't clean that way. Clear."

"A coward."

"Rory, you're saying things to me that only a woman could get away with. If a man said them to me I'd drop him on sight."

"Ah, then I must somehow get this Hunt Lawton to call you a coward."

Cain balled up his fist slowly and slowly he hit the table. Dishes jumped. His own cup popped out of its saucer and tumbled over on its side. Canned milk frothed out of the punched holes in the airtight.

Joey broke in, "Unk, don't you think it's time you taught me how to draw?"

"What?" Cain shuddered. "Oh." He bit on his teeth, fierce, bit until the big molars under his ears grated. He sat rigid for a while, like a soul caught in a stone statue and struggling to get out. When he had himself somewhat in hand again, he said, gently, "Someday maybe I'll show you, son."

"What if there ain't no someday, Unk?"

Cain made a brush-off gesture. "It'll take too long to teach you, kid. At least just now."

"You told me once you should let the gun shoot itself and not you shoot it. Where the gun sorta takes you by the hand and helps you point it. Ain't that right?"

"What a waste," Rory murmured to herself. "What a terrible waste."

Gram spoke up from where she'd been contemplating her leaking toe in the pan of warm salt water. "It's a good thing pore Mabry didn't live to these times. His blood wiped out to the last man." The old clock on the mantel tocked the time away. "Oh, tomorrow I'll be with Him in glory! Tomorrow."

Cain looked down to hide his face. "I don't like this, Rory. You wanting a man's revenge."

"All I know is this: it's time Gramp and our dads and Dale was avenged."

214

"My God! What's this tarnal world comin' to? Women wanting revenge?"

"Somebody must wipe out the shame."

"How come you don't ask Harry to do the job? He bears the Hammett name too."

"Your name is Cain Hammett. You are the firstborn brother. It is more beholden for you."

"Rory, Rory, what makes you so all-fired hot for a killin'? What's eatin' you? What awful misery is gnawin' your innards?"

"We've got to take our stand somewhere. If the law won't."

"It's onnatural, that's what it is. A woman wanting a man's revenge. Why, it's always been the women who've been hot for peace. And bright lights and Sunday morning promenades."

"When you leave this house, don't ever come back again unless you can tell us that you've walked between his head and his shoulders."

Cain looked down at his hands. "A hag of hell, that's what she's become."

"I've often wondered how any woman could have stood bein' married to that hairy old Timberline. Well, maybe I looked at that wrong. Because he at least knows when to kill."

Gram cackled in her rocker by the fire. "Old Timberline. Now there is a man like my old Mabry. To men like them a woman is like a cookstove. Nice and handy when needed. My Mabry hardly knew a woman was in the world except at mealtime. And in bed. Mabry never worried his head about a pore wife's troubles, about her private problems thirteen times in the year. Neglect and insults beyond compare. And when she got caught, he figured she could throw her kids as easy as a mare threw her colts. Euu." Gram rocked, and on each rock her swollen foot came out of the water and then splashed back into it. "But I loved the old rough son-of-a-gun. He was a wild devil but he was all hair and man."

Joey asked, "How come they hang some people and shoot the others, Unk?"

"Rustlers they can hang. Because they won't be blamed for it too much. But they can't hardly hang an honest settler. That's a tougher nut to crack. So they hire killers to dry-gulch them."

Rory hid her head. "That it's come to this. We have a first-born man in the family and yet he won't do what needs to be

215

done. When, doing it, the old way of killing might pass away with him."

The old clock tocked on. Gram's rocker creaked. The fire sagged in the fieldstone hearth. Lungs breathed.

Joey said, "But how come they hung Dencil, Unk? Wasn't he honest?"

All of a sudden baby Cain began to cry in the lean-to, loud, unceasing, as if terrorized by some baby nightmare.

"Coward," Rory said, more to herself than to Cain.

"All right then!" Cain roared. He started to his feet like an old bull branded across the rear with a cherry-red iron. "All right then! Tomorrow morning I'll go in and find him. I'm agin it. But I'll go in anyway. Maybe it is right to do wrong sometimes if it is for the women."

He snapped on his black hat, buttoned up his black leather coat, slipped on his black gloves. Then, with a last outraged look at Rory and Gram, he rammed outdoors.

Cain

When he stepped down off Lonesome in front of Dad Finfrock's livery stable, Cain knew he had pushed his horse too hard. Despite the cold out, Lonesome was sopping wet with lather and sweat. The hide over his withers and rump was wavy with it.

Cain led Lonesome in through the big door which Dad Finfrock opened for him. Stench of urine-soaked straw and hay-stringy horseballs was a fire in the nose. Cain said, "Hope I didn't ruin the hoss."

Dad caught his sloppy hat between his finger and thumb; lifted it a trifle; scratched his gray hair with his pinky. Dad was a poorly scarecrow, bent and slabsided. "That's it."

"Shouldn't've used the rib wrenches so much."

Dad looked down at Cain's spurs, and nodded.

A horse in back whinnied lonesomely. A stallion in a box stall whirled around and around, and let off a guttural stud call.

Cain said, "Brush him down good, Dad. Throw a blanket over him and give him a lot of dry straw."

Dad gave himself a deep goose; coughed.

"Don't know when I'll be back for him. I'll probably stay the night."

Dad nodded. He pried a scab out of his nose.

"What time you got?"

"Three."

"Good. That gives me a couple hours before the stores close."

"That's it." Dad led Lonesome into the dark back of the barn.

Cain straddled down main street. The frozen planks of the walk boomed hollowly under his tomping boot heels. There were no buggies or wagons or saddled horses anywhere along the street. Only the humpbacked stagecoach from Sundance in front of the Feed Rack Hotel and smoke rising from every chimney showed the town was alive at all. The sky had clouded over and twilight seemed to be coming in from the Big Stonies to the west.

Cain stomped up the stoop into Great Western Outfitters, opened the heavy door, and clanged it shut behind him. "Hi, Homer."

Homer Fox looked up from behind his old beat-up roll-top desk. "Well, Cain Hammett. What brings you in town?" Homer seemed nervous.

"Bullets. Lots of 'em." It was warm inside the store and Cain took off his gloves and opened his leather jacket.

"Going hunting?"

"Might call it that."

Fat Homer got to his feet. He was smoking a cigar. Ashes had sprinkled down the vest of his black suit. "What make?"

"Colt .45." Cain picked up a box of shells from a counter. He shook it. The waxed bullets rattled solidly inside. He liked the smell of well-kept guns and oiled leather and the fresh gunnysacks they were packed in. He decided that running a hardware store would be just the thing for him when he got too stove-up to ride the range any more. "Say, one thing, Homer, can I put this on tick?"

"Guess so. Personal, I've always known you to be about as straight as a wagon tongue."

A voice piped up from behind a stack of new shiny tan saddles. "Personal, I wouldn't let him charge it, Homer." It was a high voice. "Jesse Jacklin tells me Cain runs his slow-brand outfit with a sticky rope."

Homer's eyes rolled in their fat sockets.

Cain whirled. His own eyes still hadn't quite adjusted to the dark interior of the store. "All right, Alias, wherever you are, come out. You're just the one I'm lookin' for."

Hunt stepped into the main aisle, tall, lean, cold smile cutting back into his cheeks. He had on a dark winter overcoat with the beaver collar open at the throat. His cartridge belt gleamed some in the low light. His gun hung hidden under a fold of the coat.

Cain's left arm hung half-crooked over his gun. He studied Hunt's face. It galled him that Hunt had eyes hard to hold up to. Cain said, "Alias, I might's well come right out with it. I've come to town to kill you. Have you got your affairs in order?"

Hunt stood with his legs wide apart, both hands down, calm, easy. "As good as I'll ever have them."

"You're all set then for Judgment Day?"

"As set as I'll ever be."

"Take off your overcoat."

"Why?"

"So you can draw better and faster, you murdering black-hearted bustard. I want this to be a fair shake."

Fat Homer shimmied behind the roll-top desk, ready to duck. "Boys," he said, weak, "boys, if you must shoot, how about tryin' the street?"

Cain said, "Take off your coat."

"No."

"Well, I gave you your chance. You are ready then?"

"I am."

"No regrets over all the murderin' you done?"

"Who's talking about murder?"

"You ain't killed then?"

"Yes, I've killed. Sure. Because the law said someone needed killin'. But murder? That's something else again."

"What about Gramp?"

"He needed killin'. And I was glad to do it."

"What? What'd he ever do to you or to the law that he needed killin'?"

Hunt showed teeth. "That's my affair."

Homer Fox tried again. "Uhh . . . Cain, what make of bullet did you say again?"

"I said, Colt .45." Cain set his bowlegs wide too. "But now that you mention it, give me a couple of boxes of .38-56's." He watched Hunt's face. "For a certain Winchester I found up in the hills last month."

Hunt's gray eyes held steady.

"Draw, you high-headed devil you. Draw!"

"This ain't my fight. I didn't pick it."

"I'm next on your list to get shot in the back, ain't I? I'm giving you your chance to get your shot into me frontside."

"Hammett, let me ask you something." A mocking smile

218

moved under Hunt's mustache. "You sure no one ever did you a favor?"

Fat Homer bubbled, "Hunt, deuce take it, but every time you call on me, seems like somebody's always gunning for you."

Cain barked, "Draw!" His left hand hung clawed and ready to strike.

"Boys!" Fat Homer cried.

Cain said, "Draw."

Hunt stood with both hands down, gun still under the fold of his coat.

"Hunt, tell Homer here what your real name was back in the States. Before you was run out of the country and you took on your present summer name."

For the first time hatred glittered full in Hunt's eyes.

Homer Fox suddenly broke for the door.

"Hey! Where do you think you're going?" Cain called, trying not to follow Homer with his eyes.

"Get Sheriff Sine. I don't want my store all shot up."

Cain allowed himself a quick look after Homer. "Homer, hold up. I want you as a witness to this shooting bee."

The quick look gave Hunt his chance. He spun on his heels and dove for the back door. When Cain looked around again, Hunt was gone.

It was just after supper when Cain next ran into Hunt.

Hunt was in Butcherknife Bain's saloon smoking a pipe. He stood alone at the far end of the bar, one leg up on the brass rail. He'd been nursing a shot of whisky. At the other end of the bar, back to the door, stood Sheriff Ned Sine. Butcher-knife was at his usual stand.

Two oil lamps with reflectors glowed over the mirror. Three lanterns hung from a wagon wheel up on the ceiling. The gentle smell of fresh sawdust was laced with the pervasive stench of horse manure.

Cain legged up beside Sheriff Sine. "Hi, Ned."

"Hi, Hammett." Ned Sine was a good half-foot taller than Cain. He had a flushed face and a knowing offhand manner. He wore gray with black boots and a silver star. His feet and hands were small. He carried a .41 six-gun on the theory that it had less kickback than the conventional .45 and was faster for close-in work. "Well, and what brings you in town, Cain?"

"Him." Cain nodded in Hunt's direction.

Hunt smiled back. He took pipe from mouth and said,

219

"Yeh, how about that, Sheriff? Hammett says he's come to town to kill me."

Sheriff Sine slowly straightened up.

Hunt said, "Sheriff, I know Cain and his gang elected you into office. That you ain't exactly friends with Jesse. But you will see that right is done, won't you, Sheriff?"

Sheriff Sine puffed some. "Law is law. No matter who makes it or breaks it."

Cain said, "Alias, I see you've took your coat off. That you wear your holster tied to your leg. I hope you've got your back up finally to fight me."

"Boys," Butcherknife said, "have some tarantula juice on the house."

"Not for me," Cain said. "I aim to stay clearheaded tonight."

"No more for me," Hunt said. "This dram has fixed me up just right."

"And no more for me," Sheriff Sine said. "I already got on a talking load."

Butcherknife gave all three a wise rolling look; then turned to face his own image in the mirror. "Well, how about you, Butchie old boy, have one on the house, huh?" He allowed himself a smile at his own wit. "Don't mind if I do." He drank up in one throw of the shot glass. "Ah, it's like I always say—whisky is the juice of beautiful sentiment."

Cain said, "Sheriff, have you found a witness yet to my brother Dale's murder?"

"Not yet."

Cain grunted. "You won't find him either. Our friend Alias there always makes sure about that."

Sheriff Sine said, "Now wait a minute. Are you accusing someone?"

Cain said, "Ask that tiedown man Alias there to see what I mean."

Hunt laid his pipe on the bar. "Butcherknife, you got a piece of sandpaper handy?"

"How so?" Butcherknife stared at Hunt a moment. "No," he said then.

Hunt said, "Well, maybe this knife will do." Hunt got out a bone-handle jackknife. He clicked open the big blade. Slowly, patiently, he began scraping the surface skin off the inside of his trigger finger. The steel blade gleamed slow silver in the mellow oil light.

Cain watched the scraping. He knew that in a close squeak a sensitive trigger finger was sometimes the difference between a shot past the ear and a shot in the eye. Hunt with his coat off looked like he was going to fight after all.

"Boys," Butcherknife said, "have some tornado juice on the house."

"Thanks," Cain said, "but I don't like bein' pickled just as the ball is about to commence."

"Thanks," Hunt said.

"That goes for me too," Sheriff Sine said.

"Oh, come on, boys. You know as well as I do that whisky has been branded for lots it didn't do. Let's all be friends tonight."

Cain said, "Hunt, tell me, what is it you've got against us Hammetts?"

"The same thing you've got against yourself. What's eatin' you."

Cain said, "Sheriff, I'll have to ask you to leave."

Sheriff Sine reared back. "Me leave? What fer?"

Cain said, "I'm about to make Alias here draw on me. And I wouldn't want you to get an eyeful."

Sheriff Sine took out his blue .41 and laid it on the bar in front of him. "Gents, if there's any shootin' to be done around here I'll do it."

Cain stepped around Sheriff Sine and edged toward Hunt. He was careful to stay well away from the bar to make sure his left hand would be free for action. "Alias, how about stepping outdoors with me?"

Hunt said, "You sure no one did you a favor?"

"Hell's fire!" In his rage Cain had to set his teeth to keep them from chattering. He said through set teeth. "Hunt, that's the second time you've said that. What are you tryin' to tell me?"

Hunt closed his knife and put it away. "You figure it out." He took up his pipe and sucking hard got it going again.

Cain said, "I see you got your shootin' finger honed down finally. All right. Fill your hand, blast you, and may the Lord have mercy on your miserable soul. Because where I'm sending you they'll fry you crisper'n Christ."

Sheriff Sine picked his gun off the bar and held it on Cain. "Draw, either one of you, and by the Lord we'll all go down and get fried."

Butcherknife said, "How about a drink on—"

Hunt said, "You ask about my killin's. All right. Let me tell you something. When I kill lice I don't play favors."

Cain said, "Draw, you murderin' blackhearted bustard. Draw, and be a man."

221

"And have the sheriff here lock me up after? When I'm part of the law myself? No, thanks. I value my job as stock inspector too high for that. I ain't finished the job for Jesse yet."

"Hah. That means I'm next on the list to get shot in the back. Strapped to my hoss, toes down. As a warning to all the other little stockmen around."

Hunt cocked his head. "The man I'm now after has got winnin' ways with cows. He can talk a cow out of its calf. Calves just naturally follow his saddle across the prairie."

"Hunt, ye're a liar."

"Cain, that's enough now!" Sheriff Sine roared. Clapping a heavy hand on Cain's shoulder, Sheriff Sine tried to turn him around.

Cain slid out from under the hand. "Ned, stay out of this. Each man to his own snakes." Cain turned back to Hunt. "Alias, ye're not only a liar, ye're a coward."

Again Sheriff Sine put a gripping hand on Cain's shoulder. "That's enough of that now!"

Once more Cain slid out from under the hand. "Alias, ye're not only a liar, and a coward, but ye're a thief t'boot."

Hunt's eyes flickered. Yet his hands lay quiet, at rest, before him on the bar.

"Hunt, by God, I've called ye the worst three fightin' names I know, and yet, by God, ye still hain't filled your hand. Do you wear that gun as a watch fob? Or what?"

Hunt said, "Where do you get that 'thief' part?"

"Hunt, I don't know if you ever stole a calf or not, but I'm calling you a thief anyway. Because I want you to go for it. Now, throw lead, damn you, because it's time you took the big jump."

"I pick my own time to fight."

"Hunt, I knew there was a coward in you. But I didn't think you had it that bad."

"I'll fight when it's my fight. And run it off my way."

"All right, Hunt, if not with guns, let's fight it out knuckles and skull then. We'll let the sheriff hold our guns and knives."

Butcherknife leaned heavily across the bar. "Listen, I don't give a hoot in hell how smoky you two old stubhorns want to get, but I want you to go outside to do it."

"So you go on the theory it's safer to pull freight than pull your gun, eh, Hunt?"

Butcherknife finally had enough. He reached under the bar and came up with a blunt sawed-off shotgun. "All right. That's enough. The first man that breaks or raises gets a quart of buckshot in the belly."

All three, Cain, Hunt, Sheriff Sine, looked at the shotgun.

After a moment, Hunt clopped out his pipe in his hand and dropped the burnt tord into a brass spittoon at his feet. Then he turned his back on Cain and went over to the wall and took down his black coat from a peg and put it on and went out into the night.

Cain followed Hunt in the dark. Weak lamplight from an occasional house or store just barely lit the way. Cain stayed a good block behind Hunt, taking the frozen street instead of the booming plank walk. Hunt walked rapidly, long-legged; he didn't look back once. Cain walked light, sure-footed, across rough wagon ruts and deep hoof pocks.

Cain thought: "It ain't that he's without guts. You got to hand him that. Because even to shoot a man in the back takes some kind of guts. Because it is killing. And you're adding to the load inside. No, it ain't that. It's that he wants to kill cold-blooded. Not hot-blooded. And that he don't mind the load. Because he hates, cold."

Cain thought: "But he's nobody's fool. He ain't going to grab the branding iron by the hot end. He ain't going to kick a loaded polecat in the arse. He's going to wait until the iron has cooled some. Till the polecat has unloaded his tail."

Cain thought: "But I aim to make him fight anyway. My way. I've got to."

Somewhat to his surprise, he saw Hunt head straight for Dad Finfrock's livery barn. "Ah, he's going to ride out to Jesse and make a report. Good. I meant to look in on Lonesome anyway afore this. Two birds with one stone, as the man says."

The big barn door rolled back and Hunt's long figure showed briefly in the opening against lantern light. Then the door rolled shut.

Cain approached the big dark door cautiously. He thought: "That devil. He knows I'm following him. Yet he's pretending he don't know. The better to throw me off guard and get me when I follow him inside."

Cain drew his gun. He stood a moment outside the door listening. He tried to peer through a crack of light in the door but couldn't make out anything. Vaguely he heard voices inside. One was Dad's. The other was low, indistinct. A horse neighed. The lone stallion in his box stall sounded his primordial stud call.

After a bit, listening, all ears and feelers, Cain changed his mind. Hunt wasn't waiting for him on the other side.

Cain set his teeth. "This time I'll get him. I'll make him want to draw on me. I'll cut loose my wolf and throw part of it into him and make him rear up. If he ain't got animal enough in him I'll borry him part of mine." With a lunging jerk he rolled back the big door and sprang sideways through the lighted opening into the first stall. Frozen horseballs crunched underfoot.

There was no shot.

Then Dad yelled from the back of the barn, "Close that door! We got us a sick horse here. There's a draft."

A sick horse? Cain stepped out of the stall, gun still in hand. Near the back, in wavering lantern light, stood Dad and Hunt. Dad looked up from a crouch, glaring; Hunt stood stiffly erect, smiling.

"Close the door!" Dad yelled again. "And what's the idee of all that hardware?"

"I forgot," Cain muttered, feeling foolish, putting gun away. He rolled the door to with a slam.

It was yeasting warm in the barn. Four lanterns burned in a row down the center. There was hardly enough light to make out the individual stalls down the sides. A few of the stalls were occupied: a span of teams on one side, Sunday riding horses on the other. Manure had been pitched into the middle aisle, making the footing considerably higher than in the stalls. The footing gave on each step, juicy with moisture, rustling with straw.

As Cain slowly approached the pair in back, Hunt said, "Like Gramp, I see you Hammetts are still hard on horses and women."

Cain said, "How's Lonesome, Dad?"

"Bad off." Dad held a lantern into the open stall. Orange light fell on Lonesome lying in deep yellow straw. A red-striped gray blanket lay over his ribcase. His eyes were half-closed. His noble head lay in an awkward, even ugly, angle to the body as if it were not a part of the carcass. Lonesome breathed loud and hoarse, just barely guttering through lard-like phlegm.

"Pneumonia," Hunt said.

"That's it," Dad said.

Cain settled on his heels. He put his hand on Lonesome's

224

neck and shook him, gently, lovingly. "What's the matter, old man, huh?"

Lonesome's gaunt black head lifted level. His eyes fluttered open. Clots of bubbling snot ran out of the hollows of each nostril. Lonesome tried to whinny; couldn't quite make it. His head fell into the yellow straw again, loosely, like a bass fiddle dropped to one side.

"Pneumonia all right," Hunt said again, teeth showing yellow-white.

"What's the matter, old boy, huh?" Cain said low, petting Lonesome.

"Just like your Gramp all right," Hunt went on, smiling, fingering the ends of his mustache. "Never learned that rib wrenches was to be used as reminders, not punishers."

"That's it," Dad said.

It galled Cain that he'd been caught at wronging a horse. Had it not been for Rory and Hunt he would never have committed the wrong in the first place. He rarely used spurs. Some time ago he had even taken the trouble to file down his spurs, making them blunt, and had done it out of love for horseflesh. The dark hollows in his cheeks showed as sharp and as deep as the dents in his black hat.

Hunt said, "Now you take my horse there"—Hunt pointed across the way at a deep bay with a black tail—"take Fireball there. Give him the least motion of the knee and he minds. I never have to dig him. That's the way to use a horse."

"You can shut up now," Cain said.

Hunt laughed, low.

The laugh burned Cain. He jumped up, squaring and setting himself all in one motion. He roared, deep, powerful, "Go for it! Now." He bellowed so loud that echoes came out of the mouths of the stalls one by one, little and big, then all together.

Hunt only smiled.

Dad's mouth dropped open, showing pink gums and four old yellow teeth and a snakelike quivering tongue tip. The lantern in Dad's hand suddenly cocked off to one side, stiff, the flame fluttering on the wick, once twice. The four lanterns overhead swayed too.

"Go for it!" Cain threw his will power, deliberately trying to set it in Hunt. "Now!"

Hunt smiled, black-edged gray eyes gleaming. He stood mesmerized, as if in bondage to Cain's will rather than hot with it.

Cain took a step forward in the loose straw. Bent forward

225

from the hips, head jutted forward, veins and tendons white through walnut-dark skin, strike in the set of his hands and shoulders, he threw all his force into Hunt. "Draw, you Devil's own bastard!" His voice roared and echoed all of a piece inside the barn. "Fill your hand!"

Still Hunt didn't draw.

"Do it! Now!" Cain came forward another step, slowly, spurs catching in the straw, moving full of violent silence, eyes blazing white. "Or say something so I can hate you enough to kill you in cold blood."

And yet Hunt held off.

All of a sudden Cain had enough. He'd gone beyond where he cared to go. He let go inside. "Be damned to you then," he said. "I've talked more the last couple hours than I ever did in all my life and still I hain't been able to cut your wolf loose. So the hell with it. If you won't fight, I guess there's nothing I can do about it." He shook his shaggy head. " 'Tain't human. Heaven and hell is my witness I tried everything onreasonable. Everything."

"That's it," Dad said, mouth snapping shut.

Released, Hunt turned to his bay and saddled up and rode off into the night.

Cain hung his gun and leather jacket on a peg at the end of the stall. He sat on his heels again and put a hand on Lonesome. He swabbed out Lonesome's nostrils with rags dipped in alcohol. He noted the single veins wriggling across the tender insides of the fluttering nostrils. He stroked the noble black head. He combed the curly black mane. He put more fresh straw under Lonesome's neck and back. He took off blankets when Lonesome broke out in a sweat; piled them back on again when Lonesome began to shiver. He selected a straw from the bedding. He chewed. He waited. Dad hovered over him.

"Lonesome, boy."

At midnight, Cain raised haggard eyes. "Dad, you better go hit the hay. I appreciate it, but there's no use a you stayin' around. If anybody comes, I'll take care of the business for you."

Dad nodded. "They's a cot in back with some blankets you kin use. Sometimes in a pinch I sleep on it."

"No, I'll just set here until the crisis is past." Cain looked down at Lonesome. It was with an effort that he kept from choking on the words. "I let my best friend down and now I've got to make it up to him."

226

"That's it."

Sitting alone, listening to the slow gargling breaths, chewing on a straw, brooding, he thought of the many times he and Lonesome had ridden the range together: up under the Old Man hunting bighorn; across the prairie of an evening to take in a barn dance at Red Jackson's; up the valley to attend meetings of the little stockmen; and, yes, down the Shaken Grass to visit Rory.

"Lonesome, boy."

There was the time when he got lost in a blizzard. It was Lonesome who'd saved his life. Stiff with cold, he'd fallen off into a snowbank and all night long Lonesome kept nuzzling him to keep him awake, again and again, until finally just at dawn Lonesome pawed him with a hoof, gently, moving him and making him get to his feet and stumble on.

"Come, boy."

There was the time when Lonesome saved him from a raging prairie fire north of Casper. Lonesome smelled it first, and ran against the bit and Cain's curses all the way back to town, brought him inside the plowed fireguard just as the cinders fell thick around them and the air got too stifling hot to breathe.

"Lonesome, boy."

There were the many times they'd drunk from the same stream together, with Lonesome lipping the water's surface after he was full, in play, letting big drops fall back.

"Steady, boy."

He got a pail of water. Straddling Lonesome's neck, he lifted his head to help him drink. Lonesome lipped the water, but did not take any of it. After a bit, Lonesome's lip twisted some, and Cain took it to be a smile, a weak one, as if in thanks.

"Lonesome, boy."

He got out brush and currycomb and groomed Lonesome. He brushed down the short black hairs tufting out in a sort of cowlick above the coupling. Gently he brushed where the veins ran like gorged angleworms under the belly. The size of the veins made Cain wonder if a tight cinch hurt the flow of blood much. Gently he brushed along each stroke of bone and each length of muscle. He brushed until the hair shone in the lantern light. Tenderly he combed over the white sock on the left leg, the one sweet blemish in all of Lonesome's black glory coat.

Choked lungs breathing coarsely, Lonesome suffered it. Once he flipped an ear in appreciation.

Toward morning, Lonesome coughed, explosive. Phlegm hit the wall in splats. Lonesome raised; got one crooked front hoof up; collapsed.

"Boy!"

The horse's entire carcass worked at getting breath; couldn't make it.

"Throat's plugged."

Again Lonesome tried exploding it out. Couldn't.

Cain grabbed for his pocketknife, opened the leather-auger blade, and deliberately, grimly, bored a hole into the horse's windpipe just above where it entered the broad chest. There was first a trickle of blood; then a sudden tiny whistling; and finally, after a rip of the blade to one side, a gush of wind and froth and clot. Lonesome breathed easier.

"Ahh."

At dawn, Lonesome tried to raise once more. This time he managed to get up on both front feet; held up his noble black head a moment—and then, with a falling slide, collapsed in the straw, moving a little as the great chest slowly closed on a sigh. Dead.

"Lonesome!"

Unthinking, Cain threw his arms around Lonesome and cried in his mane.

But only for a moment. He remembered someone might catch him at it. Especially in Dad's public livery barn. He got to his feet. For a long time he stood looking down. Tears twinkled in his eyes. In the soft lantern light, in his eyelashes, the tears hung like low gold clouds, obscuring his vision. "I never did believe in pompering a horse with apple pies. Making a pie-biter out of him," Cain cried. "But I wish now I had with you, boy. No man ever had a truer friend."

Later in the day, Sheriff Ned Sine found Cain shearing off Lonesome's curling black tail and mane.

"Dead, huh?"

"Guess so."

"That tail'll make a nice braid rope."

"Guess so."

"What do you want for it? My daughter's beggin' me to get her one."

"The deuce with your daughter. This is going to be mine."

Sheriff Sine reared back. His star glinted in the dim light.

"Well, you don't need to bite my ears off. After all, it's just a horse. And a black one at that."

Cain looked up from under the peak of his black hat. His eyes bored up at the sheriff like the muzzles of two guns. "Just what do you mean by that?"

"Nothing. Just said it."

Cain said, "If you don't mind, I'd like to enjoy my grief alone."

"Oh." Again Sheriff Sine reared back, dark face flushing. "Well, anyway, I came to tell you, thanks for the tip, Cain."

"What tip?"

"On Hunt. I've finally got a witness."

Cain slowly rose to his feet, swelling. "To my brother Dale's killin'?"

"To your brother Dale's murder. Ed Turnbull saw the whole thing. You know, that wolfer Jesse hired last fall? Ed was baiting traps in the draw near the bridge when he saw it. He saw Hunt cache himself under the bridge; saw Dale come; saw Dale shot; saw Hunt run for it. Said he didn't talk up before because he knew Jesse had hired Hunt just like he hired him. To get rid of pests."

"Hah."

"But he said his conscience finally bothered him so much he had to come in and tell me. He come to my house in the dark last night right after I saw you at Butcherknife's. He come secret."

"At last."

Sheriff Sine coughed, apologetically. "The heck of it is, Hunt got wind of it somehow. Just as I was set to serve him with a warrant this morning. Some weasel in the court-house must have tipped him off. Because he skipped the country."

"Didn't you chase him?"

"He had a half-night's start on me. By now he must be halfway to Cheyenne."

"Where the law is dealt out by the big augers."

"Yeh."

Cain stood silent a while. "Well, at least we've got him over a barrel in Bighorn County. That's something. He won't dare show his nose around this neck of the woods no more. That should please Rory a mighty lot."

Rosemary

Rory saw him come walking across the snow in the pink twilight. She had just finished washing dishes and happened to look out.

Her heart leaped up. "Ah! Now we can live in peace."

She turned. "Joey, go open the door for Uncle Cain."

Both Joey and Gram looked up from the hearth, Joey from a hardback chair, Gram from her rocker.

Joey said, "I knew Unk was the best shot in Bighorn County." Joey went calmly and manfully to the door. He opened it wide. Pink twilight flowed into the cabin.

Rory's heart fell at Joey's calm. Too late. Poison had got into the boy. And the boy in turn would poison baby Cain when he became old enough to understand. Too late.

She looked out of the high window again. And then it struck her that something was wrong. Cain was walking. A man afoot was no man at all. He had not shot Hunt.

She thought: "A dream should stay a dream, whether it's daydream or nightmare. Even if both of us dream it."

She thought: "I wanted all three. And wanting them, I missed the best."

She met him at the door. "Come in where it's warm, Cain."

Cain stepped in. He tried to smile. "I could use some warm all right." He looked down at Joey. He ran a hand through the boy's throw of gold hair. "Hi, son."

"How many shots did it take, Unk?"

Cain looked at her across the boy's head.

She said, "Let's talk about it later. After we've set out some food for your uncle." She closed the door against the cold and snow.

Cain said, "Oh, as for that, I can talk about it any time. Because there ain't much to tell." Cain gave her steady smoke-blue eyes. "Rory, I'm sorry, but he just wouldn't draw." Cain shook his head. "He just would not draw. It turned out to be nothing more than a square backdown. A looking contest."

"I know," she said, "I know. Come by the fire."

She helped him into a chair. She took his black leather jacket and black hat. Joey took off his wet black boots. Cain himself took off gun and cartridge belt. She chafed his feet, first one stocking foot, then the other.

After a while, rolling and lighting a cigarette, Cain told some about it.

She said, "I was afraid of that too. But like you say, maybe it's just as well this way. Maybe a warrant hanging over his head will keep him out of the country for a while."

Joey got out his toy belt and gun and paraded around with it. "Say, Unk, how come you came home walking? Lonesome come down lame?"

"Lonesome is dead, son."

"Hey! How come?"

"I pushed him too hard, and he caught a cold and died." Cain held his hands to the fire. He held his head so she couldn't see his face.

She set out a plate for him. "I'll miss Lonesome. He always liked my perfume."

Gram began to rock in her chair. "Caught a cold and died. Caught a cold and died. Oh, God, deliver my darling soul from the power of worms."

Part FOUR

That winter there were two cattlemen meetings: one in Antelope and the other in Cheyenne.

The one held in Antelope took place in Butcherknife Bain's whisky-sweet saloon and was attended by many of the little stockmen of Bighorn County. Most were honest ranchers. But there were also a few rustlers—those who ranched and rustled on the side, those who rustled and ranched on the side.

Cain was there. So were Shock Lamb who'd bought out Clara Jager, and old neighbor Red Jackson from Red Fork, and Baconsides Murdoe who'd taken over Cattle Queen's spread, and Henry Urine just newly settled in six miles south of Cain's ranch, and Sagebrush Mason the new hired hand for Rory. So were Harry and his Red Sash gang. Also in the crowd, disguised as cowboys and settlers, were the big stockmen's detectives.

It was decided, first, to hold the next spring roundup a month early, May 1 instead of June 1. This was agreed upon partly in revenge for Jesse's early roundup the previous fall and partly in self-protection—to brand their own calves and such mavericks as they might find before the wagons and men of Lord Peter. Senator Thorne, and Governor Barb could get on the ground. "Turnabout is fair play and that goes all around."

It was resolved, second, to call themselves the Bighorn Farmers & Stockgrowers Association. "Us outlaws will make us our own laws."

It was agreed, third, that Cain should be roundup boss. Both the honest small ranchers and the occasional rustler agreed to the choice. "He's a good shot and his word is good. That's the measure of him." Cain accepted but not without first giving a short speech.

"This is one time," Cain said, "when we've got to play it straight poker. No wild cards. No aces off the bottom of the deck. No betting on the side. You come in with your openers and no questions asked. We don't care what you did last year, or the year before that. We don't care what your handle was back in the States, or down in Texas. We work from where we are and who we are—starting today. We have our own sheriff now, our own judge, our own courthouse. We don't need to beg, borrow, or steal. If we keep her honest from here on in, and stick together, them big cattle barons down in the southern part of the state, and them foreign suckers from the Atlantic States and from England, let alone the three big spreads around here, they'll never lick us, either by law or by bullets. And, if we keep her this way long enough, them big alligators, the state legislators, will finally have to take us for what we are: a county mostly full of small stockmen who believe in free grass, free water, free range, and the right to rope our own calves when, where, and how we find 'em."

The other meeting, held in Cheyenne, took place in the pomade-scented Cactus Club and was attended by the elite of the cow country, the very flower of the state. Some of the men present were pioneer western ranchers who by hard work and brilliant enterprise had conquered a wilderness and had established a magnificent, even historic, way of life—generous, courtly, heroic. They were the true kings of the American earth. Also present were certain speculators from the Eastern Seaboard and from England, men who had got into the cattle business not because they believed in it as a good way of life but as a good way to make a lot of money.

Jesse Jacklin was there. So were Senator John Thorne and Governor Dexter Barb, representing the old-time big outfits still active in the Big Stonies country. So were Wallace Tascott, Irving Hornsby, Enoch West, Bat Wildy—all of them kingly ranchers from the southern half of the state. So were Peter Caudle, the Earl of Humberwick; Oliver Twetmouth, a member of the Mayfair elegants; and Allen Stone, field manager for a combine of bankers in Scotland. Also in the crowd were Hunt Lawton, stock detective and peace officer now wanted in Bighorn County; Clayborne Rodney, a tall Dakota-born marshal hired especially to deal with rustlers; and Texas Ike, a smiling young daredevil hired to scare out the nesters.

The Cactus Club as a meeting place was quite different from Butcherknife Bain's hangout. It was swank, built of brick, was of rambling design, had a mansard roof with a skylight above the main hallway, had wide verandas fronting the streets. Here the monocled Englishmen and the mannered

236

blue-bloods from the Eastern Seaboard hobnobbed with the plain-speaking ranchers from the plains. Imported servants hovered in the background, whist and billiards were played in the gaming room, some reading was done in the library. Scotch and bourbon and fine wines were served all hours of the day in the bar, while caviar and champagne were served in private dining rooms. Paintings and other art objects from decaying Old Europe hung on many of the walls—in the main hallway, in the dining room, behind the bar, in the private clubrooms. During hot weather spring-driven fly-chasers flapped air on every room. Members had their own engraved shaving mugs and drinking cups. The only touch of the true West permitted in the whole establishment stood in the main hallway—a hall rack made of cattle and buffalo horns. As one elegant, a member, once put it: "On an Eastern basis, the Cactus is a good club." Just one mile away from it spread the raw West of green cactus and silver sagebrush and fenceless, endless prairies.

The meeting in question took place after the regular meeting of the State Cattleman's Association. The regular meeting, held in the afternoon, had been short and sweet. Only the most perfunctory business was handled. The Association was a legal organization and as such had to keep accurate minutes of all proceedings. It was agreed beforehand that the real business would be taken care of in a secret gathering attended by certain select members and thus kept from the eyes of nosy reporters from the one newspaper friendly to the small stockmen and farmers, the Cheyenne *Tribune*.

It was evening. The private dining room in the Club was jammed. Mellow lamplight glowed on the dark walnut walls. Dinner was over. Brandy had been served and cigars lighted. Private hates and frustrations were being gradually aired for all to hear.

Wallace Tascott, or Walrus as he was nicknamed in honor of his mustache, presided informally. Every now and then Walrus tried to cross his legs; couldn't quite make it. He was a short pompous man with short fat legs and quick fat hands. He had a wry neck as a result of a bullet wound. In his mind crossing his legs had something to do with unlocking his neck. He had a round head and swift shrewd brown eyes. He was a strutter with the barking manners of an army officer—picked up while a major in the Union Army in the Civil War. He owned a big ranch along the Platte and had almost been cleaned out by the deadly blizzard of '88. By hard work he had got back on his feet financially, only to see, as he said, "the railroad come poking in, bringing pauper grangers, folks you can't shoot down like you can redskins. To get even, I guess I'll have to go into the banking business."

One of the men expressed the opinion the members had better remember that some Americans prided themselves in the fact the U.S.A. offered the poor of the world a chance at a new start.

Walrus snapped, "Well, not out my way it don't. On my range, farms for the poor is a romantic absurdity. It's just not poor man's country. You either got to be big or get wiped out."

High-headed Jesse nodded over his booming brandy snifter. "It's like I always say—you can't squeeze eight married couples into the same bed."

Autocratic Allen Stone, the field manager for Scottish bankers, shook his head sadly. "The devil of it is, the rustlers are using the good small ranchers as a screen. My men on the scene who keep me posted report that the names of rustlers just do not appear on the membership rolls of that new Bighorn Farmers & Stockgrowers Association."

Walrus nodded. "Which means we'll probably have to wipe out the good with the bad if we should have to make a move."

Bluff Enoch West lipped his cigar, groused, "The devil of it is, none of us old-timers've got clean hands. Some of us got our start just like these boys are trying to get their start now. When the longest rope got the maverick. Every time we point a finger, we point at a mirror."

Irving Hornsby blew an enormous cloud of cigar smoke toward the ceiling. For a second the room dimmed with it. Irv had a ranch back on the Salt Creek. He was a short heavy-bellied man. For all his bowed worklegs, he was a man of considerable learning and experience. He had graduated from Harvard; had traveled the world; had tried all sorts of enterprises and had made small fortunes out of them; had finally come back home to try ranching. He was now married and had a big family of nine children. Allen Stone had once jokingly said of him that he was "a man who had experienced every thrill in life except religion and childbirth." He was a hard drinker, a hard rider, had a violent temper when aroused, and was known to have killed at least three tough Texas cowboys in gunfights. Irv had been having trouble with the new settlers too. "The poor buggers haven't got the money to buy barbwire and fence in their property. No. What they do instead is turn a furrow around the margin of their homesteads and call that a fence." Irv took a long sip. "Well, naturally, my cows aren't so smart they can play the furrow is a fence. So what happens? When some of my dumb cows stray across this play fence, those buggers shoot them down, claiming they're protecting their land. The loss from such killings has just been terrible out our way." Irv took another drink. "And it wouldn't be so bad if they'd just kill for their own table use, but they kill just to kill. Boys, that has just got to stop or we can close up shop and apply for a room at the poorhouse."

Stone brushed ashes from the front of his tuxedo. "One thing I must add. My clients and I want to go on record to the effect that the hanging of Cattle Queen and Avery Jimson was a bad mistake." Stone turned to Jesse. "Yes, Jesse, lynching that woman was a horrible piece of business. It gave the opposition a moral point, gratis. It was not necessary. She could have been scared off, chased out, instead."

Jesse reared up. His bad leg was no better and his temper was shorter. Also, Lord Peter still had not sold the Derby property to him. "Goldurn it, Allen, what the blazes are you going to do? Sit still and see your property ruined right before your eyes with no redress in sight?"

"Hear! hear!" Lord Peter called out from his leather chair.

"I say!" Lord Cecil echoed from his chair. With an easy languid gesture he flipped ashes from his Norfolk jacket. Like Lord Peter, red-faced Lord Cecil used his home in the upper Big Stonies basin more as a royal hunting lodge than as ranch house. Every fall he held elaborate hunting parties for his roving Mayfair friends and every summer his country home was loud with endless house-partying. He shipped fox and hounds from England and hothouse flowers, both plant and human, from Boston. Young British elegants who hardly knew the difference between a steer and a heifer discussed with much enthusiasm the latest bonanza, cattle raising, over port and nuts. The visiting chaps and chippies all said they loved the raw West and only wished there was some way of getting rid of that eternal smell of horse manure.

Hunt said, "Dead men tell no tales."

"I don't know as to that, Hunt," Bat Wildy said, twisting uneasily in his chair. "I ain't hardly ready for such doings yet." Bat was a former cowboy who had struck it rich late in life.

Jesse broke in. "Say, Bat, how does your team of elk get along in the city?"

Bat had tamed a pair of elk bulls and had driven into town

239

for the meeting. It was Bat's way of leveling himself up to the lords. "Oh," Bat said, "all right, I guess. Have a little trouble on the corners. They go too fast." Bat caught the hint of humor in Jesse's question. "But I tell you what really throws them. All them geldings in the livery barn. They can't make hide nor hair of them."

Chuckles went around the jammed room.

Clayborne Rodney said, "We've been here an hour now beating around the bush. Now by golly, what I want to know is, just what are we supposed to be up to, meeting here?" Clayborne, or Clabe as the boys called him, was a great hulking cowboy. He had soft eyes the color of bluebird eggs. He'd married a pert little spitfire named Liza who had insisted he quit dirty cowpoke work. He loved Liza very much, was anxious to please her, and had got himself the local U. S. Marshal's job. She thought being marshal a sight more respectable. Clabe himself, however, didn't care much for it. He didn't tell Liza, but he knew it would eventually pit him against his old buddies. He was a simple-minded man, tender and true as a woman, and was totally miscast as an officer of the law. "It sounds to me like you fellows all got a wholesale killin' in mind."

Walrus barked from his end of the table, "Well, what else?"

"No!" Clabe exclaimed. Clabe had difficulty showing outrage.

Governor Barb spoke up quietly from his corner. He'd once been a doctor and had sat observant during all the talk. He was a well-built man, always neat and close-shaven, had a keen eye, a duke's bold nose, and gold teeth. He liked Clabe. "Well, now, perhaps not to that extreme, Clabe. Though it has become a question of life or death for some of us ranchers. It's either them or us. That's why we're meeting here tonight to see what can be done."

"I don't believe in wholesale killin's," Clabe said, depressed.

Walrus barked, "We simply have to take the gun to them, Clabe. It's that or quit."

Senator Thorne put in his two bits' worth then too. "It's that, or declare an insurrection in Bighorn County and call out the National Guard." In polite circles Senator Thorne was a sort of fop—there was always a faint hint of perfume about him—but out on the range he could be as rough and as ready as the next. He was very vain; loved to do the grand thing; had an overbearing manner; and had a very jealous disposition. He was a close friend of the President and had talked him into investing heavily in his ranch near the Big Stonies. Senator Thorne continued. "Why, it's got so bad up our way, one small rancher just to the north of us by the name of Holdout Johnson has cows that throw twins almost every time. Sometimes even triplets, by God. Yes. While my cows just outside his fence are always barren. Poor things, my cows seem to miss motherhood so much they spend most of their time hanging around Holdout's corral, envying his cows their numerous progeny, lamenting their own childless fate." Senator Thorne coughed, spat a brown gob into a spittoon at his feet. "Well, you know what we did about that. My foreman Tine Breader made a call around that way one day and threatened to hang Holdout if his cows got any more twins. Yes, gentlemen, we've simply got to stop a situation where small bands of cattle belonging to one-time cowboys grow beyond the natural rate of increase."

Governor Barb said, "Making the cowboy prove ownership at the stockyards when he comes in to sell his beef hasn't really worked. It hasn't smoked out the rustler, since the rustler uses a fence. And it's angered the honest little rancher, since now his beef is looked upon with suspicion too at the market."

Jesse sighed. "Compared to now, it sure was good in them old days." Jesse sipped from his brandy snifter. "Them days, all a man had to do was brand his calves when dropped, ship his beeves when fat. He could keep the calf tally on a shingle. Why, the checkbook was the only book kept and the balance or the overdraft at the bank showed the whole business." Jesse sighed again, deep. "Yes, times has sure changed."

Walrus snapped, "Them organizing into an association of their own and planning that early roundup, an illegal roundup . . . I say that's the last straw."

Stone nodded over his cigar. "Yes, I'm afraid the glory has departed all right."

Irv raised, eyes fiery. "Not if we fight, it won't be."

Jesse said, "That's what I say."

Stone said, "Well, what do you suggest we do?"

Walrus whacked the table with his puffy hand. "I guess it's time for me to trot out my plan."

"What plan?" Stone asked, gray brows lifting high over florid cheeks.

"Make a surprise march on Antelope, the capital of Bighorn County. Secretly. Imprison the present sheriff, the district attorney, the district judge. Impound all the records at the courthouse. Hold a new election to put in our own men. Start with a new slate in our favor."

Governor Barb asked, quietly, "What are you going to march with?"

"Why, ourselves," Walrus roared. "Arm our foremen and our loyal cowboys and ourselves. And if that ain't enough, get Texas Ike here to bring up a delegation of some of his Texas toughs."

Stone exploded at that. "Why, you're suggesting civil war!"

"So I am. It won't be the first one we've had in this country."

"But . . . but . . . that sort of thing just can't be done!"

"Then are you prepared to give up all your holdings? Because that's just what you'll have to do if those nesters and rustlers get their way up north. Let their idea get a foothold in one county and it'll sweep the whole state. Or, if not that, they might even decide to secede from us. And you know what that means to Lord Peter, and the governor and the senator here. Clean out what holdings they still have left along the edges of Bighorn County. For myself, I say: Wipe out this nest of insurrection and save our way of life."

This was too thick for Stone. He got to his feet very perturbed. "I say . . . but my clients just will not have any part of inciting armed civil war." Stone stood trembling a moment; then, with a low curse, he muttered, "I just won't hear any more of this," and lunged out of the meeting.

Walrus smiled. "Anyone else want to pull out? Because this meeting was called to see what we could do about putting down that insurrection in the north."

No one else got up.

"Good. Good." Walrus leaned forward from the edge of his chair. "All right, now I further propose"—he drew a slip of paper from a vest pocket—"I further propose that we exterminate some twenty of the rebel leaders."

Everyone drew a sharp breath.

"How?" Clabe finally asked.

Walrus went on. "Either by shooting or hanging. Hunt, here, has drawn up a list for us. From Cain Hammett the boss of the illegal roundup to his brother Harry Hammett the chief of the rustlers." Walrus looked over at Hunt. "I see some have been checked off. I presume this means they've already been got rid of."

Gray eyes glowing, Hunt nodded grimly over his pipe.

Bat shook his head. "Well, you're probably right about

242

that Harry Hammett. I know him well. Used to ride with him. How such a nice feller can house such a hellish mind is something I just never have been able to savvy."

Walrus turned to Texas Ike. "Think you can round up some Texas fighters for us?"

"Reckon." Ike had hair as red as carrots, a boyish smiling face, and eyes that were grave and old-gray. "What's there in it for my boys?"

"One thousand dollars apiece. All expenses paid. Fifty dollars' bounty to each fighter for every rustler killed, no matter who kills him. That sound all right to you?"

"Reckon."

"Wait a minute," Bat said. "Who's going to pay all this money?"

"We're going to pass the hat round-robin."

Jesse smiled knowing at Hunt. "Well, Hunt, after we get through burning the records in the courthouse up there, you won't have a worry in the world."

Hunt's gray eyes half-closed.

Irv said, "Yes, when we get through with it, Antelope will be known hereafter as the doomed city of the plains."

"Hear! Hear!" Lord Peter called.

Walrus turned to Governor Barb. "Suppose, before we get there, suppose Sheriff Sine calls out the state militia to help him put down civil insurrection in Bighorn County?"

"Well . . . I think we can handle that."

"How?"

"This way. Send out an order to all state company commanders that they shall obey only such orders to assemble their commands as may be received from my office."

Walrus smiled. "Ain't that in direct violation of the laws of the state?"

"Perhaps."

Walrus turned to Senator Thorne. "What about you, John? In case of extreme necessity, can we count on the President to order the federal troops out as needed? As you can see, I want all bets covered."

"I think I can promise you the fullest cooperation from the President's office."

"I say!" Lord Cecil called.

Again Walrus smiled. "That too is in direct violation of the laws of the land, is it not?"

"Perhaps."

"All right. Good. Good. Remember now. The raid must be kept a surprise to be effective. It must be made quickly and efficiently and secretly. Afterwards we won't care what happens. Because then we'll be in control."

Hunt

Wednesday.

Dawn was just breaking.

Both the train and the Platte River emerged from a rocky gorge. The shining rails curved off to the left, hugging the base of the Bear Creek Mountains, while the rippling river immediately swung off to the right, going far out across a low narrow valley just now greening over with early April grass.

Going along at a little more than twenty-five miles an hour over an uneven roadbed, the special train from Cheyenne rolled and pitched, sometimes violently, first the blunt engine, then in order down the line, the baggage car, the chair car, the caboose, three stock cars loaded with saddle horses, a flatcar heavy with wagons and camp equipment. Everyone in the chair car complained about the rough jolting ride. Reading was impossible. Even to keep a small object outside the window steadily in eye was difficult. Only the large outlines held steady, the looming dark green mountains immediately to the south, the occasional ranch-house buildings along the way, the great rising sweeps of prairie going north on and on forever. Gun belts hanging from hooks overhead swung back and forth with every roll of the car.

Hunt sat alone. He'd reversed the front seat and so, riding backwards, had a view of the whole chair car all the way to the rear. Two lamps burned above him, adding some to the light of breaking dawn. Pipe in mouth, puffing on it now and then, he was busy working fresh rawhide into a tight neat braid. The smell of the rawhide pleased him. Every now and then an involuntary smile worked back into his lean cheeks.

Halfway down the aisle were the Texas fighters Ike had hired, some twenty-five of them. They sat apart, silent. Every now and then their keen eyes flickered over him and then looked away. They'd managed to get but short fitful naps during the night and were owly. Smoke hung gray and thick above them against the brown wood ceiling.

Hunt didn't like Texans. He'd spent several years in Texas as a marshal and had come to know them a little. He and a Texan just didn't hit it off. He sensed that these devil-may-

244

care toughs were like all the others he'd known. They were suspicious of all Northerners, held human life of little value, and were clannish. When aroused, a Texas cowpoke could be terrible in a fight. At the same time, grudgingly, Hunt had to admit that as horsemen they were top hands. They could sweep around a herd in great style, never missing a point. After all it was the Texans who'd taught the boys in Colorado and Wyoming and Montana how to ride the range. They'd been the best.

In the back of the rocking car sat the rest of the raiders, some thirty-five of the local boys: Walrus, Jesse, Bat, Clabe, and certain select cowboys who could be trusted. A friendly newspaperman from Chicago had also joined the party. To make sure of the National Guard and the state militia, both Senator Thorne and Governor Barb had stayed behind in Cheyenne.

The trucks under the chair car whacked into a sharp dip in the roadbed. The jolt almost shook the pipe out of Hunt's mouth. Some of the hairs in his mustache moved on his pipestem. Biting down, he managed to keep his pipe fixed firmly between clenched teeth. He set his back in a bow, ready for the next jolt.

One of the Texans, a beardless boy of some seventeen years, opened up a blue duffel bag and began to mend a brown sock. It took him a while to thread the eye of the dancing darning needle. The jolts from below kept throwing him off just as he was about to make an entrance with the wetted end of green yarn. He concentrated. Gradually the pink tip of his tongue worked out of the corner of his mouth; began to ululate like uneasy proud flesh. Finally the boy got the needle threaded. He slipped a much-pocked darning egg into the sock. Slowly, with infinite patience, he worked a neat green weave across the ragged heel of the sock.

Hunt jerked the four thongs of his braid into a round even tightness, each thong in turn. He took pride in the rawhide reatas he made. He liked to fondle giving leather. Soft leather felt alive; bristly hemp felt dead.

Over the years he had become an expert at selecting just the right kind of hide for reata-making. The best came from old skinny starved cows. Such hides usually had little or no fat, and much glue. He'd even worked out a recipe, and it went as follows: "Split the hide in two. Cut off arms and legs. Soak both halves in cold water until thoroughly wet. Cut narrow strip along outer edge, circlelike, around and around, toward the center, until gone. Same for other half.

Divide strips in half to make four thongs sixty-seventy feet long. Soak in water again until soft. Stretch each thong on pegs as tight as possible and let dry. Scrape off hair with knife. Slice off thick sections. Braid into round rope. Grease with tallow. Work it often, the more the better."

Hunt lifted up the braided portion in his lap and rolled it back and forth between palm and knee. He put it to his nose and smelled. The reata was rich with animal musk. And clean. He just barely managed to hold back an impulse to bite it, wolflike, hard, vicious.

He worked the braid some more. Sweat, body oil, its own moisture soon made each thong shine glossy where it showed in the braid. He looked down at the coiled piles of thongs still left to do and saw that if given another hour he could get the reata finished before the train pulled into Casper.

Bat down the aisle got up and bowlegged toward him. Bat's seamed leathery face was drawn too from lack of sleep and his pale blue eyes brooded. Bat's hand toyed with the brass tops of the bullets in his cartridge belt. With his gun butt sticking out, his elbows jutting, his knobby ears bent forward as if by clothespins, Bat had the blunt look of a bulldog.

"Hi," Bat said, and sat down across from him.

"Hi."

Bat got out his makings and rolled himself a cigarette. He lighted up. "Walrus wants to know what's eatin' you."

The question griped Hunt. He liked being a loner. He took pipe from mouth. "Nothing, Wildy. Just that I think two's a crowd."

"Walrus in command is all right with you then?"

Hunt looked down the aisle to where Walrus and all others sat together in the back end of the car. He saw their eyes hard on him. "I have no quarrel with Wallace Tascott."

"And it's all right that Texas Ike is to act as captain of the Texans?"

"I have no quarrel with Ike either."

"And it's all right too that you're to act as captain of the other half?"

Hunt allowed himself a sliding smile. "I have no quarrel with myself either."

Bat looked out of the window. The trucks below the chair car cracked through another deep dip in the roadbed. The jolt tossed Bat's hat to the back of his head, revealing a balding grizzled dome. A single pale vein wriggled exactly down the middle of his forehead, dividing in two just at the level of his blond eyebrows. "You ain't carryin' a grudge agin anyone here then?"

"No."

"I'm asking because Walrus wants to be sure this raid goes off as planned."

"Somebody think it ain't?"

Bat flicked a look back at the Texans. "We're beginning to wonder about them."

"Why?"

"They've asked Ike if we got warrants for Cain and his bunch."

"What did you tell them?"

"That we did."

"Good."

Bat gave Hunt a close look. "You have got the warrants, hain't you, Hunt? From the federal government?"

Hunt held steady under the look. "You worried about it?"

"You have got them warrants, hain't you, Hunt?"

"Don't worry about it."

Bat nodded. Bat looked out of the window. April-pale prairies slid by but Hunt noticed that Bat didn't seem to see them.

Hunt went back to working his reata.

Bat crushed out his cigarette. "Hunt, I guess I got a question to askt you."

"Shoot."

"Before this ever came up, I take it you didn't like Cain none."

Hunt smiled, velvet. "What gives you that idee?"

Bat persisted. "You didn't, did you?"

"Don't we all hate him now?"

"Not like you, Hunt."

Hunt clopped out his pipe. He got out his tobacco pouch and spilled in a fresh load. He lit up. He held silent.

Again Bat pressed in. "Not like you, Hunt."

Hunt decided to play a little with Bat. "Well, Wildy, you know how it is with me. Killin' is my specialty. I hire out to do it. I don't do it on my own, but for others. You know. For the government. For the law. For private business concerns. I look at it as a business proposition." Hunt smiled, thin. "Maybe that's what gets you."

"Mabbe."

"When I'm hired to exterminate rats, I don't play favors."

"You sure are warlike, all right. I've knowed men that

would kill if they had cause. But you seem to kill for the love of it."

Hunt looked over at his Winchester standing in the near corner. It was an exact duplicate of the one he'd left behind in Hidden Country the time he and three others raided a cabin hoping to capture Cain, an 1886 carbine, .38-56 caliber. He loved that particular model. It burned him that Cain had got hold of the other.

Hunt said, "You like Cain, don't you, Wildy?"

"I do."

"Let me ask you something. If Cain is so dummed honest, how come he keeps running around with a known crook. And the chief of the Red Sashers t'boot."

"Well, he and Harry is brothers."

"Sure. But blood don't have to run that thick. That a man has to stick close to an outright crook."

"Well, that's true."

"Sure. And another thing. What would you say if I told you that Harry now lives with Cain?"

"No!"

"Sure. Harry lives with Cain now. Which makes it even worse."

"You mean they're living together in Cain's cabin on the Shaken Grass?"

"That's exactly what I mean."

Bat's face saddened over. "I got to give you that. Harry is a rascal."

"Harry is a rustler."

Bat sat still a while.

Hunt braided.

Bat said finally, "How come you was so careless as to leave a trail in that other Hammett killin'?"

"Dale's? I didn't. I couldn't've. I went barefooted."

"In that terrible cold? With all them pricklepear underfoot?"

"I went barefooted."

"How come they got out a warrant for your arrest then?"

"Some range bum thought he saw me."

"Did he?"

"He couldn't've."

"Hunt, how many men have you actually killed?"

Hunt shrugged a smile. "I don't cut notches."

"How many?"

"Can't rightly recall. Never bothered to count 'em."

"How old was you when you made your first killin'?"

248

"Seventeen. He was a dead-tough devil-mean man and he needed killin'."

"Was that Gramp Hammett?"

"It was. I gave him a deadhead ticket straight to hell and I ain't regretted it."

"Hunt, what have you got agin the Hammett bunch?"

"Are you trying to work me about them?"

"Hunt, I've heard you've gone as much as five days without food when out on one of your killing bees. How can a man who weighs near two hundred pounds go without eating that long?"

Hunt couldn't resist it. "I run like the loner wolf does. When I got meat, I eat. When I don't, I wait."

The rails clicked monotonously beneath them. The chair car rolled. A horse whinnied loud on the stock car behind them. A veil of black smoke wisped past the window and after a moment the smell of burning coal was in the car.

Bat cocked his grizzled head to one side. "You never married, did you, Hunt?"

"No."

"But you've had you she-stuff?"

"Oh, I had me she-stuff all right. One. A schoolmarm." Hunt snorted as he jerked a thong into place in the braid. "She sure was smooth people, too. She once wrote me a letter. It turned out to be as long as the governor's message, all about reforming, and that was enough for me."

"That was Abigail Adams the schoolmarm from Boston, wasn't it?"

"It was."

Bat got to his feet. "Then you ain't got a mad agin anybody here?"

"Why should I have? We're going to clean out the rustlers, ain't we? And burn the courthouse records?"

"Hunt, something is burning you."

Hunt said nothing.

Bat sighed. "Well, God knows, I wouldn't blame you if there was. Me, I wish I'd never've agreed to come on this trip. It ain't going to be easy to shoot down a man who's sided you on the trail. So maybe it's all in my head that things ain't going bore-smooth."

Hunt

Hunt braided. He was almost done.

Something was burning him. As long as any male Hammett blood was left alive on earth something would always be burning him. He still had Cain and Harry to get, and Dale's two bull calves. There was also this record of a warrant for his arrest at the Antelope courthouse that had to be wiped out.

Hunt's lips thinned. His mustache moved under his sharp nose. He pulled viciously on the thongs. Once he jerked too hard and had to undo a portion of the reata and rebraid it.

Gramp Hammett's words he'd never forget. "Old Abraham in the Bible was wrong to let Isaac go, even if Isaac was his first and only son by Sarah. Abraham should have gone ahead and killed him."

His mother had burned it into his mind. Over and over. Ma Keeler always told it the same, eyes burning, mouth set in hatred. She had heard Gramp say it and she swore to avenge him for it.

That wasn't all. Dad Keeler already had been bad enough without having high-headed Gramp around to egg him into being devil-mean.

. . . One day Ma and Dad had a fight. Dad was getting the worst of it and he threatened to take the boy, little Link, and drown him if she didn't shut her trap.

"What!" Ma gasped.

"Yes. Drown him. You think more of him already at two than you ever did of me your lawfully wedded husband."

"Did our dear neighbor Mayberry give you that idea?"

"Gramp Hammett? What if he did? A good idee is a good idee."

"Him and his way of making women the equal of cows."

"But he's right. If you want peace in the house you should probably drown the first boy."

"You monsters."

"Well, ary a man kin see with half an eye that ever since Link's come I ain't been nothin' more to you than a dirty toad. Nothin'. I might's well be married to a sawhorse for all the good you're to me now."

"You murderers. My little baby boy."

"What good is he to me so long's I've lost you?"

250

"What beasts you men are! Monsters! 'Of course, Keeler, if you want to know the truth, and you want yourself a good obedient wife, you should really drown that firstborn boy. I've bred cattle and read Shakespeare, and that's what I've come to see.' What an awful thing to say."

"I wish I'd a had the guts to ha' follered his advice. Maybe you'd a knowed your place by now."

"My place."

"Where is the boy?"

"What?"

"I say, where is the boy?"

"I don't know."

"Give me him."

"Are you crazy?"

"Well, by Grab, I'll soon know where he is if you won't tell me."

"No."

"Ah. There he is. Behind the hollyhocks there. C'mere, Link. Your dad's got something for you."

"Stay away from him, Linkie."

"C'mere, boy. Look what yore dad's got for you."

"Linkie! Stay away! Run! He'll kill you!"

"C'mere, boy. See?"

"Oh, my baby boy, run run, he's going to kill you!"

"That's it, boy."

"Help! Help!"

"Come, boy, we'll go see if you can swim." ...

Beyond that, Hunt's mind would not go. At that point his mind always became a whelming rage of hate, blixon hot. At that point all the milling tails of hell let go in him.

His trigger finger worked involuntarily. He found himself gasping for breath. It was all he could do to keep his arms from windmilling in the presence of others. His eyes misted over black-red. The little Adam in the back of his head who always laughed at things he did disappeared. He was drowning again. Christ the Son might be his friend, because Ma had taught him so, but God the Father was an enemy.

There was a song which sometimes ran through his head:

I dreamt I went to heaven and saw my darling there,
She played a golden harp and had a ribbon in her hair.
I dreamt I went to kiss her, call her Abigail,
And woke up broken-hearted with a yearling by the tail.

251

Forgive me, Mother dear, it's you who's best for me,
Forgive me, dear my love, you are the girl for me.

Gradually the sharp cracking of the rails fell away to a clicking. The chair car began to ride with less of a rolling motion.

Hunt looked out and saw they were approaching the stockyards on the outskirts of Casper. He looked down at his hands and saw that he had come to the end of the four thongs. They'd come out about even. Except for the final knot, the leather reata was done.

Clayborne

Right from the start, overgrown Clabe sensed they were in for trouble. Things kept happening.

Gun belt slung from the shoulder, coat over an arm, the raiders slowly shuffled down the aisle of the chair car and out the door and down the iron steps into the chill air of dawn.

Ike took a breath and shuddered. "Why do them damn Yankees always keep it so frio up here," he griped in his low drawling Texas voice. "A man kin hardly swallow in this freeze."

Despite his wry neck, tubby Walrus managed to whirl around sharp. "You boys getting cold feet?" The major leaned forward from his toes, as if getting set to strike with his fists.

Ike's face hardened over instantly. He stared back, slow, young.

"If you are," Walrus continued, "you can get right back aboard and go back to mother."

Ike stared back, slow, measuring.

Jesse spotted the trouble and limped over. "Here, here," he growled, good-natured, "here, we're among friends. Let's get along."

Big Clabe wished he had complained about the cold. Almost. Because he just might have accepted Walrus's offer to go back to mother. Clabe didn't care much for Walrus either. It was that thick stiff neck. Walrus's neck was enough larger than his head so that he could back out of his shirt without unbuttoning his collar.

Clabe looked up to where the mountains to the south loomed blue and green, with silver night mist still sliding down the canyons and ravines. Clouds with rain falling under them rode high above the peaks. Showers were always high in that part of the state.

Clabe thought of his sweet little wife Liza still probably asleep in their warm bed, curled up like a warm puppy under the suggans. He longed to be with her. His soft blue eyes closed in memory of her warm smells. "If I could just lay my hand on her hip," he thought, "if I could just put my big hand on her little hip I'd ask for no more." It continually astounded him that her little body could accommodate his big one. Their mating was like the coupling of a St. Bernard with a lap dog.

Walrus strutted back and forth. "All right, men, let's get moving. You there, get a couple of them planks by the chutes there. Stand them up to the flatcar and roll down the wagons."

Quick hands brought planks. The ropes lashing down the wagons to the floor of the flatcar were loosened. Wheels rolled.

The last wagon, however, somehow got out of control. It slipped sideways and with a crash its gears landed on one of the planks.

Walrus exploded. "Holy Moses and the prophets! There goes another half hour. When we're already two hours late. Should have been out of here before it got light. Now we're liable to be seen." Walrus threw a nervous look toward Casper. Some of the chimneys were already pouring smoke into the gray dawn.

"Don't worry," Jesse said. "By now my men've got the telegraph wires cut between here and Antelope."

"That won't prevent a man on horseback from getting through."

"I've got that taken care of too. Mitch is riding down from the north to join us at Irv Hornsby's ranch. He'll keep a weather eye peeled for strange riders."

Clabe stood looking north, across the tree-fringed Platte River, gun riding heavy on his hip. Out of the corner of his eye he could see his silver star. It rode winking on his vest. Clabe thought of his former cowboy chums Cain and Harry and Timberline and all the rest. They were probably, right now, still sleeping under the stars, not knowing that a small army was coming for them and would probably kill them before the week was out. He felt awful thinking about them.

Walrus barked, "Come on, you big clabberlipped dreamer! Pitch in a little, will you?" Walrus stood under Clabe's elbow, glaring up at him. "We can use some of that muscle to help lift the wagon off the plank."

With a groan, hating him, Clabe turned to help the men.

Walrus next pointed toward the stock cars. "You men over there, Ike and the rest of you, let's get them horses off. Hurry now. March."

Glowering, Ike and his Texans pitched in. They moved with a quick and swaying walk. They wore their guns low and tied down. The heavy guns were sometimes in the way and caught on things.

"Rustle now, you men," Walrus clipped. "We're burning daylight."

Out of the corner of his eye, Clabe watched the Texans. The thought struck him that their guns were as handy to them as hammers were to carpenters. The major had better be careful not to rile them up too much or there'd be another civil war.

Walrus bawled, "Bat? Come here. There's still more to unload from the baggage car. The dynamite to blow up houses with."

"Comin'," Bat said.

When the wagons were finally loaded and most of the men had mounted their horses, Clabe discovered he had been given a small pony to ride, a bay. Clabe looked over to where Ike sat easy, insolent, on a great rangy black. Clabe said, friendly-like, "How about trading?"

Ike drawled, "I'll take my chances with this one."

"But I can't ride this puppy," Clabe said. "If I step across he'll fall down sure."

"Try it," Ike said.

Clabe did. The second Clabe settled into the saddle, the pony spraddled out all four legs and let out a great groan.

Clabe touched the pony's flanks lightly with his spurs. "Hup-a, sport, let's see how you do."

The pony groaned again, took a few staggering steps, and fell to the ground with a crash of bones, Clabe just barely having time to hop to one side.

There was a gleeful shout from the Texans. Ike drawled, "Three men all inside one hide. No wonder the bay gave up."

Walrus came riding over. Walrus sat high. Balancing in his saddle he looked more like a boar on a horse than a man. "What's the matter here? A horse down already?"

Clabe looked down at his fallen pony. "Major, how about putting me aboard a real hoss? I can't ride this puppy."

Walrus looked the crowd over, the Texans, the cowboys,

the cattlemen. "Well," he finally snapped, "will no one offer to trade with Clabe?"

Ike drawled, "I'll take my chances with this one."

One of the Texans, a grim fellow named Daggett, said slow, casual, "Tell y'u what, Major. Why don't you put the saddle on Clabe and let the poor pony ride." The grim Texan wore flaring weather-worn chaps. He had on a checker-patched pair of pants, a ragged gray shirt, a black vest full of holes where he'd snagged himself on greasewood. "Or better yit, put that newspaper fellow aboard Clabe. Then he kin use Clabe's back for a table and write us up as we go."

There was a short sardonic laugh from the rest of the Texans.

From behind the group came a well-dressed man. His name was Charles Exon. He rode a big lively sorrel. Exon was a young doctor just in from Philadelphia. His family had money invested in a large ranch near Cheyenne. As a gesture to show that he and his family had their heart in the right place, he'd offered to go along. He thought the raid a wonderful lark so long as their side was in the right. "Here, Major, I'll trade with him. My horse is twice too lively for me as it is."

The trade was made.

The sun was up an hour by the time the raiders got rolling. Wagons rattling, horses nickering, the party crossed the plank bridge over the Platte a mile above town. Once across, the major placed outriders some three hundred yards to either side with orders to warn off stray horsemen and keep them far enough away so they couldn't identify anyone in the group.

Two hours out of Casper, well over the first hogback, one of the wagons bogged down in a wet draw. It took a dozen ropes tied to saddle horns to pull the wagon out of the muck. The delay put the major in a rage. And the major's high and mighty airs in turn threw the Texans in a deeper pet.

Four hours out, young Doc Exon, who'd never ridden horseback before, discovered he'd developed a blister on his Philadelphia behind. When he complained about it, the major told him to climb down and get aboard a wagon.

Six hours out, tough old Bat Wildy developed a bad nose-bleed. Clabe sided him, trying to help him stanch it. With Doc Exon offering suggestions from the wagon, they tried everything: sage leaves, gunpowder, cotton plugs. Bat even tried standing in his stirrups with giving springy knees. It didn't help. The front of Bat's coat was a mess of blood. To cap it, Bat finally fainted and fell off his horse.

255

At that, the major called a halt. After Doc Exon had old Bat comfortable, the major ordered the cooks to make a warm meal for all hands. The rear ends of the wagons were let down, fires were started out of dry clumps of sage, horses were unsaddled and staked out to graze in a nearby draw, and the men were told to stretch out on blankets and get such rest as they could until the cooks had chow. The joshing talk around the fires and the hot coffee soon revived Bat.

They were riding again, near evening, when the sky clouded over and snow began to drift down.

" 'Y godies!" grim Daggett cursed. "Snow. That's Yankee country for y'u all right."

Men pulled down their broad-brim hats, tied silk kerchiefs over ears, edged a shoulder into the white furry wind.

The raiders climbed a long swell in the land. Horses on the wagons leaned into it, head to one side, tails clapped down.

Lightning flashed, strangely. It hit near a chuck wagon, knocked loose an empty pail, sent it rattling away through the silver sagebrush.

A cookie named Perley Gates was driving the wagon. He tipped back his old soggy hat and looked startled up at the snow clouds. Then his bearded face darkened over in outrage. He shook his fist at the sky. "All right, you old bald-headed son-of-a-gun up there, if you're after me you better raise your sights some!"

Before anyone could laugh or protest at the blasphemy, lightning strangely struck again. It hit a greasewood bush almost beside Clabe and his horse, not a half-dozen feet away. For a second both he and his sorrel were caught up in a seething ball of pink fire. It stunned him, stiffened him, knocked his tan hat sailing. The sorrel's yellow mane crackled, burst into racing edges of searing fire. The sorrel's yellow tail shot straight up, also burst into searing racing edges of fire. Sparks flew out of the pupils of the horse's eyes, popping them. Slowly, in slow motion, like a stone statue of a man on a horse, both stiffened man and stiffened horse tipped over and fell to the ground. Blackness rushed in where a moment before blue-white lightning and pink illumination danced.

"Whoa!" Walrus roared, reining in his prancing horse.

Everybody stopped, stood enstatued, staring, jaws dropping.

"My God," Jesse said softly, "struck down by lightning!"

"And in the middle of a snowstorm," Irv whispered, flushed face paling to ashen gray.

"Holy Moses and the prophets! If it ain't one thing it's another," Walrus raged.

256

Doc Exon hopped down off the wagon and ran over with his little black bag. He knelt down, put a hand on Clabe.

"What a way to go," Bat said softly.

"Look at his face turn blue," Jesse said.

Clabe was still vaguely conscious. He couldn't move, couldn't see, but he heard the commotion around him. He felt the sorrel between his legs slowly hardening over with the stiffness of death. He felt the young doctor's hand slide warm and brotherly over his face. The smell of burnt air stung fiercely in his nostrils.

"Couple of you men give me a hand here," Doc Exon ordered. "Quick."

Jesse and Bat and Irv jumped to the ground, heels tomping. The thin film of snow made the gray ground greasy and the men slid around some as they warily approached the fallen giant. Jesse and Bat and Irv lifted up part of the singed sorrel while Doc dragged Clabe free.

"Water," Doc called. "Quick."

Perley Gates hopped down off his spring seat and, grabbing another bucket, dipped it in a water barrel tied to the side of the chuck wagon. He came hobbling and sloshing toward them. He threw half of the water across Clabe's blue face.

Clabe came up gasping. "Hey!"

"He's alive!" Bat whispered. Others picked it up. "He's alive!" "Alive!" The murmuring wonder of it passed through the raiding party.

The wind rose. Snow whistled over the long swell. Snow on the new sage and the new spring bunch grass shoots took on the color of creamy green.

Doc Exon chafed Clabe's face; rubbed his hands.

Rain began to fall mixed in with snow. The rain froze the moment it hit. Curiously the snow melted.

Jesse looked up at the sky. He lipped some of the rain. "Sure is a strange spring," he said, nodding.

Bat looked at the frozen drops of water gathering on a tip of gray sage. "Silver thaw," he said.

Irv said, "A year of extremes. Strong ones." The color of Irv's face slowly returned. "A hard winter and now a late spring. We're liable to have a tough summer."

Bat said, "It'll try to catch up with itself."

Irv said, "Nature always seems to even things up."

Ike edged his horse up to the kneeling group. He looked down, lips curling. "I've seen it all now. Lightning in a Yankee snowstorm."

Walrus's horse shied at the dead horse. Walrus spurred him

257

close anyway. "Holy Moses!" Walrus cursed again. "If it ain't one thing it's another."

Bat stood up, groaning. "For godsakes, Wallace, this man was hit by lightning. What'd you expect, that we'd let him lay out here for the wolves? It's a miracle he's alive, man. Be thankful."

"Any more delays," Walrus snapped, "and we might as well give up Bighorn County without a fight."

Ike looked down. "Is the horse daid?"

Bat went over and kicked the horse. The horse's burnt popped-out eyes moved as if alive. Bat said, "Knocked stiffer'n a peetrified tree."

Walrus called, "Here, someone, help these men lift the big fellow onto a wagon."

Four men grabbed at a corner of Clabe.

"Hey," Clabe said, robin-egg eyes opening wide in astonishment, "hey! I can stand. Let go." He wrestled free. With a hand on Bat's shoulder, he righted himself. He staggered around a little, trying to get his balance back.

The men watched him, staring up at his blue face.

"Put him on a wagon," Jesse said, "like Wallace says."

Doc looked anxious. "He should rest a while."

"We haven't got time," Walrus snapped.

"Besides," Ike reminded them, drawling, leaning with arms crossed on the pommel of his saddle, "he ain't got him a hoss anyway."

"What a helluva way to conduct a war," Walrus growled, twitching atop his horse. He still had trouble keeping his mount near the fallen sorrel.

"War, eh?" Ike said. "Well, Major, maybe it's a good thing we ain't wearin' uniforms."

"How so?" Walrus's mustache moved quick, once. His dark eyes looked black at Ike.

"Half of us would be in gray."

Walrus humphed.

Snowflakes fell thicker. It blurred the outlines of horse and man.

"Besides," Bat put in, looking up at Walrus, "who knows, maybe the lightning was meant as a sign."

"Paugh!"

Bat said, "Don't it strike you funny it struck twice in the middle of a snowstorm? And in the same place?"

"Not at all. I've heard of it many times."

"In the same place? You know what they say: Lightning never strikes twice in the same place."

"Wife talk."

Ike drawled, "Maybe it does in Yankee country."

Walrus wried his stiff neck around at Ike again. "How would you know? You come from Texas."

Ike's face fell into a set glare. He backed his horse, gently, spurs and bit gingling, until he was once again grouped with the rest of his Texans. They looked on, silent, sullen, leaning with arms across the pommels of their saddles.

Clabe staggered around, his stunned brain gradually opening up. Slowly too the blue pallor washed out of his face. His right cheek began to show a spot of pink.

Clabe saw his hat lying to one side in the snow-tufted sage. He went over and picked it up. He stared at it. Snow fell on his matted blond hair.

"Hey!" he called. "Looky here." He stuck a finger through a black singed opening in the dented crown and held it up. "It burnt a fresh hole right through the top of it." With his other hand he felt of his hair. A sharp smell of burnt ozone rose from the hat. He thought he could smell it in his hair too.

The men came over to look. They examined the little black hole in wonder.

A meadowlark whistled cheerfully out of the snowy distance. Its swift clear warble seemed to say, "Wheu! Wheu! See you in the morning."

"I don't like it atall," Bat said.

Doc stepped in front of Clabe. Reaching high, he lifted the lid of each of Clabe's eyes. "How do you feel, Clabe?"

"Well," Clabe said, turning his burnt hat round and round on his big finger, "well, I don't know yet. I'll have to wait till I find out."

A smile broke along the young doc's grim lips. "Good."

"I don't like it nohow," Bat said. "Maybe it is wrong to dry-gulch men like Cain. It's a sign all right."

Hunt came riding in through the snow. He'd been an outrider the last while. He overheard Bat's remark. His white teeth gleamed in the snowy dusk. "You weaseling out on us, Bat?"

Walrus was still having trouble with his horse. When he touched him with spurs, the horse reared, held rampant a second with front hooves pawing, then came down with a thud. "It's a sign, all right," Walrus barked. "A sign to move on. Get aboard that wagon, Clabe. Or we'll throw you aboard."

"I can make it alone," Clabe said. He walked heavily, still staggering some, and climbed in the nearest wagon. Doc Exon got in beside him.

"Somebody take that saddle off Clabe's horse," Walrus ordered. "The rest of you move on."

"Cookie shouldn't've said that," Clabe murmured. "Perley knows the Big Boss up there don't stand for sass."

They rode on. The snow thickened. Men got out their yellow slickers one by one. They rode slowly, steadily, through a blind smother of white. Horses began to slide on the gummy gray ground. The spans of four on the wagons had trouble getting traction. Men cursed.

"It's like riding on the knob of the North Pole itself," grim Daggett said, casual, slow. "I swear."

"Fust thing we know we'll bump into an iceberg," Ike drawled. "This country!"

A meadowlark flitted from bush to bush. It whistled cheerful, clear, pure. "Wheu! Wheu! See you in the morning, boys!" It flew up some twenty feet high; sang once again. "Wheu! Wheu! In the morning!" Then, with a turn of wing, was gone.

Night came on. Mist and snow continued to mizzle down. Eyes became bloodshot from facing the wind. Icicles grew on the tips of walrus mustaches. Snow blew blindingly up under the hats.

Soon the gumbo became very greasy. Horses began to flounder badly and the wheels clogged all the way to the axle. The drivers had to climb down again and again to pry off the fat sticky clods. The pulling horses became white with frozen foam and sweat and sleet. Some fell in their traces and had to be prodded up. And again and again the wagons had to be helped through gulches by the boys on horseback.

Ike rode up alongside Walrus. "This is turrible."

"We all know that," Walrus snapped.

"When do we camp for the night?"

"We don't."

"What's that?"

Irv heard the question. Irv tried to smile in the dim sleet-lighted dark. "We're riding until we hit my ranch."

"How fer is that?"

"Oh, some twelve miles, I judge. We would have been there long ago if this sleet hadn't slowed us up."

"At this rate," Ike said, slow, "we won't get there until morning."

"I guess not." Irv looked across at Walrus. "Maybe we better lay over a day after we get to my place. So the men and horses'll be fresh when we make our final run for Antelope."

260

"And let them get set for us? Not on your tintype."

"How can they? Jesse's men have cut the wire. We ain't met anybody yet who might snitch on us. And Mitch is riding this way to make sure nobody passes him going north. So they can't know about us. One day more won't hurt."

Walrus swelled red on his horse. He wasn't used to being contradicted.

Ike said, "Then you think it'll be morning afore we get there?"

"I'm afraid so," Irv said.

"My boys won't like it," Ike said.

"Nobody likes it," Walrus snapped.

Clabe heard them vaguely. He let his stunned body roll with the jolting crashing wagon. He lay drifting in mind. Perley Gates, the dummed fool, shouldn't't've called down God's wrath. One bolt of lightning in a snowstorm was a God's plenty.

Clabe wondered where Liza was. Probably cuddled up in bed and waiting for him to cozy up against her. He could see himself with his nose into her soap-sweet curly hair, great chest pressing against her cunning back, crooked knees under her knees. And warm together. Murmuring. Slowly drifting off to sleep. And later, half-waking, having her suddenly turn in his arms, passionately seeking his embrace and all his hot potence.

"Liza, Liza, what you got me into makin' me a marshal."

Snow lightning was a sign all right. The raid was doomed. Something terrible was going to happen.

It was wrong for the raiders to take the law in their own hands; wrong to plot the death of men who happened to see the cattle business another way. It was one thing to go to war in defense of one's country; it was another to fight for a "set of corporation cormorants" as the *Tribune* put it. Cain and his settler friends had as much right to public grasslands as did the big cattle kings. It was wrong to seize Cain's cattle at the stockyards and then require him to prove they were his. God couldn't help but be against the raiders for rising superior to the laws of the land.

"Liza, Liza, what you got me into makin' me a marshal. I'd give my eyeteeth, right now, to be riding the range with the boys again."

Clabe wondered what Cain, right then, was doing. Probably asleep in his bunk along the Shaken Grass. All unknowing that in a few hours he'd be shot full of holes.

What strange throws came out of the dice box. Goodhearted Clabe here in the wagon hated his life as an officer of the law, while out there riding in the dark, mean-eyed Hunt liked it.

"Perley shouldn't've sassed the Big Boss, calling His hand like that."

It was dawn, Thursday, when they pushed through a series of bump gates and arrived at Irv Hornsby's ranch in a narrow valley. The horses were immediately put in the barn, and curried and fed. All the hands were given a big ranch-style breakfast of pancakes and ham and coffee. Then all spread out their bedrolls, some in the barn, some in the bunkhouse.

Later, Irv made the rounds with a lantern. "Sleep tight, boys, we'll take a couple days' rest. After that bitch-bear of a night in mud, we've got to let the horses get back in shape."

The last thing Clabe saw just before he fell asleep was Walrus's fat hand. It stuck out of Walrus's blanket. On the ring finger burned a big white diamond.

Mitch

Sly Mitch smiled to himself as he played around with it in his mind. He would do it. He would pull their leg and at the same time show Jesse he wasn't afraid of Cain. Jesse once might have hoped that Cain would rejoin him and become his new foreman, but he, Mitch, would show Jesse he wasn't buffaloed by a Hammett.

The same morning the raiders left Casper to go north, Mitch left the Derby ranch to go south. Mitch bade his goose of a wife good-bye, and his little boy, and saddled up and rode over the hill. He wore his .45, butt out, under his yellow slicker, and his rifle, butt to the front, under his left leg. He carried the rifle on the left side to have it handy should he have to shoot quick when he got off.

He rode a dun-gray, a color that blended well with the fresh spring sagebrush. The dun-gray was a big fat snorty boy. Until put into a full run, he ambled along in a half-racking half-shuffling gait. Despite a touch of the weed, which caused him to whistle when he breathed, which sometimes even led to puffing flights of temper, the horse had a very high life. Mitch called him Whistling Bullet.

Every now and then Mitch climbed a crest and got out the field glasses for a look around. To the west the Big Stonies still gleamed white with winter snows. To the east the

Cucumber Hills were turning barren gray. He saw no riders, coming or going. He did see Derby cattle and occasionally threw them to the right toward the mountains where the grazing would be better. A good horseman, he never went faster than a trot. He had a long way to go.

As he headed along, meadowlarks fifed at him from all sides. Some even whistled at him from overhead. He hardly noted them.

It was just dusk of the second day, Thursday, when he guided Whistling Bullet across the gurgling Shaken Grass toward Cain's cabin. Whistling Bullet's iron shoes chinked loud on the pebble slope. Some snow and rain had fallen and the ground breathed with the sticky fumes of spring. He saw smoke hanging low over the cabin, saw a light in the middle window. He glanced toward the barn. There were no extra horses in sight that he could see.

He rode up to the door and reined in. "Hello in there. Anybody home?"

The door opened inward and square carven-faced Cain stood in it. Cain looked up at him.

Mitch said, slanted eyes smiling, rolling his sloping shoulders under yellow slicker, "I come to pay back your visit of last fall."

"Step down. The beans are on. And there's an extra bunk, I guess."

"I don't need a bunk. I've got my bedroll with."

"Whatever you want."

"Home alone?"

"Nope. Harry and Tim are here. Why?"

"Just wonderin'."

"Step down. You can put up your hoss in the barn. Plenty of hay down, I guess."

"Thanks."

After he had stalled Whistling Bullet, and curried and fed him, Mitch bowlegged it to the cabin. He found Cain and Harry and Timberline around a plank table, hats off and lamplight in their faces, talking low and already eating. They clammed up when he entered.

Mitch threw his bedroll on the floor in a corner, set his rifle behind the door, laid aside his hat and slicker and coat. He also took off his six-gun and hung it over a chair. He saw that the others around the table were still armed. He smiled.

Mitch washed up in a basin on a stand. He dried himself on a towel made out of a two-bushel canvas sack. He noticed that the towel was extraordinarily clean for a bachelor's den.

263

Many and many a time he'd found towels so stale and dirty in line camps he'd had to dry himself on his shirttail.

Cain set out a plate and pushed a pot of beans and some fried bacon in a black pan and a plate of sourdough biscuits toward him. "Nothing fancy tonight," Cain said.

"Looks plenty good to me," Mitch said, pulling up a hide-bottom chair. "After a long day's ride beans sometimes looks better than homemade ice cream."

"That's a gut," big Timberline grunted. The kerosene lantern in the center of the table burned with a weak flickering orange light. It cast a rosy glow over the bald dome of Timberline's head just above the timberline of his red hair. When Timberline swallowed, muscles tight on his skull moved under the bald spot, making it look as if the brains underneath were troubling around.

Mitch noted that Harry wore his customary flashy clothes: pink shirt, checkered vest, yellow bandanna, blue trousers, studded belt, and the inevitable red silk sash. A wary smile seemed to be lurking in Harry's eyes. Mitch felt more at ease with Harry than he did with the others. Cain in his blacks was too solemn for him. Timberline with his great red beard was too big and wild for him.

A fire burned in the fieldstone hearth. Three Winchesters leaned against one side of it while a violin stood against the other. All four walls of the log cabin had been carefully chinked with sticky gumbo and then whitewashed. Even the floor had a scrubbed look, while the table and chairs gleamed hand-clean. Clothes, leather straps, belts hung neatly in rows from pegs along the outer wall.

Harry caught Mitch's roving eye. "You can thank Cain for having the place all redd up. He's something of a woman that way. Drinks too much wild mare's milk."

Cain's lips held steady under his heavy mustache.

"Wild stallion milk, you mean," Timberline said.

Harry laughed. "Well, I guess a stallion is neater than a mare at that."

After the meal, Mitch and Cain and Harry shoved back and rolled themselves smokes. Timberline took a chew. Cain put another dry cottonwood log on the fire. Presently the chinking in the wall crinkled from the rising heat. Rain pittered on the dirt-covered pole roof overhead. Some water worked through occasionally and once a drop fell exactly in the center of the table.

They watched the fire. They sat, wary. They moved slow, smoking, chewing, scratching.

Mitch said, "I'm on my way to Irv Hornsby's. He's putting on a party there."

Harry's bright gray eyes laughed at him. "Think there'll be much of a crowd there?"

The question startled Mitch and he showed it. "That I wouldn't know. I hope so. The more the merrier, you know."

Mitch noticed that Cain kept stroking a long braid of black horsehair lying across his lap. It was one of the longest quirts he'd ever seen. Cain stroked it over and over, softly, as if both in reverie and in loving memory. Mitch remembered the time Cain quirted him in the presence of Jesse high on the Red Fork.

Slyly, perverse, Mitch thought to rib him about it a little. "See you got yourself a new quirt, Cain."

"What? Oh. Yeh."

"Just braided, I see."

"Yeh."

"Long black hair. That come from your fancy riding horse Lonesome?"

"Yeh."

"That from his mane or his tail?"

"Parts of both."

"Got any left for sale?"

"No."

"You fancied Lonesome."

"I did."

"What happened?"

"Rode him too hard too long."

"Too bad."

"Yeh." Cain's eyes shone. "He was a dandy. Could run all day. Good for a hundred miles and still be ready for the next day. Wish I had a picture of him."

"Too bad."

"Let's change the subject. It's too sad to think about."

Timberline grunted to himself, then roused up and asked, pig eyes rolling at Cain, "How's your new ridin' hoss workin' out?"

"Who? Whitefoot?"

"Him."

"Not too good."

"What's wrong with him?"

"He acts ground shy. Like he's afraid the grass might tickle his feet."

"Maybe it's them white hoofs of his'n. I've heard say they don't wear like black ones."

"Could be."

Mitch asked, "How is he otherwise?"

"Who?"

"Whitefoot!"

"Oh, him. Oh, he tries."

Silence.

Mitch wished he hadn't asked about the new black quirt. He sought around in his mind for something else to talk about.

Harry seemed to have caught his unease. Harry sat smiling like a possum eating yellowjackets. He put both hands around his own neck, and gestured.

Mitch blanched. He let his slope shoulders slide.

Harry said, "You Derby boys planning to join our early roundup next month? In May?" Harry's eyes glittered with mocking laughter.

It was a good shot and it hit home. Mitch shivered. What a bold devil that Harry was. There was no shame in him whatever.

Timberline picked up a mail-order catalogue and began paging through it. He stopped at the women's corset section. He looked wonderingly at the women's underwear. He stared at the women's hosiery.

After a while Timberline broke out of his rapt gazing. "Yep. There's some born shorthorn, and some born longhorn, and even some bighorn. That's the luck of the draw. Me, I'm beginning to be glad I'm getting plain old."

Harry laughed.

Presently Mitch got up and spread out his bedroll and slid into his suggans.

Mitch felt down. His legpull about turnabout hospitality hadn't come off. It burned him that Harry could always outface him; that Cain acted as if he hardly knew he was around.

Hunt

Hunt raged inside.

It was Friday noon at Irv Hornsby's ranch. The sky had cleared off. The footing was dry again. And just as plans were being completed for the raiders to make a run for it, hoping to get to Antelope before dawn and catch Sheriff Sine and Judge Traves and all the townsfolk still in bed—just then, that sneak Mitch Slaughter came riding in with his idea.

"The party ought to make a detour west and nab ringleaders

266

Cain and Harry Hammett and big Timberline on the way in," Mitch suggested. "The beauty of it will be we can bag 'em all in one grab. Hang them and you've got half the war won."

It was like throwing a red rag in amongst a bunch of already mad bulls. The whole thing exploded into the open.

Except for the few men tending horses and supplies in the barn, most of the raiders were gathered around the big square table in Irv Hornsby's living room. Irv and a group sat on one side, Jesse and his bunch sat on the other, with the glowering Texans sitting in a corner. Hunt himself sat alone by the fire. Most of the men were smoking cigarettes and cigars, and the pole roof ceiling was almost hidden by a fog of smoke. Irv had set out several bottles of whisky and everyone, except a man named Champagne, had a glass of it in hand. Champagne had taken along his own liquor, a bottle of cognac. The country room stank like a saloon.

Irv was swearing drunk. He said, loud, coarse, "Mitch is right. Let's saddle up and first put on a party at Shaken Grass. Hck. Right now."

Walrus nodded. "I think Mitch's right too. We can easy nab them on the way in. And with little loss of time."

Jesse stomped his bad leg on the floor. He was in severe pain. "Maybe my opinion don't count. But I think it's a durn-fool stunt."

"Why?" Irv demanded, contorted face rolling forward. "I think it's a great idea. Hck."

Jesse reared back his proud head. "I'm for taking over the fountainhead at Antelope first. Make sure of the rustler capital. As well as the help I got lined up waiting for us there."

Irv whacked his short square hand hard on the table. All the bottles and glasses jumped. "And I say the fountainhead is over t'Shaken Grass."

Walrus nodded. "Hang those three rascals over at Shaken Grass, Jesse, and you've just about broken the back of the Bighorn rebellion."

Jesse appealed to Hunt by the fire. "What do you think?"

Hunt's lips thinned. The whole thing was obvious to him. His eyes glowed. "Jesse is right. We should march on Antelope first and seize the sheriff and the judge and all the records and install our own men. Then we take our time rounding up the strays." To emphasize his points Hunt tapped his glass with the stem of his pipe. "And there's this too. Suppose no matter how careful we are trying to nab Harry and Cain and Tim, suppose one of them somehow got away?

Why, we'd be done for. One of them getting away would spread the alarm all the way to Antelope and we'd have a thousand wild men on our necks."

Jesse said, "Hunt's right. And Mitch, you durn fool, I ought to fire you for wanting to make this a personal grudge war. I know you got it in for Cain, special, and in its time that's all right by me, but right now we want to keep our eye on the main play. We've all come this far to wipe out the rustlers the best way we know how, the whole kit and kaboodle of 'em, and we'll get around to your Cain at the proper time and place."

Mitch threw Hunt a vicious look. "Knowing how some of us hate Cain's guts, I only thought it would be handy to nab them on the way in."

Hunt stiffened proud in his chair. "Mitch, I guess I don't have to tell you I think I got better reason for getting Cain out of the way than you. Yet I still say, march onto Antelope first."

Mitch lowered his head and snickered, sly. "That warrant for your arrest comes first then. Not Cain the ringleader of the rebellion."

"Shut up, Mitch," Jesse bellowed.

Tough young Ike leaned forward on his side of the table. He and his Texans had been listening with increasing restlessness. "I thought we were going after bad men."

A sudden chill moved through the big ranch room.

Ike turned his bland yet deadly gaze on Walrus. "Have you got warrants for the arrest of these so-called rustlers?"

Silence.

"I wonder if you all know that some of our grandpappies got their start rustlin'. Right after the Civil War."

Walrus looked across at Hunt.

"Or is this a personal grudge war after all, like Jesse here let slip?"

Walrus's fat face swelled very red.

"Have you got those warrants? If you ain't, count us out."

Walrus couldn't look Ike in the eye. "Hunt, here, he's got the warrants. Ask him."

Ike looked at Hunt. "Have you?"

Hunt blinked. "I've got them in my saddlebags."

"Get 'em. We want to see 'em. Now. Pronto. Or we're pulling out. Pronto."

"Here, here," Jesse said. "Let's not lose our heads now. We're among friends."

" 'Friends'?" Ike echoed.

268

Bat broke in, "Hunt, you have got them?" Bat began to look very worried.

Irv tossed down another full glass of whisky. His face was almost black with rage and alcohol. "T'hell with whether we got warrants or not. The main thing is that we're out to break up them blackhearted rustlin' Red Sashers and I say let's nab ringleader Cain and his boys on the way in."

Bat said, white, quiet, "You have got them, Hunt?"

Hunt sat immobile. He stared down at the fire in the hearth.

Young Doc Exon broke in next. His pink face was lined with new and sudden anxiety. "You mean there are no warrants?"

Silence.

Doc Exon tried to catch Jesse's eye. "You mean, in some people's minds there is some doubt that these men are rustlers?"

Irv swore. "Of course Harry Hammett and Timberline are rustlers. Hells bells, ain't they the head guys in the Red Sash Gang?"

"But this Cain Hammett you mentioned. What about him?"

More silence.

"Or is he one of these small but honest stockmen we sometimes hear about?"

Jesse stomped his sore leg on the floor again. "Cain was elected foreman of the illegal roundup he and his bunch are going to hold next month. A full month too early."

Doc Exon pressed still more. " 'Illegal'? You mean, the roundup they are going to hold is against the laws of the state?"

"Well, not exactly against the state. But it is against the rules of the State Cattleman's Association."

Irv snapped, "It's the same thing, Jesse."

Doc Exon pushed in further. "Well . . . what makes the rules of the Association more legal than, say, the rules of Cain Hammett's group?"

"Enough of this!" Walrus cut in. "If you want my opinion, I'd say we ought to take a vote on it. Those in favor of marching on to Shaken Grass first—"

"Now wait a minute!" Jesse roared, pushing back his chair. He turned on Walrus as if he were going to draw on him. "You goldurn ass. Take a vote and you'll split this party wide open."

Irv roared out then too. He in turn pushed back his chair and faced Jesse. "You bloody blockheaded bustard! This is

269

my ranch and what I say goes. We're headin' for the Shaken Grass first."

Walrus turned to Ike. "Well, and what do you say?"

Ike said, "If you got the warrants, I don't care where we go first. Just so we get down to business."

Jesse snarled, "Irv, you old rumhound you, if you want to make a fight of it, go ahead, draw, and be durned to you."

Irv whitened along the edges of his nostrils. He turned slowly in his chair. His hand hung, ready to go for it.

Walrus jumped to his feet. His pouch belly almost popped with it. "Wait! Wait now!" he roared. He waved smoke away from his face to see the better. "Wait! Let's have no foolishness now. As long as I'm in command there'll be no fightin'. If there's any fightin' to be done, I'll do it."

"You and whose army?" Ike drawled.

At that point Doc got to his feet. He was white. His lips trembled. He looked terribly upset.

"Hey, where do you think you're going?" Walrus said.

Doc shook his head, sadly, and stumbled toward the door.

"Hey, where do you think you're going?" Walrus called again.

"Back to Cheyenne."

"But why? We may need a doctor come tomorrow."

"That's just it. You fellows are planning a murder. And not the defeat of rebels. The more I listen to you fellows talk, the more I'm convinced that Cain Hammett and his boys have their side too. I don't doubt that they've done wrong. Yes. But yours is going to be the greater wrong. You've taken the law into your own hands. You seek to win by force what Cain and his boys already have won by the ballot. No, not for me." And with that Doc left the room.

Doc's leaving took the fight out of Jesse and Irv. They let out great breaths; leaned back in their chairs. Every man there knew what Doc's going meant. There was sure to be bloodshed in another forty-eight hours and a doctor's skill would be downright necessary. Furthermore, there was also the chance that Doc might spill the beans when he got back to Cheyenne. If he did, there was little they could do, since Doc's Philadelphia family had invested heavily in a big ranch near Cheyenne. To touch Doc was to touch the powerful back East.

Hunt sneered from his side of the room. "Just like an Easterner. Comes to a tight and he gets a case of the gunorrhea."

All the while, grim Daggett had been staring at Cham-

270

pagne's open bottle of cognac. Daggett got to his feet and reached for it. "Mind if I sample some of your froggy stuff?" Without waiting for an answer, Daggett tilted the cognac into his mouth and took a long drink of it.

Champagne came sputtering to his feet, his dark Frenchy face in a rage. "You pig! How about usin' a cup or a glass like the rest of us?"

Daggett set the bottle on the table. He drew a face. "What you frogs won't drink. Bah!"

Walrus got out his six-gun and, using the butt of it as a gavel, tapped for attention. "Men, I still say we ought to take a vote."

Hunt gave up. "T'hell with it. Jesse is right. A vote'll split us. No, I agree now. Let's do what the major here says, even if what he wants is a dead-fool stunt."

Done. It was agreed to pull out for Cain's cabin after dark. In the meantime Mitch and a scouting party of two were ordered on ahead to make sure no one left the Shaken Grass before the main party arrived. The supply wagons were to follow as best they could.

Hunt raged inside. For two cents he could have plugged Mitch. He hated Mitch's sly slanted face, hated the way Mitch sat in the corner, smirking to himself because his idea had been accepted after all.

Hunt cursed. There was now a chance that the warrant for his arrest might stay on the books forever.

Clayborne

That afternoon, after checking guns and horses and supplies, the major ordered all hands to their bedrolls for a nap. A night march lay ahead. Some unrolled their beds in the ranch house, some in the bunkhouse, some in the barn. Quite a few of those in the barn slept in triangles, head on each other's ankles, to keep warm and off the prickly hay. Clabe happened to unroll his tarp and suggans in the haymow of the barn, and beside him lay Hunt Lawton.

Clabe lay on his left side, half-curled up. It was the same position he took when sleeping with Liza. He'd been asleep an hour or so, when a rustling in the hay next to him awakened him. Opening an eye, he saw a man's big back shuddering not two feet away. It took him a moment to realize it was Hunt's back, that Hunt was having a nightmare.

Half-awake, Clabe watched Hunt. He himself often had

271

nightmares so deep and gripping, so overpoweringly real, that his shudders rattled the bedstead in its coasters. Generally a touch on the shoulder by Liza brought him out of it.

Half-wondering if he should touch Hunt, yet half-reluctant to do so because he didn't care for the man, Clabe lay caught between the doing and the not-doing, one eye open and the other eye closed, cozy and warm between his blankets on the sweet and giving slough hay.

Hunt's shudders reminded Clabe that his dog Sparky often had nightmares too as he lay sleeping beside the hard-coal burner back home. From Sparky's convulsive jerks, from the way he sniffed and smelled as if in the grip of fierce dog passion, it was easy to see Sparky was on the chase again, or was after the bitch in heat next door.

Clabe wondered what could be bothering Hunt. Maybe Hunt wasn't such a dead-tough man after all. Maybe Hunt's deadly velvet surface hid a bad conscience. A law man who was said to have a man for breakfast every morning was bound to make a few mistakes somewhere along the line. God knew that he, Clayborne Rodney, had tried to be a law man with a heart, and yet, the Lord forgive us all, he had made his share of mistakes.

Presently Hunt's shudders became more pronounced. After another while he began to moan; then to mutter.

At first Clabe couldn't make out the muttering. But after a bit, lifting his ear off his blanket pillow, he began to make out the words.

"Get a crossfire on the door." A really big shudder shook Hunt then. "Sorry, but I always play a lone hand. I don't need any help to get him." Hunt breathed loud for a moment or two. "S'all right, Maw. If it's the last thing I ever do, I'll get them all for you before I die." His back stiffened. "He needs killin'." His arm set for the draw. "Don't think you can stompede this officer with lightning bugs and corncobs." His trigger finger crooked. "If you ever drop another one that hits the ground as close as that last one, I'll crack your crust wide open." His trigger finger trembled. "Wait. Take your time. Patience and you'll have them in your trap just the way you want them." His trigger finger steadied. "What? Are they coming? Hammett?" His whole body tightened. "Ah. Here they come!" His back crimped over like a stepped-on grub convulsed in agony. "Got the dead drop. Now! Now!" Then his tensed hand jumped and the crooked trigger finger worked, worked fast, almost blurring in its swift triggering.

Clabe shuddered. The blurring trigger finger was exactly like the buzzing tail of a rattler.

Clabe reached out a hand and shook Hunt. "Hunt."

Hunt muttered. "If you want to know the truth, and you want yourself a good obedient wife, you should really drown that firstborn boy."

"Hey, you. Hey."

"I dreamt I went to kiss her, call her Abigail, and woke up broken-hearted with a yearling by the tail."

"Hunt! Hey."

"Wha . . . ?"

"Wake up. You're dreamin'."

"What?"

"You're dreamin', man. Wake up."

"Oh." Silence. "Ohhh."

Cain

That same Friday evening, Old Bon Hamilton the cook dropped in on Cain. Old Hambone had been out wolfing and was on the way back to the Derby outfit to get ready for the spring roundup in June. He came with his sourdough keg and his fiddle.

Cain was glad to see Hambone. A Hambone visit always meant a couple of days of first-class cooking plus a lot of fun jawing about the old days. A lot of old things would be made to happen again.

Outside it was snowing and the four of them, Cain, Hambone, Harry, and Timberline, were ringed cozy around the fire in the hearth. Their boots were off and they sat roasting their toes. Their guns hung handy from pegs on the wall behind the door. A brown jug of whisky stood at their feet, half empty. All four took turns guggling from it.

Harry sat on the far end, hat cocked at just the right jack-deuce angle over his left eye. Timberline sat next in line, eyes brooding strangely on the jumping fire. Hambone slouched in a hide-bottom chair next in line, his completely bald dome gleaming like a bloody dinosaur egg. Cain brought up the end near the door.

Cain toyed with his new black-hair quirt, working it some, stroking it some. "Hambone, from your side of the fence, does Sheriff Sine look honest to you?"

"Him? Honest?" Hambone's head swung around from its neck anchor. "As up and down as a cow's tail I'd say."

273

Harry smiled, easy. "He better be. Come May first, when we start our own roundup, there's going to be a showdown for fair."

Hambone's old eyes mused in thought. "Could be you fellers are a mite hasty callin' your roundup that early."

Timberline touched his bearded jaw. "By the Lord, but I sure got me a full-sized toothache. Man oh man oh man."

Hambone got out his papers, dug up a small handful of tobacco from his pants pocket, and rolled himself a cigarette. A few crystals of strychnine were mixed in with the tobacco. Licking the cigarette into shape, Hambone asked, "Say, Cain, how's the widder Rory makin' it these days?"

Cain fell silent. So did Harry.

Hambone craned his old bald head around and looked Cain in the eye. "Don't you see her much any more?"

"Sometimes," Cain said, slowly. "I guess she's doin' all right."

"Well, Cain, I don't know as to you, but me, if I was just ten years younger I'd build me a stack to her that'd be the marvel of the ages."

Harry said, "Sagebrush Mason is working for her now, you know."

"You don't say. Well." Hambone nodded. "Now there's one mean man."

Harry smiled. "I hear Jesse swore a blue streak when he heard Rory hired Sagebrush. Except for Cain here, Sagebrush is probably the best shot in the whole state."

Cain said, "I guess she got him mostly for watchdog. He ain't much around sheep. Like Dale was."

Timberline groaned, still holding his jaw. "Man oh man oh man." His eyes closed over in misery.

"Tim, you old moose you," Harry laughed, "you ain't dyin' off on us, are you?"

Timberline groaned. "I swear, I've got me a toothache built for a grizzly."

The others laughed. Firelight flashed across their gleaming teeth and the whites of their eyeballs.

Cain reached down for the brown jug. "Here, take another long suck of this. Help deaden the pain some."

Timberline slugged down a long one. When he finally let loose of the jug his eyes looked a little glazed.

A coyote suddenly yowled lonely and eerie outside. Cain listened to it, his ear idly noting how the call began as a series of short yipping barks, the yips then gradually coming

274

faster and faster until they ran together and became a long rising wail.

Hambone helped himself to the brown jug next. He guggled down a long one too. Wiping his old thin lips, Hambone happened to catch the flash of silver on Harry's hat. Slowly a sly smile worked across Hambone's ancient leathery face. He examined in detail Harry's new pink shirt and new blue trousers, and finally Harry's clean smooth-shaven face. He tolled his old head. "How a purty boy like you never got married . . . I don't understand it. Cain here now with a face that looks like a used-up old chopping block . . . that the she-stuff here'bouts never tied onto that ain't such a mystery to me. But you."

Harry seemed to like what he heard. He slid his hands in his pockets and leaned back on two legs of his chair.

Smile still growing, Hambone said, "Harry, and I hate to say this, but Harry, after a couple of long snorts, by golly, you look so darn purty I feel like I should take my hat off to you."

Harry came down on all four legs. His face darkened over some.

"Well, it's all right, Harry." Hambone nodded at the fire. "I know just how you feel. We punchers is just too busy follerin' a cow's tail around to bother about marrying nesters' daughters." Hambone ran a gnarled hand over his gnome head. "Yeh, a puncher usually makes a poor married man. A sheepman like Dale, that's one thing. Or a clerk in town like pinchpenny Alberding. But a puncher, when he gets married, he either makes a spoon or spoils a horn."

Cain laid his quirt aside. He got to his feet; rose to his toes and stretched long; then put another log on the fire. He stood watching the fire. For a moment the fire choked over with yellowish-gray smoke, seemed smothered, then a quick bright rim of fire moved across the rough ocher bark of the fresh log. Cain sat down and took to stroking his black quirt again.

The coyote outside set up another howl. Again Cain listened idly, picking out the first quick yips and then the rising wail.

Somehow, perhaps because of the lonesome coyote call, the talk got around to the question of life after death. Old Hambone advanced the opinion that there was no afterlife. When you died, that was it, he said, and there was no returning. That was why all critters, including man, fought so hard to hang onto life. If heaven was such a fine place to go to, and man believed in heaven, why wasn't he in a rush to get this life over with?

275

Cain said, quiet, "Funny thing is, he is."

"Is what?"

"In a rush to get killed."

"Name one."

"Well, this Alias Hunt fellow is. He craves it. That's why he's in the killin' business."

Hambone nodded, reluctantly. "Well, him, yeh."

Timberline grunted, eyes glaring at the fire. He rose in his chair. "Tell you what I think. When we die, all of us will go back to what we was before we got this life. Now take me. I know you rannies always laugh when I tell about how I was once a moose in the other life. And that's all right. Because you wasn't there. While I was. So I kin say. Because I *was* a moose. And a good moose too. In fact, so good a moose, the good Lord rewarded me with a chanct at human life in this here life. Well, you can see what a bad mistake that was. I made a botch of it. Not because being a human being is harder, and better, but because my heart warn't in it. So I know the Big Boy up there is going to give me a chanct at bein' a moose again."

It was one of the longest speeches Cain had ever heard Timberline make and he sat back and laughed.

Hambone, however, seemed to consider it gravely. "Well, now, Cain, Tim here may be right. You never know about them things."

"Hey," Cain said, "I thought you just got through saying you didn't believe in another life."

"I don't. But one look at Tim and you know some kind of mistake was made. He actually does belong with the mooses."

They all laughed.

Timberline took it all good-naturedly. "You can snort all you want to, boys, but what I say is truth."

Harry said, "You better not die close around here, Tim. Because one of us is just as liable as not to gutshoot you to make a meal of you. Why, I can almost taste you already."

Timberline's great red brows rose. "Now looky here, Harry. If it should happen I die afore you, and you've liked me atall in this here life, you better pay close attention to what moose you shoot, or you will be eating your old sidey." Timberline fixed his eyes on Harry. "Here's how you'll be able to tell if it's me you've got in your sights or just some other ordinary bull moose. See this here red hair all over on me? Well, I was a red moose in the life before this and I'm liable to be a red moose again in the next life. So watch for a red moose. And looky here." Timberline pulled his shirt out of his pants

276

and turned his hairy right side to the fire. "See this patch of white here? Like it was snow? Like I once had the lousy scab? Well, I had that in the life afore this and will probably have it again. It's where some son-of-a-gun actually did take a snap shot at me and nearly got me." Timberline's little eyes narrowed. "I'm layin' for him in the next life and I'm going to get him, believe you me, the blinkered bustard. Couldn't he see I was a human moose? So, Harry, you be careful when you eat moose, or I'll give you the darnedest bellyache you ever had."

Cain crimped back a smile. "Well, now, Tim, we'll probably never run across you. So I wouldn't worry about it."

Timberline snapped around on Cain. "But you just might. Because I tell you I've taken a fancy to this fine meadow of yours along the Shaken Grass here. And I've made up my mind that I'm going to make it my next pasture. I made a big mistake when I sold it to you not knowing what I was sellin'."

Then, before anyone could make further comment, or laugh, Timberline had another thought. "Dog eat it, Hambone, there is too an afterlife. How about all them times Joel Adams came back from the dead after Irv Hornsby hung him? Seven times Irv hung him and seven times he revived him to get him to tell where he hid them horses he stole. If Joel was dead, where was he so he could come back when he was revived?"

Hambone studied the jumping fire.

"Or take Harry. Last fall, before Cain cut him down from his cottonwood tree out here on the yard, where was he then?"

Cain said, "Wal, as to that, I'll have to say he wasn't dead. His heart was still beating. I felt it."

"Wait a minute," Harry said. "Why don't you ask me? It was me that was hung, wasn't it? Maybe I got an opinion on what happened. Cain, I never talked much about it, but I was gone somewhere. My ears was dead, my eyes was dead, my skin was dead, my mouth was dead, my nose was dead. They was all dead because I wasn't here for a couple of minutes."

Old Hambone looked at Harry steadily. "Where do you think you was then?"

"God only knows. I know I don't. Because I wasn't here."

Silence fell among them. All hands repaired to the brown jug.

Talk then got around to what the world was like before God made Adam and Eve.

Hambone's leathery face screwed up into thoughtful wrinkles. "I say this. If there warn't no humans about, there warn't no sin around either. Nor no happiness. No. Caze there wasn't no souls around to spoil life or enjoy life."

Cain considered this gravely. Firelight played over his dark face.

Old Hambone said, "And there wasn't no talking nor singing neither. Because they wasn't no mouth to make the singing and no ear to hear it."

Timberline said, "What about the birds? They was singing, wasn't they? And they was hearing the singing, wasn't they?"

Hambone said, "Well, they heard something all right. But they didn't know it was singing. Because singing is a human bein' idee. So the birds didn't know they was singing."

Timberline asked aghast, "You mean to say, as long as there was no human being ears around there really wasn't no singing?"

"No, they wasn't. In fact, they wasn't even no noise."

"No!" Timberline reared back on two legs of his chair and stared at Hambone in shock.

"No," Hambone continued, "as long as they wasn't no human bein' around to hear, they wasn't no noise." Hambone pointed at the ceiling. "If the roof of this cabin was to fall in, and they was no human ear around to hear it, they wouldn't be no noise of it."

Timberline dropped his chair to the floor on all four legs. "Hell, Hambone, that's where I fall out. Supposin' Crimson Wall back there was to fall down—you can't tell me there wouldn't be a hell of a racket whether anyone heard it or not."

Cain burst out laughing. So did Harry.

"And besides," Timberline said, "you talk about this ceilin' fallin' and no human bein' around to hear. What I want to know is: who built this ceilin' in the first place so it could fall?"

Hambone thought a moment; then laughed too. "You got me. Pass the jug again, Tim. And don't hog it all."

Cain had been eyeing Hambone's fiddle. "How about twisting the tail of your friend there some, old-timer? A couple tunes afore we hit the hay would be just the thing."

"Hey," Harry said, "that's a great idee. C'mon, Hambone, play us a hymn or two."

"No," Timberline said, "no hymns. I ain't of a mind to sing dirty ditties right after we get through talking about the afterlife."

Cain said, "Let Hambone decide. It's his fiddle."

Hambone soberly considered the fire for a few moments.

278

Finally he decided he was in the mood. While Cain put on another log, and while Harry and Timberline rolled cigarettes, Hambone tuned up.

Soon Hambone was sawing them off, one after another. Every now and then the boys would join him for a few bars, voices rusty and raw, like frogs warming up for a concert.

When Hambone swung into "Sweet Betsy from Pike," they all joined in. They bayed full blast. This excited Hambone and his fiddle began to cry. Like beads on a string, one song led to another: "The Old Chisum Trail," "Pretty Quadroon," "Little Mohee," "Lament of a Cowboy."

Timberline liked the last one especially. He bellered it with great hoarse gusto, completely drowning out the others. Only the sharp whining cry of the fiddle rose above it:

> *"Oh, I walked down the streets of Laredo,*
> *Oh, I walked through Laredo one day,*
> *And spied a poor cowboy all swathed in white linen,*
> *All swathed in white linen and cold as the clay."*

Cain quit singing halfway through the song. He watched bald-top Timberline roar out of his great mustache-fringed mouth. Bemused, Cain shook his head.

Timberline caught the headshake. When he finished the song, he demanded, "What's the matter? Your ears hurt?"

Cain laughed. "Tim, I like you. You know that. But durn me, when you sing, you sound like you're gargling axle grease."

"You don't like it?"

"Listening to you, I'm ready to believe you was a moose in the life before this."

"You don't like it then?"

"As a human bein' in this life, no, I don't."

"By God, this is a free country, and so long as I'm still in this life, I'll sing as I please."

Hambone discovered yet another tune in his head, one Cain hadn't heard. He sang it alone:

> *"There ain't no hoss that can't be rode,*
> *There ain't no man that can't be throwed.*
> *There ain't no woman that can't be duped,*
> *There ain't no man that can't be ruped."*

Harry said. "Now there's a song I've heard sung in places where a rattlesnake would be ashamed to meet his mother."

"Well, you would know," Hambone smirked.

"Say, that reminds me," Cain exclaimed. "We ain't sung the best one of all."

"What's that?"

" 'Riders of Judgment.' "

Hambone thought a moment, and nodded. He closed his eyes, searching within for the tune. When he found it, he quickly swung into it.

After a few bars, getting the rhythm and the beat of it, all joined in, even moose-voiced Timberline:

"Get along, little leppy, she's agetting late,
It's time you was earmarked and branded by fate.
Hup up, you windbellies, move along, old sucks,
It's time you was tallied in the Old Man's books.
Oh, some will be cut for the butcher in town,
Oh, some will be cut for the evergreen hills.
Leppy oh.

"When the Riders of Judgment come down from the
sky
And the Big Boss fans wide His great circle drive
And critters come in from low and from high
And critters rise up both dead and alive—
Will you be ready for that Roundup of Ages?"

"Roll out, you rannies, she's abreaking day,
The Big Boss has come to see about your pay.
Rise up, you waddies, roll out of your bed,
The Big Boss has come for the quick and the dead.
Oh, some will be cut for the Devil in hell,
Oh, some will be cut for the garden of God.
Waddy oh.

"When the Riders of Judgment come down from the
sky
Will you be ready for that Roundup of Ages?"

When they finished, Hambone said, "I don't agree that's the best. Me, I prefer 'Pretty Quadroon.' "

Harry said, "I don't agree either. My favorite is 'Little Mohee.' "

Timberline said, "You know mine. 'Lament of a Cowboy.' "

Hambone said, " 'Pretty Quadroon' has got good poetry. That's why I like it the best."

Harry said, "But it's about coons, Hambone. While my 'Little Mohee' is about the red man. Now we all know the coon don't come up to the noble red man for blood."

Timberline said, "You're both wrong. 'Lament' is best because it's about death and that's tarnal matter."

Cain said, "Now I'll tell you why I think mine is best. Because it's classic."

Hambone reared back. " 'Classic'? What's classic?"

"Classic is when a song has got some judgment in it, and has got it in the best. Now you take 'Riders.' It's got heaven in it, and hell, and a lot of other tarnal matter. But better yet, it has got judgment in it. Man judgment and God judgment. It's just plum full of judgment all the way through. Now I say, with all that judgment in it, that not only makes it classic, but that makes it plumb classic."

"All right," Hambone said. "All right. You got me. I know when I'm throwed."

"Play it again, Hambone," Cain said.

They went back to singing and drinking.

Cain

At first Cain had trouble sleeping. The moment he fell away, the roaring voices and the crying fiddle and all the argument about afterlife would start in again and wake him up. He tried all sorts of new positions but each time a loud bray in a dream would kick him out of it again. Or else Old Hambone's wailing violin would raise him. Cain turned and twisted in his bunk, trying his left side, then his right. He heard Harry turning and twisting on his bunk, too, on the other side of the room. He heard the fire in the hearth fall slowly with soft tushing sounds. He heard Hambone snoring in the far room.

Finally, toward morning, Cain got up in his shirt and underwear and socks and had himself a drink of branch water from the bucket on the washstand. He felt better right away. And, once again cuddled under brown-black buffalo robe, he fell into a deep and untroubled sleep.

When he awoke later, he wasn't sure what it was that had pricked him up out of slumber. He had the notion that there'd been some kind of noise like the cracking of a wagon wheel on stone. He also had the feeling that he'd lost something.

He lay very still, sleepily wondering about it. He heard a

meadowlark whistling cheerily at the breaking day. He heard Hambone snoring in the other room, heard Timberline groaning in his sleep. He was sure it hadn't been any of those noises.

"No," he thought, "it was some kind of cracking some ways from the cabin. Not the usual kind around the place."

As for the feeling of having lost something, he finally decided it was probably the onset of his usual morning blues over the death of his good horse Lonesome.

In any case, it was Saturday and time to get up. He planned to ride into town later in the morning to buy some supplies, maybe even have himself a fun, before the spring chores and then the early spring roundup caught up with him.

He sat up and put on his hat. He rolled himself a cigarette, stuck it in the corner of his mouth, and lit it with a match from his hatband. He put on his vest, slipped on his pants under the brown-black robe, and, swinging out of the bunk, drew on cold boots. Stretching, he glanced over at Harry's bunk. And instantly became wide awake. Harry was gone.

"Ah," he thought, "so that was the noise I heard."

He stomped into the middle room. It was damp and cold. He swung his arms around his chest a couple of times to warm his finger tips, then settled on his heels before the fireplace and scratched through the ashes until he found live pink coals. He put on a few pieces of kindling and blew the coals into fire. Once the flames got a good start, he threw on some sticks and three logs crossed over each other.

He warmed his hands; then his back; then his front. He lit a funk and started another fire in the round wood stove in the back of the room near the door to the root cellar.

Stretching again, yawning, he went over to the washstand beside the door and poured some water out of a bucket into the basin, laid aside his hat, opened his black shirt, and sloshed his face and his ears, even wetting well up into the roots of his dark hair. He dried himself off briskly in the rough sack towel. He made a point of drying his mustache tips and rolling them. He combed his hair in a broken mirror. He emptied the used water into the slop pail under the washstand.

There was a waking groan in the back room. Cain went over and poked in his head. He saw Hambone stirring on his bedroll on the floor. His blanket seemed humped up unnaturally high in the middle. Timberline on his side was still dead to the world.

Cain smiled. "You take on company during the night, Hambone? Who you got in bed with you?"

"Who? Me?" Hambone's old rheumy eyes cracked open, red along the lids. "Oh. That's my sourdough keg. Started to get cold in here last night and I thought I better sleep with it. Keep it warm and working."

"Say," Cain said, "now there's something I never thought of."

"I done it afore."

Cain studied the high hump under Hambone's blanket. "How about me using some? I'll make you some splatterdabs so thick and light you'll think them wasp nests."

Hambone sat up in bed. He put on his hat first and then rolled and lighted himself a cigarette. "Sourdough flapjacks, eh? Now there is a great idee. I've heard about your pancakes." Hambone puffed a thick cloud toward the ceiling, some of it smoke, most of it chilled breath. "Make me some and I'll go get you some fresh branch water for coffee."

"Done." Cain went over and picked up the warm five-gallon wooden keg. An ancient yeasting smell rose from it.

Hambone watched Cain lift the keg in his arms. "Don't drop it now." Love for the keg shone in Hambone's old eyes.

Cain said, "Say, by the way, Harry's gone. You hear him pull out in the night?"

"No."

"Wonder where he went?"

"Don't look at me. I know less about the habits of that ramblin' ranny than you do."

Timberline groaned on his bedroll on the other side of the room.

Hambone looked over. "Tim, you old moose you, if you ain't out a bed by the time I get back with the water, I'll throw it all on you."

"That's right, Tim," Cain said. "We ain't in the habit of servin' breakfast in bed around here."

"What a headache!" Timberline groaned. "The toothache was a little thing compared to this."

Cain laughed and, still holding the warm keg in his arms, went back to his fires in the middle room. He tied on a cook's leather apron. A couple of helpings of the sticky gelid yeast and he was soon busy mixing batter.

As he worked, tongue caught between teeth, he continued to wonder why Harry had left in the night. Harry hadn't mentioned going anywhere the previous evening. In fact, they'd half agreed that he should stay close to home while he, Cain, went to Antelope.

283

Hambone came scuffing in on old tottery boot heels. "Where's the bucket?"

"Over by the washstand. There's still a little in. You might like to wash off last night's scut first."

Hambone grunted. He hoofed it to the bucket, poured out what water was left, snorted in the gray basin a couple of times, loud, like an old gelding testing strange water, and then pawed over the towel. He said, "Cain, remind me to wash out my canyon before I head back to the Derby ranch tomorrow, will you? Jesse always complains about the way I smell after a long winter wolfin'."

Cain smiled. "Well, the ice is out of the crik and it's full of fresh mountain water. Help yourself."

Hambone picked up the bucket. He was about to open the heavy log door, when he saw something. He said, "You say Harry is gone?"

Cain looked up from mixing batter. "Yeh. Why?"

Hambone pointed. "Look at that log you propped against the door last night when we went to bed. It's still there."

"Say, that's right."

"You sure he still ain't in his bunk? Or under it?"

"No." Just to make sure, though, Cain stepped into the bedroom. After a moment, he came back. "No, he's not in there. And he didn't climb out of the window either. Because there's an old spiderweb over that."

Hambone stared down at the propped-up log. "Now how do you suppose he got out?"

Cain went into the back bedroom where Timberline lay sleeping. He examined the window carefully; came back out. "Spiderweb there too."

"Funny," Hambone said.

Cain settled on his heels and looked at the log. Then he saw something. "Hah," he said, "he went out through here, all right."

"How do you figure?"

"See this scratch here above where the log ends? Harry lifted the log away, stepped through the door, reached in a hand around the corner and set the log in place, and let it slide back when he closed the door."

"I'll be dogged."

"Thoughtful of him. With the country full of night riders."

"I'll say."

"But I don't like it," Cain said.

"Neither do I," Hambone said.

284

Then Hambone put on his coat and went out to get the water.

Cain went back to mixing pancake dough.

Hunt

Hunt heard the cracking of the wagon wheel on stone too. But Hunt knew what it was. Going down the head of a deep draw, one of the supply wagons whacked into a boulder, dishing both wheels on the left side. The coupling pole underneath snapped too. In the falling snow and half-dark, driver Perley Gates had failed to spot the boulder.

Hunt cursed under his breath. Perley had the dynamite and it was lucky he and all the rest hadn't been blown to hell.

Ahead and below in the draw, Walrus held up a hand. He signaled for the men to dismount. He came strutting down the line and said low to each man, "We'll light a fire here and have us all a good warm first."

Hunt didn't like it. "Can't hang around here too long."

"Why not?"

"I know for a fact Cain is an early riser."

"It's all right," Walrus said. "We just had a message from Mitch that all is quiet."

"How far is it yet?"

"Less than a mile."

"Well . . . all right."

Hunt and a dozen half-frozen men rustled up some dry sagebrush and got a good fire going. Luckily the wind was in the northwest and it carried the scented yellowish smoke away from Cain's cabin. Perley and the other cooks quickly made coffee and served it piping hot in tin cups.

The boys barely had themselves two sips of coffee, when the snow quit all of a sudden. Presently the sky lightened in the west, toward the Big Stonies, instead of the usual east, and boulders and bushes came up clearly for the first time since the raiders had left Irv Hornsby's ranch. The warm coffee and the hot fire thawed the men out and soon they took off their yellow slickers and overcoats and tied them up behind the cantles.

Every face was grim, tight-lipped. Every face was reddened over by wind and firelight. There was no joking. All knew death might come to some that day. Ike and his Texans wore cold hard expressions. They seemed to be relieved that they were at last going to get action. Irv and Jesse and their loyal cowboys also moved about with stony faces, eyes squared and drawn with terrible gravity. Planning the invasion had been one thing; making it come to pass was another.

Hunt found himself admiring Wallace Tascott some. The major had ridden at the head of his men all the way from Hornsby's ranch, straight up as if on parade, never once lifting a hand to wipe ice and snow from his mustache. That was one thing the army did for a man—toughened him into tolerating any kind of rough riding.

Walrus came strutting on fat legs through the men again. He had new orders to give. Four men were to help the wagon drivers hold the horses close in the draw, out of sight, while the rest were to deploy around Cain's two buildings in the meadow. Hunt was to lead a bunch across the Shaken Grass and go around to the north behind the barn, picking up Mitch on the way. Ike and his Texans were to swing around still further to the west, and hide behind the bridge and the ditch. Irv and Jesse were to take yet a third group and go around to the south side of the buildings, creeping through sagebrush and greasewood to the top of the ridge or bench overlooking the meadow. One side, the east, was to be left unguarded, but that was open meadow, and a man running across it could be cut down by a good crossfire from the other positions.

"The orders are simple." Walrus rocked back and forth on fat stub legs. "Place your shots well and shoot down every man that shows out of that cabin!"

The raiders nodded. They tightened cartridge belts; gave their carbines a last look; then trailed off in three groups.

Most of the snow had melted. But the going was greasy. Men had to stop every so often and clean off their boots.

Hunt found himself at the head of ten men, among them big Clabe and knobby Bat Wildy. Hunt didn't like either one and was sorry they had been assigned to his bunch. He thought them too sympathetic to Cain. They should have been left behind with the horse guard.

Hunt led them across a greasy stretch of mud, then through a clump of willows, then down across the shallow murmuring Shaken Grass, then up another greasy bank and onto the north ridge. Skulking down, spurs gingling, clothes brushing through sagebrush and greasewood, they filed in a long curve until they were directly in line with the barn. Here they picked up Mitch and two of his boys hiding behind a rock. From there on, carefully keeping out of sight behind the barn, Hunt led them straight down the ridge, across the creek again, and in through the corral. At no time could any one of them have been seen from the cabin. They moved on toe tips. They entered the barn, one by one, quietly.

"At last!" Hunt exclaimed softly. "Now we've got him hived!"

A horse whinnied in a far stall.

"Go over and pet that critter down," Hunt whispered, fierce. "You, Clabe. Quick."

Moving slow, Clabe swung his long legs over a manger and got in beside the horse. It was a dun buckskin. It seemed to know Clabe. "It's Cain's Bucky," Clabe said after a bit. He petted the horse; rubbed its nose. "Here now, Bucky. Quiet, boy."

"Good," Hunt said. "You fellows line up along the windows. Careful. Don't wipe off any of the dust or cobwebs. Stay well back, three feet at least, so they don't catch sight of your face or your shadow moving."

Bat said, "They's three more hosses in a box stall back there."

Hunt whirled. "Where?"

Bat said, "Looks to me like they is strange hosses." Bat shivered. "Maybe Cain has company." Bat pointed at the harnesses hanging on the wall. "Two of them is trotters."

"He can't have," Mitch said, "we watched all night."

Bat said, "Another thing. Where's Cain's black riding hoss? Maybe Cain himself ain't here."

Hunt said, "Cain rode the black into a pile of staves last fall."

Mitch said, "When I dropped in on them last Thursday, they talked about him having a new hoss by the name of Whitefoot. Had white hoofs."

Bat went over to look. "No hoss with a white hoof here." Again Bat shivered. "I got a hunch Cain's gone."

"But he can't be," Mitch cried. "We watched all night."

Hunt fixed Bat with a hard eye. "What are you up to, Bat?"

Bat wouldn't look him in the eye.

"Balls of fire! What an army this has turned out to be. Half of 'em secretly sidin' in with the enemy."

A meadowlark whistled cheerily out in the pasture south of the barn. The men listened, their eyes meeting fleetingly. For a moment the birdsong seemed to bring them back to themselves.

Walrus came puffing in to check their position. "Everything shipshape here?"

287

"No," Hunt said, swearing. "There's three strange horses in here. And Bat here thinks Cain ain't t'home because his riding hoss ain't here."

Walrus's wind-burnt face darkened over. "And we just spotted a buckboard standing in the yard on the other side of the house. Where the lane comes down off the road there."

"That means somebody is here we didn't expect. Somebody with a pair of trotters and a buckboard."

Walrus whirled around on Mitch, wry neck turning with his body. "I thought you said you watched the place close."

"I did."

"Who's this in the buckboard then?"

"I don't know."

"What do you know? Do you know if Cain is home?"

"Well, so far as I know I think he is. We heard a lot of singing in the cabin last night. Till late. We thought we heard him."

"You saw no one leave?"

"Not one."

"You're sure now?"

Mitch rolled his sloping shoulders. "Well, I wouldn't swear absolute of course. The snow was falling heavy now and then. And it was plumb dark."

"Holy Moses and the prophets!" The major swelled until he looked tall. "That means he maybe did get away." Walrus stood thinking. His brown eyes wicked wide, almost went cockeyed. In his black overcoat, for all the height of the men around him, he bulked large in the barn.

Bat said, eager, "Maybe we better not shoot on sight. Could be some of our men stayed overnight. Like Mitch did the other night."

"That's so. Damn this cow country courtesy anyway."

Hunt swore too. "Blast you, Mitch. Here's still another time you bulloxed up the ball."

Mitch couldn't hold up to them. Slowly his eyes slid off to one side. Slowly his eyes heated over with hate.

Walrus said, "Any of you men ever see these hosses before?"

After a silence, Clabe called from the stall where he was busy making friends with the dun buckskin. "I think . . . that sorrel there . . . belongs to Timberline."

"You sure?" Walrus asked eagerly. "You sure? Because he's on our list too."

"It's his hoss . . . all right."

"What makes you think so?" Hunt questioned close.

288

"Well . . . he's a big man . . . and I just naturally notice . . . the hosses of other big men."

"Let's hope you're right." Walrus stomped around in the alley. The hay crackled underfoot. "Just the same I think I better countermand that order to shoot on sight. We wouldn't want to shoot down one of our own boys. Men! Until we've found out who's in the cabin, make sure of them first as they come out."

Hunt bit at his mustache. "Maybe we should head for Antelope first anyway, now that we're not sure who we got hived up here."

Walrus was emphatic. "No. If Clabe here is right we at least got Timberline in there. And we want him. It won't take too long."

Hunt shrugged and went back to his post at the window.

Walrus left to tell Ike and Jesse of the new development.

Hunt and his men waited. They watched through the dusty windows. They couldn't spot their own men behind the bridge, or on the bench across the meadow, but they knew they were out there. It was warm in the barn. Morning light increased very slowly. It was going to be a dark gloomy day.

"Somebody's up!" Mitch whispered, loud. "I just saw a puff of smoke."

Hunt watched too. A bit later another puff rose from the largest of the two low chimneys. The wind shoving down from the northwest caught it and trailed it southeast along the ground. After another wait, the second chimney began to throw smoke.

Mitch said, "Now he's got the cookstove going. In a minute now somebody'll come out for fresh water from the crik behind us. That is, if they do like they did the other morning when I stayed over for breakfast."

Hunt said, "Ready with your rifles, men. Get a crossfire on the door if you can."

They waited.

At last the door opened.

"Ah!" Hunt exclaimed softly, almost gleeful. "Here they come. Get the dead drop on them, boys! And don't shoot until I give the word."

A bowed old man came down the stoop with a bucket in hand. He took a few steps toward the barn and then stopped for a look around. His hat was tossed back, revealing a balding dome. He sniffed the air like an old wolf enjoying yet one more morning of life. He set the bucket down on the ground and casually unbuttoned his pants and peedoodled in a low drift of snow. He shuddered halfway, once, deep. He threw a look up at the clouds, then toward the Big Stonies to the west. He shivered again as he finished and buttoned up. Then, picking up his bucket, he drew his overcoat up close around his neck, pulled down his hat over his old nose, and came on toward the barn.

Hunt and his men waited, ready to let fly.

"Hey!" Mitch suddenly whispered, loud. "That's Old Hambone our cook!"

"Who?"

"Hambone. You remember him? The roundup last fall when Cain and his boys came over and cut their cattle out of the bunch we was holding on the bench? Hambone was our cook then."

Hunt watched the old man's shambling walk. He wiped clean a corner of the dusty windowpane for a closer look. "You're right. I remember him now."

Bat said, shivering, trembling, "God! Good thing we didn't shoot on sight at that. Good Old Hambone."

Mitch said, "He's coming without his gun too. That probably means nobody suspects nothing in the cabin yet."

"Can't shoot . . . an unarmed man," Clabe said, slow, dull.

Hunt was suspicious. "What's he doing staying out here with Cain? You sure he knows which side his bread is buttered on?"

Bat said, "Oh, well, with Hambone now there ain't no sides. He's a cook and is over and above such digglements as range wars."

"Not so loud," Hunt whispered. "Here, Mitch, let's you and me form a reception committee around behind the barn. Out of sight. The rest of you keep watching the house."

Hunt and Mitch stepped outside in back. They waited, rifles at ready at the hips, tense.

Presently the sound of dragging boot heels came to them. A moment more and the peak of Hambone's hat, then his old leathery face, then the rest of his old bowed body, came around the corner. Hambone saw them but it didn't seem to register with him at first. He walked until Hunt's Winchester caught him in the belly. Then he stopped, bent over the rifle.

"Not a peep out of you!" Hunt said, low, deadly. "Or it's a one-way alley through your guts."

Hambone only blinked.

"Step this way." Mitch grabbed Hambone by the belt and pulled him forward and then shoved him into the barn.

Hunt grabbed Hambone by the collar of his overcoat and

drew his face up to his, almost choking him. "Who's in the cabin there with you?"

Mitch said, "Yeh, what you doin' stayin' here at Cain's?"

Hambone blinked. Slowly he came to. His wise old eyes rolled around, looking at all the armed men, then narrowed to slits.

One of the raiders in the barn took a bead on Hambone.

Hunt waved the gun down. "None of that now. He's all right. On the dead square."

Hambone cleared his throat with an old man's wet cough. He shook his head sadly. "Me for the luck of a lousy calf. For the first time in years a man offers to make me breakfast and then I run into a sight of men bent on killin' me." He continued to shake his head. "And I sure was looking forward to them splatterdabs of Cain's too."

Hunt's eyes opened with burning light. "Ah! Then Cain is in the cabin after all!"

Too late, Hambone realized he had let something slip. "My God! Look what I have gone and did." Hambone looked down at the bucket in his hand. "Now I do have a turrible dry."

Hunt said, "Yes, old man, you might as well know it. This is hell with the hide off."

Cain

Inside the log cabin, Cain had about a dozen crisp brown pancakes piled up, when Timberline showed at the door, stooped over, bald pate against the doorheader. His red whiskers were askew and wild, his red pig eyes were squinted down at the griddle, and his pug nose was working overtime like a pig's snout.

"Mornin'." A smile cracked across Cain's face. "I was about to call Your Bullship."

"Uh." Timberline stomped over to the gray wash basin. He dipped in his fingers, wetted his lips and the tip of his nose, and dried himself off on the sack towel.

"You can set out the cups and plates," Cain said. "Three sets."

"Who's left us?" Timberline shuffled back to the table, and from one stance, using his long arms, set the table.

"Harry. Sometime in the night."

"Uh."

"Hambone went to get some fresh water for the coffee."

"Uh."

"You know how an old coosie is. Got to have the best for his coffee."

"That's a gut."

They sat down and helped themselves, each taking four cakes. Cain liked to spread his around in his plate in the shape of a four-leaf clover and then pour on the strap molasses. Timberline fancied his pancakes all in a pile with the molasses streaming down the sides.

After Cain had made another batch of pancakes, he began to wonder what was keeping Hambone so long. "The old man don't get fits in the morning, does he?"

"Hambone? Naw, not that I know."

"It's sure taking him a long time to get that bucket of water."

Cain got up and peered out of the window looking toward the creek. "Trouble is, my barn is in the way. Can't quite see if he fell in that water hole in the turn there or not."

"He'll show," Timberline said, mouth full of pancakes and molasses. "He likes cakes even better than I do."

Cain stood troubled over his stove. "Something's wrong out there," he said finally. He remembered waking to the sound of what he thought was a wagon wheel cracking against stone. Could Hunt be out there trying to pick them off like he got Dale and all the others? Yet what would Hunt be doing with a wagon?

On a hunch Cain stepped to the back window. Hambone's buckboard stood where he'd left it the day before, at the end of the lane beside the house. Wal, it couldn't have been Harry driving off with it in the night.

Gooseflesh pimpled out over his arms and body. He felt it. He looked down at the bumps. When the animal in him roused up it was time to take notice. It hardly ever missed. It always knew better than he did. Something was wrong. He nodded to himself.

He reached around and began untying the strings to his leather apron. "I'm going out and hunt the old man up. He didn't take his gun with him and something could have happened to him."

Timberline looked up from his gorging. His small eyes blinked. He looked at the sizzling griddle and then at the bowl of mix on the back of the stove. He shoved back his chair with a crash and got to his feet. He spoke with his mouth full, spraying bits of food to all sides. "Better let me see. No use ruining prize pancakes. I can make coffee, or boil a potato,

but pancakes that float like calf slobber, that I can't make."
Cain hesitated.

Timberline put on his hat and started for the door.

Cain said, "Better hitch on your belt and gun."

"Why?"

"Wal, I got a feelin' somebody's out there. Somehow."

"Sure somebody's out there. Hambone is." Timberline stared down at Cain. "It ain't gettin' you finally, is it, Cain?"

"No. Just a strong feeling somebody's out there waiting for us, is all."

"Naw."

Timberline stooped out through the door and headed slowly for the barn, shambling along easy.

With half an eye Cain watched through the window as he caught up three new steaming fluffy brown pancakes and flipped them onto the platter. About a dozen yards from the door, Timberline stopped and cocked an ear toward the barn. It struck Cain that Timberline looked exactly like a red bear up on two legs listening intently at somethinng.

Cain poured some more batter.

The next time Cain looked up, he saw Timberline still standing motionless and listening. He was about to tell Timberline to get a wiggle on, when a shot, then a whole barrage of shots, cracked across the yard. First one bullet, then a hail of bullets, whacked into the side of the cabin. Two of the windowpanes right in front of Cain's eyes shivered into a shower of pieces. Chinking fell to the floor. Still looking out, out through the new blanks in the window, Cain saw Timberline, in a great slow fall, slide to the ground. From the barn windows and the barn door rose puffs of gun smoke.

"Hell's fire and little fishes!" In a whip, Cain tore off his leather apron and buckled on his gun and cartridge belt. "I was right!" He ran to the heavy log door, jerked it open, and left-handed let fly a hail of bullets of his own, working over the barn window, knocking out the panes, and then the barn door, hoping to catch some of the unseen enemy. Immediately more shots cracked from the barn and bullets hit all around him. Smoke trailed out of the windows. From the cracking reports he knew they were using high-powered rifles. They had a better chance to hit him, taking dead aim, than he them. He jumped back inside and slammed the door shut. Quickly he ran to the window again. He saw Timberline slowly turning on the ground, saw him inch toward the cabin, bloody fingers scratching in the ground. There was blood on Timberline's bald pate and his right hand looked badly shot up.

He smelled something burning besides gunpowder. Looking around, he saw that his last batch of pancakes was burning on the griddle. The room was almost full of the burning stink. Two swift lunges and he was beside the stove. He jerked the griddle to the back. He lifted a stove lid and flipped the black crisps into the galloping flames. Then, reloading his .45, and grabbing up the Winchester by the fireplace—the same gun Hunt had left behind in Hidden Country—Cain ran back to the window looking out onto the barn. He stood well back so they couldn't catch a glimpse of his face or his moving shadow.

He watched Timberline. The men in the barn were still taking potshots at him. Every few seconds pellets of mud sprayed all around him.

Cain agonized with him. The stricken giant was still crawling slowly, very painfully, across the yard toward the cabin door. He'd come a dozen feet, leaving a sloughing rut across the snow-sloshy yard. The rut was like the trail of a giant slug in mud.

"Poor devil!"

Cain boiled inside. Yet he stood calm. He took stock of the situation. Hambone was already caught and so was out of the fight. Timberline lay wounded on the ground outside. Even if he did manage to crawl to safety, he'd be in no condition to help. And only God knew where Harry had gone. He hoped Harry wasn't too far away, that he would hear all the gunfire and come on careful to take stock of things and then go for help. One word and the whole county would come piling down to help him. He had no doubt about who the invaders were. They were killers hired by the big cattlemen. Hunt was sure to be in the mob. Maybe even Jesse and Mitch. Maybe even some of the big cattlemen from around Cheyenne and Casper. If so, it would mean his cabin was at that very moment completely surrounded, that besides the gunmen in the barn there'd be some behind the bridge to the west and others up on the ridge to the south. The long low meadow to the southeast would be left unprotected. For a reason, too. The killers would hope he would make a run for it that way and thus catch him in a crossfire.

"Not this waddy," Cain swore.

It occurred to him that the raiders might not know just how many were in the cabin with him. If Mitch was with the raiders—that spying son-of-a-bugger pretending he was only a neighbor dropping by the other day!—he'd probably tell them there were at least two others in the cabin with him. Timberline and Harry. Hambone they had caught but Hambone's being there might suggest he had brought others with him. Cain nodded. The gunfighters would hardly rush the cabin even if Timberline was out there lying on the ground.

"What I better do is fire a shot from each window every little while. Make it seem they's a half-dozen of us tough hellions in here."

He made the rounds. With the Winchester he pinged a shot off the first support of the bridge, splintering off bits of wood. He next creased one through the largest clump of greasewood on the ridge to the south. On the barn side he dropped one low and off to the right of the barn door on the theory that someone might just be kneeling for a look through a knothole he remembered seeing there only yesterday. He had been meaning to plug it but had forgotten it.

He watched Timberline crawl on. The big man had covered another dozen feet. Shots still came popping at him intermittently and mud flew up in little black geysers around him.

"What lousy shots!" Cain muttered. "Onless they're in such shape they can't get a good bead on him. Maybe they dassent show for fear I'll get 'em." Cain smiled grim. "Or all of us get 'em. The ones they think are in here with me. If Hambone ain't snitched on us."

Again he made the rounds of the windows, this time changing the order, to keep up the pretense that there was more than one in the cabin with him. When he shot out of the window to the south he saw that the wind had come up again from the northwest. He could see it moving like waves across the new grass in the meadow.

He looked out of the window on the barn side. Timberline was still coming on, inching on, undulating like a wounded caterpillar. They'd kept after him with an occasional shot and he bled like a riddled wine barrel.

The sight of Timberline's terrible determination made Cain shiver all over.

Intent on Timberline, he forgot himself, let his head come too close to the window. There was a loud pop in the barn and then a ping through one of the remaining windowpanes. His black hat flew off. Instantly, instinctively, he dropped out of range.

He picked up his hat. Seeing the neat hole in its crown, he calmed over some. He even saw humor. "Now how could that duck know how much of my head was in this hat and still not hit it?"

And seeing humor, it began to close over him, the inevitability of it. Unless help came, unless Harry or some stray cowpuncher heard the shooting, he was done for. He was lost. He was sure that by now they had tortured Hambone into telling how many were in the cabin with him. If Hambone told, they would eventually rush the cabin and either put a crossfire on the door and windows or burn it and shoot him down when he flushed.

The terrible feeling that life was slowly unraveling out from under him, that, worse yet, he could do nothing about it, moved over him like a great storm cloud. Life was falling apart, it was all slipping away from him, and he could do nothing to stop it. Calamity was coming down on him like a sliding rockfall falling down on a man already pinned to earth. No matter what desperate measures he might take, no matter how he might jack first one way and then the other, in the end, finally, he was doomed, and no longer would he be around to enjoy his green meadow and life beside the Shaken Grass.

Then he rallied. Like a grizzly tormented into one last desperate lunge and bite, his animal came up and rose terrible in the back of his head, rampant. His eyes opened terrible under his dark brows, glowed like balls of silverish fire. His carven walnut face set rock hard. Who was Hunt or Mitch or Jesse or any of the hired killers to cow, even kill, a Hammett? He was a grandson of the great Gramp Hammett. All his life he'd had to hold his wild one in check for fear of going too far, of hurting someone, of overstroking when a light stroke would serve. Here now was a chance to let it out full force without having to worry about hurting the good. The odds were more than equal at last. A young army was out there to get him and he now had the right to fight with all he had. And he would. They might get him, but he would get some of them too, a lot of them.

He made another round of the windows, placing shots where he thought the killers might be hiding.

When he turned his attention to Timberline again, he found him almost at the foot of the stoop. Timberline's trail through the mud looked like someone had dragged a heavy log across the yard.

Cain set aside his rifle and got out his six-gun again. He set himself at the heavy door; gave it a sudden jerk inward and emptied his gun in the direction of the barn as a covering

296

fusillade; then threw his gun into the house behind him and leaped down beside Timberline. With all his might, grunting, he hauled Timberline up by his great shoulders and dragged him up the stoop. Timberline's limp legs and boots clumped on the two steps. Instantly another hail of bullets came rattling from the barn, wild, spraying all around them in the doorway, singing like swift hummingbirds. Cain's mind raced. Cain's mind raged. So clearly did it see and feel all things, so clear and wide and deep did it reflect the moment, he found he could actually see bullets winging toward them, coming on as straight as whistling wheat spears in a gale, coming on like swift blunt bumblebees. The bullets came on and at the last second seemed to veer off just enough to miss them. Except one bullet. It nicked his mustache, giving it a tick as if someone were trying to pull out a hair with tweezers. With another heave he pulled Timberline over the doorsill. Just as he was about to reach for the door, still one more bullet came singing straight for them. It did not veer. It splashed into Timberline's belly. Then he got the door shut.

Pouncing, he grabbed up the Winchester and made the rounds of the windows to let them know that he and his army were at their posts again.

He was immediately answered by a splintering shattering barrage of flying lead, from the barn, from the bridge, from the low bluff. Windows exploded out on the west and south sides of the cabin and fell to the floor with a brittle tinkling sound. Old dust stived up. Hard chinking spilled to the floor.

Cain nodded. The barrage from three sides told him an army of killers was out there just as he'd guessed. The fight was now bigger than a mere grudge fight between himself and a vengeful Hunt, between himself and a Jesse. A whole way of living was now at stake. The thing had finally come down to this: Would the state go big cattlemen or little cattlemen? Yes, a whole army of big cattlemen and their killers, including even a governor and a United States senator, were out to destroy the small-holder way of life. And he was plumb in the middle of it. Even the President was in it. He too had invested money in a ranch near Cheyenne.

"Well, there's nothing for it but to battle them all, if that's the way the cards want to fall. Hold out till help comes."

He noticed mud on his boots. He went over and carefully cleaned them on the gunnysack by the door.

He shot off yet another round through the windows to let them know he and his army were still on the alert.

The smell of gunpowder in the cabin became nauseous. It

297

reminded him powerfully of an old heavey mare's loose flates in the night.

He knelt beside Timberline to see what he could do for him. Timberline's old patched shirt and pants and vest were soaked with islands of blood. Cain got out an old washed shirt of his own from a shelf and ripped it into strips and cleaned and bandaged Timberline as best he could. There was a wound across Timberline's scabby unwashed pate where a rifle bullet had creased him. It wasn't deep. But it had nicked him enough to stun him and make him fall. There were a dozen punctures in his arms and shoulders, most of them flesh wounds and not fatal. Cain found only two thigh wounds; not deep, just bleeding slowly. Worse was the right hand. The thumb had been completely shot off and the palm was badly shattered. But the very worst was the belly wound, where the last shot had hit him. Greenish blood oozed from it. Cain guessed it had plowed into the liver and gall bladder, that it was fatal.

He noticed a bump in Timberline's near pocket. He reached in. He came up with a money bag. It was made of a leather he had never seen before, neither horsehide, nor cowhide. Nor for that matter even sheep hide. He turned it over; smelled it; turned it over. The rough side was turned out, the smooth side in. He felt silver coin inside, and curious to see how much Timberline carried about on him, he untied the buckskin thongs and looked in. He found two silver dollars and an assortment of small change. There seemed to be a lump stuck in a fold, so he opened the maw of the bag wider and turned it over. Out rolled a dried-up human ear.

He cried out. The last time he'd seen a severed ear was when Clara Jager showed him one she'd got in the mail. Hah. This was Dencil Jager's other ear. He and Dale had found Dencil's body without ears hanging from a tree. Cain looked at the money bag in his hands again, looked closely, and suddenly an idea, a horrible idea, struck him. He turned the bag completely inside out. There they were. Two little bumps on the smooth side of the bag exactly like dried-up dog dugs. So that was why the front of Dencil's chest had been skinned.

Cain's face first went as black as bile, then as pale as winter grass, then as blue as a dead man's cheek.

Jesse and his men hadn't hanged Dencil after all.

He gave big hairy Timberline a rough shake. "You black-hearted bustards!"

298

Timberline groaned. "Uh."

"Buzzards!"

"My thumb."

"T'blazes with your thumb. Listen, you big moose, can you hear me?"

"Uh."

"Listen! Did you and Harry hang Dencil?"

"Uh?"

"Did you and Harry string up Dencil Jager?"

"Not—Harry."

"But you did?"

Silence.

Again Cain shook big hairy Timberline, rough, fierce. "Listen! Can you hear me? Did you hang Dencil Jager?"

"Uh."

Cain's teeth set down tight together. He raged within; was calm without. "But why? Dencil was a wonderful fellow. I got my horse Lonesome from him. He was as honest as the day was long. And he was making it out with that nutzy Clara when any other mortal man would long ago have left her. And on the run."

"Thumb."

"T'blazes with your thumb, you strangling son-of-a-bugger. I ought to let you lay there and die, you bloody-minded beast. That was a terrible cowardly thing to do."

Timberline stirred. His eyes opened some. "No," he gasped, slow, "no. We thought—killin' him—would rouse the valley—get rid of Jesse."

"Tell me. Tell me honest Indian. I've got to know, Tim. Did my brother Harry have a hand in this too?"

"I did it alone."

"Don't lie now, Tim. Tim, you're dying now and you wouldn't want to die with a lie on your lips, would you? So tell me the truth. Did my brother Harry order you to kill Dencil?"

Silence.

"Did he?"

Timberline groaned.

Cain sensed instantly the groan was show. Timberline was covering up for his pardner. Harry had given the order then.

He was outraged at the idea of his brother Harry's ordering so gruesome and so cruelly wrong a killing. Yet at the same time he couldn't help but admire, a little, Timberline's loyalty. The Red Sashers did stick together. Even with death in his belly Timberline was no squealer.

"Thumb."

"Yeh, your thumb's all right." Cain let out a long shuddering sigh. So many things. Men waiting to kill him. Now this. "Once a wild one always a wild one."

"Thumb."

"Your thumb is going to be all right."

"It feels like it's gone." Timberline tried to raise his arm and look at it; couldn't quite make it.

"Lay quiet. I've got it all bandaged up."

With an effort, he recalled the waiting enemy outside. He got to his feet and, straddling, made another round of the three windows, firing one shot out of each. Again there were answering broadsides from all three barricades. Lead whistled and cried around his ears.

Cain took stock of his ammunition. With both Timberline's and Hambone's supply on hand, plus his own and Harry's, he had enough to hold out for a week provided he was saving with it. "Cowards get murdered; brave men get killed. So I'll have to do what I have to do. Shoot when necessary. Save my cartridges. Place my shots one by one, careful, steady."

"Rum?"

"Tim, you know I never drink rum."

"Drink?"

"Hambone went to get the water, remember?"

"Uh."

"Just lay quiet. Maybe tonight I can sneak out across the meadow and get you a hatful."

"A—good—drink—of—water—beats—all."

Cain stared out of the window. He saw the vague movement of a human form deep in the open barn window. He fired at it; saw the form jerk out of sight.

Dust itched in the corners of his eyes. "Well, I guess at that a man has to die sometime. And it might as well be one time as another." He fired again at what he thought was a second form in the open window. "And what better time than this—holding off a whole army for the boys."

He thought of Gramp Hammett getting shot in the back. Same with their fathers Gordon and Raymond Hammett. Same with brother Dale.

He thought of Rory. Of Gram. Of Joey and little Cain.

"Now I can think of it," he said aloud. "Now at last I can think of it." He nodded to himself, grim. "Yes, life might have been better had I married Rory. It might have been richer bein' father to Joey. Yes, I know that now."

He thought of Hunt. "He did do me a favor in a way, like he says. Though it was too late when he did it. And yes, maybe Rory was right after all that I should've killed him on sight to avenge Gramp and our fathers and Dale. And all the others that low-down skunk may have dry-gulched."

He thought of Hunt some more. "He did me a favor, yes. But now I am free to kill him if I can. I never did kill for pleasure or profit, having always preferred peace. And I am right sorry I had to shoot down Cecil Guth, even if everybody said I done right because he was no good and had it coming. But now at last I've come to the place where I must kill to live and where I will kill to live. I am free to kill now because I have no chance."

He thought: "My God, then I am going to die at that!"

"Cain?"

"Say it."

"Be sure to tell the boys—to watch out for a red moose—with a nick in the right front hoof."

"I will."

"Be sure now."

"Don't worry."

Blood began to froth from Timberline's lips and run down into his red whiskers.

Cain made the rounds again, carefully selecting points to shoot at. Again a hail of bullets rampaged against the cabin. Old dust rained on him. Chinking fell underfoot.

Through one of the cracks came a solitary bullet. It hit the wood stove, caromed off, narrowly missed him, finally spent itself in Hambone's old fiddle, splitting the dark wood open. A second later, as if in protest, the bass string punged loose with a half-smothered gulplike sound.

"But who will know how it went," he thought, "and who will care?"

He thought: "The boys will."

He thought: "Dead men tell no tales."

On an impulse, he dug out an old stub of a pencil from a pocket. From under the clock he got a small red book given to him by a cattle commissioner in which to keep accounts and addresses. The pages in the back were blank, marked *Memoranda*.

"Here's one killin' they're going to know all about. How it happened," he muttered to himself. "There'll be no story in the papers about how Cain Hammett came to his death by parties unknown to the jury. I'll leave a kind of last will and testament behind me so they'll really know."

He sat down at the plank table. He wetted the point of his pencil with his tongue and wrote in dark blunt strokes.

Me and Tim was making breakfast when the attack took place. An old man was here with us. The old man went to get a bucket of water. When he didn't come back, Tim went to see what was the matter. I told Tim to watch out, there maybe was somebody out there waiting for us. Tim said he thought it had finally got me.

Tim called from the floor, weakly, "Cain."

Now Tim is shot, but not dead yet. He is awful sick. I must go and wait on him.

Tim called again, this time stronger, clear. "Cain."

Cain put down his pencil and went over and knelt beside Tim. Gently he brushed back Timberline's red whiskers. "Here I am."

"Cain, you'll take my word for it?"

"For what, man?"

"You will, won't you, Cain?" Timberline tried to raise his head off the floor; couldn't quite make it. His eyes burned out of his whiskery face with a feverish almost holy light. "You will, won't you?"

"Lay down. Rest."

"Harry had nothing to do with it."

"It's all right, man."

"You won't take my word for it?"

"Quiet now. Rest."

Timberline's eyes closed over, very slowly. He moaned to himself. "He won't take my word for it."

Cain thought: "I know how he feels. I've been oncommon fond of Harry myself."

Cain got to his feet, hand to a knee. As he stepped toward the table, the raiders in the barn caught the movement deep within the window. A barrage of shots peppered all around the window frame.

"The more I think on it," Cain thought, "the more sure I am Harry knew this attack was comin'. It ain't the first he's slid out from under. Like that time up in his Hidden Country cabin." Cain pushed his hat to the back of his head. When he grimaced both his scalp and his stub ears moved. "He knew they was comin' for me all right. That's why he left early in the night."

He sat down to the plank table again.

It is now about three hours since the first shot. Tim is still

302

alive. They are still shooting and are all around the cabin.
He thought he heard the noise of someone running toward the cabin from the west. They were rushing him at last. Quick as a cat he leaped into his bedroom; peered out of the west window.

There was nothing. Nothing. The space between the cabin and the bridge was clear. Nor was there anyone coming down the lane.

He saw that the clouds had raised and that the sky had lightened some overhead. He could see the Big Stonies far to the west, where clouds streamed over a long comb of white peaks, past and over the Old Man and the Throne, whose very topmost tips were hidden. There was a storm on the other side of the Big Stonies because every few seconds sheet lightning played along the summits.

As he looked at the old familiar peaks, it came to him that he would miss them more than all else, more than his little spread beside the Shaken Grass, more than Rory and her boys. The never tiring winds might hone and chisel the Big Stonies down a little each millennium, but so far as he was concerned, thirty years of him, they had always been there and they would always be there, pure, white, high. If a man held his head just right he was sure to hear the wind soughing across them like a breath playing a harmonica.

" 'Tain't possible. I will be alive tomorrow."

The slow turn of the seasons, would he never experience them again? Summer, when the yellow sickles of grama grass quivered in the heat. Fall, when the Good Lord got out his color box and showed what He could do. Winter, when it was silver and gray in the Bitterness valley and the Stonies always blue. Spring, the best of all, when all things, grass and sage, greasewood and buckbrush, red willows and gay-feathers, became a tender light green, so tender and so sweetly light green a man had to argue with his animals not to get down on all fours and join the grazing horses and cows.

" 'Tain't possible."

He remembered the moonlit nights when he went hunting bighorn sheep under the Big Stonies, when the peaks above him seemed to glow with an inner fire of their own. He remembered the day when he sat just under the Throne looking down at the great Medicine Wheel, when it seemed to him he could see again the ancient dark ones come streaming up from the valleys to worship the sun.

Sharp eyes behind the bridge caught a glimpse of him. Puffs of smoke broke out along and under the bridge and

303

from the road ditch. Bullets rattled into the cabin like an avalanche of stones. Cain spotted several faces as they raised to fire. From the style of the hat, from the way they wore it cocked over the eye, from the knot in the bandanna, he guessed they were Texans. The big boys had to go to Texas for their gunmen? Maybe things hadn't gone as planned for the big cattlemen at that. Maybe there was some hope after all for his Association boys if the big cattle kings had to hire men from other states to fight their battles for them.

The meadowlark out in the pasture called from a low perch in a clump of greasewood. "Kuk, kuk," it said, and then it rolled out a low wooden plaint, "b-r-r-r-r."

He wrote in his little red stock book.

Boys, there is bullets coming in here like it was hail. Them fellows is in such shape I can't get at them. They are shooting from behind the barn and the bridge and back of the cabin on the rise. Boys, they are all dead-hard men. They commenced firing without saying a word.

The meadowlark called out again, this time cheerily, "Wheu! Wheu! See you in the morning, men!"

He was looking out of the middle window, watching, waiting, eyes lidded low—when he suddenly saw something that made the animal in him rear up on two feet, ears out, mouth open. A stocky fellow had stepped out from behind the barn.

Cain recognized him. It was Major Tascott, or Walrus, as the boys called him. Cain remembered a story the boys told about the major. On one of their escapade rides in Old Cheyenne, they'd had themselves too wild a fun and got haled into court by the local constable. Walrus was justice of the peace at the time and he sent them to the calaboose for a month. Later the boys learned that Walrus automatically sentenced anyone appearing in his court, no matter what the charge might be, on the theory that a man was probably guilty anyway, if not of the charge, then of something else.

Walrus called, loud, "You there, Cain Hammett, come out!"

Cain smiled some.

"Come out and talk."

Cain smiled, grim.

"We've got you surrounded, Hammett. You haven't got the chance of a good cold glass of water in hell. We know you're alone in there. We're bound to get you. Put down your guns and come out with your hands up."

Cain smiled.

"Come out and we'll give you a chance."

"A chance, my eye." Cain's left hand came up slow, almost

304

casual. "And an awful hell to you, my fat friend." He pulled the trigger. His .45 jumped and roared in the open window.

Walrus ducked; jumped back out of sight. The bullet skipped harmlessly across the rippling pink waters of the Shaken Grass.

Cain heard a long and shuddering groan behind him. It was like the welling groan of an old dog who hated to lay down his old bones yet once again on a hard floor.

Cain knelt beside Tim. He touched his brow. "Tim."

There was no movement in the long hulk.

Cain leaned down and put an ear to Tim's high chest. There was no heartbeat. Cain next rolled back an eyelid. The red eye looked at him sightless. Huge Timberline lay dead.

He was alone. For a second blind rage possessed him. He ran from window to window, firing the Winchester, ejecting and shoving in shells until the barrel began to blister his hands.

Later, calming, he got a blanket from his bunk and spread it over Timberline, hiding the old friendly boar face.

Tim is dead. He died at eleven by the clock. Boys, I feel pretty lonesome just now with Tim dead. I wish there was someone here with me so we could watch all sides at once. It is pretty hard doing it alone.

Between rounds at the window he ate the pancakes he'd left uneaten in his plate in the morning. They were soggy with black molasses and bitter with dust from the ceiling.

It is now noon by the clock. One of them ducks in the barn is throwing a rope at the door. He has a weight at the end. Now he is pulling it back and trying it again. I can't figure what he has in mind to do. He can't catch the door latch and hope to pull down the door, because it opens to the inside. I wish he would just stick his neck out a little more and I'd get him. He looks like Mitch Slaughter who is a good roper. They may fool around just long enough for me to get in a good shot before they leave.

He turned over the page; wetted the point of his pencil.

I just seen a smoke down by the barn. I guess they mean to fire it. They probably figure the wind will carry the burning brands to the cabin here and burn me out. They are dead-hard men. They won't let me get away this time. Well, there will be a lot of new faces in hell with me tonight.

He had just made the rounds of the windows again, when he heard galloping off to the southwest. Ears out, alert as a wolf, he went to look out of the bedroom window. There was a horse, with a man astride. The man was wearing flashy clothes. Then he recognized the flapping ends of the red sash. It was Harry. Harry was coming back. He had come back to help him.

Then he saw that Harry was riding in easy, as if he didn't realize what he was getting into. "Hell's fire and little fishes! He don't know about the raid then. Hah. Then he left us in the night for another reason. Glory be!" Cain nodded to himself. "Wal, and I forgive him for it. Even if it was Rory he went to see."

Cain shouted a warning. "Look out, Harry!" He yelled for all he was worth, letting his animal into it, willing his roar of a voice out through the window, far out, so it would explode all around Harry. "Look out!" Then, steady, he fired at the log railing of the bridge just ahead of Harry. The bullet landed just where he wanted it to hit. Splinters of raw wood shot up.

Harry either heard him or heard the shot. Or saw the splintering. Harry reined in, hard. His horse pawed the air.

A barrage of shots cracked out. For once there was no sound of bullets rattling into the cabin. They popped all around Harry instead. Harry ducked instinctively; whirled his horse around. Spurring, he galloped up the creek a ways, again reined his horse, then shot across the creek, water splashing, and up the rise. The last thing Cain saw, running to the window on the barn side, was the top of Harry's hat bobbing over the rise to the north toward Antelope, then gradually vanishing, bullets cracking all around him in the sagebrush. Off to the right, a good quarter of a mile away, bent on cutting him off, a half-dozen riders came galloping out of the draw.

It is three by the clock now. I just saw Harry. They fired at him but I think he got away. I seen lots of men from out of the stable and from behind the bridge run out and fire at him. I seen some on horseback take out after him. I don't know if his horse is fast enough or not. If he gets away we are saved.

He turned over another narrow page.

I shot at them ducks in the barn just now. I think I got one. I must go and look again.

He wetted the pencil point; scrounged around uneasy on his hide-bottom chair.

It doesn't look as if there is much show of my getting away. I see a dozen men standing across the river. One of them is Hunt. I took a long shot but missed. I hope they didn't catch Harry.

306

Still later he turned yet another page.

They are shelling the house like hail. I must go and look. It may be a trick.

He heard a noise behind the house. He looked. They had pulled a trick all right. He came back and wrote some more.

They managed to get a rope onto Hambone's buckboard while I was busy on this side. They got it behind the barn now. I hear them splitting wood. I hear them hammering. I guess they are going to fire the house tonight. I guess I will leave Tim and make a break when night comes, if alive.

He took off his black hat and hung it on a peg behind the door. He took down the black hair quirt he'd made out of Lonesome's mane and tail and stuck it in his pocket. He took off his boots and looked at them fondly and then slipped on an extra pair of socks. If he had to make a run for it, he would go as light-footed as possible, with yet enough on to protect a little against pricklepear cactus.

Clayborne

Hunt handed Clabe the ax. "Get to work."

Clabe said, slow, dull, "What—am—I—to—do—with—this?"

"Cut some kindling out of them knotty boards in the mangers."

"What—are—you—going—to—do?"

"Make a go-devil?"

" 'Go-devil'?"

"Yes." Hunt's eye glittered. "We're going to load down Hambone's buckboard with dry hay and wood. Then we're going to roll it against the cabin and fire it. We will get that left-handed son of Satan yet."

"You—are—going—to—smoke—him—out."

"Yes. We would have dynamited him out but that durn Perley Gates let the caps get wet when he cracked into that stone this morning."

"You—are—going—to—smoke—him—out."

"Chop wood, you big lummox. Bat, will you help him get started? Mitch and me will nail some heavy planks onto the back of this buckboard here. For protection. Make a kind of ark of safety out of it. We plan to push it backwards toward the cabin, so he can't hit us while we're pushing it, using the tongue to steer it with."

307

Clabe fell to, slowly, swinging the ax. Bat gathered up the raw broken pieces of knotty wood, slowly.

Jesse and Irv held up the boards on the tail of the buckboard while Hunt and Mitch hammered them in place. All four worked away swiftly, grimly.

The meadowlark out in the meadow called for his mate. He caroled sweetly. "Here's the place! Here's the place!"

Walrus came strutting in. "Men, I've got another idea. I figure that if Hammett makes a run for it, he'll try one of two things. He'll either take the meadow to the east, the side we left unprotected, or he'll skedaddle straight south for a ravine that cuts back through the ridge. He'll figure that once he gets into the ravine, he can hold us off. In fact, he is almost sure to try for the ravine instead of the meadow. He's smart enough to guess by now that we got the meadow set for crossfire. So I want two men to hide back in that ravine, in the sagebrush, one on each side. I will give that job to Mitch and Hunt here, the best shots we got."

"What if he don't try either of them two?" Mitch asked, rifle at ready. "Because I want to be the one to send him to hell."

"Listen, Mister Mitch Slaughter, I'm not picking you because you got the best revenge. I'm picking you because you're the best shot."

Mitch fell into sullen silence.

"In case Hammett makes a break to get back up the creek, we'll have plenty of men waiting for him there too."

"Sounds good to me," Hunt said. "We'll take the ravine."

"All right. Now the rest of you. Listen. When that cabin starts to burn, I want every man jack of you to be ready to fire at Hammett the second he shows in that door!"

Just then Clabe caught sight of Bat's eyes. Bat was crying.

Clabe broke inside. He took the ax and smashed it into a six-by-eight timber support. "I'm—through!" Clabe said, slow. He spoke the word "through" with such vehemence that spittle shot from his mouth in a shower. "I—can't—stand—it—any—more."

Hunt whirled around. He snarled, "You overgrown coward! You're not through." Hunt dropped his hammer and ran over and grabbed the ax by the handle and tried to jerk it out of the timber.

But Clabe had sunk it in so deep Hunt couldn't budge it. Clabe said, low, "Leave—that—ax—be!"

Hunt whirled again. He drew on Clabe. "Pull it out! Get! Hurry!"

Bat saw the drawn gun. He stepped back out of range. And in so doing, he stumbled over a fork and fell on his back in the hay.

"Draw—on—me—will—you," Clabe said, slow, gathering. "Why—you—murdering—killer—I'll—teach—you—to—draw—on—me." With huge slow steps, with huge slow hands, Clabe grabbed the ax by the handle and in a single springy motion jerked it free. He raised it over his head, the blade flashing against the ceiling, and advanced on Hunt.

"Clabe!" Walrus roared. "Hunt!"

Hunt shot. The bullet mashed into Clabe's belly.

"Liza!" Clabe dropped the ax. Like a bear outraged, he tore at his wound. His eyes opened very wide and white. "Liza!" He stumbled forward. He picked up the ax again and raised it, flashing. He staggered; wobbled to one side; swung the ax. Swerving with him, the ax came down with a rush and cleaved Bat's hatted head in two.

Hunt shot again.

Liza.

Cain

It is not night yet. They have made a go-devil. They have loaded down the buckboard with hay and wood. They are rolling it to the house. The men are in such shape behind them planks I can't get at them. I smell smoke.

He heard the fire against the house gathering and growing. He thought: " 'Tain't possible. It ain't happening to me. It's some other time. It ain't now."

Smoke began to seep into the cabin around the window. He thought: "It is true. In a minute I'll have to make a run for it."

The north wall became hot. He thought: "Well, if I have to go, I'm going to live it up to the very last. Full. Die fighting. Hold a high note and sing it for all I'm worth."

Flames began to lick along the ceiling. He thought: "Just the same, my neighbor is my god."

His skin began to prickle all over. Sparks spat off in his head. His eyes glowed white.

Not without humor did he notice that they'd rolled the buckboard well away from the door. They were inviting him to make a run for it across the meadow to the east.

He sat down to the table yet once more. He wetted the pencil point. He wrote each letter carefully, hard, painfully, as if he meant to print it through the little red stock book into the very wood underneath.

The house is all fired.
Good-bye, boys, if I never see you again.
Cain Hammett

He closed the little red book and stuck it in a shirt pocket and buttoned it down. He looked around. The old cork-dry walls and ceiling were already raging with jumping flames. Smoke was swooshing down toward the floor.

He made a last survey of his home. From the south window he noticed that the north-by-northwest wind was carrying the yellow-tinged black smoke from the burning house low across the meadow toward the south. He saw how it trailed straight for a ravine that led back through the ridge.

An idea came to him. Instead of making his run across the meadow where they were all set for him, he would hit for the ravine. Jump out and run inside the low trailing dark smoke. Cloud his trail. They would have a tough time making out his black clothes in the smoke. And once he got to the ravine, he'd have them all behind him. There was even a chance he might hold them at bay in the ravine until he got help or until night fell and he could sneak away. He recalled there was a side gully a ways into the ravine. He'd dart into that and wait for them to come after him. Even if there wasn't a chance to save himself, he could at least bring down a good dozen men with his .45 and the Winchester. They would know they had been in a fight.

He stepped over to Timberline and, lifting the blanket in the thick smoky suffocating haze, had a last look at the old friendly whiskered face.

Heat seared down at him from the blazing roaring roof. Roof dirt began to fall all around. Tightening up his cartridge belt another notch, making sure of his .45, making sure the Winchester was loaded, he ran to the low door by the wood stove and on hands and knees crawled into the dugout. The dugout had a low dirt roof. It would be the last place to burn.

It was damp inside. Potatoes with long pale sucker stems rolled queazily under his hands. He scuttled across them.

He found himself smiling. They would wait, and wait, for him to pop out of the front door. They wouldn't figure him ducking into the dugout. Waiting and waiting for him to pop out, they might even get the notion he'd shot himself rather than run the crossfire in the meadow. To help the idea

310

along, he fired off his .45 a couple of times into the house behind him. He reloaded.

Smoke followed him into the dugout after a minute. He choked in it. The air became acrid, close. He burrowed his nose down into the potatoes. They stunk like rutting toads.

Smoke next seemed to come out of the dirt floor. He waited. "They'll think me dead by now." He waited until he could feel heat on his rump.

The time had come. "Well, boys, here's where I play a lone hand in a dark room with my eyes shut. So long, Tim."

Gasping, he raised. He pushed against the low dirt roof. When it didn't budge, he bowed his head and set his back against it. With his short powerful haunches he heaved his whole body up. Dirt trickled into his neck. He heaved again and the low roof poles gave way and his head popped through. Dirt rolled off his dark hair. He winked; cleared his eyes. He took a mighty breath before flames and smoke could follow his head out. Then smoke puffed up around him; hid him for a second. He rammed up his shoulders and climbed out.

"There he goes!" a voice shouted from the rise in front of him.

Cain legged it for all he was worth around to where the low plume of smoke streaked across the meadow. He ran, shaking lead out of his .45 as he went, trying to hit the sudden forms rising out of the sagebrush on the ridge, trying to lay down a covering barrage for himself. Bullets whistled and whined past him from all sides. He slipped once in a cow plotch; regained his balance. His feet were suddenly wet. When his .45 clicked empty he stuck it inside his belt.

The moment he got inside the twisting plume of yellowish-black smoke, the shots fell off. The smoke hid him. It was hard to breathe. Holding his breath, he ran hard, bowed. For so short a man he bounded along with incredibly long strides. He willed himself into great speed.

Running, he was minded of the many times he had ridden in the clouds under the Old Man and the Throne with Lonesome under him. He stepped on a pricklepear cactus. It stung all across the sole of his foot. He stepped on a tiny sagebrush. It tickled. He kicked through a pile of horseballs and sent them rolling. The ground was damp underfoot, sweet with wet grass and snow-candied wild clover. His feet became sopping wet up over the ankles.

"By golly!" he thought. "I'm almost there! I'm going to make it!"

At the end of the meadow, near the mouth of the ravine, he

noticed the smoke lighten more at his feet than above him. He saw his socked feet stroking.

Then, too late, he saw that the smoke plume didn't go up the ravine as he'd thought; that a countercurrent of wind coming out of the ravine seemed to push it up and away from the ridge.

And also too late, after he was in the ravine a half-dozen steps, he saw two men, Hunt and Mitch, crouched over and waiting for him in the side gully. They were down on one knee and had dead aim on him. They had seen him emerge, feet first, a good dozen steps before he'd seen them. He quick tried to jerk up the Winchester for a running snap shot.

But he was too late. Their barrels both blazed and two punches hit him in the chest, each like the kick of a horse hoof. The punches stopped him in full flight. The two colliding momentums caused him to fly up. It looked as if he were trying to leap up over the bullets. He landed, tottering. Again the two barrels blazed. And again two separate kicks caught him square in the chest. They knocked him over on his back.

He fell with the Winchester gripped tight in his hand.

Good-bye, boys.

Hambone

They came running out of their holes, from behind the barn and the bridge and the rise. They closed in. Hambone swung behind the limping Jesse to see what there was to see.

They circled Cain from a distance, rifles cocked and at ready, still afraid he might strike. Yellowish-black smoke from the burning cabin streamed past; rose and fell over both them and him.

Hambone left from behind Jesse and went up close. Cain's trigger finger still worked. His right hand was gripped white around the barrel of the Winchester.

Mitch saw the finger move too. He shot. He shot again. Then some of the others shot too.

Hambone tolled his old leathery head. He cried, "You cowards! Can't you see he's dead at last? Or are you shooting at his ghost?"

"I've killed diamondbacks before," Mitch snarled.

"Who are you to talk?" Hambone cried.

"That's enough out of you too, you old buzzard, or you'll get some of the same."

"This is a free country," Hambone cried. "Or ain't it?"

312

Hunt walked up. He sat down on a heel and looked at the Winchester in Cain's grip. He looked for a mark. He found it. He threw aside the rifle he was carrying and with both hands jerked the Winchester out of Cain's hand. Hunt said, "At least I got back my favorite .38-56."

Hambone said, "Yes, I guess it is finders keepers at that."

"What do you mean by that remark?" Hunt demanded, leveling the Winchester on Hambone.

"This is a free country," Hambone cried. "Or ain't it?"

Irv Hornsby came up. His face was flushed with liquor. Irv gave the body a kick. Blood momentarily welled out of the wounds. Then Irv got out a card and wrote on it in pencil and pinned it to Cain's vest. It said:

Cattle Thieves Beware!

Hambone snorted. He reached down and ripped it off and tore it to bits. "I dare you to put another'n on him," he said.

Walrus came strutting up. His neck was crooked to one side. He walked around the body twice. Gradually a new look came over his chub face and he stood a while. Black smoke swooped down over him and the body; then it raised to the sky.

Jesse said, "He was a brave man. Game to the end. It was almost a shame to kill him."

Walrus snorted. The motion shook all of him. He said, "Yes, and if I had fifty men like him I could lick the whole state inside of a year."

Hunt snorted too. He set the Winchester stock down to the ground. He turned his back on Walrus and the crowd.

Hambone looked down at Cain. "Maybe he was a rustler once years ago when he worked for Jesse. I don't know. We all made mistakes when we was boys. But grown up he was my friend and I knew him to be honest. He was the whitest man that ever wore boots. He was the nerviest man I ever knew. I never knew him to start a fight. Yet, when one was started, I never knew him to back down. That is the best I can say for any man."

Ike came up, light-footed, young face like he was at his mother's funeral. After a while he said, "If they're all fighters like that up here, we Texans might as well quit."

Jesse said, "Too bad he was on the wrong side."

Then they all relieved themselves on the young light green grass in the meadow. Hambone would not join them.

The meadowlark landed nearby. It hopped onto a clod; then

onto a stone. Its yellow breast shone in the low dusk. It whistled wild, pure, clear, nervously opening and shutting its tail, flashing its white tail feathers. "Wheu! Wheu! See you in the morning, men!"

Hunt turned. "That durn bird has been in my ear all day." He took a snap shot at the meadowlark. He missed. The meadowlark soared off into the high dusk over the land.

"Well, men," Walrus said at last, strut coming back, "on to Antelope, the doomed city of the plains."

Later in the night, after the invaders had been surrounded and captured near Antelope by the army Harry had raised, Sheriff Ned Sine and Harry came out to Cain's cabin. They came with their horses sobbing for breath and dripping wet.

Hambone met them with a lantern. He showed them where Cain lay. Some new snow had fallen and the wind had blown a little drift off Cain's nose. Light from the swinging lantern momentarily quickened Cain's half-lidded staring eyes.

They stood looking down at him.

At last Hambone said, "So long, cowhand, and good ridin'. You was the best. We'll never forget you so long as we live."

Harry went white then, and he turned around and threw up in the snow. "I come too late," he said.

Hambone gave Harry a steady look. He said, "Now, now, Harry boy, don't take it so hard. You know you did the best you could."

"No," Harry said, "no, I didn't. I should have come sooner."

"But how could you, Harry?" Sheriff Sine broke in. "It was already too late when we ran into the raiders south of town there. You know that. He was already dead by then."

"I know that," Harry said. "I don't mean then."

"What!" Sheriff Sine said. "When do you mean then?"

"I mean I should have come back sooner from Irv Hornsby's."

Hambone reared back. "What the hell was you doing t' Irv's? He's on the other side."

"Mitch told us they was having a party there. And I got a wild hair in the night and snuck over to have a look at it. You know how it is when you're full a beans."

"When you might have known the kind of party Irv might throw?"

"Yes," Harry said. "When I might have known."

Hambone stared at Harry in the lantern light. So did Sheriff Sine.

Harry cried. He hid his face. "Oh, Cain. My brother, my brother."

Hambone put a hand on Harry's shoulder. "Now, sidey, now."

Harry said, "But when I got to Irv's, the party had already left. And then I knew for sure, but too late, what kind of party Mitch meant. So I came back as quick as I could. But it was too late. Too late."

At that Hambone let out a big gushing sigh. So did Sheriff Sine.

Hambone said, "It's all right, Harry. Don't take it so hard, boy. You did the best you could."

"Too late. My brother. My brother."

Sheriff Sine couldn't stand to look at Harry. He turned. He looked at the dead man a while. Then, groaning, he got down on one knee and rolled the body over. He counted the bullet holes in reverent awe. "There's at least thirty holes in this man. One for every year of his life."

Harry again turned and threw up.

Sheriff Sine searched the body. He found the little red stock book. After he had read it aloud in the lantern light, he said, "He sure put up a fight, all right. Holding them off all day alone. From the last count the coroner and the doc made, he got five of them and nicked at least a dozen others."

"Yeh," Hambone said, scuffing the ground with a boot toe, trying to think of something to draw Harry off his grief, "yeh, he put up a fight all right. But what I'm wonderin' is, what state will Hunt Lawton do his peace-officerin' in next?"

Sheriff Sine slowly got to his feet. "Hunt Lawton ain't goin' to no other state. We've got him behind bars now. With witness galore agin him."

Hambone shook his old head. He watched Harry out of the corner of his eye. "Ned, you know damn well you'll never bring Hunt to trial. Nor any of them other'n either."

Sheriff Sine stiffened. "How do you figure?"

"There's too much power behind them. Them millionaires in the East own them big alligators our state legislators. Body and soul."

"We'll try Hunt here if I got anything to say about it."

Hambone smiled, sad. His old head continued to swing back and forth from his hump spine. "No, you won't, Ned. They'll claim they can't get a fair trial in this county. Which they won't of course. So their lawyers will ask for a change of venue to another county. And once they're out of this county, they're gone. You know that."

315

Sheriff Sine swore.

"Swear all you want to, Ned, but they'll get off." Hambone watched Harry. "Oh, they probably won't bother us much again. Make another raid. But they'll get off."

Harry finally got up enough courage to look down at Cain again. Slowly Harry settled on his heels beside him. With just barely touching finger tips he closed his brother's half-lidded staring eyes.

Hambone nodded to himself. He said, "What burns me, though, is that that snake Hunt should get off. Them other'n was fightin' for what they thought was their right. They thought they had a side. They thought they had to do it. So they did it. But Hunt, he came here and killed just to kill. While wearin' a star. And that's wrong. That's plumb wrong."

Harry stood up. His face was still white. "Will you go get a wagon, Hambone? So we can ride him into town?"

Hambone said, "I'll be glad to."

Rosemary

They were in the cemetery. It was a very cold day. Everyone puffed white breath.

Wearing black, Rory stood with Joey on one side of her and cousin Harry on the other and baby Cain in her arms.

The wooden hearse backed slowly through the crowd. The pallbearers picked up the bodies and carried them carefully across the slippery ground and set them beside the open clay graves.

Rory saw that Cain's pine-board coffin was closed. In her mind's eye she could still see his grim face and his bullet-ridden body. The baby casket in which Timberline's burnt stump of a body lay was also closed.

The crowd was as still as mice and as grave as owls. Beyond and above a little grove of seedling cottonwoods rode the Big Stonies. The white peaks were combing out a huge bank of fleecy clouds.

Hambone led Cain's cow pony, Bucky, beside the grave. The dun buckskin was saddled. A black-hair quirt hung from the saddlehorn.

Rory felt the crowd around her. They had come to honor him. Her tongue moved behind her teeth. Her teeth tasted bitter.

Reverend Creed stood in black, short, bowlegged. He was

a cowhand turned preacher. He had an old face, stiff, like the sides of a woman's old leather purse. He raised the Bible in his hand and spoke quietly in the hush.

"These men have been sent into eternity. We know why. They fought the invaders and lost their lives to them. Yet by fighting they saved the homesteader way of life in Bighorn County. One of them died early in the fight. The other prevailed until the sun went down. Together they died so that others might survive. We lost a dear brother in the flesh, but we gained a hero in the spirit in return."

Reverend Creed's voice raised some. "We all know what happened afterwards. By holding on bitterly all day, Cain Hammett gave his neighbors time to rally and beat back the invaders and later surround them. We all know too that it took a presidential order to save the invaders from certain death. Had not the President sent out the U. S. Army and put the invaders in jail, they would all have been massacred. We do not condone killing and we are glad lives were saved. But now that they are safely behind bars we hope that justice will be done."

Reverend Creed's voice soared. "It is doubtful that the world will ever remember the names of the invaders, yes, even the senator and the governor and the President who aided and abetted the invaders. But the world will never forget the name of Cain Hammett. Wherever cattle graze or homesteaders live, Cain Hammett will always be remembered as the man who alone overthrew the feudal system of the old frontier and turned the cattle kingdom into a free country. In future times to come the story of Cain Hammett and his bravery will always be quoted in history. Our children and our children's children will point to him as the coolest and bravest American of them all."

Reverend Creed's voice became solemn. "He was a true hero. He fought to save his own life, yes. He fought to save the lives of his boys, yes. He fought to save all our lives in Bighorn County, yes. But he did more than that. He fought not knowing his side would win. That is his true glory. He fought because he was a man and because bravery was expected of him. He fought because he had lived by a code and because he wanted to die by that code. Though his heart might be in mortal anguish, though the terror of death might be in his throat, he fought anyway, calmly and well. He shed his blood that men might once again learn that you cannot force a free people to accept something they do not want."

Reverend Creed closed his Bible. He gestured.

The pallbearers silently lowered the two bodies into their graves.

Reverend Creed said, "We stand at his grave. Now it is for us to examine our own hearts. Some of us do not have clean hands. Yes, the cattle barons made an illegal attack upon us. But on our side of the fence our hands are not clean either. By no means. Some of us have stolen. Some of us do have blood on our conscience. Some of us have coveted our neighbor's ox and ass. The same enemy that rode with the invaders rides with us. He is the Devil."

Reverend Creed picked up a handful of clay. He crumbled it in his hand. In turn he scattered the clay over the coffins deep in the ground. One of the larger crumbles hit the top of Cain's pine box. A tiny wisp of steam spurted out of a crack into the cold air. The inside of the coffin was still warm from having been in church. The puff rose and vanished against the clouds over the Big Stonies. Rory saw it and thought of the time when Cain went to get her a bighorn.

Reverend Creed said, "Forgive us our trespasses as we forgive them that trespass against us. Amen."

Rory wept bitterly. Wearing black, she stood with Joey on one side and cousin Harry on the other and baby Cain in her arms.

She thought: "And I am left with Joey, Harry's boy. And with little Cain, Dale's boy. While Cain is but a memory."

Reverend Creed touched her shoulder. "I commend you to God."

In hushed silence, old Hambone unsaddled Bucky from the wrong side. It was solemn announcement that none of the mourners present had been Cain's equal in life.

At Wrâlda
December 8, 1956